NEGL
CHIL

Dedicated to my gentle and loving father,
Nathan Paul Dubowitz (1923–1980).

NEGLECTED CHILDREN

Research, Practice, and Policy

Howard Dubowitz Editor

SAGE Publications
International Educational and Professional Publisher
Thousand Oaks London New Delhi

For information:

SAGE Publications, Inc.
2455 Teller Road
Thousand Oaks, California 91320
E-mail: order@sagepub.com

SAGE Publications Ltd.
6 Bonhill Street
London EC2A 4PU
United Kingdom

SAGE Publications India Pvt. Ltd.
M-32 Market
Greater Kailash I
New Delhi 110 048 India

Printed in the United States of America

Library of Congress Cataloging-in-Publication Data

Neglected children: Research, practice, and policy / edited by Howard Dubowitz.
p. cm.
Includes bibliographical references and index.
ISBN 0-7619-0853-6 (cloth: alk. paper)
ISBN 0-7619-1842-6 (pbk.: alk. paper)
1. Child abuse—United States. 2. Abused children—Services for—United States. 3. Social work with children—United States. I. Dubowitz, Howard.
HV6626.52 .N44 1999
362.76'8'0973—dc21
98-40296

99 00 01 02 03 10 9 8 7 6 5 4 3 2

Acquiring Editor: C. Terry Hendrix
Production Editor: Diana E. Axelsen
Editorial Assistant: Nevair Kabakian
Book Designer: Lynn Miyata
Typesetter: Christina M. Hill
Cover Designer: Michelle Lee

Contents

Preface

"The neglect of neglect" has almost become a cliché, and like many other clichés, there is ample justification for the phrase. Abuse, particularly sexual abuse, has evoked an intense response from the media, the public, and professionals. Neglect has attracted far less attention. Journals and conferences pertaining to child maltreatment have had relatively little on neglect. At the same time, it has been clear that neglect is distressingly prevalent and that the effect on children can be immense. The importance of child neglect as a major clinical and social issue is not in question.

Despite not getting its due attention, a great deal has been learned about child neglect. Because cases involving neglect constitute more than half of cases reported to child protective services, the child welfare system and practitioners in several disciplines have had enormous experience addressing neglect. There has also been increasing research on neglect, particularly supported by the National Center on Child Abuse and Neglect (now, the Office on Child Abuse and Neglect). The main goal of this book is to synthesize our knowledge of child neglect in one text, in a way that will be valuable for clinicians, researchers, and policymakers. Obviously, much remains to be learned, but here is an opportunity to examine the state of our knowledge and, sometimes, the "state of the art." I hope this book will in some small way help enhance efforts to protect children and support families and provide a foundation for further developing the knowledge base and new theory, programs, and policies related to the neglect of children.

It is inevitable that an edited volume will include divergent views; this book is no exception. This offers an accurate reflection of our field, and I have resisted the temptation to present a single or my perspective. The lack of consensus on a definition and causal pathways of neglect, for example, poses challenges for clinicians and researchers. The link between child neglect and political and ideological values makes it likely that certain differences will continue. At the same time, substantial overlap in views and interpretations of the research exists; I believe that the differences are not as huge as they may appear.

The range of topics covered in this book should be of broad interest to professionals in the field of child maltreatment. Clearly, neglect often co-occurs with other forms of child maltreatment. It is hoped that clinicians, researchers, and policymakers will find useful guidance in these pages. Ultimately, neglected children and their families should benefit.

ACKNOWLEDGMENTS

There are many people who have contributed to my interest and development in the field of child maltreatment; I feel very fortunate to have had such terrific colleagues. Robert Reece and Eli Newberger were early role models introducing me to this area of pediatrics in the early 1980s. The faculty and fellows at the Family Development Program at Boston's Children's Hospital taught me the value and pleasure of interdisciplinary collaboration. Maureen Black, Diane DePanfilis, Donna Harrington, Wayne Holden, Charles Shubin, Raymond Starr, and Susan Zuravin, all at the University of Maryland, have helped make work in this difficult area stimulating and rewarding.

I am also grateful to my colleagues in the Longitudinal Study on Child Abuse and Neglect and the American Professional Society on the Abuse of Children; I have learned so much from them. Terry Hendrix at Sage has been an enthusiastic supporter of this project, and Jan Roberts has been a whiz with word processing challenges. I want to thank the authors who contributed to this book. Life is not dull for any of them, and these chapters required a great deal. Behind the scene, my wife, Diana, and children, Nikki and Andy, have been an important source of support and inspiration.

Child Neglect

The Family With a Hole in the Middle

1

JAMES GARBARINO
CYLESTE C. COLLINS

It has become commonplace in the field of child maltreatment to recognize "the neglect of neglect." Much as we may use the phrase "child abuse and neglect," the overwhelming focus of child maltreatment research, theory, and practice is on abuse, not neglect. For example, a quick review of the listings in a popular psychology index indicated 5,848 entries for child abuse and only 559 for child neglect.

If we take it as a given that neglect is neglected, the obvious next step is to address the question of "why?" Why has the topic of neglect been neglected in the literature? Empirical reality does not suffer from this problem. From national surveys of child maltreatment cases known to child protection units and other child-focused professionals, we know that more children are neglected than abused (Sedlak & Broadhurst, 1996) and that this number has been increasing.

The most recent National Incidence Study of Child Abuse and Neglect (Sedlak & Broadhurst, 1996) reports an overall rate of child maltreatment of 1,553,800, defined by the Harm Standard. The Harm Standard requires that demonstrable harm has occurred. This overall rate includes a rate of 743,200 for child abuse and 879,000 for child neglect. We also learn that the rate of neglect is increasing more quickly than that of abuse (Sedlak &

Broadhurst, 1996). The number of abused children under the Harm Standard increased from 507,700 in 1986 to 743,200 in 1993, whereas the number of children identified as neglected went from 474,800 in 1986 to 879,000 in 1993 (Sedlak & Broadhurst, 1996). Thus, abuse increased by about 45%, whereas neglect increased by nearly 100%. Others have noted that the effects of neglect are more severe than those from abuse (Wolock & Horowitz, 1984). Indeed, recent research by Perry, Pollard, Blakely, Baker, and Vigilante (1995) supports this view by documenting the especially damaging effects of early deprivation on brain development associated with neglect—greater than those associated with trauma (which could stand as a surrogate for abuse).

Why the discrepancy between the importance of neglect and its salience in the professional literature? Some have tried to explain the discrepancy between prevalence and attention by pointing out that our culture is obsessed with violence (Wolock & Horowitz, 1984), and physical force grabs more attention than acts of omission (i.e., neglect). The sight of a child who has been severely beaten commands more attention, whereas the scars left from neglect are less dramatic. Indeed, in a society obsessed with violence, we are more interested in what is tangible, what is dramatic, and what is vivid to our senses. A person who sees a child's scars is more likely to act on his or her behalf (or at least to demand action from someone else).

On the other hand, a child who has been neglected may have more insidious problems, ones that are not as easy to see. What is more, the child protection issues differ. In the case of abuse, the task may be conceptualized as an *act* of protection—stopping the caregiver from assaulting the child—whereas in the case of neglect, the task is clearly a *process*—creating or restoring an ongoing pattern of caregiving behavior. This difference may feed a professional prejudice: Treating child abuse seems more sophisticated than treating neglect.

Another possible reason for the neglect of child neglect is the role of poverty. More than 30 years ago, Michael Harrington (1968) sought to make the poor visible in his book *The Other America.* He succeeded, and the subsequent "war on poverty" was evidence of that success. Today, poverty is not so much invisible as it is déclassé. This lack of interest in poverty—except as an indicator of the moral failures of poor people—contributes to the neglect of neglect. The 1980s saw increasing disparities between rich and poor—the rich getting richer and the poor getting poorer. At present, the United States has the dubious distinction of leading developed nations in the *magnitude* of this discrepancy. This tends to make the poor less connected to the rest of society, and it may contribute to the marginalizing of neglect. The loneliness, lack of social supports, social isolation, and social distancing of many neglecting families (Gaudin & Polansky, 1986; Gaudin, Polansky, Kilpatrick, & Shilton, 1993) may well accentuate this phenomenon and contribute to the sense of poor families being "silent but dangerous."

In this chapter, our goal is to introduce the topic of child neglect, to provide both a conceptual and an empirical road map for other chapters that will delve more deeply into issues of theory, research, policy, prevention, and treatment. We will do this by matching up the concept of neglect with some important concepts and issues in child development. We start from the issue of how and when it is appropriate to speak of the universality of basic developmental needs in contrast to a radically ecological view—a perspective asserting that in matters of child development, when the question is "does X cause Y?" the best answer is always, "it depends." This issue of definition leads us to a concern with two principal issues: the intrinsically contextual nature of efforts to define child neglect and the centrality of "psychological availability" in concepts of neglect.

AN ECOLOGICAL PERSPECTIVE ON DEVELOPMENTAL CONTEXT

For development to proceed effectively, basic needs must be met. Each culture and society plays a role in defining these needs, but to what extent are developmental needs universal? The differences that may be observed across time and space mainly affect the implementation of commonly recognized basic needs. For example, societies and cultures differ in their interpretation and understanding of "hazards to development," but virtually all agree that children require some protection from hazards (however they may be defined in a particular time and place).

This is one foundation for the concept of neglect. Child neglect is a pattern of behavior or a social context that has a hole in the middle where we should find the meeting of basic developmental needs. Infancy provides the easiest context in which to observe this because the needs of infants exist within a much narrower range than those of older children and adolescents. Non-organic failure to thrive is an example of a specific form of unmet needs that may reflect neglect and that is highly relevant in infancy and generally irrelevant to later childhood and adolescence (although eating disorders, such as anorexia nervosa and bulimia, can be understood as child-initiated non-organic failure to thrive).

A systems approach helps clarify the complexity we face in understanding the interplay of biological, psychological, social, and cultural forces in neglect. An ecologically grounded systems approach helps us discover connections that might otherwise remain invisible. Forrester (1969) concludes that because systems are linked and therefore influence each other ("feedback"), many of the most effective solutions to social problems are not readily apparent and may even be counterintuitive. According to Hardin (1980), the First Law of Ecology is that "You can never do just one thing." Intersystem feedback ensures that any single action may reverberate and produce intended or unintended consequences.

As individuals develop, they play an ever more active role in an ever-widening world, and this is one reason why the developmental significance of such universals as do exist can be understood only in an ecological context. Development is about the content of experience, not simply developmental processes. Newborns shape the feeding behavior of their mothers, but they are confined largely to cribs or laps, and they have limited means of communicating their needs and wants. On the other hand, 10-year-olds influence many adults and other children in many different settings and have many ways of communicating. The world of adolescents is even larger and more diverse, as is their ability to influence that world.

We cannot reliably predict the future of one system without knowing something about the other systems with which it is linked. Even then, prediction may be very difficult, because individuals and environments negotiate their relationships over time through a process of reciprocity, if they are effective systems. In the case of neglecting families, these "normal" systems processes may be distorted; for example, the link between early developmental delay and later IQ deficit appears to differ across social class groupings in the kind of social system present in most United States communities. In one classic study, 13% of the lower-social-class children who were developmentally delayed at 8 months showed an IQ of 79 or less at 4 years of age. In contrast, only 7% of the middle-class children who were delayed at 8 months were retarded at 4 years of age. For the upper-class children, the figure was only 2% (Willerman, Broman, & Fiedler, 1970).

Does developmental delay predict IQ deficit? It would seem that *it depends* on the family and community environment in which one is growing up.

We might hypothesize that the social class effect linked to family status would be exaggerated in some communities and diminished in others. Neglect can bring out into the developmental open whatever disabilities or vulnerabilities a child possesses. What is more, this example makes it very clear that neglect is not simply or absolutely a matter of negligent parents. It also is inescapably a judgment about communities—communities that differ in the level of support and supervision they offer to individual parents. If the community defines parenting as a private, individual act, it may rightly be judged neglectful, in contrast to a community that recognizes parenthood as a social contract (Garbarino, 1995).

Looking through the lens of the ecological perspective, we see the individual's experiences as subsystems within systems, within larger systems, "as a set of nested structures, each inside the next, like a set of Russian dolls" (Bronfenbrenner, 1979, p. 22). In asking and answering questions about development, we can and should always be ready to look at the next level of systems "beyond" and "within" to find the questions and the answers (Garbarino et al. (1992). If we see parents and visiting nurses in conflict over supervision issues in early childhood (the family system), we need to examine the community that establishes laws and policies about minimum standards of child care (and where societal neglect may be defined as the lack of these standards). We also should look to the cultures that define the range of normal supervision practices.

But we must also look within the individual, as a psychological system that is affected by conscious and changing roles, unconscious needs, and motives, to know why and how each adjusts in ways that generate willingness to consider supervision and competing values and interests. In addition, we must also look "across" to see how the several systems involved (family, social services, social network, and economy) adjust to new conditions. Interaction among these social forces is the key to an ecological analysis of child neglect. They exist as linked social systems, implying that intervention can take place at each system level and that intervention at one level may well spill over to others.

This system approach examines the environment at four levels beyond the individual organism—from the "micro" to the "macro." These systems have been detailed elsewhere (Bronfenbrenner, 1979, 1986; Garbarino et al., 1992). The goal here is to introduce them briefly to provide a context for discussing the ecology of child neglect.

Microsystems are the immediate settings in which individuals develop (e.g., the family). Microsystems evolve and develop, much as individuals do, from forces generated both within and without. The quality of a microsystem depends on its ability to sustain and enhance development and to provide a context that is emotionally validating and developmentally challenging. This, in turn, depends on its capacity to operate in what Vygotsky (1986) called "the zone of proximal development," that is, the difference between what the child can accomplish alone (the level of actual development) and what the child can do when helped (the level of potential development). In a neglecting family, there is an interactional hole where there should be action in the zone of proximal development.

Children can handle (and need) more complex social environments than infants. Adolescents can handle (and need) more complexity than children. We measure the social richness of an individual's life by the availability of enduring, reciprocal, multifaceted relationships that emphasize playing, working, and loving. And we do that measuring over time, because microsystems, like individuals, change over time. Risk, on the other hand, lies in patterns of abuse, neglect, resource deficiency, and stress that insult the child and thwart development. Most destructive among these is psychological neglect (Garbarino, Guttmann, & Seeley, 1986); thus, the principal microsystem issue for students of neglect is the responsiveness and affirmation of those in direct contact with the child.

The "same" day care center is very different in June from what it was in September for the "same" infants who, of course, are themselves not the same as they were at the beginning of the year. The setting of the family, as the firstborn child experiences it, is different from that experienced by subsequent offspring. Naturally, children themselves change and develop, as do others in the setting. It is also important to remember that our definition speaks of the microsystem as a pattern experienced by the developing person. Individuals influence their microsystems, and those microsystems influence them in turn. Each participant acts on the basis of an emergent social map. Neglect distorts these social maps as they develop in children.

Mesosystems are relationships between microsystems in which the individual experiences reality. These links themselves form a system. We measure the richness of a mesosystem in the number and quality of its connections. Consider the example of an infant's day care group and his or her home. We ask, do staff visit the child at home? Do the child's parents know his or her friends at day care? Do parents of children at the center know each other? A second example concerns the hospital and the home for a chronically ill child. What role do the parents play in the hospital regimen? Do the same health care professionals who see the child in the hospital visit the home? Is the child the only one to participate in both? If he or she is the only "linkage," the mesosystem is weak, and that weakness may place the child at risk. Research suggests that the strength of the mesosystem linking the setting in which an intervention is implemented with the settings in which the individual spends most significant time is crucial to the long-term effectiveness of the intervention and to the maintenance of its effects (Whittaker, 1983). Neglect in mesosystem terms is the isolation of the microsystem from potentially supportive links with other systems (e.g., home, school). Once again, there is a hole where there should be active relationships.

Exosystems are settings that have a bearing on the development of children but in which those children do not play a direct role. For most children, the key exosystems include the workplace of their parents (for most children, as they are not participants there) and those centers of power, such as school boards, church councils, and planning commissions, that make decisions affecting their day-to-day life. Note that the same setting that is an exosystem for a child may be a microsystem for the parent, and vice versa. Thus, one form of intervention may aim at transforming exosystems into microsystems, by such methods as initiating greater participation in important institutions for isolated, disenfranchised, and powerless clients—for example, by getting parents to visit the family day care home or by creating on-site day care at the workplace.

In exosystem terms, both risk and opportunity come about in two ways. The first is when the parents or other significant adults in a child's life are treated in a way that impoverishes (risk) or enhances (opportunity) their behavior in the microsystems they share with children. Examples include elements of the parents' working experience that impoverish or enhance family life—such as unemployment, low pay, long or inflexible hours, traveling, or stress, on the one hand, in contrast to an adequate income, flexible scheduling, an understanding employer, or subsidies for child care, on the other (Bronfenbrenner & Crouter, 1983).

The second way in which risk and opportunity flow from the exosystem lies in the orientation and content of decisions made in those settings that affect the day-to-day experience of children and their families. For example, when the state legislature suspends funding for early intervention programs, it jeopardizes development. When public officials expand prenatal health services or initiate specialized day care in high-risk communities, they increase developmental opportunities (and may reduce infant mortality and morbidity).

Albee (1980) has gone so far as to identify powerlessness as the primary factor leading to impaired development and mental disability. It certainly plays a large role in determining the fate of groups of individuals via public policy and may even be very important when considering individual cases—such as whether or not parents have the "pull" to get a medically vulnerable child enrolled in a treatment program. In many cases, risk and opportunity at the exosystem level are essentially political matters. And neglect almost always has an exosystem dimension in the sense that it thrives when those in positions of power over high-risk families abdicate their responsibility to care for every child in a community, to recognize that every child has a right to be cared for in ways that meet the minimal standards of care needed to sustain development, that every child deserves a whole life—not one with a hole in the middle where the caring should be.

One of the most useful aspects of the ecological approach is its ability to highlight situations in which the actions of people with whom the individual has no direct contact significantly affect development. The following example illustrates the relationship between social policy and individual child development. Because of a leveraged corporate takeover, a board of directors decides to shift operations from one plant to another. Many families with young children are forced to move to new locations. Local services are underfunded in a period of escalating demand. Parents lose their jobs and thus their health insurance. The quality of prenatal and well-baby care declines; infant mortality increases. This is a classic illustration of an exosystem effect. It highlights the fact that exosystem events may shape the agenda for early intervention on behalf of children at risk.

At this point, it is worth emphasizing that the ecological perspective forces us to consider the concept of risk beyond the narrow confines of individual personality and family dynamics. In the ecological approach, both are "causes" of the child's developmental patterns and "reflections" of broader sociocultural forces. Mark Twain wrote, "If the only tool you have is a hammer, you tend to treat every problem as if it were a nail." Inflexible loyalty to a specific focus (e.g., the parents) is often a stumbling block to effective intervention. However, the obverse must also be considered: "If you define every problem as a nail, the only tool you will seek is a hammer." Viewing children at risk only in terms of organismic and interpersonal dynamics precludes an understanding of the many other avenues of influence that might be open to us as helpers or that might be topics of study for us as scientists.

Those who limit their attention to parent education may be missing the potential importance of kin and neighbors as influences of the quality of care a child receives. This message provides a crucial guide to our discussions of early intervention. In exosystem terms, neglect is a matter of influences on caregivers that lead to lowered morale, deteriorated functioning, and depression and on institutional policies that ignore the needs of children ("institutional neglect").

Meso- and exosystems are set within the broad ideological, demographic, and institutional patterns of a particular culture or subculture. These are the macrosystems that serve as the master "blueprints" for the ecology of human development. *Macrosystem* refers to the general organization of the world as it is and as it might be if policies or institutional practices change. These blueprints reflect a people's shared assumptions about how things should be done, as well as the institutions that represent those assumptions. Macrosystems are ideology incarnate. Thus, we contrast differing societal blueprints that rest on fundamental institutional expressions, such as a "collective versus individual orientation." Religion provides a classic example of the macrosystem concept because it involves both a definition of the world and a set of institutions reflecting that definition—both a theology and a set of roles, rules, buildings, and programs.

Historical change demonstrates that the "might be" of a macrosystem is quite real and occurs through either evolution (many individual actions guided by a common reality) or through revolution (dramatic change introduced by a small cadre of decision makers). The collapse of the Soviet Union in the 1990s, for example, overturned a communist society and embodied a changed institutional and ideological landscape that shaped the most basic experiences of childhood. Current efforts to "modernize" in China include a massive shift from "collective reward" to "private initiative" as the dominating economic force. More directly relevant still is the "one-child policy" that has altered the demography of the family and appears to be altering the social fabric at each level of the human ecology (Schell, 1984).

In the United States, the increasing concentration of high-risk families in a geographically concentrated "underclass" (Lehmann, 1986; Wilson, 1987) is dramatically influencing the need and the prognosis for early interventions. For example, in Cleveland in 1960, 23% of all poor families lived in neighborhoods where a majority of the residents were poor. By 1990, that figure was 65%, indicating increased geographic concentration of poverty. Pockets of marked vulnerability show poverty and infant mortality rates many times those found in unafflicted communities. For early intervention services to be plausible in such high-risk areas, they must target "ecological transformation" as the program goal. Home health visiting offers one such model (Olds, Henderson, & Kitzman, 1994; Olds, Henderson, Tatelbaum, & Chamberlin, 1988) in which the basic relationship between the community and the child is altered by "injecting" a new caring adult into the family equation as a representative of the larger society—a nurse skilled in child care and child developmental issues. Such efforts together with thoughtful evaluation research can serve as "transforming experiments" that advance an ecologically valid science of early intervention (Bronfenbrenner, 1979).

An ecological perspective has much to contribute to the process of understanding child neglect. It gives us a kind of social map for navigating a path through the complexities. It helps us see the relationships (potential and actual) among forces in the lives of families and communities—how, for example, some human service programs are complementary, whereas others may be competitive. It aids us in seeing the range of alternative conceptualizations of problems affecting children and points us in the direction of multiple strategies for intervention. It provides a checklist to use in thinking about what is happening, and what to do about it when faced with developmental problems and social pathologies that afflict children. It does this by asking us always to consider the micro-, meso-, exo- and macrosystem dimensions of developmental phenomena and interventions. It constantly suggests the possibility that context is shaping causal relationships. It always tells us "it depends" and stimulates an attempt to find out "on what." With this as a foundation, we can move to consider issues of definition.

DEFINITION IN CONTEXT: CHILD NEGLECT IS CHILD NEGLECT IS CHILD NEGLECT

As noted earlier, human development always occurs "in context." However, this does not mean that there are no universals. A particularly relevant example comes from the work of anthropologist Ronald Rohner (1975). Rohner studied the meaning and implications of rejection transculturally. Using the Human Area Relations Files, he demonstrated that although cultures differ in the way the rejection is expressed, across all cultures, rejection is a "psychological malignancy." Thus, it is associated with whatever is defined as a negative outcome *in that culture.* This, we believe, is a crucial insight for understanding neglect in terms of psychological unavailability, for it offers a universal perspective on our central metaphor of neglect representing a hole in the center of the child's life. What do we know about the meaning of that hole in U.S. culture?

Child maltreatment does not exist as a concept apart from social and cultural context in historical time and place (Garbarino et al., 1986). At any given time, child maltreatment is a social judgment about the minimal standards of care. Child neglect is the failure to meet these minimal community standards of care. These standards evolve and are bound to change as a function of a negotiated settlement between science and professional expertise on the one hand and culture and community values on the other. For example, in the United States of the 1950s, there were no minimal standards of care for children in automobiles. By the 1980s, knowledge had stimulated changes in community values, and now it is considered neglectful to permit a young child to ride in a car without a car seat. This value arose from the knowledge that more than two thirds of injuries and 90% of fatalities in automotive crashes can be prevented through protective action on the part of parents. This is the basic model for defining neglect: historical advocacy based on increased knowledge of childhood processes.

It may be said that the research on child maltreatment has a hole in the middle, where the concept of neglect should be filled in. Child neglect may be thought of as central to the study of child maltreatment because of its high and increasing incidence in our society. Research is lacking, however, largely because of difficulty in defining what constitutes neglect. Definitional issues are critical. How is neglect to be defined today so that child care researchers and professionals can come to agreement about how to effectively study and treat it? How will we define it now so we can fill the hole in neglect research and end the neglect of neglect?

The National Incidence Studies break up the concept of child neglect into three categories: physical, educational, and emotional neglect. All of these definitions involve inadequate care or the failure to provide; all of them assume that children have basic needs that must be met. These needs involve being physically cared for—making sure a child is properly fed and clothed, that a child is allowed to learn and thrive, that a child is treated well emotionally. Under Third National Incidence Study (NIS-3; Sedlak & Broadhurst, 1996) standards, educational neglect was the most prevalent type of neglect, followed by physical and then emotional neglect. One concept is common to these three types of neglect: They all deal with a parent or caregiver's *failure* to meet a child's basic needs. One main problem in coming to a universal definition is how we define these basic needs. Standards established by NIS-3 are neither universal nor unchanging definitions. The process of coming to a universally agreed on standard is a struggle, as we must take into account not only community standards but professional ones (Barnett, Manly, & Cicchetti, 1991; Garbarino et al., 1986), as well as ones that are relevant across cultures, while keeping in mind the centrality of basic needs.

How should we define child neglect? Wolock and Horowitz (1984) define child neglect as "the failure of the child's parent or caretaker who has the material resources to do so, to provide minimally adequate care in the areas of health, nutrition, shelter, education, supervision, affection or attention, and protection" (p. 531). *Failure* is the key word here. Neglect is easily distinguished from abuse operationally. Neglect is an act of omission; abuse is one of commission (Garbarino et al., 1986; Wolock & Horowitz, 1984). The failure to provide is critical. Wolock and Horowitz's definition is consistent with the other attempts to wrestle with definitional issues (e.g., Garbarino et al., 1986; McGee & Wolfe, 1991; Thompson & Jacobs, 1991).

The struggle to establish a definition of neglect that would be relevant across cultures is a particularly challenging one. LeVine and LeVine (1981) point out that in sub-Saharan Africa, it is common for pre-school-aged children to stay at home and care for their younger siblings and complete basic domestic chores while their parents go out to work. In the West, we may see this practice as a clear case of neglect. Looking at the situation through an ethnographic lens, however, we will see that context is everything. Looking deeply, we will see that, given the greater sense of community in some African cultures, it is rare that the aforementioned children are completely alone. Rather, grandparents and neighbors are rarely more than earshot away, and the children's mothers are likely to be doing agricultural work not far away as well.

This type of arrangement seems impractical for U.S. society, as our lives have been increasingly moving farther from the home—workplaces in some large cities may be hours away, and the sense of community that is present in some African communities is diminishing in the United States as Americans move much of their lives away from the home. The sense of the "rugged individualist" that permeates U.S. society further contributes to the disregard for community and wider kinship networks. Thus, should we hear that a mother has left her 2-month-old in the care of her 4-year-old in a downtown Los Angeles apartment, for example, it is likely that our society would be outraged and consider her to be neglectful of her children. Again, we must look at the context. Our society does not accept the caretaking of a 2-month-old by a 4-year-old, in any context where an adult would not be present. In the African case, however, we could not make the same judgment. It is important, then, to consider the cultural context of neglect before making judgments that would apply to only one culture. The social and cultural context is critical, because so many factors must be taken into account. We must also be sensitive to value judgments, while keeping the basic needs of children at the forefront of discussions. In the United States, we view the bond between the mother and child as one of the most important to a child's successful emotional development. In the societies studied by LeVine and LeVine (1981), however, the bond between mother and child is not as strong as is the bond between siblings.

Different standards of what is important in child development further complicate the definitional issues. Polansky and Williams (1978) found that women in the middle classes felt that cognitive-emotional interactions were more important to childrearing, whereas working-class mothers felt that basic physical care was more important. Indeed, in the different life situations that these mothers must face, this makes sense. For middle-class mothers, it is likely that basic physical needs simply are easier to meet, whereas for working-class mothers, this may be more of a challenge. Cultural differences abound here as well. Women in the African society studied by LeVine and LeVine (1981), for example, do not make eye contact with their infants past 3 months of age for fear that they will encourage their children to be playful—a characteristic that is not encouraged between mother and child. The role of the mother is strictly functional by Western standards, in that the mother provides basic physical needs, but the children are not completely without social interaction. Siblings, grandparents, and others are permitted to engage the children in play, thus, the children's cognitive and emotional needs are met elsewhere. LeVine and LeVine point out that a child would not be considered deprived unless these alternative sources of stimulation were unavailable. Their research harkens back to the work by Polansky and Williams that shows us that middle-class, white

American definitions of child neglect certainly are not universal or even necessarily the best standards by which to decide how to define neglect, but there is definitely a sense here of what constitutes basic needs and generally how to meet these needs. In what ways and how elaborately these needs are met differ, but we can agree that there is some consensus that basic physical, emotional, and educational needs are most important.

As researchers struggle to find a clear operational, universal definition of child neglect, at least one study has found that there is a surprisingly high level of agreement among mothers of both the middle and working classes and social workers on what constitutes basic, adequate child care (Polansky & Williams, 1978). As stated earlier, these authors found that, whereas middle-class mothers tended to place greater importance on cognitive-emotional care, working class mothers tended to feel that basic physical care was more important. Thus, it seems that definitional issues and basic standards for care can be agreed on to some extent in the general population, and it stands to show that class standing alone does not explain the higher rates of neglect reported among the poor (Sedlak & Broadhurst, 1996). Indeed, it has been reported that simply taking poverty into account does not explain child neglect—many mothers in extreme poverty and isolation have been found to be wonderful caregivers, whereas others were not (Polansky, DeSaix, Wing, & Patton, 1968). Poverty, however, is a definite risk factor (Drake & Pandey, 1995), and thus allowing our children to live in poverty might be thought of as a type of societal neglect. It seems then, that because there is some agreement, some sort of "transclass" definition with children's basic needs at the center should be within our grasp.

Difficulties in defining what constitutes neglect may stem from changing cultural norms on what standards of behavior are acceptable. On the one hand, there is much continuity across time and space in how societies and parents conceptualize the basic needs of children, despite the fact that there are important cultural differences in how children are treated (Garbarino et al., 1986). Standards of care are sociohistorical constructions that are vulnerable to change. Examples of this abound in our culture and others. The first author, in a paper on the poor in America (Garbarino, 1998), discusses how standards determining who is "rich" in China have changed. He reports talking with a young man who declares that not many people used to be rich in China, but now many were. When asked what determined that someone was rich, the man declared that now many people have radios and bicycles when not many used to.

In the United States, we see similar changes in standards. For example, smoking has been banned in many public establishments across the country. But a few years ago, when the smoking laws were not so strict, few would have blinked an eye to see a smoker in a public restaurant. In the future, smoking in the presence of a child may be seen as neglect. That is, parents may be accused of failing to protect their child from something harmful or even deliberately exposing them. Would this then be taken further? Could this be considered abuse? Recently, television shows have come under a rating system. Will it eventually be considered neglect to allow our children to watch violent or R-rated television shows? Perhaps yes. But any such change is related in part to the degree of personal blame and the repercussions of such a definition of neglect. Perhaps the key is that child neglect is fundamentally about the responsibility of parents to protect children from *known* hazards. As understanding of hazards increases and as the capacity to protect children from those hazards increases, the minimal standards of care change. Thus, neglect evolves.

Our views change with the social norms and attitudes of the day. Although this is a human trait, we cannot help to feel worried for children who won't be protected tomorrow because of the flexible or inconsistent cultural norms of today. This is where our call for a universal definition of child neglect begins and ends. We must be able to protect children, and to do this efficiently requires that child care professionals and researchers are on the same page when considering child neglect.

PSYCHOLOGICAL AVAILABILITY: WHAT DOES A PARENT HAVE TO OFFER A CHILD?

Unfortunately, the research on psychological availability of a parent in terms of child neglect tends to focus on mothers. This may be because so many mothers are single parents or primary caregivers. If we consider fathers who abandon their children physically, financially, psychologically, and otherwise as neglectful of their responsibilities to their children, we might not seem to be placing so much responsibility on the mothers. In any case, the reader should keep in mind that this focus on mothers is a limitation of the research on child neglect.

Polansky, Gaudin, Ammons, and Davis (1985) provide us with some important insights about characteristics of the mother who neglects her child. These authors found that the neglectful mother envisions herself to be surrounded by unsupportive people, and she feels lonely and isolated, whereas non-neglecting mothers feel they have more social support and feel less lonely. This feeds what Polansky (1979) has called the apathy-futility syndrome, which is characterized by feelings of despair, detachment, and alienation, that may occur because of social isolation, lack of social supports (Gaudin et al., 1983), and the greater stress accompanied by poor coping skills characteristic of neglectful families (Gaines, Sandgrund, Green, & Power, 1978).

Social distancing (Gaudin & Polansky, 1986) is also characteristic of neglecting families, as mentioned earlier in this chapter. Polansky (1979) points out that neglecting families tend to relocate frequently, contributing to their social isolation. Thus, a mother who neglects her child may be distancing herself socially from others, not only geographically but emotionally as well, and others in turn respond to this, distancing themselves from her isolation and loneliness. It is also likely that the mother is distancing herself from her own child, and neglect of that child is the result. Burgess and Conger (1978) and Bousha and Twentyman (1984) report that abusive and neglectful parents are likely to interact less and more negatively with their children. Of all mothers in the Burgess and Conger (1978) study, neglectful mothers were the most negative in their interactions with their children. The difficulty demonstrated here shows us that when others are not psychologically available for the neglectful mother, she cannot be psychologically available for her own child.

The process, as we can see, appears to be cyclic and requires early intervention if we are to reverse the trend of rapidly escalating rates of child neglect. Social service agencies should have the resources to help at-risk families, and social support and networks are essential, education on the part of social service agencies primary. In addition, Polansky et al. (1985) suggest parenting support groups and social skills workshops as ways to provide help to the neglecting parent. Thompson (1995) suggests that the integration of formal support networks into the informal support networks of families might be a good way to intervene with neglecting families. Home visitation is one of these suggestions, and his book *Preventing Child Maltreatment Through Social Support* provides a detailed and thoughtful analysis of the issues so critical to intervention efforts.

Probably the most critical and most difficult issue, however, is that of the neglectful society. This is a much larger problem and the one more difficult to solve. Intervention on the behalf of the parent is important, but we need to make society aware of the ways it is contributing to child neglect by neglecting the poor. We already know that rates of neglect are higher among the poor. So when we as a society ignore the poor, we contribute to child neglect. We fail to allow poor parents access to social supports, both on interpersonal levels (by believing they are lazy) and on institutional levels (by failing to provide adequate resources for poor parents and, by extension, children). We run into difficulty as well, when we define community standards of neglect but we fail to consider the ways in which neglect and poverty are connected (Drake & Pandey, 1995). Research has shown that children whose families experience long-term economic hardship have more psychosocial difficulties and that this effect is mediated by parental behavior (Bolger, Patterson, Thompson, & Kupersmidt, 1995). From this same study, we can see that harmful effects of poverty are transmitted to children in part by the harmful effects it has on their mothers. In addressing these issues from a systems perspective, we can see the ways in which the different issues feed into and affect one another. We cannot address one problem without addressing others with which it is connected.

In 1924, a study was conducted on the characteristics of family life of a midwestern city called Middletown, which was supposed to be representative of U.S. family life at that time. In 1977, the study was replicated and the results reported. The Middletown study (Bahr, 1980) offers a provocatively illuminating perspective on what children want from their parents. Children were consistent in one trait that they most expected and wanted from their parents. Kids reported that they simply wanted their mothers and fathers to spend time with them, "reading, talking, playing, etc." (p. 47). "Making plenty of money," "Being well-dressed," and "Being a college graduate" were all items that were rated relatively low on the scale. It is clear that what a child requires from his or her parent is relatively simple. It has little to do with money or prestige or outward appearances but, rather, has to do with parents simply being there for their kids. Being psychologically available for a child is the most coveted characteristic of a parent by the child. The fact that this quality was the most desirable for both parents indicates that children's desires have not changed very much and that what a child needs is quite far from material but must emanate from within the parent. When that parent is unavailable or neglectful, the child suffers greatly.

The fact that children want their parents to spend time with them is quite basic. This doesn't seem to be terribly demanding, but for parents who are financially strapped, who lack social supports and are lonely, this desire may seem overwhelming. These parents may feel that they have little to offer their children, either in sheer time spent with them or the quality of that time. Any one of these factors can place a child at risk for neglect. Another issue seems relevant here, as well. It might be the case that upper-class or middle-class parents spend enormous amounts of time away from the home for their work, or are otherwise occupied, and a substitute parent, such as a nanny or other caregiver, is the primary caregiver for the child. As several studies have shown and LeVine and LeVine (1981) demonstrated, as long as the child's basic needs are fulfilled by some caring person, it is likely that the child will function normally. This comes back to the idea of there being very basic needs that are critical to prime developmental outcomes for a child. As noted earlier, there are many different ways of meeting these basic needs.

In considering the African case, again, we can see that wider kinship networks provide a stand-in for the unavailable parent. Grandparents there are more involved than many grandparents in the U.S. today, participating more in caregiving. LeVine and LeVine (1981) found that some of the closest relationships reported in the community were between siblings. Thus, in line with the findings of Erickson, Egeland, & Pianta (1996), we can see that if there is an adult who "fills in" for the inadequate parent, normal development of a neglected child is possible. These researchers remind us that parenting practices today considered maltreating may not have been at other times. Thus, in considering both standards for parental behavior in particular and definitions of neglect in general, social, historical, and cultural contexts must be taken into account but not necessarily accepted as adequate care for children. Again, we must keep the idea of children's basic needs in mind.

LaRose and Wolfe (1987) point out that, in contrast to the abusive parent, the neglectful parent demands little from his or her child and uses strategies of avoidance in dealing with stressors. This strategy does not appear to be effective, as we have seen from earlier mentioned studies, as neglectful parents tend to be more lonely, tend to feel more isolated, and lack social supports. This is not surprising, given the tendency to avoid difficulties rather than being assertive and expressive about feelings and desires. Thus, avoidance breeds loneliness, and loneliness breeds isolation, and the cycle continues. This is likely to lead to the overall poor psychological adjustment reported by LaRose and Wolfe (1987). These authors go on to point out that neglectful and abusive parental interactions are not always as distinct as they might seem. In fact, there is substantial overlap in the ways abusive and neglectful parents deal with stress. Both have been found to have poor coping skills. The outcome of interactions is what differs, however.

Whereas an abusive parent might lash out at the child, a neglectful parent might avoid the child, which can lead to inadequate supervision and not meeting basic needs and can even lead to injury or death.

Several investigators have found that neglectful parents do not respond well to their children's attempts to garner their attention, so important to the children, according to the Middletown study (Bahr, 1980). Neglectful parents, consistent with the definitions of neglect involving acts of omission, fail to stimulate their children verbally or socially. It seems, then, that as soon as parents decline social interaction with their children, they are denying and threatening basic developmental needs (and desires) of their children. Again, we must keep in mind the social context of this. It is hardly likely that we would consider an African mother's lack of eye contact and verbal intercourse with her child alone as threats to the child's development. In this culture, that is normative behavior, and goes along with the course of the child's normal developmental course. We must take into account the fact that these needs are fulfilled elsewhere. In the United States, however, and in the context of the middle-class standard of having good emotional and cognitive relationships with one's child, the requirement that a *parent* fulfills his or her child's cognitive needs stands tall. We must keep in mind that a community's standards for what is normative behavior are not always in the best interests of the child, particularly in the case of attitudes about poverty, discussed earlier, and current issues on welfare reform, which we will discuss at the end of this chapter.

What effects does neglect have on children? Erickson et al. (1996) report that neglected children tend to be uncooperative with adults, that they have low positive affect, and do not express a sense of humor. The effects of neglect are most devastating at early ages when children are developing most quickly. Children who have been neglected early in life showed the most dramatic declines "in cognitive and social-emotional functioning and their behavior was of great concern" (p. 676). Children in their study who had been neglected often appeared unkempt. The combination of their poor physical appearance and their deviant behavior was a recipe for disaster with the children's peers, as well as the teachers. This example is one outcome of a child who is a victim of neglect. We see here that a parent's physical and psychological unavailability to a child is devastating, and the child's reactions probably perpetuate the cycle, through an interactional pattern (Gaensbauer & Sands, 1979). The child's rejection by his or her peers, felt rejection by his or her parent(s), and lack of resources for coping with difficulties leads us to a situation for which we cannot help but grieve.

Our task then is to ask ourselves whether these signs of maltreatment should be as neglected as they are. Indeed, the question should not be how much time we should spend on abuse over neglect, or whose wounds are worse, but what we can do to become aware that the neglected child needs just as much help as a child who has a bruise on his or her body. We hope that this work, along with the other works in this volume, can serve as just one "call to arms" for ending the neglect of neglect and filling the holes—both in neglectful families specifically and in child maltreatment in general. Impoverished families must be given the attention and the resources that can break the cycle of systematic deprivation that makes a child's environment toxic (Garbarino, 1992). We feel this ideal can be made a reality when we make a commitment to meet children's needs, "regardless of race, creed, national origin, or income-generating capacity" (Garbarino, 1992, p. 235), and are able to agree on definitional issues to forge forward and give neglected families the attention they so desperately need.

This analysis is particularly relevant to the U.S. public policy arena at the close of the 20th century. The specific legislation and the larger social movement known as "welfare reform" necessarily evoke a broad discussion of societal neglect. In its hard-line form, welfare reform can lead to further deterioration in the care of at-risk children if it means increasing reliance on the income-generating capacity of parents as the basis for a child's access to what is needed to meet basic developmental needs. The United States already has the biggest gap in incomes between rich and poor (after taxes and income transfers). Anything that exacerbates this gap will probably increase neglect among children at the bottom of the socioeconomic ladder. All this makes for increasing social toxicity for poor children, as the vulnerabilities of high-risk parents are exploited by a market-economy-driven social policy (Garbarino, 1995). If things deteriorate far enough, we may see ever more clearly that the neglect experienced by children in families flows *from* the larger social environment *through* the parents. Neglect, then, reflects not just the family with the hole in the middle but the society with a similar hole in its moral core.

REFERENCES

Albee, G. W. (1980). Primary prevention and social problems. In G. Gerbner, C. J. Ross, & E. Ziegler (Eds.), *Child abuse: An agenda for action.* New York: Oxford University Press.

Bahr, H. M. (1980). Changes in family life in Middletown, 1924-77. *Public Opinion Quarterly, 44*(1), 5-52.

Barnett, D., Manly, J. T., & Cicchetti, D. (1991). Continuing toward an operational definition of psychological maltreatment. *Development and Psychopathology, 3,* 19-29.

Bolger, K. E., Patterson, C. J., Thompson, W. W., & Kupersmidt, J. B. (1995). Psychosocial adjustment among children experiencing persistent and intermittent family economic hardship. *Child Development, 66,* 1107-1129.

Bousha, D. M., & Twentyman, C. T. (1984). Mother-child interactional style in abuse, neglect, and control groups: Naturalistic observations in the home. *Journal of Abnormal Psychology, 1,* 106-114.

Bronfenbrenner, U. (1979). The ecology of human development. Cambridge, MA: Harvard University Press.

Bronfenbrenner, U. (1986). Ecology of the family as a context for human development research perspectives. *Developmental Psychology, 22,* 723-742.

Bronfenbrenner, U., & Crouter, A. C. (1983). The evolution of environmental models in developmental research. In P. Mussen (Ed.), *The handbook of child psychology* (pp. 357-414). New York: John Wiley.

Burgess, R. L., & Conger, R. D. (1978). Family interactions in abusive, neglectful, and normal families. *Child Development, 49,* 1163-1173.

Drake, B., & Pandey, S. (1995). Understanding the relationship between neighborhood poverty and specific types of child maltreatment. *Child Abuse and Neglect, 20(11),* 1003-1018.

Erickson, M. F., Egeland, B., & Pianta, R. (1996). The effects of maltreatment on the development of young children. In D. Cicchetti & V. Carlson (Eds.), *Child maltreatment: Theory and research on the causes and consequences of child abuse and neglect* (pp. 647-684). New York: Cambridge University Press.

Forrester, J. (1969). *Urban dynamics.* Cambridge, MA: M.I.T. Press.

Gaensbauer, T. J., & Sands, K. (1979). Distorted affective communications in abused/neglected infants and their potential impact on caretakers. *Journal of the American Academy of Child Psychiatry, 18,* 236-250.

Gaines, R., Sandgrund, A., Green, A. H., & Power, E. (1978). Etiological factors in child maltreatment: A multivariate study of abusing, neglecting, and normal mothers. *Journal of Abnormal Psychology, 5,* 531-540.

Garbarino, J. (1992). The meaning of poverty in the world of children. *American Behavioral Scientist, 35(3),* 220-237.

Garbarino, J. (1995). *Raising children in a socially toxic environment.* San Francisco: Jossey-Bass.

Garbarino, J. (1998). The stress of being a poor child in America. *Child and Adolescent Psychiatric Clinics of North America, 7*(1), 105-119.

Garbarino, J., Guttmann, E., & Seeley, J. W. (1986). *The psychologically battered child: Strategies for identification, assessment, and intervention.* San Francisco: Jossey-Bass.

Gaudin, J. M., & Polansky, N. A. (1986). Social distancing of the neglectful family: Sex, race and social class influences. *Children and Youth Services Review, 8,* 1-12.

Gaudin, J. M., Polansky, N. A., Kilpatrick, A. C., & Shilton, P. (1993). Loneliness, depression, stress, and social supports in neglectful families. *American Journal of Orthopsychiatry, 63(4),* 597-605.

Hardin, G. (1980). The tragedy of the commons. In H. Daly (Ed.), *Economics, ecology, ethics: Essays toward a steady-state economy.* New York: Freeman.

Harrington, M. (1968). *The other America: Poverty in the United States.* New York: Macmillan.

LaRose, L., & Wolfe, D. (1987). Psychological characteristics of parents who abuse or neglect their children. In B. Lahey & A. E. Kazdin (Eds.), *Advances in clinical child psychology: Volume 10* (pp. 55-97). New York: Plenum.

Lehmann, N. (1986). The underclass. *The Atlantic Monthly, 254,* 1-25.

LeVine, S., & LeVine, R. (1981). Child abuse and neglect in sub-Saharan Africa. In J. Korbin (Ed.), *Child abuse & neglect: Cross-cultural perspectives.* London: University of California Press.

McGee, R. A., & Wolfe, D. A. (1991). Psychological maltreatment: Toward an operational definition. *Development and Psychopathology, 3,* 3-18.

Olds, D. L., Henderson, C. R., & Kitzman, H. (1994). Does prenatal and infancy nurse home visitation have enduring effects on qualities of parental caregiving and child health at 25 to 50 months of life? *Pediatrics, 93*(1), 89-98.

Olds, D. L., Henderson, C. R., Tatelbaum, R., & Chamberlin, R. (1988). Improving the life course development of socially disadvantaged mothers: A randomized trial of nurse home visitation. *American Journal of Public Health, 78*(11), 1436-1445.

Perry, B. D., Pollard, R. A., Blakley, T. L., Baker, W. L., & Vigilante, D. (1995). Childhood trauma, the neurobiology of adaptation, and the "use-dependent" development of the brain: How "states" become "traits." *Infant Mental Health Journal, 16*(4), 271-289.

Polansky, N. A. (1979). Help for the help-less. *Smith College Studies in Social Work, 49*(3), 169-191.

Polansky, N. A., DeSaix, C., Wing, M. L., & Patton, J. D. (1968). Child neglect in a rural community. *Social Casework, 49*(8), 467-474.

Polansky, N. A., Gaudin, J. M., Ammons, P. W., & Davis, K. B. (1985). The psychological ecology of the neglectful mother. *Child Abuse & Neglect, 9,* 265-275.

Polansky, N. A., & Williams, D. P. (1978). Class orientations to child neglect. *Social Work, 23*(5), 397-401.

Rohner, R. P., (1975). *They love me, they love me not: A worldwide study of the effects of parental acceptance and rejection.* New Haven, CN: HRAF.

Schell, O. (1984). *To get rich is glorious: China in the eighties.* New York: Pantheon.

Sedlak, A. J., & Broadhurst, D. D. (1996). *The third national incidence study of child abuse and neglect.* Washington, DC: U.S. Department of Health and Human Services.

Thompson, R. A. (1995). *Preventing child maltreatment through social support.* London: Sage.

Thompson, R. A., & Jacobs, J. E. (1991). Defining psychological maltreatment: Research and policy perspectives. *Development and psychopathology, 3,* 93-102.

Vygotsky, L. (1986). *Thought and language.* Cambridge, MA: MIT Press.

Whittaker, J. K. (1983). Social support networks in child welfare. In J. K. Whittaker & J. Garbarino (Eds.), *Social support networks.* New York: Aldine.

Willerman, L., Broman, S., & Fiedler, M. (1970). Infant development, preschool IQ and social class. *Child Development, 41,* 69-77.

Wilson, W. J. (1987). *The truly disadvantaged: The inner city, the underclass, and public policy.* Chicago: University of Chicago Press.

Wolock, I., & Horowitz, B. (1984). Child maltreatment as a social problem: The neglect of neglect. *American Journal of Orthopsychiatry, 54*(4), 530-543.

2 Child Neglect

A Review of Definitions and Measurement Research

Susan J. Zuravin

To promote the development of reliable and valid operational definitions of child neglect, this chapter has three objectives: (1) to review recent methodologies for defining neglect, (2) to examine recent measurement research on neglect, and (3) to make recommendations for future research. A review of the literature reveals no publications that have centered on either of the first two.

Focusing on child neglect is justified on a number of bases. First, it is the most prevalent type of maltreatment (U.S. Department of Health and Human Services [U.S.DHHS], 1996). Second, it has received much less definitional attention than other maltreatment types, particularly physical and sexual abuse (Wolock & Horowitz, 1984). Third, it has received less research attention than the other maltreatment types. More than 10 years ago, the lack of a standard definition was recognized as a critical problem for developing our knowledge of neglect (National Center on Child Abuse and Neglect, 1987). This problem still prevails today.

AUTHOR'S NOTE: Work on this chapter was supported by a 1997 grant from the Lois and Samuel Silberman Fund of New York.

BACKGROUND

This section of the chapter provides a context for examining current methods for defining neglect. It is divided into two parts: Part 1 provides information about problems and recommendations for defining maltreatment and its various types (i.e., physical abuse, sexual abuse, emotional maltreatment, and neglect), whereas Part 2 focuses on neglect.

Part I

Since the publication of the article by Kempe, Silverman, Steele, Droegmueller, & Silver (1962) on the battered child, child maltreatment has attracted considerable media, policy, and research attention. Given widespread concern, one might expect to see a relative consensus regarding definitions of maltreatment. Unfortunately, this is not the case. Statutory and legal definitions are vague and differ among states. Clinical definitions vary from agency to agency as well as among professionals. Research definitions also are not standard and universal. Today, as when Zigler (1980) wrote about controlling child abuse, "no standardized definitions of child abuse have been developed or accepted by all professionals and social service personnel who work in the field" (p. 5).

The importance and consequences of this definitional problem are summarized by Martin (1979) in an article in *Pediatrics:*

> The issue of defining abuse and neglect is one of central importance and logically precedes a discussion of incidence, etiology, (sequelae), and treatment. The vagueness and ambiguities that surround the definition of this particular social problem touch every aspect of the field—reporting system, treatment program, research, and policy planning. (p. 56)

Definitional debates have centered around numerous issues, impeding arrival at a standardized, well-operationalized definition. Should definitions be broad or narrow? In other words, should they be restricted to clear instances of serious physical harm, should they encompass neglect incidents of emotional harm, or should they include all acts that jeopardize the development of children? Should definitions be general or precise? The main proponents of the general definition are judges who argue that they need flexibility for their decision making. Should the definition focus on harm to the child, the parental act, or both? Should definitions require intentionality of the parent as a key issue? Should research definitions be based on statutory definitions, or should they be developed independently and for their own purposes?

This last controversy is vociferously debated (see Barnett, Manly, & Cicchetti, 1991). It is a backlash, in part, to a recommendation made in the early 1980s (Ross & Zigler, 1980) that separate standardized definitions be developed for *different purposes:* "Many discussions would be clarified by the development of separate working definitions of child abuse for legal, clinical, social service, and research purposes" (p. 294). They predicted that the "standardization of a range of definitions actually being used informally by members of different professions would facilitate accurate communication about child abuse" (p. 294).

The opponents (e.g., Barnett, Manly, & Cicchetti, 1991; Garbarino, 1991; Giovannoni, 1991) of separate definitions for different purposes, particularly research, counter that (1) "the conclusions of the research will have no relevance to existing social policy" (McGee & Wolfe, 1991a, p. 120) and (2) "if the research itself is included under the rubric of maltreatment only on the basis of the researcher's definition of maltreatment, there is danger that the results themselves might be added to the ongoing definitions" (Giovannoni, 1989, p. 30). McGee and Wolfe (1991a) responded (1) that "science demands that research operate from invariant 'universal' operational definitions," whereas "social definitions of maltreatment are in continuing evolution" and (2) that "researchers are often interested in thoroughly exploring a phenomenon—even those aspects that the state has not identified as problematic" (p. 120).

Notwithstanding these controversies, many articles call attention to the problems with, ramifications of, and needed improvements in research definitions. It is probable that more effort has been spent discussing the shortcomings of existing definitions and providing guidance for the development of new ones than on the formulation of standardized and well-operationalized definitions and on measurement research.

Several authors (e.g., Besharov, 1981; Cicchetti & Barnett, 1991; Zigler, 1980) have called for the development of a classification system for maltreatment. For instance, as Zigler (1980) notes,

> The nature of child maltreatment is . . . in need of a more differentiated and conceptually based classificatory system. It is a phenotypic event having a variety of expressions and causes, and we will make little

> headway so long as we insist on viewing every act of maltreatment as the equivalent of every other. (p. 172)

Cicchetti and Barnett (1991) concur. They assert that "research on maltreatment would benefit greatly from the utilization of structured classification schemes" (p. 360).

Some (Manly, Cicchetti, & Barnett, 1994; Wolfe & McGee, 1994) conclude it is important to incorporate into the classification system several dimensions, including maltreatment type, frequency, chronicity, severity, and perpetrator. For example, Manly et al. (1994) noted that most research has "focused on maltreatment as a dichotomous variable" with "scant empirical attention being devoted to the multidimensional nature within the broad rubric of maltreatment" (p. 121).

Many (Besharov, 1981; Cicchetti & Barnett, 1991; McGee & Wolfe, 1991b; National Research Council, 1993; Zuravin, 1991) have called for clear operational definitions. For example, the National Research Council (1993) recommended development of "sound clinical-diagnostic and research instruments for the measurement of child maltreatment" and that the "reliability and validity of these instruments be established by sound testing with economically and culturally diverse populations" (p. 212). Cicchetti and Barnett (1991) noted the following:

> The establishment of a set of operational criteria would have the effect of maximizing the precision in the definition and description of different types of maltreatment. With the development and validation of such a precise nosology and a standardized set of assessment procedures, clarity of communication and language across investigators will be facilitated. (p. 360)

They also concurred with the National Research Council (1993) in advocating "development of a structured, clinically sensitive procedure useful to researchers investigating all subtypes of maltreatment" (p. 360). They noted that such a procedure "would have the advantage of making more standardized and uniform the means used to assess the particular form or forms of maltreatment experienced" (p. 360).

Giovannoni and Becerra (1979), in their book *Defining Child Abuse,* identified and critiqued three approaches to an operational definition: (1) giving an incident the label applied by agency personnel—a dominant past trend, (2) using a combination of the official designation and the researcher's own definition, and (3) the researcher's own definition. The first approach is problematic due to interjurisdictional and intrajurisdictional differences as well as caseworker variation in definitions. This method bars knowledge building because it impedes the comparison of results across studies. The third approach is problematic because it may not have any bearing on cases of maltreatment and may have little relevance for formulating social policy. Giovannoni and Becerra prefer the second approach. It focuses on cases seen by agencies, thus having the most relevance for policy and service delivery, and it clarifies what the researcher means by the maltreatment type, enabling comparisons across studies.

Besharov (1981) has two further recommendations. He noted that (1) information about a study's conceptual classification and operational definitions should be presented clearly when reporting a study and (2) the report should identify any limitations due to definitional inadequacies. This is necessary to figure out why findings conflict, to generalize results to other populations, and to compare conclusions across studies.

Part 2

Review of the recent literature identified only two articles (Dubowitz, Black, Starr, & Zuravin, 1993; Zuravin, 1991) that focused on critiquing existing neglect definitions and formulating recommendations for future work. Like other types of maltreatment, there are no standardized, objective criteria for identifying when neglect has occurred. The dominant trend for operationalizing neglect, as for other types of maltreatment, has been to use "the label assigned to an act by responsible agencies, including hospitals, CPS, police, and courts" (Giovannoni & Becerra, 1979, p. 14).

In defining neglect, both conceptually and operationally, several considerations are important (Zuravin, 1991). First, it differs clinically from other types of maltreatment. It refers to omissions in care, rather than commissions, that endanger or harm children. Because of this difference and the likelihood that the etiology and sequelae of neglect may differ from those of other types, neglect should be a distinct type in any classification. Second, it is phenotypically diverse, encompassing many different subtypes (i.e., inadequate supervision, medical care, housing, etc.). Because of this heterogeneity and the possibility that the etiology and sequelae of different subtypes of neglect may differ, their classification should include conceptual and operational definitions for each subtype. The classification should be multidimensional, including at least subtype, frequency, and chronicity. Third, behaviors or lack thereof need to be considered in the context of the child's developmental level. For example, needs for supervision are very different in endangering young children and adolescents. Fourth, the provision of daily, routine care for a child is a parent's or a primary caregiver's responsibility. Failure to provide such care is the parent's problem; consequently, neglect should be restricted to omissions in care by parents (and primary caregivers).

REVIEW OF RECENT DEFINITIONS OF CHILD NEGLECT

The purposes of this section are to examine the current status of methods for defining child neglect and to determine whether recent definitions meet the recommendations noted earlier. For the second purpose, I examined whether any type of classification system was used, the dimensions of the system, the type of operational definition according to the Giovannoni and Becerra (1979) schema, and whether the definition was reliable and valid. In addition, I examined whether the definitions met the recommendations of Zuravin (1991).

The child maltreatment literature is published in an array of different journals. Some of these journals are highly specific (e.g., *Child Maltreatment, Child Abuse and Neglect*), while others are broadly focused. To achieve the first objective, all articles pertinent to child neglect published during the 5-year period from 1992 to 1996 in *The International Journal of Child Abuse and Neglect* were reviewed to assess methodologies for defining neglect. *Child Abuse and Neglect* was chosen because it is the oldest of the specific journals. To be included in the review, an article had to report empirical findings on child neglect only or separately from findings on other types. Before examining the results of the review, there are two caveats. Contrary to Besharov's recommendation (1981) for detailing one's conceptual and operational definitions, many of the eligible articles failed to do this. Consequently, this review is less precise than it could have been. Also contrary to Besharov's recommendations, none of the authors discussed how their definitions may have limited the conclusions.

Of the 489 mostly empirical articles, 25[1] reported findings on child neglect. Study objectives focused on five different topics: epidemiology—3 studies; etiology—7 studies; reporting—1 study; sequelae—9 studies; and treatment—5 studies. Study designs also varied, including retrospective, prospective, and cross-sectional types. The sources of data were child protective services (CPS) case records, caseworker reports, central registries data, or parent-child reports.

In the 25 studies, 23 reported findings for multiple types of maltreatment. Only 2 (Ethier, Lacharite, & Couture, 1995; Gaudin, Polansky, Kilpatrick, & Shilton, 1996) focused exclusively on neglect. All 23 reported findings for physical abuse, and some reported findings for sexual or emotional maltreatment or both. Some also reported when multiple types occurred to one child or in one family. Given the scant information provided on definitions, only 1 study (Tjaden & Thoennes, 1992) characterized the maltreatment types in terms of other dimensions (frequency and severity).

The most common method of operationalizing neglect as well as the other types of maltreatment was by use of the label applied by official agency personnel—14 articles did so; none of these studies reported on neglect subtypes. Four articles used the agency label plus the researcher's own definition. Even though information about definitions was hardly covered by most articles and definitions differed considerably across the studies, all either required that the neglect meet certain operational criteria or used some instrument that described the neglect in greater detail than an agency label. For instance, Benedict, Zuravin, Brandt, and Abbey (1994) used the Zuravin definitions (1991) for neglect subtypes. This procedure requires that the case be substantiated for neglect (agency label) and meet operational criteria for at least one neglect subtype. No information, however, was provided on the assessment instrument. Christensen, Brayden, Dietrich, McLaughlin, and Sherrod (1994) used CPS case records reviewed by coders. The information recorded by the raters was reviewed by pediatricians, who decided whether cases met the definitions of maltreatment. No information was provided about the operational definitions. Herrenkohl, Herrenkohl, Rupert, Egolf, and Lutz (1995) used the agency label and an observational rating of parent-child interaction to create a neglect index. Coohey (1996) classified his cases into neglect only, physical abuse only, and neglect plus physical abuse by screening neglectful parents with a question asking whether the parent had punched or hit a child with an object at least once per week.

The remaining 7 studies used the third approach, the researcher-designed measure only. Two (Ards & Harrell, 1993; Jones & McCurdy, 1992) were reanalyses of data from the National Studies of the Incidence and Severity of Child Abuse and Neglect (NIS-1 and NIS-2) ([U.S.DHHS, 1981, 1986). Four studies examined sequelae, and maltreatment was measured retrospectively, typically with questions developed by the researcher.

The examples described in the discussion to follow reveal that none of the studies with the exception of the two U.S.DHHS (1981, 1988) reanalyses used the same operational definition, and only one (Rosen & Martin, 1996) employed a measure with known reliabilities and validities. Rosen and Martin's study of the impact of childhood abuse on psychological symptoms among male and female soldiers in the U.S. army used the Childhood Trauma Questionnaire (Bernstein et al., 1994), a self-report instrument designed to provide brief, reliable, and valid assessments of a range of childhood traumatic experiences, including emotional neglect, physical abuse, sexual abuse, and physical neglect. Egeland and Susman's (1996) study of dissociation as a mediator of child abuse across generations used two measures of maltreatment types. For the mothers' generation, they asked questions about how they were raised, including the makeup of their families, their living conditions, feelings toward parents, how affection was expressed, how they were disciplined, the degrees of emotional support given, as well as whether they were physically abused, neglected, or sexually abused. For the children's generation, they used in-home observations of childrearing practices and maternal attitudes at many points in the child's life up to 48 months of age. They rated physical abuse, psychological unavailability, and neglect. Chaffin, Kelleher, and Hollenberg's (1996) study of the relationship between physical abuse and neglect and substance abuse and social risk factors used four questions from the antisocial personality disorder module of the Diagnostic Interview Schedule. These questions inquired about leaving very young children alone for extended periods, inadequately feeding or caring for children, and having a health care provider suggest the children were neglected. Sheridan's (1995) study of an intergenerational model of substance abuse, family functioning, and physical abuse and neglect used researcher-developed questions concerning omissions in care, including not being fed enough, not being clothed properly, being left alone when they were too little or couldn't take care of themselves, and ignored or treated like they didn't matter. Ney, Fung, and Wickett's study (1994) of the impact of combinations of types of maltreatment interviewed children with their Child Experience Questionnaire and covered physical abuse, physical neglect, verbal abuse, emotional neglect, and sexual abuse.

REVIEW OF MEASUREMENT RESEARCH

Measurement research should provide information on the psychometrics of existing methods as well as develop and assess new measures. To examine the extent and content of measurement research, 5 years (or from date of origin) of five journals—*The International Journal of Child Abuse and Neglect, Child Maltreatment, Journal of Family Violence, Child Welfare,* and *Journal of Interpersonal Violence*—were hand searched for pertinent articles on child neglect. Despite repeated calls for psychometric research (National Research Council, 1993), only six articles were found. Of the six, two (Kaufman, Jones, Stieglitz, Vitulano, & Mannarino, 1994; McGee, Wolfe, Yuen, Wilson, & Carnochan, 1995) compared the adequacy of different sources for gathering information on maltreatment; two (Wolfe & McGee, 1994; Trocme, 1996) reported on the development of an assessment instrument (operational definition); one (Manly, Cicchetti, & Barnett, 1994) examined the construct validity of a classification and operational scheme; and one (Gaudin, Polansky, & Kilpatrick, 1992) examined the validity of a subset from the Child Well-Being Scales (Magura & Moses, 1986).

Adequacy of Different Data Sources

Given the heavy reliance of studies on operationalizing neglect and other types of maltreatment by "the agency label" and case records to obtain additional data, the most fascinating and relevant papers are by Kaufman et al. (1994) and McGee et al. (1995). Both groups examined whether sources of data in addition to CPS records or caseworker reports would provide important additional information about children's maltreatment. Findings suggested that exclusive dependence on data from CPS sources leads to misestimation of prevalence and severity for all types of maltreatment as well as the incidence of multiple types of maltreatment per child or family.

McGee et al.'s (1995) study obtained maltreatment history and severity data on 160 adolescents from three sources—the CPS caseworker, the CPS case record, and the adolescent. Ratings from 0 to 3 in severity were assigned for five types of maltreatment, for each of three possible perpetrators from the three data sources. Overall, findings show that 94% of the adolescents had experienced multiple types of maltreatment. With regard to differences in results among the three data sources, neglect had the largest discrepancies in prevalence rates. The CPS caseworker and case record researcher agreed 82% of the time that neglect had occurred, whereas the caseworker and case record researcher agreed with the adolescent only 59% and 65% of the time, respectively. There were also discrepancies relative to severity. There was a moderate correlation between CPS caseworkers and case record researchers (.52) but low correlations between these two and the adolescents (.32 and .02, respectively). Adolescents characterized their neglect experiences as much less severe than the other two sources. McGee and colleagues comment that "it would almost appear that maltreated youth and official report sources are rating different experiences" (p. 241). To assess the validity of the different sources of data, regressions were performed using the Achenbach Youth Self Report Internalizing and Externalizing Scales. Findings "indicated that ratings made by adolescent victims significantly improved prediction of self-reported behavior problems above and beyond the ratings of 'official' sources" (p. 243), whereas "ratings by official sources never added unique variance above that explained by adolescent ratings" (p. 243).

Although the results of Kaufman et al. (1994) were not as dramatic as those of McGee et al. (1995), probably because the children were not used as a data source, they did show discrepancies between sources. The researchers integrated maltreatment history and severity information on 56 children from four sources—a checklist filled out by the CPS caseworker, parent interview, medical record, and research assistants' observations. Ratings from 0 to 4 in severity were assigned to each of four types of maltreatment—physical abuse, neglect, sexual abuse, and emotional maltreatment—based on all four sources. For a type to be considered present, the child had to obtain a severity level of 2. For neglect, this meant that two forms of neglect were experienced. Overall, findings showed that most children experienced multiple types of maltreatment—91% experienced two or more types. With regard to neglect, (1) two cases of neglect were identified through review of the medical records that were not identified by the caseworker, (2) five cases classified as neglectful by the caseworker were not classified as neglectful by the research raters who compiled the data from the four sources, and (3) three cases of mild neglect turned out to be serious on review of the medical records. To assess the validity of the maltreatment ratings compiled from the four sources, three multiple regressions with the four types of maltreatment as predictors were performed. Findings revealed that only neglect was negatively associated with intellectual functioning. Unlike physical abuse and emotional maltreatment, however, neglect was not associated with acting out behavior or depression.

Development and Psychometrics of Two Measures

The first article, one by Wolfe and McGee (1994), had two objectives. First, "to examine the composition of the ROME (an assessment instrument called the Record of Maltreatment Experiences) to determine the underlying factor structure defining child maltreatment" (p. 170). This was to determine if the factors corresponded to the main types of maltreatment—sexual abuse, physical abuse, neglect, and emotional maltreatment. The second objective was to examine the construct validity of the ROME factors. To do this, the authors examined whether "individual types of maltreatment had independent effects on current adjustment or they interacted in a manner that improved the prediction equation significantly" (p. 170). Subjects included 162 adolescents receiving CPS services.

The ROME is a comprehensive assessment of a child's maltreatment experiences. It gathers information about the severity, perpetrator, and developmental age at occurrence (early childhood, later childhood, and adolescence) for five types of maltreatment—physical abuse, sexual abuse, exposure to wife assault, psychological maltreatment, and neglect. Each type is operationalized by a different set of items constructed by the researchers. Information for this assessment was gathered from CPS records.

Items from the ROME pertaining to psychological maltreatment, partner abuse, physical abuse, and constructive parenting practices (for operationalizing neglect)—57 of them—were subjected to two principal components analyses, one for maltreatment occurring during early childhood and the other, for middle childhood. The sexual abuse items were not included. The factor structure for both developmental periods was very similar. For early childhood, the factors accounted for 57% of the variance. They were, in order of amount of variance accounted for, psychological maltreatment (19 items "depicting unpredictable, threatening, and denigrating acts" [Wolfe & McGee, 1994, p. 171]), partner abuse (7 items), child neglect (8 items depicting omissions in care), positive childrearing (7 items), and physical abuse (6 items). Overall,

> [this] factor structure supports the contention that dimensions of maltreatment corresponding to the major categories described in the literature are valuable and reliable aggregated variables; that is, actions commonly associated with child neglect, for example, cluster together and are distinguishable from other types of maltreatment. (p. 177)

To examine the construct validity, five scales were used. Four were created "by summing scores on variables loading on the four factors of primary interest to the investigation" (Wolfe & McGee, 1994, p. 171). The scales were psychological maltreatment, physical abuse, partner abuse, and neglect. A fifth scale was created by using 16 of the 17 sexual abuse items. Internal consistency-reliability (alpha) for all five scales was high. The dependent variable for analyses, carried out separately for boys and girls, was the Achenbach Child Behavior Checklist (CBCL; Achenbach, 1991) completed by the adolescent's primary caregiver. Analyses were performed on the total behavior, internalizing, and externalizing scores.

For males, not one of the five maltreatment types occurring during the early developmental period had an independent effect on subsequent behavior. Examination of the interaction terms revealed that adjustment was poorer when both physical and psychological maltreatment were present and when partner abuse was lower and neglect was higher. During middle childhood, only neglect affected the three behavior scores.

For females, none of the maltreatment types in early or middle childhood were associated with later behavior. Two interactions (neglect during early childhood × neglect during middle childhood as well as the same term for psychological maltreatment), however, were predictive of adolescent behavior. Examination of these terms revealed that (1) "increases in neglect ratings from early to middle childhood were associated with greater adjustment problems" and (2) "adjustment problems were at their worst when psychological maltreatment ratings were high during both early and middle childhood" (Wolfe & McGee, 1994, p. 177). Overall, these findings suggest that the ROME scales do have good construct validity—they predict what they are supposed to predict, poor adjustment—and that neglect is an important construct associated with behavior problems in both boys and girls.

The second article (Trocme, 1996) described the development of the Ontario Child Neglect Index (CNI), an instrument that "is designed to serve as a substantiation tool that can be used by child welfare researchers and practitioners as an operational definition of neglect and the severity of neglect" (p. 145). It was developed by a panel of six individuals knowledgeable about neglect using an expert-based index developed by Gustafson et al. (1986). The CNI has six scales representing different subtypes of neglect: supervision, nutrition, clothing and hygiene, physical health care, mental health care, and developmental-educational care. Each scale is graded on either a 1 to 4 or 1 to 5 severity scale where 1 equals adequate care and 4 or 5 equals omissions that have resulted in harm or are highly likely to result in harm. The perpetrator is restricted to the child's primary caregiver(s). Criteria for various subtypes are age graded. The scoring model "combines the score on the scale receiving the highest severity rating with an age score" (Trocme, 1996, p. 147). This score "is best interpreted as a rating of severity of neglect rather than a categorical measure of neglect versus no neglect" (p. 147).

Several types of psychometric analyses were done on 127 intake cases. Concurrent validity—"extent to which an instrument is correlated with other instruments designed to measure the same construct" (Trocme, 1996; p. 148)—was assessed by "comparing CNI scores to the NIS (U.S. Department of Health and Human Services, 1981) maltreatment classifications (neglect vs. other types of maltreatment) and scores on the Child Well-Being Scales (CWBS; Magura & Moses, 1986) neglect scales" (Trocme, 1996, p. 148). Findings revealed good concurrent validity, with findings for both instruments suggesting that the CNI "is specific to child neglect" (p. 149). Predictive validity—"extent to which instruments accurately predict a subsequent event related to the measured constructs" (p. 149)—was assessed by comparing scores on the CNI and the CWBS with regard to providing continuing child protective services. Findings revealed better predictive validity for the CNI than the CWBS. Test-retest reliability was assessed by "having the intake workers complete the CNI twice within a 2-week period" (p. 149). There was very good reliability, with the average for all scales being .86 weighted kappa. Interrater reliability was assessed by having two additional individuals provide CNI ratings on a subsample of 87 intake cases. Findings revealed a very good average reliability of .79

weighted kappa for individual scales. To examine whether the six scales and age ratings were nonredundant, correlations were conducted. Findings revealed low correlations between all scales except for mental health care and developmental care.

Construct Validity of the Maltreatment Classification System

The objective of this study (Manly et al., 1994) was to "examine the impact of dimensions within maltreatment, such as the severity, frequency, chronicity, and subtypes of maltreatment and their relationship with child outcome" (p. 121). The Maltreatment Classification System is a multidimensional classification and assessment instrument using CPS records abstracted by trained raters. It includes six types of maltreatment: sexual abuse, physical abuse, emotional maltreatment, two categories of neglect—failure to provide and supervision—and moral-legal-educational maltreatment. Frequency is operationalized by the total number of indicated reports on a family. Chronicity is operationalized by the total number of months the family received CPS services. Severity ratings were "summed across subtype and the most severe rating and the average ratings were computed" (p. 130).

To examine the construct validity of the system, several analyses were conducted, with child adjustment as the outcome. Adjustment was operationalized by three measures: two rated by adults who served as counselors at the 1-week camp the children were attending and the other rated by the children's peers. The measures included The Achenbach Child Behavior Checklist-Teacher Form (CBCL-TRF); the California Child Q-Set, a measure of social competence; and peer ratings of prosocial behavior, aggression, and disruption. Subjects included 235 children, 145 from maltreating families and 90 from non-maltreating families.

The two most important analyses examined (1) the effect of maltreatment, frequency, severity, and chronicity, and the interaction terms between these dimensions and (2) the effect of the first five maltreatment types. Findings of the former analyses for most of the outcome variables were quite similar. After controlling for maternal education, years on Aid to Families With Dependent Children, and number of children in the home, severity, frequency, and the interaction between the two were significantly associated with social competence, the CBCL-TRF, and cooperation. Only for social competence was maltreatment versus non-maltreatment a significant predictor. As severity and frequency increased, outcomes worsened. Examination of the interactions showed some differences for different outcomes; however, generally, they revealed that at high levels of severity, increases in frequency had little effect. For disruption, the only predictor was the interaction between maltreatment severity and frequency. At high levels of severity, frequency had little effect on the outcome. For "starts fights," the only significant term was chronicity. As chronicity increased, peer ratings of aggression increased.

For the latter analysis, "presence or absence of each of the five types was entered into regression analyses" (Manly et al., 1994, p. 139) for each of the outcomes. "This strategy was employed to more closely approximate the naturally occurring complexities in the maltreatment experiences of the children while using statistical means of controlling for shared variance" (p. 139). Sexual abuse and physical neglect reduced social competence, whereas only physical neglect was associated with behavior problems.

Known Groups Validity of the Child Well-Being Scales

The primary objective of this study (Gaudin et al., 1992) was to determine if 23 of the Magura and Moses (1986) CWBS scales discriminated between two groups of families—53 confirmed as neglectful by CPS and 80 low-income control families not known to CPS for neglect. Of the 23 scales, 12 "were selected to represent physical care and five to measure psychological care" (p. 323). Three analyses were performed to determine if the scales discriminated. First, the mean scores for the neglectful families on all but one of the physical care scales and all psychological care scales were significantly lower than those for the control group. Second, 60% of the neglectful families, compared with 8% of the controls, were classified as "outright neglectful at the time of data collection" (Gaudin et al., 1992, p. 326) on the basis of their scores on at least one of the 23 scales. Third, discriminant analysis using 17 of the scales divided into three factors established by the authors of the CWBS revealed that the "three combined factors correctly classified 79% of 59 neglectful cases as neglectful and 87% of 80 controls" (p. 326). Of the three factors—household adequacy, parental disposition, and child performance—the first was the strongest.

DISCUSSION AND RECOMMENDATIONS

This chapter focused on reviewing current methods for defining child neglect and examining measurement research on child neglect. Before summarizing the results, it is important to repeat an earlier warning—articles failed to provide details about definitions of neglect. Consequently, findings from the review and measurement literatures may not be as precise and accurate as they could have been.

Summary of Findings

First and very important, the review of methods of defining neglect revealed that it is still an underresearched topic. Of the 489 articles in the five volumes of *Child Abuse and Neglect,* only 25 pertained to neglect. Findings showed that most researchers are cognizant of the phenotypic differences between maltreatment types. Notwithstanding much criticism of the "agency label" method for defining neglect, studies (14 of 25) predominantly used this time-but-not-honored method. Studies (11 of 25) that did not employ the agency label used a wide array of definitions, ranging from observational methods to interview methods to case record abstractions to various combinations of methods. Given the variety of methods, it is not surprising that the sources of data for the definitions varied substantially—from interviews with mothers or the maltreatment victim to home observations of mother-child interaction to case records or some combination. Generally speaking, definitions of neglect did not comply with the recommendations of Zuravin (1991).

Scant as the body of measurement research was, it yielded both interesting and useful findings. Given the number of researchers that used the agency label definition or relied on case records as a primary or sole source of data for establishing neglect, it is particularly important to consider findings from the two articles (Kaufman et al., 1994; McGee et al., 1995) that compared information from data sources other than CPS caseworkers or records. Their results suggested that exclusive dependence on CPS data can lead to underestimation of prevalence and severity for all subtypes of maltreatment as well as the incidence of multiple types of maltreatment per child or family.

Studies (Manly et al., 1994; McGee et al., 1995; Wolfe & McGee, 1994) of the construct validity of classification systems and operational definitions' sequelae also have implications for future measurement. Manly et al.'s (1994) as well as Wolfe and McGee's (1994) findings suggest that multidimensional classification systems are important for predicting sequelae. Even though these studies, as well as McGee et al.'s (1995) used different classification systems, operational definitions, and sources of data, all found neglect to be an important predictor of children's adjustment, suggesting that all three definitions of neglect are valid. Dimensions of importance were frequency, severity, chronicity, type, and age at which maltreatment occurred.

Trocme's (1996) evaluation of a measure of neglect identified important findings with regard to a neglect nosology. Correlations between the six subtypes of neglect in his classification revealed little overlap, supporting the need for neglect subtypes. Concurrent and predictive validity were good.

Implications for Future Measurement of Child Neglect

This last section of the chapter has three purposes: (1) to integrate findings from the review of methods and examination of measurement research for the purpose of recommending directions for the future measurement of maltreatment and child neglect, (2) to suggest areas for measurement research, and (3) to recommend topics pertinent to definition.

1. Use multiple sources of data to obtain information on neglect and other types of maltreatment. Whereas only two measurement studies looked at the adequacy of different sources of data and both need to be replicated before firm conclusions are drawn, both suggested the predominant source of data—CPS case records or caseworker reports—was inadequate for estimating the prevalence of maltreatment types and their severity. One of the articles (McGee et al., 1995) found this to be particularly true for neglect, interpreting discrepancies between case record-caseworker report and adolescent self-report to mean that victim perceptions of what happened may be more closely linked to adjustment than factual events alone (those from records). Although the recommendation to use multiple sources of data appears sound, the question of which sources to use remains and may have to vary according to type of research (e.g., epidemiologic, sequelae, etiology), study design (e.g., prospective, retrospective, and cross-sectional), and age of the victim. It appears from McGee et al.'s (1995) research that victim self-report may be an important source. Another difficult question is how to integrate data from the different sources when they differ, as they inevitably will. Only further research will solve these important issues.

2. *Use a multidimensional classification scheme for conceptualizing maltreatment and include neglect as a type.* Findings from two of the construct validity studies suggest that multiple dimensions, including type, severity, chronicity and frequency of maltreatment, as well age at which the maltreatment occurred, are important predictors of sequelae. An important unanswered question, however, is whether these dimensions are important predictors for all types as well as the etiology of maltreatment. Does etiology differ according to type or any of the other dimensions? Should a different classification scheme but identical operational definitions be used for etiology? Certainly, operational definitions should be the same for research on etiology and sequelae; otherwise, we will never know whether the dimensions that have negative sequelae are the same as those that are etiological in nature. Whether dimensions other than type need to be used for etiology as well as different types requires further research.

3. *Use a multidimensional classification scheme for conceptualizing neglect.* That neglect is an important type of maltreatment was well illustrated by the research. Manly et al.'s (1994) findings suggested that physical neglect may be a more important predictor of sequelae than supervisory neglect. Whether the subtype classification systems used or recommended by various authors (e.g., Manly et al., 1994; Trocme, 1996; U.S.DHHS, 1996; Zuravin, 1991) are valid for etiologic and sequelae research at all or what system is optimal remain as important questions. It is still unclear whether chronicity, frequency, severity, perpetrator, and age are important for each type of maltreatment.

4. *Researchers should strive to limit the number of classification and operational schemes in use by adopting those with the best psychometric properties.* The review very clearly revealed that investigators still have no standardized and

> systematic procedure for describing the maltreatment experiences of their subjects, . . . that little consensus has been achieved regarding appropriate operational definitions of particular expressions of maltreatment, . . . and that no commonly accepted nosological system exists by which researchers can classify the diversity of maltreatment within their samples. (Manly et al., 1994, p. 122)

These problems are likely to "obfuscate our understanding of the complexities within the phenomenon" (p. 122)—and bar comparison of results across studies. To build knowledge in general as well as to determine if nosological and operational schemes are valid for all racial and ethnic groups, it is important to adopt those systems with known psychometric properties—ones with good interrater reliability, internal consistency, and construct validity. In addition, studies of concurrent validity are important.

5. Researchers should publish articles that describe in detail their classification and operational schemes as well as pertinent measurement research. To date, there are very few articles that describe in detail the classification systems and in particular the operational definitions used by maltreatment researchers. This is important to include for three reasons. First, there is insufficient space in most articles to completely detail a system. Second, such articles will aid the integration of findings across studies and facilitate reviews such as this one. Third, they will promote the adoption of the better systems by other researchers.

NOTE

1. See the appendix at the end of this chapter for the list of the 25 articles that were reviewed.

APPENDIX: The 25 Articles Reviewed

Ards, S., & Harrell, A. (1993). Reporting of child maltreating: A secondary analysis of the national incidence study. *Child Abuse and Neglect, 17*(3), 337-344.

Bath, H., & Haapala, D. (1993). Intensive family preservation services with abused and neglected children: An examination of group differences. *Child Abuse and Neglect, 17*(2), 213-225.

Benedict, M., Zuravin, S., Brandt, D., & Abbey, H. (1994). Types and frequency of child maltreatment by family foster care providers in an urban population. *Child Abuse and Neglect, 18*(7), 577-585.

Chaffin, M., Kelleher, K., & Hollenberg, J. (1996). Onset of physical abuse and neglect: Psychiatric substance abuse, and social risk factors from prospective community data. *Child Abuse and Neglect, 20*(3), 191-203.

Christensen, M., Brayden, R., Dietrich, M., McLaughlin, F., & Sherrod, K. (1994). The prospective assessment of self-concept in neglectful and physically abusive low income mothers. *Child Abuse and Neglect, 18*(3), 225-232.

Coohey, C. (1995). Neglectful mothers, their mothers, and partners. The significance of mutual aid. *Child Abuse and Neglect, 19*(8), 885-896.

Coohey, C. (1996). Child maltreatment: Testing the social isolation hypothesis. *Child Abuse and Neglect, 20*(3), 241-254.

Drake, B., & Pandey, S. (1996). Understanding the relationship between neighborhood poverty and specific types of child maltreatment. *Child Abuse and Neglect, 20*(11), 1003-1018.

Egeland, B., & Susman, E. (1996). Dissociation as a mediator of child abuse across generations. *Child Abuse and Neglect, 20*(11), 1123-1132.

Ethier, L., Lacharite, C., & Couture, G. (1995). Childhood adversity, parental stress, and depression of negligent mothers. *Child Abuse and Neglect, 19*(5), 619-632.

Garland, A., Landsverk, J., Hough, R., & Ellis-MacLead, C. (1996). Type of maltreatment as a predictor of mental health service use for children in foster care. *Child Abuse and Neglect, 20*(8), 675-688

Gaudin, J., Polansky, N., Kilpatrick, A., & Shilton, P. (1996). Family functioning in neglectful families. *Child Abuse and Neglect, 20*(4), 363-377.

Goldman, J., Graves, L., Ward, M., Albanese, I., Sorensen, E., & Chamberlin, C. (1993). Self-report of guardians ad litem: Provision of information to judges in child abuse and neglect cases. *Child Abuse and Neglect, 17*(2), 227-232.

Herrenkohl, E., Herrenkohl, R., Rupert, L., Egolf, B., & Lutz, J. (1995). Risk factors for behavioral dysfunction: The relative impact of maltreatment, SES, physical health problems, cognitive ability, and quality of parent-child interaction. *Child Abuse and Neglect, 19*(2), 191-203.

Jellinek, M., Murphy, J., Poitrast, F., Quinn, F., Bishop, S., & Goshko, M. (1992). Serious child maltreatment in Massachusetts: The course of 206 children through the courts. *Child Abuse and Neglect, 16*(2), 179-185.

Jones, E., & McCurdy, K. (1992). The links between types of maltreatment and demographic characteristics of children. *Child Abuse and Neglect, 16*(2), 201-215.

Kendall-Tackett, K., & Eckenrode, J. (1996). The effects of neglect on academic achievement and disciplinary problems: A developmental perspective. *Child Abuse and Neglect, 20*(3), 161-169.

Kurtz, P., Gaudin, J., Jr., Wodarski, J., & Howing, P. (1993). Maltreatment and the school-aged child: School performance consequences. *Child Abuse and Neglect, 17*(5), 581-589.

Mollerstrom, W., Patchner, M., & Milner, J. (1995). Child maltreatment: The United States Air Force's response. *Child Abuse and Neglect, 19*(3), 325-334.

Ney, P., Fung, T., & Wickett, A. (1994). The worst combinations of child abuse and neglect. *Child Abuse and Neglect, 18*(9), 705-714.

Perez, C., & Widom, C. (1994). Childhood victimization and long-term intellectual and academic outcomes. *Child Abuse and Neglect, 18*(8), 617-633.

Prino, C., & Peyrot, M. (1994). The effect of child physical abuse and neglect on aggressive, withdrawn, and prosocial behavior. *Child Abuse and Neglect, 18*(10), 871-884.

Rosen, L., & Martin, L. (1996). Impact of childhood abuse history on psychological symptoms among male and female soldiers in the U.S. Army. *Child Abuse and Neglect, 20*(12), 1149-1160

Sheridan, M. (1995). A proposed intergenerational model of substance abuse, family functioning, and abuse/neglect. *Child Abuse and Neglect, 19*(5), 519-530.

Tjaden, P., & Thoennes, N. (1992). Predictors of legal intervention in child maltreatment cases. *Child Abuse and Neglect, 16*(6), 807-821.

REFERENCES

Achenbach, T. (1991). *Manual for the Child Behavior Checklist/4-18 and 1991 profile.* Burlington, VT: University of Vermont Department of Psychiatry.

Ards, S., & Harrell, A. (1993). Reporting of child maltreating: A secondary analysis of the national incidence study. *Child Abuse and Neglect, 17*(3), 337-344.

Barnett, D., Manly, J., & Cicchetti, D. (1991). Continuing toward an operational definition of psychological maltreatment. *Development and Psychopathology, 3,* 19-29.

Benedict, M., Zuravin, S., Brandt, D., & Abbey, H. (1994). Types and frequency of child maltreatment by family foster care providers in an urban population. *Child Abuse and Neglect, 18*(7), 577-585.

Bernstein, D., Fink, L., Handelsman, L., Foote, J., Lovejoy, M., Wenzel, K., Sapareto, E., & Ruggiero, J. (1994). Initial reliability and validity of a new retrospective measure of child abuse and neglect. *American Journal of Psychiatry, 151*(8), 1132-1136.

Besharov, D. (1981). Toward better research on child abuse and neglect: Making definitional issues an explicit concern. *Child Abuse Neglect, 5,* 383-390.

Chaffin, M., Kelleher, K., & Hollenberg, J. (1996). Onset of physical abuse and neglect: Psychiatric substance abuse, and social risk factors from prospective community data. *Child Abuse and Neglect, 20*(3), 191-203.

Christensen, M., Brayden, R., Dietrich, M., McLaughlin, F., & Sherrod, K. (1994). The prospective assessment of self-concept in neglectful and physically abusive low income mothers. *Child Abuse and Neglect, 18*(3), 225-232.

Cicchetti, D., & Barnett, D. (1991). Toward the development of a scientific nosology of child maltreatment. In P. Grove & D. Cicchetti (Eds.), *Thinking clearly about psychology: Vol. 2. Personality and psychopathology.* Minneapolis: University of Minnesota Press.

Coohey, C. (1996). Child maltreatment: Testing the social isolation hypothesis. *Child Abuse and Neglect, 20*(3), 241-254.

Dubowitz, H., Black, M., Starr, R., Jr., & Zuravin, S. (1993). A conceptual definition of child neglect. *Criminal Justice and Behavior, 20*(1), 8-26.

Egeland, B., & Susman, E. (1996). Dissociation as a mediator of child abuse across generations. *Child Abuse and Neglect, 20*(11), 1123-1132.

Ethier, L., Lacharite, C., & Couture, G. (1995). Childhood adversity, parental stress, and depression of negligent mothers. *Child Abuse and Neglect, 19*(5), 619-632.

Garbarino, J. (1991). Not all bad developmental outcomes are the result of child abuse. *Development and Psychopathology, 3,* 45-50.

Gaudin, J., Polansky, N., & Kilpatrick, A. (1992). The Child Well-Being Scales: A field trial. *Child Welfare, 71*(4), 319-328.

Gaudin, J., Polansky, N., Kilpatrick, A., & Shilton, P. (1996). Family functioning in neglectful families. *Child Abuse and Neglect, 20*(4), 363-377.

Giovannoni, J. (1989). Definitional issues in child maltreatment. In D. Cicchetti & V. Carson (Eds.), *Child maltreatment* (pp. 3-37). Cambridge, UK: Cambridge University Press.

Giovannoni, J. (1991). Social policy considerations in defining psychological maltreatment. *Development and Psychopathology, 3,* 51-59.

Giovannoni, J., & Becerra, R. (1979). *Defining child abuse.* New York: Free Press.

Gustafson, D., Fryback, D., Rose, J., Prokop, D., Detmer, D., Rossmeisl, J., Taylor, C., Alwmi, F., & Carnazzo, A. (1986). Severity index development methodology. *Medical Decision Making, 6,* 27-35.

Herrenkohl, E., Herrenkohl, R., Rupert, L., Egolf, B., & Lutz, J. (1995). Risk factors for behavioral dysfunction: The relative impact of maltreatment, SES, physical health problems, cognitive ability, and quality of parent-child interaction. *Child Abuse and Neglect, 19*(2), 191-203.

Jones, E., & McCurdy, K. (1992). The links between types of maltreatment and demographic characteristics of children. *Child Abuse and Neglect, 16*(2), 201-215.

Kaufman, J., Jones, B., Stieglitz, E., Vitulano, L., & Mannarino, A. (1994). The use of multiple informants to assess children's maltreatment experiences. *Journal of Family Violence, 9*(3), 227-248.

Kempe, C., Silverman, F., Steele, B., Droegemueller, W., & Silver, H. (1962). The battered child syndrome. *Journal of the American Medical Association, 181*(1), 17-24.

Magura, S., & Moses, B. (1986). *Outcome measures for child welfare services.* Washington, DC: Child Welfare League of America.

Manly, J., Cicchetti, D., & Barnett, D. (1994). The impact of subtype, frequency, chronicity, and severity of child maltreatment on social competence and behavior problems. *Development and Psychopathology, 6,* 121-143.

Martin, H. (1979). The abuse and neglect of children. *Pediatrics, 55*(3), 56-61.

McGee, R., & Wolfe, D. (1991a). Between a rock and a hard place: Where do we go from here in defining psychological maltreatment? *Development and Psychopathology, 3,* 119-124.

McGee, R., & Wolfe, D. (1991b). Psychological maltreatment: Towards an operational definition. *Development and Psychopathology, 3,* 3-18.

McGee, R., Wolfe, D., Yuen, S., Wilson, S., & Carnochan, J. (1995). The measurement of maltreatment: A comparison of approaches. *Child Abuse and Neglect, 19*(2), 233-249.

National Center on Child Abuse and Neglect. (1987, August). *Proceedings of the neglect grantees meeting.* Washington, DC: Author.

National Research Council. (1993). *Understanding child abuse and neglect.* Washington, DC: National Academy Press.

Ney, P., Fung, T., & Wickett, A. (1994). The worst combinations of child abuse and neglect. *Child Abuse and Neglect, 18*(9), 705-714.

Rosen, L., & Martin, L. (1996). Impact of childhood abuse history on psychological symptoms among male and female soldiers in the U.S. Army. *Child Abuse and Neglect, 20*(12), 1149-1160

Ross, C., & Zigler, E. (1980). An agenda for action. In G. Gerbner, C. Ross, & E. Zigler (Eds.), *Child abuse: An agenda for action* (pp. 293-304). New York: Oxford University Press.

Sheridan, M. (1995). A proposed intergenerational model of substance abuse, family functioning, and abuse/neglect. *Child Abuse and Neglect, 19*(5), 519-530.

Tjaden, P., & Thoennes, N. (1992). Predictors of legal intervention in child maltreatment cases. *Child Abuse and Neglect, 16*(6), 807-821.

Trocme, N. (1996). Development & preliminary evaluation of the Ontario Child Neglect Index. *Child Maltreatment, 1*(2), 145-155.

U.S. Department of Health and Human Services. (1981). *First national study of child abuse and neglect.* Washington, DC: Author.

U.S. Department of Health and Human Services. (1988). *Second national study of child abuse and neglect.* Washington, DC: Author.

U.S. Department of Health and Human Services. (1996). *Third national study of child abuse and neglect.* Washington, DC: Author.

Wolfe, D., & McGee, R. (1994). Dimensions of maltreatment and their relationship to adolescent maltreatment. *Development and Psychopathology, 6,* 165-181.

Wolock, I., & Horowitz, B. (1984). Child maltreatment as a social problem: The neglect of neglect. *American Journal of Orthopsychiatry, 59,* 377-389.

Zigler, E. (1980). Controlling child abuse: Do we have the knowledge and/or the will. In G. Gerbner, C. Ross, & E. Zigler (Eds.), *Child abuse: An agenda for action* (pp. 100-128). New York: Oxford University Press.

Zuravin, S. (1991). Research definitions of child physical abuse and neglect: Current problems. In R. Starr, Jr., & D. Wolfe (Eds.), *The effects of child abuse and neglect: Issues and research.* New York: Guilford.

Child Neglect

Causes and Contributors

3

PATRICIA MCKINSEY CRITTENDEN

Child neglect is a perplexing problem. On the one hand, it appears to be "caused" by socioeconomic factors. On the other hand, interventions to remediate these root causes have not effectively improved families' social and economic status, nor have they reduced the incidence of neglect (Mayer, 1997; Sedlak & Broadhurst, 1996). This chapter first addresses the issue of socioeconomic causation of neglect; it is proposed that such causation is not sufficient to explain child neglect. Then an alternative perspective is discussed: specifically, that something else causes both poverty and child neglect. This cause is identified as distortions of mental processing of information. Last, three types of child neglect (labeled *disorganized, emotionally neglecting,* and *depressed*) are discussed; each type differs in the kind of mental processing used by the adults. For each type of neglect, it is suggested how analysis in terms of differential critical causes would lead to differential styles of intervention.

AUTHOR'S NOTE: I wish to thank Peter Stratton for his helpful comments on an earlier draft of this paper.

DEFINING THE PROBLEM

What Is the Best Explanation for the Occurrence of Child Neglect?

Because of its association with neglect, low socioeconomic status has universally been identified as a major cause of child neglect (Garbarino, 1982; Pelton, 1981; Russell & Trainor, 1984). Low socioeconomic status, however, includes a wide range of factors associated with poverty, such as unemployment, limited education, social isolation, large numbers of children, and childbirth to unmarried adolescents. Many policymakers and researchers, including myself, have argued that alleviating poverty on a national and international scale is essential to ameliorating child neglect (Crittenden, 1992a). It is also true, however, that three decades of effort to improve the economic status of poor families in the United States have, on the whole, been ineffective at preventing child neglect. Although living conditions have improved appreciably (in terms of housing, health, nutrition, and possession of consumer goods) among poverty families, the proportion of families living in poverty is unchanged. Ironically, it could even be argued that recent policy has fostered an increase of precisely those families that are least prepared to improve their condition and to care adequately for their children. Because these families now have large numbers of surviving children, their proportion of the population is not decreasing, in spite of an improved standard of living. Thus, a core of chronically impoverished families whose children experience high rates of physical and psychological neglect has been maintained. It is these families that require a fresh perspective on the causes of child neglect.

It could be said, with some accuracy, that we just haven't made the necessary economic commitment, that our economic relief is below the threshold at which it can begin to take effect. We could even say that a major restructuring of society is necessary. Both of these might be true, but it is unlikely that they will persuade policymakers who must appropriate the necessary funds. Indeed, the current political climate makes it very clear that neither politicians nor the population that elects them find these arguments convincing. Moreover, it may be that although economic factors often contribute to neglect, they are neither necessary nor sufficient to cause neglect. A systemic understanding of social, familial, and personal functioning suggests that those factors that cause a condition may not be the same as the factors needed to change or eliminate the condition once it exists. A more focused approach to addressing the needs of neglected children may be to seek the so-called critical causes of neglect—that is, those causes that, when changed, will precipitate a pattern of systemic changes that will reduce or eliminate neglect (Crittenden, 1992c).

Previously, quality of human relationships has been offered as a possible critical cause of child maltreatment (Crittenden, 1992c). Current work on the relation of information processing to attachment relationships between parents and children suggests another way to view the problem. First, however, a brief reexamination of the relation between neglect and socioeconomic factors is warranted

Why Economic Help Isn't Enough

There are several fallacies in the argument that poverty is a sufficient or necessary cause of child neglect. First, large numbers of families live in poverty. Only some of them neglect their children. Knowing what enables most families to successfully care for their children, in spite of poverty, limited education, and so forth, might help us to understand neglect better.

Second, most human children, over our history as a species, have been born to poor families. Indeed, most poor families in Western countries would be considered rich on an international or historical scale. Therefore, it is unlikely that income or lack of material goods is the primary impediment to successful childrearing.

A similar conclusion can be reached with regard to the other aspects of socioeconomic status that are related to neglect. Large numbers of children and the failure to use birth control have always been typical of human families. The primary difference today in Western countries is that most infants now live, so parents are spared the pain of frequent loss of children. Similarly, formal education does not typify human parents nor does parent education. Thus, both historically and currently, observable patterns of childrearing can be used to cast doubt on the explanation that poverty causes neglect. Thus, although transferring financial resources to impoverished families increases the health and happiness of many families, it seems not to have reduced the incidence of child neglect (Sedlak & Broadhurst, 1996). An alternative perspective is needed—one that both generates a sound and intellectually satisfying thesis and also leads to effective action.

The Failure to Establish Enduring Human Relationships

That leaves being unemployed, unmarried, and socially isolated as aspects of low socioeconomic status that might "cause" child neglect. These probably are not typical of human parents from an international or historical perspective; that is, most human parents probably have worked for their families' resources, have been committed to the other parent of the child, and have lived and raised their children in a community of other familiar humans.

On the other hand, these three characteristics have in common the failure of individuals to successfully establish enduring and productive social relationships. These are interpersonal problems tied specifically to the failure to engage in enduring relationships—hierarchically with employers and reciprocally with coworkers, spouses, and neighbors. In this context, it would be surprising if the (hierarchical) relationship with children were unaffected. This suggests that there may be something other than socioeconomic status that is critical to the occurrence of child neglect. Possibly, socioeconomic failure and child neglect are both the result of something else: specifically, severe difficulties sustaining interpersonal relationships. (See Leon & Weissman, 1993, for evidence of the relation between receiving public assistance and affective and depressive disorders, and Zuravin & Diblasio, 1996, for the relation between child neglect and maternal depression.) Moreover, it may be that if we do not address this problem, we may not be able to change either families' socioeconomic status or the prevalence of child neglect (Mayer, 1997).

INFORMATION PROCESSING

This hypothesis can be explored from the perspective of current theory about how humans process information (Crittenden, 1993). Specifically, it may be that, when past experience with danger teaches humans that certain kinds of information are misleading or irrelevant to attaining safety, the meaning of such information is distorted or the information is omitted from further processing altogether. This, in turn, can lead both to gaps in individuals' understanding of reality and to limitations in their ability to construct effective strategies for resolving future problems. When these gaps and limitations are great, they will affect the ability of humans to adapt to changing conditions. This will frequently be displayed as poor interpersonal relationships. Furthermore, because functional interpersonal relationships are needed to maintain families and employment and to obtain assistance from others, poor relationships may lead to economic poverty, particularly the sort of poverty that is enduring across generations in spite of opportunities for economic success.

Research indicates that poor interpersonal relationships account for many of the most enduring and severe consequences of child neglect (Crittenden, 1985; Erickson & Egeland, 1996; Jean-Gilles & Crittenden, 1990; Polansky, Chalmers, Buttenweiser, & Williams, 1981; Tonge, James, & Hillam, 1975; Wolfe, 1993). On the other hand, poverty in the context of affectionate and supportive relationships does not have such devastating effects. Because improving interpersonal relationships may be necessary to reducing neglect, knowing how humans mentally process information about relationships may be extremely important as well.

Two types of information are particularly relevant to this discussion: cognition and affect.[1] *Cognition* is information about what actions effectively cause specific outcomes; it is information about the effects of one's behavior. *Affect* is information about the safety or danger of contexts; affect is experienced as feeling states that motivate protective and affectionate behavior and, when feelings of distress are low, that promote exploration and learning. Three types of neglect are described (Crittenden, 1988): one in which cognition is not perceived or responded to, one in which affect is omitted from processing, and one in which both cognition and affect are discarded as meaningless sources of information about danger and protection. The first and last of these describe conditions commonly thought of as neglect and associated with poverty. The omission of affective information may lead to another type of neglect, one that is found more often among economically advantaged families.

THREE TYPES OF NEGLECT

In the following sections, three sorts of neglect are described. For each, a description of the family environment, as it is experienced by professionals who work with such families, is offered first. These descriptions are intentionally quite informal; their purpose is to create a context that reflects realistically both the atmosphere (affect) of the home and also the causal contingencies (cognition). This is made explicit under the heading of "Affect and Cognition." A discussion of developmental processes for children reared in such homes follows. Each section concludes with a discussion of the implications of this perspective for case management.

Disorganized Neglect—Living From Crisis to Crisis: Defending Against Cognition

Recognizing the Families: Professionals' Perspective

The first group of neglecting parents offers *inconsistent* parenting to their children. These are multiproblem, disorganized, and crisis-prone families. Being in their homes is a confusing, frustrating experience to professionals because, as one tries to discuss problems with the mother, there are constant interruptions. For example, a phone rings: Some minor disaster now occupies the mother's attention. A child runs in crying: There is a fight outside, and another child has hurt him. The mother, when she attends to the visiting professional, wants help in solving her immediate problems: for example, the electricity being turned off for failure to pay the bills, the school suspending her oldest child, her husband being fired after getting drunk and fighting with the boss, and so on. Indeed, the mother appears to need and want professional help urgently. In the background is the sound of the TV and the intense emotions of a soap opera that, in spite of the glamour associated with wealth, mirrors her own life.

The professional tries to discuss the reasons for the visit, but these interruptions leave one feeling that they have only fragments of the mother's attention. Moreover, even when one has finally discussed all the issues that needed to be covered, one is not sure that she really understands or agrees. Indeed, the discussion is often so fragmented and disrupted that it is difficult to be certain what was said and decided. Nevertheless, in spite of the confusion, professionals often feel welcome in such homes.

Affect and Cognition

These disorganized homes can be described as those in which affect is dominant and cognition is minimized. Feelings motivate behavior; that is, family members organize their behavior in terms of how they feel. Moreover, more intense feelings attract family members' attention more than less intense feelings. On this basis, the children fighting outside dominate the mother's attention, whereas the letters from the phone company are set aside until a later, quieter time (that may never come). Under these conditions, a professional's time and resources may be hijacked to meet the mother's priorities. The alternative, of course, is to decide logically (cognitively), on the basis of probable outcomes, what topics and activities warrant attention. Presumably, on this basis, the notice from the phone company and the professional's agenda would be deemed important.

This creates an environment in which maternal response to children is unpredictable, with family members, especially mothers, responding only to the most immediate, most extreme crisis. To receive attention, their children must become the most demanding, most salient stimulus to their mothers. They accomplish this by themselves learning (preconsciously) to emphasize affect and to minimize or discard cognitive information. That is, the children exaggerate their displays of feelings so that their needs seem more dramatic than they really are. In addition, they refuse to listen to explanations, to accept delay, or to compromise. They act as though they were always in a crisis situation. In this manner, they improve their chances of getting—and holding—their parents' attention.

Developmental Pathways

There is a developmental process through which children of such mothers come to depend on exaggerated affective information and to distrust cognitive information about future outcomes. In infancy, the children of such mothers find their environments to be unpredictable; sometimes, their mothers are responsive and warm; at other times, they are angry; and at other times, they ignore their children's signals altogether. An outsider watching this could determine that the mothers respond sensitively when there is nothing more important going on, that they display anger when they are trying to do other things but their children are very disruptive, and that they ignore their children whenever the children's signals are not intense. Put another way, the mothers both positively reinforce and also punish children's negative behavior. But infants cannot understand this; they are simply left feeling vulnerable and distressed by the unpredictable outcomes and highly emotional contexts.

By about 2 years of age, however, children become able to recognize the association between their displays of anger and their mothers' responses. So they show more anger. This both attracts their mothers' attention and also causes their mothers to be angry with them frequently. The children need a way to terminate parental anger and aggression. Coy behavior is used to do this. By alternating aggressive-threatening behavior with coy-disarming behavior, children are able to coerce their mothers into doing what they want more of the time. This produces what is commonly called the "terrible twos," a period in which children heighten oppositional behavior and the display of negative feeling states. Careful observation shows that, in addition, disruptive children frequently use coy behavior to disarm parental anger.

For example, imagine that a little boy is playing while his mother works in the house. She decides to leave for a minute and starts to move toward the door. He immediately protests loudly that he wants to go with her. She says "No." He protests more and clings to her legs. Then, he drops to the floor in a tantrum. At first, his mother tries to cajole him into getting up. He cries louder. Eventually, she gets angry and shouts at him. Immediately, he flashes her a beautiful, endearing smile. She melts and comforts him. As she does so, he begins making demands of her. She stiffens—and the battle of wills is on.

Frequently, mothers win these battles by outwitting their children; that is, they use their intelligence to deceive their children and get their own way. For example, when her child protests her departure, a mother might trick him into playing with the ball and, to divert his attention to the ball, she talks about the ball as though she intended to play with him: "Look at the ball! Go get the ball!" Her child runs to get the ball. As he does so, she slips out. When he turns around gleefully with the ball, she is gone. He feels angry and afraid. Things did not turn out as he was led to believe.

What he has learned is that his mother's words and the temporal relation among events that they describe can deceive him. Cognition, in other words, is not to be trusted. Feelings and affective displays are more powerful and have more predictable effects.

At other times, such mothers bribe or threaten their children. If the bribes and threats are fulfilled, this will work. But in many families, they are used to obtain immediate changes in children's behavior, and later, when the promised outcome should occur, it has been forgotten by the parent. Children quickly learn that their behavior is being manipulated and that the promised reward or punishment is unlikely to occur. Children learn to ignore information about the future (about the temporal and causal order among events) because it is misleading.

In cases such as this, children learn that both bribes and threats are false. The message is, "Don't believe what you are told; you might be tricked." In addition, children learn not to compromise—because when they do so, they are more easily deceived. Consequently, in the future, they will tend to act on the basis of their feelings, to display their feelings very strongly, and to insist on their own way without compromise. They will be self-centered and coercive.

As parents, they themselves may use their greater intellectual competence to manipulate and deceive their own children and will respond to their children most predictably when the child's affective signal is too intense to ignore. Their strategy for solving life's problems and for managing relationships will be a coercive strategy of exaggerating affect and ignoring cognitive information about the (uncertain) future.

By organizing their behavior around feelings and not on planning that meets future needs, parents will fail to do some things that need to be done but that do not come with intense messages. For example, they will put off paying bills until there are threats of court action. They will fail to purchase enough food, leading to panic at dinnertime, and then have to make do with snacks and other less nourishing (and more expensive) foods. They will fail to attend to children's needs—of all kinds—until the situations become crises. Then, they will run from crisis to crisis, frantically trying to solve long-standing problems with quick solutions. Of course, this rarely works. But behaving in this manner keeps feelings intense and gives parents the feeling of being needed. This is important if, in their childhoods, they rarely had enough attention from their parents.

Case Management

This is one type of neglect, *disorganized* neglect (see Crittenden, 1988). It is found in multiproblem, crisis-prone families. The children are cared for but not in a predictable and timely manner. The family is always on the verge of disaster. The functioning of such families is best described as being affectively organized and with interpersonal relationships based on the use of a coercive strategy for getting what one wants.

It seems reasonable that, if professionals could just hold the families' crises at bay for a little while, the mothers could be taught to organize their lives, and then they would be able to prevent future problems. Under those conditions, mothers would be able to care for their children's physical and emotional needs appropriately.

It now seems that although these families desire to have their needs met, they do not trust the information that we give them. They want their way now and express their needs with clear desperation. They cannot wait or plan. Moreover, even if we take charge and solve the problems, they will sabotage our efforts. Without the intense demands associated with crises, they have no way of perceiving that they are important to others. Consequently, when family life is orderly and safe, they often feel let down and depressed. This creates new crises.

When professionals work with families, they usually plan their interventions cognitively, that is, around the predictable consequences of specified behaviors. Disorganized neglecting families organize their behavior affectively. The mismatch is experienced by almost everyone who works with such families. If professionals switch to the families' strategy, they can use bribery, but that usually is effective for only a short time. Alternatively, professionals can threaten families, but this will work only so long as the threats are carried out and, even so, the families tend to ignore many threats, calling the professionals' bluffs. This is both exhausting and futile for professionals. Last, professionals tend to pull back and offer less support as soon as families begin to function competently. For families such as these, that forces them to fall apart again to regain our attention.

So what can be done? A few principles (that are easy to state, but hard to implement) may help. First, feelings must be dealt with, especially mothers' need for comfort and reassurance that they are loved and indispensable to family members. Second, professionals must provide a structured, predictable environment with no surprises (i.e., they must create an environment in which cognition always works, always provides accurate information about the relation between behavior and outcomes). Third, professionals must maintain an affective relationship with the parents even after, *especially* after, the parents gain competencies (Crittenden, 1991). As with growing children, it must be the families who seek independence rather than the professional who cuts back on service. If professionals withdraw too soon, it is likely that the families will revert to the problems that brought them to attention in the first place. In addition, professionals must help the families to find the environments in which clear, direct, and undistorted communication of feelings and accurate cognitive information about future outcomes will be rewarded and in which they can learn the value of compromising without fear that, in giving an inch, they will lose all. Last, when these other steps are under way, professionals must teach parents how to use cognitive information about the effects of behavior to regulate (without denying) affect and affective display. An underlying aspect of these interventions is to teach parents, through their own experience, that attention to the temporal relations among events can yield greater satisfaction than simple reliance on feelings alone.

Emotional Neglect—Emotional Poverty in the Land of Plenty: Defending Against Affect

Recognizing the Families: Professionals' Perspective

Although both physical and psychological neglect are usually associated with poverty, parents who provide materially for their children can be emotionally neglectful. The failure to connect emotionally with others is at the heart of emotional neglect; moreover, failure to connect emotionally is inherently painful to humans. The pain comes from being unable to share feelings with others, especially feelings of fear, desire, anger, and even joy and love. The pain, in other words, has its basis in affect. Of course, the problem varies in intensity, but, for clarity, it will be presented here in fairly bold terms and without any mixture of problems.

Families with problems experiencing and using affect must depend on cognitive information as their organizing structure, as the way to make sense of the world. Thus, they become focused on predictable outcomes and on the conclusions about behavior to be drawn from experience. For example, cognition-based processing of information leads to a focus on education, performance, and learning the rules for behavior. Because these things lead to good functioning in school and (later) in careers, families who neglect children's emotional needs may become economically advantaged. When economically advantaged, they are rarely identified as neglectful. Nevertheless, they are limited in how they manage their personal lives, and this may affect the development of their children.

Typically, the homes of emotionally neglectful families, whether they are well-off or in poverty, are highly structured. There are more rules for how to behave than in other homes, and everyone has a role and knows what to do. The children often seem more mature and independent than other children. In addition, the children are often neater than others and more diligent in their housework and schoolwork. Indeed, the children are often most comfortable in settings that have clear standards for performance and clearly stated consequences (both rewards and punishments). For this reason, they often perform very well in school.

In contrast with the common knowledge of the nature of neglect, these homes are often advantaged with regard to material and educational things. The children may have many and expensive toys and clothes. They may have rooms of their own. In addition, they may go to expensive schools and have a full schedule of lessons and activities.

However, in those cases of emotional neglect, these advantages are used as material expressions of parental love and concern, in the absence of affective expression. Often, the activities cover the fact that the parents feel awkward and tense when left alone with their children. Although most of us know such families and we often are aware that the children's emotional needs are not met, we probably do not think of such parents as neglectful. Nevertheless, there are many things that children need to develop, and failure to provide an essential class of them is neglect. In the case of these parents, there is adequate attention to the children's physical and cognitive needs but not to their emotional needs.

Developmental Pathways

When infants do not experience an empathic response from their caregivers to expressions of affect, the experience is painful (Stern, 1985; Tronick, 1989). Such infants first protest their condition. If the protest leads to parental anger and rejection, they are punished for showing negative affect. If it leads to continued isolation, they experience psychological abandonment. In either case, if this happens often enough, they first learn to inhibit expression of their feelings. Later, they may block out awareness of the missing response. They may pretend that they didn't need anyone.

Later, some of these infants and children learn to be falsely cheerful (Crittenden, 1992b; Stern, 1985). In some cases, this affect is used with parents who themselves are falsely bright. It is as though both parent and child were whistling in the dark; neither feels comfortable and relaxed with the other, but neither can face that truth. So they put on brittle, bright smiles and plow forward. With a bright smile and enough attention to work, one can pretend that the loneliness is not there and that work and achievement are enough. Human relationships become defined by performance.

In other cases, the parents are themselves depressed and withdrawn. In such cases, they are not rejecting of children's feelings; instead, they don't even notice them. They are so absorbed in themselves that they are unresponsive. In such cases, children learn to use false brightness to reassure the parent that they (the parents) are safe, that the world and their child are happy. The child, in other words, becomes a role-reversing, compulsively caregiving[2] child (Crittenden, 1992b, 1992d). In such cases, children set aside their own feelings and focus on meeting the emotional needs of their parents. Ignoring their own feelings eases the pain of not having those feelings soothed. In addition, caring for the parent gives the child a role that permits some closeness to the parent, under conditions that are safer for the parent. Most important, the cared-for parent may become psychologically available should the child become endangered and need rescue by the parent.

Children of emotionally distant parents who do not respond to caregiving often become compulsively self-reliant; they act falsely mature and independent of the help and companionship from others. These children have found no way to fit into social relationships. Among peers at school, they tend to be isolated and awkward (i.e., the "nerds" and "geeks").

When children are forced to behave as though they were far more mature than they actually are, they must depend on cognitive rules to guide their behavior. In other words, right thinking leads to right behavior. Nevertheless, without affect and support from a caring adult, they cannot understand social situations. Instead, they must look for cues and signs about how to behave. Relationships become puzzles that are more or less predictable but never understood affectively. To deal with the pain of isolation, the children use a mental and behavioral strategy of inhibiting feeling and depending on cognitive rules to guide their behavior.

Such children are common in clinical work. They act like efficient little adults. Often, they seem unexpectedly resilient to the obvious inadequacies of their homes. Only their air of sadness and emptiness contradicts the appearance of competence. Often, our first reaction is to wish to give the children back their childhoods, to take away their responsibilities so they can become children again. Doing so abruptly, however, can have undesirable consequences. If removed from their parent, compulsive caregiving children may become frantic in their efforts to find the parent (about whom they may fear the worst; Bowlby, 1973). They may also try to establish a caregiving relationship with new parent figures. When that is thwarted, they feel rejected and helpless. They have been denied the only role that they know how to fulfill; if they cannot be useful caregivers, they fear abandonment by adults. They also know that showing their true feelings will drive parents away.

Separating compulsively self-reliant children from their parents can be even more devastating. When they are young, such children, who have been psychologically abandoned in the physical presence of the parent, may give up entirely when they experience physical separation. When separated as adolescents, they may turn to promiscuity as a way to bridge the isolation.

Case Management

The group of families that avoids use of affect in their childrearing falls into two groups. One is superficially successful and, therefore, does not usually receive professional attention. Nevertheless, many adults who come in contact with the family are aware that something is amiss. For this pattern of development, research is needed that explores the extent of the developmental difficulties experienced by the children. On the basis of this information, we can make the policy decisions that must precede the development of services for such families.

For the families in which there is role reversal or compulsive self-reliance, the needs are more serious. In addition, the probability of referral for service is greater. When parents are so incompetent that children must become parental or prematurely independent, there is often also failure in careers and economic management of the home that ultimately brings the family to public attention.

In all cases except the most immediately threatening, it is often best to keep children with their parents. Removal gives the children the additional problems of separation and learning to adjust to life with new people (Crittenden, 1983, 1992d). Instead, services should be offered in the home to enable the parents to learn to use others as sources of support and, eventually, to become independent. Concurrently, the parents need to be taught to engage emotionally with their children. Failure to add this component will leave children feeling abandoned. The engagement, however, must be highly structured. Neither parent nor child knows how to interact normally and spontaneously; both are afraid of affect. Therefore, activities with clear roles and rules should be taught. In a sense, the goal is to move the family toward the less withdrawn version of emotional neglect.

Summation

From a theoretical perspective, these two types of neglect are opposites in terms of the way in which information is processed. (See Crittenden, 1997, for a fuller discussion of the mental and neurological evidence.) Disorganized neglect results from limitations on cognitive processes, whereas emotional neglect results from limitations on affective processes. Considering disorganized neglect first, high-intensity stimulation and unpredictability, experienced as high levels of novelty, are processed through the limbic system, leading to autonomic arousal. If comfort is not quickly forthcoming, physiological arousal augments externally generated arousal, thus increasing autonomic arousal and, in addition, expanding the range of arousing stimuli to include bodily states associated with anxiety. The outcome is a self-generated and self-maintaining feedback loop of escalating anxiety that becomes increasingly difficult to soothe. The behavioral expression of this neurological process can include either anxious comfort seeking (i.e., "dependency") or aggression. The speed of this process precludes cortical processing, including processing of information about outcomes (cognitive information), that could modify future processing. Instead, repeated use functions to speed processing, thus reducing the probability of future cortical analysis (i.e., thinking). Thus, we observe such children to be impulsive (i.e., they act before thinking, primarily on the basis of intense and suddenly escalating feeling states).

Emotional neglect operates in a slightly different manner. Because affect and displays of affect do not change parental behavior, affect is omitted from processing. Doing as parents desire (that is, performing) does elicit approval, attention, care, or a combination of these. Thus, a cognitive, sensorimotor loop is generated that bypasses affective information. Therefore, even when the information is processed cortically, the absence of affective information leaves the self vulnerable to inappropriately rigid behavior, that is, to compelled or inhibited patterns of behavior (or both).

The importance of patterns of adult interaction with infants lies in the early establishment of these neural patterns. It may be difficult to counteract such early forming patterns of processing information at later ages, thus leading to pervasive problems in situations that call for the integration of affective and cognitive information. Childrearing is one such situation as are other relationships, including peer, spousal, and work relationships.

Correcting these neurological patterns is difficult because, in both cases, half of the necessary information—either affect or cognition—is missing from processing. Moreover, mental processes and behavior have been organized so as to preclude awareness of the absence of this information. The role of professionals is to reverse this trend. If, however, intervention increases anxiety regarding being loved or safe (including the safety of keeping one's children), individuals are likely to distort their mental processes even more to protect themselves from the "help." Put more directly, intervention itself, because it can be perceived as threatening, may exacerbate the problems associated with disorganized and emotional neglect.

Therefore, it may be necessary for professionals working with neglectful families to be aware of family members' mental and behavioral strategies. This could enable professionals to structure interventions that capitalized on the strengths of the strategies while, concurrently, building competence in the weak areas. For example, a disorganized family (one that was affectively organized and motivated) would be approached through affective means. The emphasis of professional contact would be on expressing empathy, creating a protective and soothing context, and developing feelings of trust. Doing so would require high levels of availability, patience, and predictability from the professional. Through this process (and increasingly as trust developed), the professional could provide a nonevaluative, descriptive commentary on the family's use of their affective strategy. Thus, the professional first becomes a source of understanding, safety, and comfort and, later, a mirror to help the family to observe their own functioning. Because their affective strategy does have advantages, these should be pointed out so that family members can feel pride in their actual competence and also use the strategy in a more intentional, and less impulsive, manner. Efforts to (cognitively) structure the family and attempts to use predictable outcomes to motivate behavior would be delayed until after the affective relationship was firmly established and the influence of affect on family functioning at least partly understood by family members.

The reverse approach would be used with a cognitively organized family. A predictable, contingency-based relationship would be established first and later used to explore feelings and affective motivations for behavior.

Depressed Neglect: Defending Against Both Affect and Cognition

Recognizing the Families: Professionals' Perspective

Depressed neglecting families reflect the classic image of child neglect. The individuals in these families are withdrawn and dull. They show little interest in us when we visit—neither friendliness nor anger. They seem not to understand why we are coming nor to comprehend our advice to them. Many seem mildly retarded. Worst of all, they do not seem motivated to work for their children's benefit. This is not because they do not love their children—they do. It is that they do not perceive their children's needs, even after we have explained them. In addition, they do not believe that anything that we do, or that they could do, will change the situation. They are, in other words, passive and helpless.

Developmental Pathways

Some parents are so withdrawn that they do not respond to their children at all. Of course, the infants are fed, changed, and moved from place to place. But the contact is infrequent and rarely in response to signals from the infant. In addition, there is little affectionate play or soothing contact between parent and child. Such infants first protest their condition. If, with increasing protest, there is still no parental response, the infants usually give up and become silent, limp, dull, and depressed. Without feedback about the meaning of their behavior to others, infants cannot learn. If this is applied to both affective and cognitive signals, infants eventually learn that their feelings and actions have no meaning; they are helpless.

When people, of any age, learn that their behavior has no meaning, the human mind shuts down. It ceases to perceive or interpret information. Without thoughts and feelings that can be shared with others, humans become hollow shells. In this vacuum, parents do not perceive the occasions that call for action—so they don't act. Because they do not act either on their own behalf or on that of their children, they may both sink into poverty and neglect their children.

Although this pattern of helplessness most commonly begins in infancy, it can occur at any age. When first learned at later ages, however, the child has already learned that feelings and behavior do have implications, so it will take a long period of parental failure to result in child depression. Consequently, infants, who lack prior normative experience, are more vulnerable to the impact of neglectful childrearing.

Affect and Cognition

When humans cut off their mental processes, they no longer send out signals that force others to notice their misery and to try to help. On the other hand, people who have shut off feelings and the perceptions that elicit feelings no longer hurt, because they no longer feel. They no longer focus on either affect or cognition; they no longer focus. Unlike the productive, problem-focusing aspects of depression (see Gut, 1989, regarding productive depression), this depression is both unfocused and unproductive. Because no strategy works and neither affect nor cognition proves useful, this condition becomes the learned helplessness described by Seligman (1975) as depression. As Zuravin and Diblasio (1996) have demonstrated, such depression is associated with child neglect.

Although this is similar to ordinary depression, this depression may actually be a more profound state. The majority of depressed people feel sad, desperate, abandoned, angry, or some combination of these. They hurt. It is this hurt that causes them to focus all of their resources on solving the problem, even to the exclusion of other important life tasks.

These parents experience chronic depression in which there is little feeling or thought. The failure to use either affect or cognition to organize information about reality closes the doors to both relationships and learning. Under these conditions, it will be very difficult to intervene to create change.

Case Management

Restarting this *mental* system involves much more than just teaching people the appropriate parental behavior. First and foremost, all individuals in the family must learn that their behavior has predictable and meaningful consequences and that affective states can be shared by empathic others. It is essential that infants experience contingently responsive and stimulating environments that also contain human comfort for at least a few hours every day. Given such conditions, they are likely to recover rapidly and to be able to make developmental progress. Children beyond infancy are also able to benefit from such environmental changes, but the longer they have experienced debilitating environments and the earlier in their life such experiences began, the longer and more difficult will be the recovery. For parents, of course, the task is the most difficult. This is partly because of their longer exposure to helplessness. In addition, however, it is far more difficult to place adults in new and responsive environments.

Second, parents need to learn to use appropriate expressions of affect. They need to practice smiling in appropriate situations, laughing when others laugh, and looking soothing and concerned when their children are distressed. Of course, this will be quite mechanical at first. It is likely, however, that after many repetitions, actual feelings will begin to fit expressions of affect (Ekman, 1984). In addition, the affective displays will increase their children's responsiveness and liveliness, thus initiating an upward spiral of mutual reinforcement. For children, of course, the pace of change is more rapid than for adults.

Nevertheless, even with adults, changes can be made. Some of our commonly used approaches, however, are likely to be counterproductive. Threatening or punitive strategies that are tied to parents' learning to use new and more appropriate parenting behavior are particularly likely to be ineffective. There are two reasons for this. First, the parents do not believe themselves to have the ability to change, so they may not even try. Second, even the most reasonable pressure is likely to elicit their familiar response to danger of blocking out all information. A longer-term, more supportive approach is needed. Similarly, parent education is likely to be wasted on severely depressed parents and, because judgment would not be exercised in the context of feelings and predictable outcomes, could be counterproductive by introducing potentially harmful behaviors. (For example, "time-out" can be used too often and too long and become a source of further neglect.) Medications can effectively alter mental processing of information, thus changing behavior. Nevertheless, side effects must be considered. In addition, it must be determined whether the effects of the medication can facilitate self-generated processing changes or whether the medication will be permanently necessary. Although it may still be advantageous, it would be preferable if medication permitted new processing patterns that could be maintained after discontinuation of the medication. Last, even with the medication, environments for learning previously unlearned patterns of using cognition and affect need to be carefully structured.

Thus, a central point of the processing of information about relationships as a critical cause of child neglect is that, with this perspective, potential intervention strategies can be conceptualized theoretically and tested empirically. The perspective offered here suggests the importance of differential diagnosis of processing strategies among child neglect cases. Interventions can be aimed at a variety of interlocking systemic levels of functioning (e.g., societal, familial, intrapersonal, or neurological). But ultimately, to be effective, they must change how information is processed and used to organize behavior by individuals. This will require systematic and deliberate consideration of *how* specific interventions function and *who* is likely to benefit (a) at what time, (b) with which combination and order of techniques, and (c) in what context.

CONCLUSION

In conclusion, the association of poverty with neglect needs to be reconsidered. First, both poverty and child neglect may be the effects of learning to process information in distorted and limiting ways. Second, the focus on poverty may prevent us from seeing the importance of emotional neglect in more affluent families. Last, the focus on the association of poverty with neglect may lead to the conclusion that global economic solutions are primary. If failures in the processing of information are critical to the process of neglect, it is likely that neglectful parents will continue to neglect their children's mental needs, regardless of the financial resources made available.

That is not to suggest that poverty should be ignored. Poverty both adds to life stress and confirms adults' sense of helplessness. But poverty may not be the critical cause of the harmful effects of child neglect on children; indeed, it may be one of the outcomes. In addition, this perspective suggests that parent education may be wasted on most neglectful parents. Because they are blocking out information necessary for action, teaching them new responses may be useless; they will be unlikely to identify correctly the occasions on which to use the newly learned behaviors. See Crittenden (1993) for a fuller discussion of this perspective.

Instead, we need to construct interventions (and environments that support interventions) that will assist parents to accept (i.e., to perceive) information that in the past has been useless or threatening (Crittenden, 1991, 1992c). Threats and badgering are unlikely to accomplish this. Establishing nurturant relationships with neglectful parents may be essential to enabling them to establish such relationships with their children. Because they have been hurt by essentially all of the important people in their lives, it will take time to accomplish this goal. Unfortunately, high caseloads and patterns of infrequent contacts (that are not in response to parents' signals and needs) may make it difficult to establish relationships with neglectful parents at all. Last, if we stay involved with such families for only a short time, we will once again fail them, thus making them more resistant to the next professional.

Although there is insufficient evidence to confirm the validity of many of the propositions made in this chapter, it is clear that our dual perspectives of individual pathology and societal failure have not, in the past 30 years, led to effective solutions to the problem of neglect. A new explanation that can lead to new treatment techniques is needed, and the rudiments of one such approach are offered here. Possibly, these ideas will be sufficiently intriguing to initiate fresh thinking about child neglect. It is the most serious type of maltreatment and the least understood. Careful thought, new policies, and improved interventions can't come too soon.

NOTES

1. See Crittenden (1997) for a fuller discussion of these concepts.
2. This should be differentiated from parental or "parentified" children who act as parents to their *siblings*. Depending on the ages of the children, the demands placed on the parental child, and the support offered to the child, this may be beneficial or detrimental to the parental child and the cared-for siblings.

REFERENCES

Bowlby, J. (1973). *Attachment and loss: Vol. 2. Separation.* New York: Basic Books.

Crittenden, P. M. (1983). The effect of mandatory protective daycare on mutual attachment in maltreating mother-infant dyads. *International Journal of Child Abuse and Neglect, 3,* 297-300.

Crittenden, P. M. (1985). Social networks, quality of child-rearing, and child development. *Child Development, 56,* 1299-1313.

Crittenden, P. M. (1988). Family and dyadic patterns of functioning in maltreating families. In K. Browne, C. Davies, & P. Stratton (Eds.), *Early prediction and prevention of child abuse* (pp. 161-189). Chichester, UK: Wiley.

Crittenden, P. M. (1991). Treatment of child abuse and neglect. *Human Systems, 2,* 161-179.

Crittenden, P. M. (1992a). *Child neglect.* Chicago: National Committee for the Prevention of Child Abuse.

Crittenden, P. M. (1992b). Quality of attachment in the preschool years. *Development and Psychopathology, 4,* 209-241.

Crittenden, P. M. (1992c). The social ecology of treatment: Case study of a service system for maltreated children. *American Journal of Orthopsychiatry, 62,* 22-34.

Crittenden, P. M. (1992d). Treatment of anxious attachment in infancy and early childhood. *Development and Psychopathology, 4,* 575-602.

Crittenden, P. M. (1993). Characteristics of neglectful parents: An information processing approach. *Criminal Justice and Behavior, 20,* 27-48.

Crittenden, P. M. (1997). Toward an integrative theory of trauma: A dynamic-maturational approach. In D. Cicchetti & S. Toth (Eds.), *The Rochester Symposium on Developmental Psychopathology: Vol. 10. Risk, trauma, and mental processes* (pp. 34-84). Rochester, NY: University of Rochester Press.

Ekman, P. (1984). Expression and the nature of emotion. In K. R. Scherer & P. Ekman (Eds.), *Approaches to emotion* (pp. 319-343). Hillsdale, NJ: Erlbaum.

Erickson, M., & Egeland, B. (1996). Child neglect. In J. Briere, L. Berliner, J. A. Bulkey, C. Jenny, & T. Reid (Eds.), *The APSAC handbook on child maltreatment* (pp. 4-20). Thousand Oaks, CA: Sage.

Garbarino, J. (1982). *Children and families in the social environment.* New York: Aldine.

Gut, E. (1989). *Productive and unproductive depression: Success or failure of a vital process.* New York: Basic Books.

Jean-Gilles, M., & Crittenden, P. M. (1990). Maltreating families: A look at siblings. *Family Relations, 39,* 323-329.

Leon, A. C., & Weissman, M. M. (1993). *Analysis of NIMH's existing epidemiological catchment area (ECA) data on depression and other affective disorders in welfare and disabled populations* (Report on Grant HHS-100-92-0032). Washington, DC: U.S. Department of Health and Human Services.

Mayer, S. (1997). *What money can't buy.* Cambridge, MA: Harvard University Press.

Pelton, L. (1981). *The social context of child abuse and neglect.* New York: Human Sciences Press.

Polansky, N. A., Chalmers, M. A., Buttenweiser, E., & Williams, D. P. (1981). *Damaged parents: An anatomy of child neglect.* Chicago: University of Chicago Press.

Russell, A. B., & Trainor, C. M. (1984). *Trends in child abuse and neglect: A national perspective.* Denver, CO: American Association for Protecting Children, American Humane Association.

Sedlak, A. J., & Broadhurst, D. D. (1996). *Third annual incidence study of child abuse and neglect: Final report.* Washington, DC: U.S. Department of Health and Human Services.

Seligman, M. E. P. (1975). *Helplessness: On depression, development, and death.* San Francisco: Freeman.

Stern, D. (1985). *The interpersonal world of the infant.* New York: Basic Books.

Tonge, W., James, D., & Hillam, S. (Eds.). (1975). Families without hope [Special issue]. *British Journal of Psychiatry, 11.*

Tronick, E. Z. (1989). Emotions and emotional communication in infants. *American Psychologist, 44,* 112-119.

Wolfe, D. A. (1993). Prevention of child neglect: Emerging issues. *Criminal Justice and Behavior, 20,* 90-111.

Zuravin, S., & Diblasio, F. A. (1996). The correlates of child physical abuse and neglect by adolescent mothers. *Journal of Family Violence, 11,* 149-166.

Cultural Competence and Child Neglect 4

JILL E. KORBIN
JAMES C. SPILSBURY

The relationship between culture and child neglect is complex, politically charged, and fraught with unresolved issues. In this chapter, we focus on the need for acquiring what has been termed *cultural competence* in child protection and argue that culture is central to understanding and working with child maltreatment. We suggest that cultural competence begins by acquiring the skills and knowledge that enable child maltreatment professionals both to understand their own cultures as well as to take another cultural perspective. The foundation of cultural competence, then, is the development of skills and knowledge that allow one to take multiple perspectives, to see things through multiple filters or lenses. This

AUTHORS' NOTE: The authors thank Howard Dubowitz for his helpful comments and editorial assistance, Toby Martin for assistance with references, and Sara Kersey and Christina Welter for assistance with Figure 4.1. There is considerable variation on the appropriate terms to use for any cultural group. Variation in terminology in this chapter reflects our effort to be consistent with literature cited. Furthermore, examples have been used citing particular cultural or ethnic groups. These were intended as examples and not in any way to indicate that problems are unique to the culture or ethnic group used in the example. The chapter focuses on cultural diversity within the United States. Cultural diversity in a broader cross-cultural perspective has been discussed elsewhere (e.g., Finkelhor & Korbin, 1988; Korbin, 1981, 1987, 1994, 1997; Levinson, 1989; see also *Child Abuse and Neglect: The International Journal*).

permits an understanding of both commonalities and differences across cultures.

There is no inherent contradiction between incorporating culture in child protection and ensuring child well-being. It does not follow that if cultural diversity is accommodated in child protection efforts, differing standards for different cultures will emerge and children will suffer as a result. We argue that consideration of culture is critical in child protection work—a firmly grounded knowledge base concerning if, when, and how culture affects child maltreatment can only enhance child well-being. The lack of cultural competence leads one into either accepting all behaviors as culturally appropriate, regardless of their impacts on children, or insisting on one global standard to which all societies must adhere for optimal child well-being. Although cultural factors are not necessarily involved in all cases of child neglect, culture must be considered when working within a multicultural context.

CULTURAL COMPETENCE

Cultural competence is a key to effective child protection (e.g. Abney, 1996; Cross, Bazron, Dennis, & Isaacs, 1989; Korbin, 1987, 1997). The term *cultural competence* was introduced to child protection by anthropologist James Green (1978, 1982). Cultural competence is grounded in the ability to stand in other people's shoes, to walk around a bit, and to look at the world through their eyes. According to Green, cultural competence is not merely an acquired sensitivity to cultural diversity but a repertoire of skills and knowledge that enable one to transcend cultural boundaries.

Culturally competent practice puts children's well-being and protection first but understands well-being and protection within the cultural context. Cultural competence incorporates culture in definitions of child neglect to identify cases without cultural bias. Cultural competence addresses the need for a culturally informed perspective on the etiology of child neglect to better inform culturally appropriate prevention and intervention. Cultural competence helps to sort out which aspects of a family's difficulties are "cultural," which are "neglectful," and which are a combination of factors. And, in a broader sense, cultural competence involves advocacy for cultural diversity in the entirety of child protection endeavors as appropriate in a multicultural society.

Child care practices must be viewed from an *emic,* or insider perspective, as well as an *etic,* or outsider viewpoint. Examples of practices that would be differentially defined as abusive or neglectful by different cultural groups abound in the cross-cultural record. Cross-cultural research has not yielded a universally ideal parenting strategy. Rather, what is considered optimal or deficient childrearing differs in various social and historical contexts (e.g., Green, 1978; Korbin, 1981, 1987, 1997; Sternberg & Lamb, 1991). Cultural practices in child care persist through the force of custom and because parents believe that by adhering to their culture's prescriptions and proscriptions, they will enhance their children's, and their own, well-being.

Cultural competence avoids both unmoderated ethnocentrism and unmoderated relativism. Ethnocentrism is the belief that one's own cultural beliefs and practices are not only preferable but also superior to all others. In contrast, cultural relativism is the belief that each and every culture must be viewed in its own right as equal to all others, and that culturally sanctioned behaviors cannot be judged by the standards of another culture. An exclusive reliance on either position precludes cultural competence.

An unmoderated ethnocentric position disregards cultural differences and imposes a single standard for child care practices. It is counterproductive for effective child protection because it attempts to impose the beliefs and behaviors of one group, the dominant culture, on all populations. Childrearing practices cannot be separated from the wider context in which they are embedded, and one culture's patterns have not necessarily been demonstrated to be superior to another. Change imposed from the outside has rarely been successful, and child care practices and beliefs have been quite persistent and resistant to change. An unmoderated position on ethnocentrism runs the risk of false positives, or misidentification of cultural practices as child maltreatment.

Conversely, an unmoderated relativist position suspends all standards and runs the risk of false negatives, or misidentification of neglect as cultural practice. That a behavior can be identified as part of a cultural heritage does not necessarily mean that it is "good" for children. In addition, child protection professionals need to understand the range of intracultural variability so that culture cannot be used as an excuse for neglect.

Culturally competent child protection must first assume an orientation of cultural and ethnic *difference* rather than *deficiency.* Child protection efforts can accommodate differences in child care patterns without the assumption that such accommodation permits a lesser standard of care for children of diverse ethnic groups. A deficiency approach is ethnocentric in the insistence that one cultural standard is superior to others, whereas a difference approach allows a more circumspect and contextual perspective without compromising child well-being. A difference approach allows for the possibility that a child is not faring well or even being harmed. It just does not begin by assuming that this is due to culture.

The ability to understand one's own culture is the stepping-stone to being able to understand other cultures. The cross-cultural record affords us the opportunity to look at both our own and others' cultures with an eye to both the variability and the uniformity of human behavior. It is instructive to consider European American child care practices through the eyes of other cultures. For example, common pediatric advice is that it is developmentally important for infants and young children to sleep independently (e.g., Lozoff & Zuckerman, 1988). However, rural Hawaiian-American-Polynesian women with whom one of us (Korbin) worked in the 1970s were incredulous at her verification of a "rumor" that *haole* (literally meaning outsider but more commonly used to refer to whites) parents put infants and young children in separate beds, and worse, in separate rooms, alone for the entire night. Although this seems like a benign example, many cultures believe that isolating children for the night is not only detrimental to social development but also potentially dangerous. In many cultures, contact at night is a basic need. In traditional Japanese culture, two-generation co-sleeping was preferable and expected throughout most of the life cycle (Caudill & Plath, 1966). Similarly, letting an infant "cry itself to sleep" is difficult to comprehend in traditional highland New Guinea society, in which it was believed that a crying infant's spirit could escape through the open fontanelle causing death (Langness, 1981). These same Hawaiian-American-Polynesian women responded to Korbin's explanations of the dangers of overlaying with incredulity that it would be possible for a normal person to sleep through the struggles of a suffocating infant or toddler. Indeed, looking at human behavior from an evolutionary perspective, McKenna, Mosko, Dungy, and McAninch (1990) have hypothesized that co-sleeping may be advantageous because parents and children may coordinate breathing and sleep cycles, thereby preventing apnea spells (periods without breathing) possibly related to sudden infant death syndrome.

As another example, the symptoms of colic would arouse suspicion of bad child care practices or inflicted trauma among Hawaiian-Polynesian-Americans. Hawaiian-Polynesian-Americans would attribute symptoms of fussiness, indigestion, general discomfort, and inconsolable crying to bouncing or jiggling of infants, which causes a condition known as *opu huli* (turned or twisted stomach). *Opu huli* is diagnosed by seeing which leg a child pulls up when lying down flat and can be treated by someone familiar with therapeutic massage. If child maltreatment is to be defined as an identifiable consequence to a child resulting from parental action (or inaction), jiggling a child and causing *opu huli* would certainly qualify among Hawaiian-Polynesian-Americans—thereby putting all mainlanders with colicky infants at suspicion of abuse, rather than as objects of sympathy (Korbin, 1990).

INTRACULTURAL VARIABILITY

Understanding the range of intracultural variability is an important part of cultural competence. Membership in a culture or ethnic group is too often defined by categorization based on skin color or broad geographical area from which descent can be traced. Thus, multiple, distinguishable populations are too often classified as a single homogeneous entity, such as Hispanics/Latinos (e.g., Cubans, Puerto Ricans, Mexicans, Mexican Americans, Guatemalans), Blacks (e.g., African Americans, Haitians, West Indians), Asians (e.g., Chinese, Japanese, Koreans, Thai, Cambodians), Pacific Island peoples (e.g., Hawaiians, Samoans, Tahitians), Native Americans (e.g., Navajo, Sioux), and European Americans (e.g., Italians, Germans, British). Such broad classifications (e.g., African American, Asian American) do not necessarily reflect the reality of day-to-day life. Each of the subgroups has been described as possessing a unique culture and concomitant therapeutic needs (McGoldrick, Giordano, & Pearce, 1996).

It is important to note that there is also considerable diversity *within* any culture or ethnic group along the lines of generation, acculturation, education, income, gender, age, and past experience. Because of both subcultural differences and individual variability within any cultural or ethnic group, culture/ethnicity should be viewed as an important background variable: Culture/ethnicity as a variable of interest should be on a par with age and gender.

However, no set of generalizations about any cultural or ethnic population will be sufficient to deal with child neglect across culturally diverse populations. The importance of within-culture variability and the need to specify what it is about the cultural context (to "unpack" the cultural variable) preclude the development of a library-like card catalogue of strategies for working with specific cultural groups. Care must be taken not to assume that one strategy will work for multiple cultures that have been grouped together. For example, significant differences among Native American populations "highlight the need for cultural and geographic specificity in child welfare services to Native Americans" (Nelson, Cross, Landsman, & Tyler, 1996, p. 519). Similarly, differences have been found in types of child maltreatment, including neglect, among different cultural groups usually lumped together as Asians and Pacific Islanders. These differences among Vietnamese, Filipino, Laotian, Cambodian, Samoan, Korean, and Hmong are related to cultural variation in family composition and structure, childrearing beliefs and practices, and war and refugee-related experiences (Ima & Hohm, 1991). Thus, whereas knowledge of general cultural patterns provides an important starting point, each individual and family must be assessed on their own merits.

STEPS IN CULTURALLY COMPETENT CHILD PROTECTION

As we noted earlier, culturally competent child protection should have its first priority on the child's well-being but must consider the child within a cultural context. Figure 4.1, discussed in the subsequent section, illustrates a suggested framework for culturally competent child neglect work.

1. Have the child's basic needs been met? Culturally competent child protection begins with an assessment of the child's status. We begin with

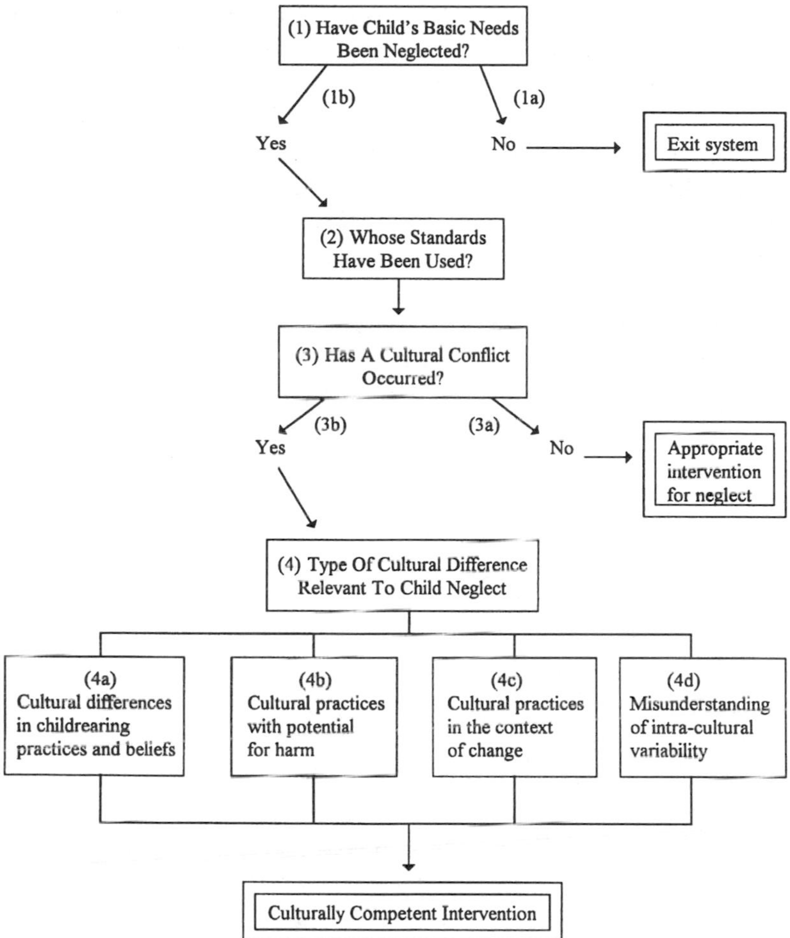

Figure 4.1. Cultural Competence in Child Neglect Intervention

Dubowitz, Black, Starr, and Zuravin's (1993) suggestion that "neglect occurs when basic needs of children are not met" (p. 12). A child can be assessed as to his or her nutritional, educational, growth, and health or psychological status. If the child's basic needs are judged to be met and there are no additional difficulties to be resolved, the child and family can exit the child protection system (see arrow at 1a). If, however, it is determined that the child's basic needs are not being met (see arrow at 1b), the next step in culturally competent practice should be considered.

2. *Whose criteria have been used to determine that the child's basic needs have not been met?* Identification of neglect is firmly rooted in cultural and societal standards within which the acceptability of parental behavior and the severity of child outcomes are judged (e.g., Sternberg & Lamb, 1991). Dubowitz et al. (1993) include contextual factors as important for understanding the situation and guiding interventions, suggesting a child-centered process of evaluating neglect. Whereas the focus on children's basic needs is an appealing way to conceptualize child neglect, most of our conceptions of children's needs are dependent on a cultural filter. What, then, are some basic needs, and how might they vary across cultures?

Survival is the most basic of basic needs. In the more clear-cut cases of child neglect, culture becomes negligible. Severely neglected and malnourished children, deprived of the most basic needs of food and shelter, look sadly similar across cultural contexts. There is international consensus on maltreatment involving the deprivation of such basic needs as food (Daro, Migely, Weise, & Salmon-Cox, 1996). In our research in Cleveland, Ohio, we asked 400 randomly selected residents of neighborhoods that differed in predominant ethnicity (African American and European American) and neighborhood risk factors for child maltreatment reports to list three behaviors that they would call child abuse and neglect. In our preliminary analysis, not providing a child with adequate food was the single most frequently reported behavior ($n = 208$, 52%). For the purposes of comparison, the next most frequently mentioned behavior ($n = 127$, 32%) was beating a child (including beating, kicking, or punching). Additional behaviors that fell under the domain of neglect included children not being supervised ($n = 93$, 23%), being left at home alone, ($n = 78$, 20%), and not being properly clothed ($n = 36$, 9%). No statistically significant differences were identified in these behaviors by level of neighborhood impoverishment (greater than 40% of residents living below the poverty line) or predominant neighborhood ethnicity (greater than 75% African American or European American). Polansky, Gaudin, Ammons, and Davis (1985) similarly found substantial agreement as to what would be considered neglect.

Child neglect, however, encompasses so many gray areas that, in practice, what constitutes neglect is often highly contested across cultures, and basic needs are not always as clear-cut as food and water. For example, one could argue that regardless of culture, preparation for the future through education is a basic need. However, the form of education varies across cultures. Among most families living in the United States, formal education is seen as basic to child and adolescent development, and this view is supported by mandatory education laws. In contrast, Amish parents view education beyond the eighth grade as wholly inappropriate for their way of life and damaging to Amish children's socialization to Amish adulthood. Is Amish society's court-supported refusal to send children to school beyond the eighth grade neglect? One would be hard pressed to identify Amish teens as neglected, yet they are not in school.

Similarly, one could argue that maintaining a child's health is another basic need, yet considerable cultural diversity is evident in meeting this need and identifying neglect (Korbin, 1987, 1997; Korbin, Brinkley, Reebals, & Singh, 1996; Korbin & Johnston, 1982; see also Dubowitz, this volume, Chapter 6; Zuravin, this volume, Chapter 2). Practices that are firmly grounded in a cultural tradition generally are not reported as medical neglect unless parents persistently refuse to obtain medical care for serious conditions in their children. Coin rubbing *(cao gio)* among Vietnamese individuals, for example, involves forcefully rubbing metal coins on the body to push out the illness, leaving a pattern of bruises that can be extensive. Nonetheless, this is recognized as a cultural practice administered with good intentions, without anger or rage, and is generally not reported as maltreatment (Yeatman, Shaw, Barlow, & Bartlett, 1976). The health care and child protection response to culturally based healing practices are examples of negotiating a balance between children's basic needs for health and for medical care, and cultural differences in how health is defined and what medical care should be.

A more controversial area of basic needs is the level of supervision required to ensure children's safety and well-being. For example, Laotian and Cambodian refugees in the United States bring with them child care practices that include sibling caregiving and community responsibility for child supervision. Some of these refugees, then, are quite surprised that the dominant culture in the United States, as reflected through schools and child protection agencies, looks askance at sibling caregiving by children as young as 8, something that is unremarkable in their indigenous setting (Ima & Hohm, 1991).

Divergence in the criteria for meeting children's basic needs, then, creates a situation that has the potential for cultural conflict, which is the next step in our framework.

3. *Has cultural conflict occurred?* Cultural conflict in defining child maltreatment generally arises because of differences in child care beliefs and

practices. The greater the divergence in child care practices and beliefs, the greater the potential for cultural conflict in definitions of maltreatment (Korbin, 1997). Neglect is particularly problematic because it encompasses such a wide range of parental action or inaction and consequences for children, from subtle parental behaviors to life-threatening inattention, abandonment, or starvation (Dubowitz et al., 1993; Erickson & Egeland, 1996; Margolin, 1990; Zuravin, this volume, Chapter 2).

The cross-cultural literature provides a wealth of examples of differential definitions of what constitutes child maltreatment (e.g., Finkelhor & Korbin, 1988; Korbin, 1981, 1987, 1997). More attention has been devoted to the more dramatic examples of cultural differences in what is perceived as physical abuse than to child neglect. We have suggested that any examination of child maltreatment cross-culturally must not confuse three levels of definition: (1) cultural differences in child care and childrearing practices, (2) idiosyncratic or individual deviance from these cultural norms, and (3) societally induced maltreatment to children (Korbin, 1981, 1987, 1997). We have also suggested that child maltreatment can be defined across cultures as those acts that are preventable, proximate, and proscribed (Finkelhor & Korbin, 1988). The criteria of preventable and proximate distinguish child maltreatment from other circumstances that have detrimental consequences for children (such as natural disasters), and the criterion of proscribed makes the definition flexible enough to encompass a range of cultural contexts.

Following our framework, if there is not cultural conflict in deciding whether or not the child's basic needs have been met (see arrow at 3a), then intervention can proceed to address the child and family issues, keeping in mind but not necessarily involving cultural considerations. If, however, cultural conflict is raised in identifying whether the child's basic needs are compromised (i.e., if the child is neglected—see arrow at 3b), then further steps in understanding culture must be undertaken.

4. What is the nature of cultural difference relevant to child protection and child neglect? At this stage of the framework, we discuss four types of cultural differences. We also suggest that the difference orientation discussed earlier is a more effective approach in child protection than a deficiency orientation. A difference orientation and approach leads one to focus on reducing the potential harm rather than attacking cultural practices and beliefs that are difficult to change.

4a. Cultural differences in childrearing beliefs and behaviors: Even if children's basic needs (Dubowitz et al., 1993), however defined, are inadequately met, different culturally based interpretations of child behavior may stimulate different solutions. For example, a malnourished child may be regarded quite differently across cultural contexts, and cultural beliefs may further compromise an already malnourished child. In areas of Mexico and Central America, a child displaying the apathetic, anorexic, and unresponsive behaviors indicative of malnourishment may instead be perceived as *chipil* or angry at the mother during weaning and envious of a new sibling. The child may then be punished or ignored for perceived bad behavior (Chavez, Martinez, & Yaschine, 1975; Foster & Anderson, 1978; Werner, 1979). If the parents believe that they are acting in the older child's best interests, by helping him or her to accept the new baby as part of the family, is this neglectful or is it malnutrition secondary to a cultural practice or belief? If we assume a deficiency orientation and define the situation as neglect, then we must take a stance that labels the parents' beliefs and behaviors as wholly in error and as bad in their outcome for at least one of their children. Our intervention strategies then are limited to imposing or insisting on changed behaviors in the parent(s) and reporting the child to authorities. If, on the other hand, we assume a difference orientation, we can ascertain the pathway by which the child became malnourished, accept it as culturally legitimate that the older child must give way to the new baby, and engage the parent in education about the behavior of children who are both displaced by a new baby *and* malnourished. Across cultures, we can begin by assuming that parents would rather be dealing with a content toddler.

4b. Cultural practices with potential for harm: Some cultural practices may cause injury or be harmful to children. These practices may not be inflicted with malintent but cause harm nevertheless. A difference orientation grounded in cultural competence facilitates intervention. In the Southwest, for example, lead poisoning in young children was linked to indigenous medications, "azarcon" and "greta," used to cure *empacho. Empacho* is an illness defined by many Hispanic groups as a bolus in the stomach that must be purged. Trotter, Ackerman, Rodman, Martinez, and Sorvillo (1983) found that in some places these indigenous medications had high concentrations of lead. Educational and community awareness efforts were successful in decreasing the use of the harmful forms of these medicinal substances, and thus the incidence of lead poisoning, while not minimizing the cultural importance or reality of treating *empacho.*

4c. Cultural practices in the context of change: A child care strategy well suited to one situation may not be suited to another. For example, Polynesian (primarily Maori) children, who compose approximately 10% of the child population of New Zealand, constitute more than half of the children reported as not being properly supervised (Fergusson, Flemming, & O'Neill, 1972). This overrepresentation results, in part, from cultural conflict in the definition of child maltreatment related to a misunderstanding of the Polynesian practice of sibling caretaking. In the indigenous setting, sibling caretaking is highly valued by both children and adults and is central to Polynesian socialization patterns (Gallimore, Boggs, & Jordan, 1974; Korbin, 1990). Polynesian adults do not view children being left alone with siblings as dangerous. However, Ritchie and Ritchie (1981) point out that it is not merely cultural misunderstanding or cultural conflict that accounts for the disparity in reporting statistics. They argue that in changing circumstances, cultural practices that are valued and adaptive in one setting may indeed be dangerous to children in another. In the move to urban settings, Maoris often find themselves living in the city's poorest sections, in substandard housing that more easily catches fire, on streets with fast-moving cars, and isolated from a larger supportive network of kin. Sibling caretaking in this changed setting may indeed pose increased risk of accident and injury to children. However, it is not sibling caretaking per se that is of concern but sibling caretaking in its new context.

4d. Misunderstanding of intracultural variability: Intracultural diversity and the continuum of acceptable and unacceptable behavior within any culture must be understood. This is the level at which cultural practices can best be differentiated from maltreatment. Unfortunately, distinguishing cultural differences from child maltreatment has been hampered in child protection largely because child protection workers are typically restricted in their community contacts to problematic individuals' and families' unacceptable behaviors rather than to the full continuum of acceptable and unacceptable behaviors.

For example, leaving children alone and unsupervised by adults is a frequent source of child maltreatment reports among the Navajo (Hauswald, 1987). Parents reported for these behaviors may justify their actions as part of traditional Navajo childrearing patterns involving sibling caretaking and responsibility training. However, in Hauswald's interviews with 30 Navajo mothers, none thought that young children should be left alone for extended periods with siblings less than 13 years of age. These mothers also disapproved of leaving children alone overnight without adult supervision. Thus, leaving children alone and unsupervised is not, in the case of the Navajo, a part of traditional, acceptable childrearing.

This Navajo example underlines the importance of child protection professionals becoming culturally informed through contact with clients and the communities in which they live. Familiarity with culture based on the literature or on consultations with cultural experts, be they community members or academics, must be validated through knowledge generated from those being served. Because of the diversity of cultures and intracultural variability, child protection professionals should approach culture as an interested learner and approach patients and their families as teachers about that culture.

5. Culturally competent intervention: By this point in our framework, we have suggested that a difference orientation allows greater flexibility and is more suited to cultural competence than is a deficiency orientation that seeks to change cultural practices and beliefs. Research on cultural issues in clinical treatment needs further development (e.g., McGoldrick et al., 1996; Tharp, 1991). A culturally competent therapeutic approach should focus not only on pathological behaviors that can be labeled maltreatment but, equally important, on cultural strengths that can mitigate risk factors.

Culturally competent treatment for different cultures may involve different approaches. One approach is to use indigenous treatments and healers. For example, *ho'oponopono* is a traditional form of family discussion and conflict resolution among Hawaiians (Ito, 1985; Shook, 1985) that has been used in child abuse intervention. *Ho'oponopono* assumes that family difficulties are deeper than those between two individuals and that the whole network must be involved in identifying the trouble and coming to some resolution of the problem.

Another approach is to design treatment modalities for specific cultures that build on cultural patterns. An example is *cuento* therapy developed for Puerto Rican children, which adapts the traditional use of folktales in child socialization to foster discussion of current difficulties

(Costantino, Malgady, & Rogler, 1986). Longress (1991) has argued that a child protection model based on cultural differences is best suited to new immigrants and refugees but that work with people of color also must attend to status differentials and a history of discrimination.

Consensus on a working definition of child neglect is an important step in a culturally informed and culturally competent child maltreatment intervention, and efforts should be made to understand clients' explanations of behavior within the context of their cultures. However, definitions of child neglect and case identification may not overlap, because of distrust of the child protection system (e.g., Long, 1986). Cultural values on family solidarity and fear that the child protection system will remove children may mask cases considered neglectful from both within and without the cultural or ethnic group.

Cultural competence is furthered when child protection professionals work to lessen the contentiousness of child protection efforts. The bias in reporting by race and socioeconomic status is not just a matter of academic interest but filters into the worldview of communities, where there is a fear of a punitive child protective system that will "take your kids" as opposed to providing help. As but one recent example, a grandmother in Akron, Ohio, was prosecuted because she left one grandchild in a running car on a cold night while she went back inside to retrieve another child. In the moments she was inside, her car was stolen (Dennis, 1997). Within the same month, an anesthesiologist in Boston was investigated for child neglect when she left her two daughters in a store parking lot while she ran inside to drop off her film. She was not prosecuted (Estrin, 1997).

CULTURE AND THE ETIOLOGY OF CHILD NEGLECT

A challenge to a culturally informed understanding of child neglect is to distinguish clearly what portion of neglect is related to cultural factors and what portion to other multiple factors. This task is exceedingly complex and does not lend itself to easy solutions. Dubowitz et al. (1993) have been important in moving the discussion away from an exclusive focus on individual parental or caretaker culpability to the involvement of parents, professionals, and a larger society. This reorientation allows for more flexibility, which should be more conducive to addressing cultural variability.

Whereas efforts were made to separate child maltreatment from poverty in public policy (e.g., Nelson, 1984), poverty has been demonstrated to be related to child neglect at both the individual and aggregate levels (e.g., Coulton, Korbin, Su, & Chow, 1995; Drake & Pandey, 1996; Pelton, 1981). One could certainly argue that poverty is, in itself, a form of societal neglect (e.g., Gil, 1970; Giovannoni & Billingsley, 1970; Korbin, 1981; Pelton, 1981).

Giovannoni and Billingsley's (1970) classic study of neglect in poor families in San Francisco highlighted differences within a population of mothers in poverty. Regardless of whether families were African American, European American or Hispanic/Latino, neglect was the most prevalent in the poorest of the poor families. In another study of families referred for child neglect in Allegheny County, Pennsylvania, African American families in the neglect sample were more economically deprived than white families reported for neglect (Saunders, Nelson, & Landsman, 1993).

Because ethnic minorities are overrepresented among the poor, it is easy to confound culture and poverty. One way to overcome this difficulty in practice is to first rule out more tangible issues that might be contributing to concerns that a child is being neglected. Does a family really disagree with a recommended course of treatment, are they medically neglectful, or do they face real difficulties and even danger in getting a prescription filled in a high-crime neighborhood if the appointment is at the end of the day? If clients are often late, does a family really have a different cultural orientation to time or are they dependent on unreliable public transportation (often in cold weather with young children in tow)?

Proponents of a "critical" theoretical perspective assert that understanding of a social phenomenon necessitates examination of that phenomenon in its larger political and economic context. Critical analyses of child neglect (Kasinsky, 1994; Swift, 1995) posit that society has historically conceived neglect as mothers' deficient care of children and that this conceptualization has served the interests of the powerful by (1) deflecting attention from societal causes of neglect (e.g., poverty and marginalization) and, therefore, from costly societal-level solutions to the problem; (2) providing scapegoats for the problem of streetwise or otherwise unruly children; (3) permitting state intrusion into "problem" families; and (4) privileging certain cultural forms of child care while penalizing others. Current social service practices contribute to the distortion of the true causes of neglect and delay efforts to help children (Swift, 1995). Even in instances when social work and child protective services acknowledge the relationship between poverty and neglect, the focus remains on individual families (Kasinsky, 1994).

Research should also consider commonalities and differences in etiological pathways across cultures (National Research Council, 1993). Spearly and Lauderdale (1983), for example, using central registry data, found that socioeconomic status of counties was the best predictor of Anglo rates of child maltreatment, whereas urbanization was the best predictor of higher rates for Blacks and Hispanics. In our research examining the relationship of neighborhoods to child maltreatment reports, we have identified a stronger relationship between an impoverishment factor and child maltreatment reports in predominantly European American neighborhoods as compared with African American neighborhoods. In an analysis of 177 residential census tracts in Cleveland, we found that impoverishment was the most important predictor of neighborhood rates of child maltreatment reports (Coulton et al., 1995). However, when we analyzed African American and European American neighborhoods separately, we found that the same impoverishment factor had a stronger effect in predominantly (> 75%) European American than in predominantly (> 75%) African American neighborhoods. An in-depth ethnographic study of four neighborhoods, two African American and two European American, suggested that the relationship between impoverishment and child maltreatment reports had the most pronounced effect on those neighborhoods at the lower end of the economic spectrum (Korbin, Coulton, Chard, Platt-Houston, & Su, 1998). Our analysis, then, is consistent with the suggestion of Garbarino and Ebata (1983) that cultural or ethnic differences in child maltreatment are most pronounced at the lowest socioeconomic levels where the stresses of poverty are the more pronounced on cultural patterns.

Unfortunately, the reasons for differences in neglect both within and between populations are rarely specified. Differences in incidence or prevalence are assumed to reflect cultural patterns, but these patterns are rarely measured. In exploring the relationship between culture/ethnicity and child maltreatment, the cultural variable must be "unpacked." That is, because culture is not monolithic, it cannot be viewed as having a uniform impact on all members. It is critical to understand intracultural diversity, to distinguish behaviors that are culturally based from those that are neglecting and related to other factors. This lack of attention to unpacking the cultural variable, or assessing specifically what it is about a culture that contributes to child maltreatment, is akin to conducting research without explaining or measuring the independent variables (aspects of culture) that explain the dependent variable (neglect). There are, however, some exceptions. For example, addressing the issue of both intercultural and intracultural variability, Dubanoski (1981) compared Hawaiian American and European American child maltreatment reports. Hawaiian Americans were overrepresented, whereas European Americans were underrepresented in Hawaii's child abuse reports. Looking within the Hawaiian American population, Dubanoski suggests that child-abusing Hawaiian American families had less *'ohana* (extended family) involvement compared with non-abusing Hawaiian American families.

CONCLUDING REMARKS

The neglect of neglect has included a neglect of cultural considerations. In this chapter, we have argued that cultural competence is a key to effective work in child neglect. Cultural factors will not necessarily be important in all cases of child neglect, but cultural factors must be considered in any multicultural setting. We have suggested that there is no inherent contradiction in putting children first and accommodating cultural diversity, providing that one takes a difference rather than a deficiency orientation. Further research and guidelines for practitioners are needed to more fully understand the implications of cultural diversity for effective child neglect prevention and intervention.

REFERENCES

Abney, V. (1996). Cultural competence in the field of child maltreatment. In J. Briere, L. Berliner, J. Bulkley, C. Jenny, & T. Reid (Eds.), *The APSAC handbook on child maltreatment* (pp. 409-491). Thousand Oaks, CA: Sage.

Caudill, W., & Plath, D. (1966). Who sleeps by whom? Parent-child involvement in urban Japanese families. *Psychiatry, 29,* 344-366.

Chavez, A., Martinez, C., & Yaschine, T. (1975). Nutrition, behavior, development, and mother-child interaction in young rural children. *Federation Proceedings, 34,* 1574-1582.

Costantino, G., Malgady, R. G., & Rogler, L. H. (1986). Cuento therapy: A culturally sensitive modality for Puerto Rican children. *Journal of Consulting and Clinical Psychology, 54*(5), 639-645.

Coulton, C., Korbin, J., Su, M., & Chow, J. (1995). Community level factors and child maltreatment rates. *Child Development, 66*(5), 1262-1276.

Cross, T., Bazron, B. J., Dennis, K. W., & Isaacs, M. R. (1989). *Towards a culturally competent system of care: CASSP Technical Assistance Center.* Washington, DC: Georgetown University.

Daro, D., Migely, G., Weise, D., & Salmon-Cox, S. (1996). *World perspectives on child abuse: The second international resource book.* Chicago: National Committee to Prevent Child Abuse.

Dennis, D. (1997, May 16). Grandma gets parenting classes. *Plain Dealer,* p. 3-B.

Drake, B., & Pandey, S. (1996). Understanding the relationship between neighborhood poverty and specific types of child maltreatment. *Child Abuse and Neglect: The International Journal, 20*(11), 1003-1018.

Dubanoski, R. (1981). Child maltreatment in European- and Hawaiian-Americans. *Child Abuse and Neglect: The International Journal, 5*(4), 457-466.

Dubowitz, H., Black, M., Starr, R., & Zuravin, S. (1993). A conceptual definition of child neglect. *Criminal Justice and Behavior, 20*(1), 8-26.

Erickson, M. F., & Egeland, B. (1996). Child neglect. In J. Briere, L. Berliner, J. Bulkley, C. Jenny, & T. Reid (Eds.), *The APSAC handbook on child maltreatment* (pp. 4-20). Thousand Oaks, CA: Sage.

Estrin, R. (1997, March 27). Mom wins battle to clear neglect accusation. *Plain Dealer,* p. 6-A.

Fergusson, D., Flemming, J., & O'Neill, D. (1972). *Child abuse in New Zealand.* Wellington, NZ: Government Press.

Finkelhor, D., & Korbin, J. (1988). Child abuse as an international issue. *Child Abuse and Neglect: The International Journal, 12*(1), 3-23.

Foster, G., & Anderson, B. (1978). *Medical anthropology.* New York: John Wiley.

Gallimore, R., Boggs, J. W., & Jordan, C. (1974). *Culture, behavior and education: A study of Hawaiian Americans.* Beverly Hills, CA: Sage.

Garbarino, J., & Ebata, A. (1983). The significance of cultural and ethnic factors in child maltreatment. *Journal of Marriage and the Family, 45*(4), 773-783.

Gil, D. (1970). *Violence against children: Physical child abuse in the United States.* Cambridge: Harvard University Press.

Giovannoni, J., & Billingsley, A. (1970). Child neglect among the poor: A study of parental adequacy in families of three ethnic groups. *Child Welfare, 49*(4), 196-204.

Green, J. W. (1978). The role of cultural anthropology in the education of social service personnel. *Journal of Sociology and Social Welfare, 5*(2), 214-229.

Green, J. W. (1982). *Cultural awareness in the human services.* Englewood Cliffs, NJ: Prentice Hall.

Hauswald, L. (1987). External pressure/internal change: Child neglect on the Navajo reservation. In N. Scheper-Hughes (Ed.), *Child survival: Anthropological approaches on the treatment and maltreatment of children* (pp. 145-164). Dordrecht, Holland: D. Reidel.

Ima, K., & Hohm, C. F. (1991). Child maltreatment among Asian and Pacific Islander refugees and immigrants: The San Diego case. *Journal of Interpersonal Violence, 6*(3), 267-285.

Ito, K. (1985). Ho'oponopona, "to make right": Hawaiian conflict resolution and metaphor in the construction of a family therapy. *Culture, Medicine, and Psychiatry, 9*(2), 201-217.

Kasinsky, R. G. (1994). Child neglect and "unfit" mothers: Child savers in the Progressive Era and today. *Women and Criminal Justice, 6,* 97-129.

Korbin, J. (Ed.). (1981). *Child abuse and neglect: Cross-cultural perspectives.* Berkeley: University of California Press.

Korbin, J. (1987). Child abuse and neglect: The cultural context. In R. Helfer & R. Kempe (Eds.), *The battered child* (4th ed. pp. 23-41). Chicago: University of Chicago Press.

Korbin, J. (1990). *Hana'ino:* Child maltreatment in a Hawai'ian-American community. *Pacific Studies, 13,* 6-22.

Korbin, J. E. (1994). Sociocultural factors in child maltreatment: A neighborhood approach. In G. Melton & F. Barry (Eds.), *Protecting children from abuse and neglect* (pp. 182-223). New York: Guilford.

Korbin, J. E. (1997). Culture and child maltreatment. In M. E. Helfer, R. Kempe, & R. Krugman (Eds.), *The battered child* (5th ed., pp. 29-48). Chicago: University of Chicago Press.

Korbin, J., Brinkley, P., Reebals, L., & Singh, N. (1996). Understanding the importance of cultural beliefs and behaviors in clinical practice. In R. Kliegman (Ed.), *Practical strategies in pediatric diagnosis and therapy* (pp. 35-39). New York: W. B. Saunders.

Korbin, J., Coulton, C., Chard, S., Platt-Houston, C., & Su, M. (1998). Impoverishment and child maltreatment in African-American and European-American neighborhoods. *Development and Psychopathology, 10,* 215-233.

Korbin, J. E., & Johnston, M. (1982). Steps toward resolving cultural conflict in a pediatric hospital. *Clinical Pediatrics, 21*(5), 259-263.

Langness, L. L. (1981). Child abuse and cultural values: The case of New Guinea. In J. Korbin (Ed.), *Child abuse and neglect: Cross-cultural perspectives* (pp. 13-34). Los Angeles: University of California Press.

Levinson, D. (1989). *Family violence in cross-cultural perspective.* Newbury Park, CA: Sage.

Long, K. (1986). Cultural considerations in the assessment and treatment of intrafamilial abuse. *American Journal of Orthopsychiatry, 56*(1), 31-136.

Longress, J. F. (1991). Towards a status model of ethnic sensitive practice. *Journal of Multicultural Social Work, 1*(1), 41-56.

Lozoff, B., & Zuckerman, B. (1988). Sleep problems in children. *Pediatrics in Review, 10*(1): 17-24.

Margolin, L. (1990). Fatal child neglect. *Child Welfare, 69*(4), 309-318.

McGoldrick, M., Giordano, J., & Pearce, J. (Eds.). (1996). *Ethnicity and family therapy* (2nd ed.). New York: Guilford.

McKenna, J., Mosko, S., Dungy, C., & McAninch, J. (1990). Sleep and arousal patterns of co-sleeping human mother/infant pairs: A preliminary physiological study with implications for the study of Sudden Infant Death Syndrome (SIDS). *American Journal of Physical Anthropology, 83,* 331-347.

National Research Council. (1993). *Understanding child abuse and neglect.* Washington, DC: National Academy Press.

Nelson, B. (1984). *Making an issue of child abuse: Political agenda setting for social problems.* Chicago: University of Chicago Press.

Nelson, K., Cross, T., Landsman, J. J., & Tyler, M. (1996). Native American families and child neglect. *Children and Youth Services Review, 18,* 505-521.

Pelton, L. (Ed.). (1981). *The social context of child abuse and neglect.* New York: Human Sciences Press.

Polansky, N., Gaudin, J., Ammons, P., & Davis, K. (1985). The psychological ecology of the neglectful mother. *Child Abuse & Neglect, 9*(2), 265-275.

Ritchie, J., & Ritchie, J. (1981). Child rearing and child abuse: The Polynesian context. In J. Korbin (Ed.), *Child abuse and neglect: Cross-cultural perspectives* (pp. 186-294). Berkeley: University of California Press.

Saunders, E., Nelson, K., & Landsman, M. (1993). Racial inequality and child neglect: Findings in a metropolitan area. *Child Welfare, 72*(4), 341-354.

Shook, E. V. (1985). *Ho'oponopono: Contemporary uses of a Hawaiian problem-solving process.* Honolulu, HI: West-East Center.

Spearly, J. L., & Lauderdale, M. (1983). Community characteristics and ethnicity in the prediction of child maltreatment rates. *Child Abuse and Neglect: The International Journal, 7*(1), 91-105.

Sternberg, K., & Lamb, M. (1991). Can we ignore context in the definition of child maltreatment? *Development and Psychopathology, 3*(1), 87-92.

Swift, K. J. (1995). *Manufacturing "bad mothers": A critical perspective on child neglect.* Toronto: University of Toronto Press.

Tharp, R. G. (1991). Cultural diversity and the treatment of children. *Journal of Consulting and Clinical Psychology, 59*(6), 799-812.

Trotter, R., Ackerman, A., Rodman, D., Martinez, A., & Sorvillo, F. (1983). "Azarcon" and "Greta": Ethnomedical solution to epidemiological mystery. *Medical Anthropology Quarterly, 14*(3), 18.

Werner, E. (1979). *Cross-cultural child development: A view from planet earth.* Monterey, CA: Wadsworth.

Yeatman, G. W., Shaw, C., Barlow, M. J., & Bartlett, G. (1976). Pseudobattering in Vietnamese children. *Pediatrics, 58*(4), 616-618.

5 Child Neglect

Short-Term and Long-Term Outcomes

JAMES M. GAUDIN, JR.

The authors of a recent review of the research on the developmental effects of child maltreatment on its victims conclude, "There is no longer any doubt that child maltreatment—whether it be physical abuse, neglect or some mixture—has significant adverse effects on the development and adjustment of children, adolescents and adults" (Trickett & McBride-Chang, 1995, p. 324). Many studies have concluded that, contrary to popular belief, the child victims of neglect emerge as the most severely negatively affected (Eckenrode, Laird, & Doris, 1993; English, 1995; Erickson, Egeland, & Pianta, 1989; Herrenkohl, Herrenkohl, Egolf, & Wu, 1991; Starr, McLean, & Keating, 1991). This chapter seeks to critically review the limited research on the short-term and longer-term effects of neglect on children.

ECOLOGICAL PERSPECTIVES ON CHILD DEVELOPMENT

The spectrum of conditions that critically influence the development of children has been considerably expanded by the work of Bronfenbrenner

(1979), Belsky (1980, 1993), and Garbarino (1982). The ecological perspective on child development demands that we consider the development of children within a context that identifies influential variables beyond the genetic, biological, psychological, and even the family systems levels (Bronfenbrenner, 1979; Garbarino, 1982). Important enabling and limiting factors from the extended family, organizational, neighborhood, and wider cultural environments impinge on and powerfully influence the ability of parents to meet the critical economic, physical, emotional, and cognitive needs for the developing child. Critical developmental needs may be met at different stages of development by a variety of sources (e.g., child care, grandparents). Yet, particularly for the infant and the preschool and young school-age child, the quality of parent-child interactions is pivotal for the child's healthy physical, cognitive, and emotional development. Neglected children are those for whom some or many of these basic needs are not met.

LIMITATIONS OF CURRENT RESEARCH

Definition of Neglect

This review is immediately complicated by conceptual and methodological problems. The first is the absence of a clear and consistent definition of child neglect. Studies of neglect lack a clear, consistent conceptual and operational definition of neglect and seldom differentiate among subtypes of neglect (Zuravin, 1991). Many studies of developmental effects fail to differentiate between neglect and other types of maltreatment or combinations of neglect and abuse (Aber, Allen, Carlson, & Cicchetti, 1989; Crouch & Milner, 1993; Lewis & Schaffer, 1981; Starr et al., 1991; Trickett & McBride-Chang, 1995; Zuravin, 1991). Clear definitions of neglect are problematic, because there are not clear, widely accepted cross-cultural standards for what is desirable or minimally adequate for children. Legislative definitions of neglect vary greatly across the United States. Some state laws exclude deprivation if due to poverty; others make no such exceptions. There is also the question of accountability of society as well as the parent for the inadequacy of care that children may receive (Dubowitz, Black, Starr, & Zuravin, 1993).

There is broad agreement that children are neglected when they are deprived of minimally adequate food, clothing, shelter, education, medical care, and nurturing. This general consensus is supported by several studies (Giovannoni & Becera, 1979; Polansky, Ammons, & Weathersby, 1983). However, differences in operational definitions have been identified across professional and ethnic groups (Giovannoni & Becera, 1979; Wattenberg & Boisen, 1995). This author agrees with Dubowitz et al. (1993) that our central interest in identifying neglect is adequate care and protection of children, regardless of who is responsible. Therefore, "child neglect occurs when basic needs of a child are not met, regardless of the cause" (pp. 22-23).

Recent studies have sought to differentiate between types of neglect that help refine our understanding of this phenomenon (Gaudin, 1995; Zuravin, 1991). One might anticipate that chronic neglect would have more severe developmental consequences than episodic neglect, and emotional neglect is quite different from physical neglect. Although a few studies have made distinctions between chronic and non-chronic, and emotional-psychological versus physical neglect (Erickson et al., 1989; Gowan, 1993; Polansky, Chalmers, Buttenweiser, & Williams, 1981), neglect is largely treated as if it were a homogeneous entity. Clearly, this is not the case.

Sampling Bias

This more complete and complex definition of neglect is not reflected in the samples used in most studies of neglect. Because of the lack of consensus among researchers on the definition of neglect, most have confined study samples to reported cases of neglect confirmed by child protective services (CPS). Because of the nationwide trend of overburdened CPS to screen out all but the most severe neglect (Alter, 1985; English, 1995; Leiter, Myers, & Zingraf, 1994), study samples are representative only of the more severe cases, which are predominantly children from very poor families.

The samples used for prospective studies have been small, with families lost to follow-up, seriously limiting the generalizability of the research (Allen & Oliver, 1982: neglect $N = 7$; Elmer, 1977: neglect $N = 17$; Egeland, 1991: neglect $N = 24$; Dietrich, Starr, & Weisfeld, 1983: neglect $N = 6$).

Mediating, Moderating, and Confounding Variables

The effects of maltreatment on children, although clearly demonstrable, are not invariant or inevitable. Child neglect is highly correlated with poverty, which is a major influence on the development of children. Child development is the outcome of a complex set of personal and environmental factors, at the personal-ontogenic, microsystems, and macrosystems levels, some of which are limiting or risk enhancing and others, enabling or protective (Belsky & Vondra, 1989; Cicchetti & Rizley, 1981; Garbarino, 1982; Starr et al., 1991). Dunst (1993) refers to these as risk and opportunity factors in relation to child development. The relationship between child maltreatment and its developmental consequences is influenced by individual, family, community, and societal factors (Belsky, 1993; Garbarino, 1982; Starr et al., 1991). As Erickson and Egeland (1995) have argued, no child can be viewed as invulnerable or unaffected by neglect, but there is great variability in developmental outcomes dependent on the interaction of a variety of potential influences (Egeland, 1991; Farber & Egeland, 1987; Starr, 1991).

Developmental Stage

Only recent studies of developmental outcomes of maltreatment have been rooted in child development theory, which considers domains of adaptive functioning specific to developmental stages and the dynamic interactions between children's needs and environmental influences (Aber et al., 1989; Cicchetti & Rizley, 1981). Failure to base studies on this more complex theoretical understanding of development has often resulted in erroneous, reductionist conclusions about the causal relationship between child maltreatment and developmental outcomes (Aber et al., 1989; Starr et al., 1991).

Exceptions to this are the longitudinal Minnesota study of high-risk dyads (Egeland, 1991) and Aber et al.'s (1989) studies. Egeland et al.'s (1989) results suggested that children maltreated as infants were more developmentally disabled than those whose maltreatment occurred later in childhood. Infant victims of emotional neglect, whose functioning had declined alarmingly over the first 2 years of their lives, did not differ significantly from non-maltreated children after school entry at age 6. However, only one third of the 24 mothers who were emotionally unavailable when the children were age 3 were still emotionally neglectful 3 years later (Erickson et al., 1989). The age and developmental stage at which the neglect occurs are critical determinants of its effects on the child.

Specific age-appropriate developmental tasks must also be considered. Aber et al. (1989) examined the relationship between a history of maltreatment and four domains of adaptive functioning considered critical during children's preschool and early school years. They compared matched samples of children with substantiated maltreatment (71% neglect), nonmaltreated children from AFDC families, and children from middle-class families on two outcomes: secure readiness to learn and outer-directedness. The latter involves children's sense of autonomy and need for external approval. The maltreated children demonstrated less readiness to learn than the AFDC children, who were worse off than the middle-class children. However, the maltreated and AFDC children did not differ in outer-directedness (wariness, imitating behavior, approval seeking), though both were higher (more approval seeking) on this dimension than the middle-class children. It thus appeared that maltreatment did not affect children's outer-directedness over and above the effects of poverty. The authors also found no differences in mothers' ratings of their children's problem behaviors between the mothers of maltreated (71% neglected) and nonmaltreated preschoolers from poorer families. However, 6-year-old to 9-year-old maltreated children were rated by their mothers on the Child Behavior Checklist (Achenbach & Edelbrock, 1983) as more depressed, socially withdrawn, and with more overall behavior problems than the children in a low-income comparison group. Much more attention to stage-specific developmental effects is required to resolve some conflicting results between studies.

Poverty and Neglect

Child neglect is highly associated with poverty. Results of the *Third National Incidence Study* (Sedlak & Broadhurst, 1996) indicate that children in families with an income under $15,000 per year are *22 times* more likely to be victims of neglect than children in families with an income over $30,000. Although, according to the study, even among the poorest families, fewer than 3% of children are neglected, almost 1 million are victims of neglect.

Currently, 20% of U.S. children live in families with income below the federal poverty level. Many of these 14 million children lack critical resources to meet their basic needs; they are victims of societal neglect. Families with income below the poverty level often cannot provide their children with adequate food, clothing, shelter, and education unless significant public support is provided. The recent federal welfare reform legislation (TANF—Temporary Assistance for Needy Families, Title I of the Personal Responsibility and Work Opportunities Act, 1996) is indicative of government's increasing unwillingness to provide the required supports. School performance and social competence are significantly and inversely related to family income (Alwin & Thornton, 1984; Barnett, Vondra, & Shonk, 1996; Herrenkohl et al., 1991). A host of poverty-related and neglect-related conditions have been shown to be related to poor school adjustment by as early as the third grade. These conditions include being an unwanted child; low birth weight; unavailability of a consistent, caring adult; untreated health problems; and entering school with poor language skills (Hess & Shipman, 1968; Schorr & Schorr, 1988; Segal & Yahraes, 1978). Poverty is also a significant predictor of school completion and employment status at age 19 (Schweinhart & Weikart, 1989).

Numerous studies have clearly identified negative developmental consequences of neglect over and above the effects of poverty (Eckenrode, Laird, & Doris, 1993; Egeland, 1991; Gowan, 1993; Herrenkohl et al., 1991; Howing, Wodarski, Kurtz, & Gaudin, 1993). In Herrenkohl et al.'s (1991) longitudinal study, after adjusting for social class, neglectful parent-child interaction still predicted poor performance on cognitive-educational measures. The combination of parental and societal neglect by reason of poverty results in even more serious cognitive, academic, and behavioral problems (Howing et al., 1993). On the other hand, Elmer's (1977) study stands alone in the conclusion that there were no significant differences in development for small samples ($N = 17$) of physically abused and non-maltreated children, all of whom were poor. She concluded that maltreatment added nothing to poverty as a significant predictor of poor outcomes for children.

Mixed Types of Maltreatment

Few studies have examined the physical and psychological consequences of different combinations of maltreatment. One study (Eckenrode et al., 1993) indicated that the neglected children and children who were both neglected and sexually abused scored lower than the non-maltreated group in reading and math. Children victimized by a combination of physical abuse and neglect and those who were only neglected had lower grades in English than non-maltreated children. The neglect and combined neglect and sexual abuse groups had more suspensions than those who were not maltreated. Barnett et al. (1996), however, found no differences by type of maltreatment on motivation toward scholastic tasks and school functioning.

Two studies found that preschool children who were neglected had expressive and receptive language inferior to those who had been abused and those who had been both physically abused and neglected (Allen & Oliver, 1982; Culp et al., 1991). All three groups of children had language and cognitive delays, although there were no differences in cognitive abilities. In another study, school-age children who had experienced more than one type of maltreatment, and especially those who had experienced sexual abuse in addition to physical abuse or neglect, were more likely to engage in delinquent behavior (Gaudin et al., 1996).

Severity and Chronicity

Chronicity and severity of maltreatment have, with a few exceptions, been largely ignored in studies of maltreatment effects on children. Where these variables have been considered, the findings have been equivocal. Erickson et al.'s (1989) longitudinal study found, in a small sample, that children who were abused or neglected earlier in life were not functioning as well cognitively and were less confident, assertive, and creative than children more recently maltreated. Those whose earlier maltreatment had abated were rated by their teachers as having poorer self-esteem and emotional health than those whose maltreatment continued. However, the authors stated that children whose maltreatment continued, regardless of the chronicity, were rated by their teachers as having greater need for closeness than children no longer being maltreated. Kurtz, Gaudin, Howing, and Wodarski (1993) concluded from their short-term, cross-sectional retrospective study of school-age children that neither chronicity nor severity was associated with academic or socioemotional adjustment in the maltreated children. In contrast to Erickson et al.'s conclusions, a puzzling finding of this study was that children whose abuse or neglect had only begun within the previous 18 months were more likely to have school adjustment problems than those whose maltreatment began earlier in life.

Fox, Long, and Langlois (1988) found preschool and school-age children who were either physically abused, mildly neglected (i.e., not physically injured by the neglect), or severely neglected (i.e., child's health was harmed or endangered by the neglect) all had poorer language comprehension skills than the non-maltreated children. Severely neglected children scored lower in language composition than those who were abused or less severely neglected.

SHORT-TERM EFFECTS OF CHILD NEGLECT

The effects of neglect on infants and preschoolers have been given the most attention. The conclusion of Egeland, Sroufe, and Erickson's (1983) seminal longitudinal study was that physically neglected infants, toddlers, and preschool children had the most severe developmental lags compared with physically abused and non-maltreated children. During infancy, more of the neglected children were insecurely attached to their mothers. There were no significant differences between the neglect and control groups at 9 months of age, but their developmental scores declined between 9 and 24 months of age. At 24 months, the neglected children lacked enthusiasm in problem-solving tasks and were more angry, frustrated, and noncompliant compared with the others. At 42 months, when confronted with a barrier box, where previously accessible toys remained visible but were made inaccessible, the neglected children showed very poor impulse control and demonstrated less flexibility and creativity in problem solving. They had low self-esteem and often just withdrew. In response to the teaching tasks given to mothers, the neglected children were incompetent on all measures, had difficulty coping, and appeared dependent and angry (Egeland, 1991, p. 50). Kindergarten teachers consistently rated the neglected children more poorly in social, emotional, and academic functioning.

Cognitive and Language Effects

Child development researchers have discovered that neglected children have the worst delays in expressive and receptive language compared with abused and non-maltreated children (Allen & Oliver, 1982; Culp et al.,

Gaudin, & Howing, 1990). These negative developmental effects have been found to be greater and more enduring for neglect than for any other type of maltreatment.

Polansky et al. (1981) found that IQ scores of neglected children in an urban, white sample were lower than those of comparison children who had not been neglected, but not outside the normal range. The quality of care, especially psychological care, was also significantly associated with children's IQ, even after the effects of poverty were accounted for.

Some gender differences have been noted in neglected children's intellectual development. Rogeness, Amrung, Macedo, Harris, and Fischer (1986) compared the IQ scores of school-age children admitted to psychiatric hospitals who were either victims of neglect, abuse, or not maltreated. Boys in the neglect group had lower IQ scores than those who were physically abused or not maltreated. The IQ scores of the girls in the neglect group were not different from the abused girls, but both groups had lower IQ scores than the children not maltreated.

Eckenrode et al.'s (1993) cross-sectional comparison of 420 school-age (kindergarten through 12th grade) abused and neglected children and 420 non-maltreated children in the same community revealed that the maltreated children performed less well than the non-maltreated children on standardized tests, had lower grades, and were more likely to repeat a grade. Maltreated children also had more referrals for discipline problems and more suspensions. Neglected children had the poorest academic performance, especially in math, and abused children had by far the most discipline problems (Eckenrode et al., 1993). These results were consisten with those of a previous study of school-age abused, neglected, and non maltreated children, which found that even after controlling for social class the neglected children had more school absences and much poorer perfor mance on standardized academic achievement tests and were rated mor poorly by their teachers than were the abused and the non-maltreate children (Wodarksi et al., 1990).

The neglected children in the Wodarski et al. (1990) study scored lowe than the non-maltreated children in language, reading, and math. The also scored lower than comparisons on author-derived indexes of hom adjustment but not on in indexes of school adjustment, peer adjustmen self-adjustment, or delinquency. (Note: The five indexes were constructe by the authors from scores on individual items from well-known sta dardized measures of child functioning and school records.) Physical abused children scored significantly lower than the neglected and the no

1991; Fox et al., 1988). The first two of these studies concluded that neglect was a significant predictor of problems in both comprehension and expression for preschool children but not for the physically abused or those both physically abused and neglected. All three groups of children had problems in language and cognitive abilities, but there were no significant differences among groups in cognitive abilities (Culp et al., 1991).

The relationship between neglect and the cognitive development of preschoolers was supported by another short-term longitudinal study (Gowan, 1993). In this study, the adequacy of children's psychological care predicted their IQ and language abilities, especially receptive language, of 2-year-olds and 3-year-olds. The IQ scores of both the maltreated and non-maltreated of lower-income children declined over time, but at ages 12, 18, 24, and 36 months, the children who received inadequate psychological care scored lower on measures of IQ than those with adequate psychological care. Physically neglected children had significantly lower IQ scores at 24 and 36 months. Children who received inadequate physical or psychological care also demonstrated less ability to engage in age-appropriate play at 36 months (Gowan, 1993).

Social or Peer Relationships

Few studies have examined the peer relationships of abused and neglected children. Most often, studies on child maltreatment exclude neglected children or fail to differentiate them from abused children or from combinations of abuse and neglect (George & Main, 1979). The studies are also often limited by very small samples. Studies that have differentiated abused from neglected children have characterized the neglected children as more passive and withdrawn and abused children as more aggressive than comparison groups (Bousha & Twentyman, 1984; Crittenden, 1992; Hoffman-Plotkin & Twentyman, 1984). These authors have also found neglected preschool and young school-age children to display less affection and to initiate less play with their mothers. Others have found abused and neglected preschoolers to be more aggressive in their peer interactions than non-maltreated children (George & Main, 1979; Herrenkohl et al., 1991; Reidy, 1977) and to exhibit fewer positive play interactions (Lewis & Schaffer, 1981). Others have observed that neglected children, especially those who have also experienced abuse, compensate for the lack of stimulation with active exploratory behavior (Crittenden, 1988), and neglected children have been described by teachers as alternately withdrawn and aggressive (Erickson et al., 1989). When Bousha & Twentyman (1984) observed mother-child interactions, both the neglected and the abused preschool and school-age children were more physically and verbally aggressive than the non-maltreated children.

Evaluations of the effectiveness of peer-initiated interventions to enhance peer interactions with small samples of maltreated children have provided mixed results. Fantuzzo, Jurecic, Stovall, Hightower, and Goins (1988) trained two prosocial preschoolers to initiate play with two or three shy, withdrawn, socially inept peers in child care settings. The goal was to assess the effectiveness of positive peer-initiated efforts to foster prosocial behavior in socially inept children. The peer-initiated interactions did improve the peer interactions of the passive, withdrawn, and neglected preschoolers. However, aggressive abused children were more responsive to adult initiations of activity and less responsive to peer-initiated activities than the passive, withdrawn children (Davis & Fantuzzo, 1989; Fantuzzo et al., 1988).

Physical Effects

Failure of parents to meet basic nutritional and psychological nurturing needs of children may impede physical growth, most often referred to as nonorganic failure to thrive (NOFTT). Organic failure to thrive results from a medical problem that impairs growth. The usual criteria are weight or height (or both) below the fifth percentile and weight or height below the 10th percentile for children of the same age. Growth retardation may be attributable to a combination of organic and psychosocial factors. Ruling out organic causes, NOFTT has been attributed to neglectful, inattentive, unresponsive parent-child interactions (Drotar, Eckerle, Satola, Palotta, & Wyatt, 1990). Crittenden (1988) has suggested that stress contributes to the impoverished mother-child interactions in NOFTT families.

Even with aggressive intervention involving hospitalization, nutrition, and emotional nurturing, NOFTT can result in ongoing developmental deficits (Singer, 1986). However, improvement from intensive intervention appears to be related to the degree of severity of the failure to thrive and the parents' awareness and cooperation with treatment (Ayoub & Milner, 1985). As the severity of the NOFTT increased, the level of parents' awareness and cooperation decreased, and successful outcomes were less likely.

Parents' awareness and cooperation were strongly predictive of good outcomes for the children. The chapter on medical neglect in this book covers other health effects when appropriate care is not obtained.

Child Fatalities

Reports from the states to the National Center on Child Abuse and Neglect revealed that 1,111 children in the United States died during 1994 as a result of child maltreatment and more than 5,400 during the 5-year period from 1989 to 1994 (U.S. Department of Health and Human Services, 1996). The National Committee to Prevent Child Abuse (1998) reported that 1,185 child fatalities related to child abuse and neglect were confirmed by CPS agencies, and 44% of those were the result of neglect. As cited in the *Atlanta Constitution* ("A nation killing its kids," 1995), a 1995 report from the U.S. Advisory Board on Child Abuse and Neglect cited a Centers for Disease Control estimate of 2,000 child fatalities per year resulting from child abuse and neglect ("A nation killing its kids," 1995).

Other estimates of deaths from neglect include 40% of the 267 child maltreatment-related fatalities in Texas attributed to neglect and 21% to combined neglect and physical abuse (Anderson, Ambrosino, Valentine, & Lauderdale, 1983) and in Iowa, 40% of fatalities related to child maltreatment were attributed to neglect (Margolin, 1990). The families in the latter study with a death due with neglect were large, averaging 4.9 members and 3.3 children, compared with an average of 1.8 children in the families of fatal child abuse. The fatalities resulted primarily from allegedly isolated life-threatening incidents (e.g., toddlers drowning when left unsupervised), rather than from chronic neglect; only 39% of the fatalities had previous involvement with CPS.

LONGER-TERM EFFECTS OF CHILD NEGLECT

Cognitive-Academic

The evidence from a number of prospective and retrospective studies is that older school-age victims of neglect have cognitive and academic deficits that impair their development (Eckenrode et al., 1993; Erickson et al., 1989; Herrenkohl et al., 1991; Perez & Widom, 1994; Wodarski, Kurtz,

maltreated children on all of these indexes of adjustment. The authors suggested that entry into school may have provided enough stimulation and nurturing to mitigate some of the serious social and emotional problems noted earlier in preschool neglected children.

Their teachers reported that more neglected children were functioning and learning at below-average levels than those who were not maltreated; 60% of neglected children versus 24% of comparison children had repeated one or more grades; however, this difference was not significant after taking social class into account. The neglected children were absent nearly 5 times more frequently on average (21.3 days) than non-maltreated children (4.5 days) (Wodarski et al., 1990). At 1-year follow-up, there were significant gains in academic performance of neglected children. There were no significant differences between the three groups in math and English-reading. However, increased grade retention and poor grades were clearly associated with lower social class, and neglected children were overrepresented in this group (Kurtz, Gaudin, Howing, & Wodarski, 1993).

Well-controlled longitudinal studies of maltreated children have revealed unique patterns of severe, continuing developmental deficits in neglected children. The Minnesota Mother-Child Interaction Research Project has followed a small sample of high-risk mothers and their children from birth through early school years (Egeland, 1991; Egeland et al., 1983; Erickson et al., 1989). The young school-age neglected children (N = 24) of poor, single mothers had serious developmental deficits.

> The neglected children demonstrated a decline in functioning during the early school years. They were significantly lower on all achievement subtests, and by second grade all of the neglected children were referred for special education services. In general, these children had difficulty coping with the demands of school. (Egeland, 1991, p. 50)

The enduring effects of neglect on intellectual functioning are supported by the results of a large (N = 413) long-term, follow-up study comparing previously abused or neglected individuals at age 28 with those who had not suffered maltreatment. Both the abused and the neglected groups scored lower than controls in IQ and reading ability. After controlling for age, sex, race, and social class, a history of neglect still predicted lower IQ and reading ability at age 28. Even after controlling for the greater truancy rates and fewer years of school completed, abused and neglected individuals scored lower on IQ and reading ability than the comparison group (Perez & Widom, 1994).

Social and Behavioral Effects

Neglected children have been characterized as passive, non-assertive, or withdrawn but with less severe behavioral problems than abused children. However, as indicated earlier, this pattern is by no means consistent in neglected children.

Herrenkohl et al.'s (1991) longitudinal follow-up study of abused, neglected, and comparison children composed of low-income Head Start children, children in day care centers, and children from middle-income families revealed a negative relationship between neglect and children's social competence. There was also a strong positive relationship between socioeconomic status and social competence of children and between higher social class and more adequate parenting. However, the authors concluded that "negative, uninvolved, neglecting parenting at the preschool age has a negative impact on social competence at school age, even when social class is controlled" (Herrenkohl et al., 1991, p. 73).

Young, school-age maltreated children (aged 6-9 years), 70% of whom were physically neglected, were rated by their mothers as having more behavior problems and being more depressed and socially withdrawn than did mothers of a comparison group of non-maltreated, poor children (Aber et al., 1989). However, for the preschool children, these behaviors were not significantly different from the non-maltreated children. The maltreated children had more behavior problems than the "normal" group reported by Achenbach and Edelbrock (1983) but not significantly more than their clinical sample.

Neglected school-age children studied by Wodarski et al. (1990) were rated by teachers and parents as having more behavioral problems at home and at school than the comparison children. However, once adjustments for social class and race were made, the differences in behavior and socioemotional adjustment were not significant. Physically abused children, however, had more interpersonal and intrapersonal adjustment problems than neglected or comparison children, even after controlling for social class and race.

Crime and Delinquency

There has been very little research on the connection between neglect and delinquency; most of the research has focused on the relationship between child maltreatment in general and delinquency. However, one study found that neglected children were only slightly less likely (12.5%) than abused children (15.8%) to be arrested (not necessarily convicted) as juveniles or as adults for violent crimes (Widom, 1989). However, this study included only serious neglect and violent crimes that had been court adjudicated. Alfaro's (1981) study of neglect and delinquency concluded that maltreatment in general was a more important predictor of delinquency than any one type of maltreatment.

Race and gender were identified as important influences in Rivera and Widom's (1990) large prospective study of the relationship between child maltreatment and arrests for violent offenses. Childhood neglect or abuse increased the overall risk for violent offending as an adult, but not as a juvenile, for African Americans and for males. This was not the case for whites or females. Abused or neglected females were at greater risk of being arrested for violent offenses as juveniles but not as adults. The abused and neglected children were delinquent at an earlier age than the non-maltreated children, and they had committed significantly more chronic and violent offenses. Because the maltreatment group was selected from cases that came to the attention of juvenile court, these results are not generalizable to most neglected children but only to particularly serious cases of neglect.

Good school performance appears to influence the relationship between physical abuse and delinquency but not between neglect and delinquency (Zingraff, Leiter, Johnson, & Myers, 1994). Neglect remained a predictor of delinquency even when the effects of race, gender, family structure, school attendance, grades, and in-class behavior were accounted for. Starr et al. (1991) argue that the link between neglect and delinquency is their common strong association with poverty and lack of social support. Poverty causes frustration, which results in aggression. Poorer families are more violent (Strauss, Gelles, & Steinmetz, 1980). Starr et al. (1991) speculate that the lack of or dissatisfaction with social support is a common link between neglect and poverty.

Intergenerational Transmission

Although the stereotype of neglectful families includes a cycle of intergenerational repetition, the evidence suggests that this applies only to a minority of chronically neglectful families. Most studies are retrospective and flawed by the unreliability of recall over time and the inconsistency in definitions of neglect.

Only 15% of neglectful mothers in Polansky et al.'s (1981) study reported a clear history of neglect during their own childhoods. However, 57% reported feeling unwanted as a child, and 41% had experienced long-term removal from their parents.

Giovannoni and Billingsley (1970) found no differences between neglectful and non-maltreating mothers in terms of parental dominance, stability, and structure in their families of origin. A more recent study of neglectful families similarly found few differences between neglectful and non-neglectful mothers and fathers in their reports of the stability and nurturance in their families of origin. More of the neglectful parents did feel unwanted as children (24% vs. 13%) and felt that the discipline in their families of origin was unduly strict (Gaudin, Polansky, Kilpatrick, & Shilton, 1996).

Kaufman and Zigler (1989) found that the intergenerational transmission rate for any of the three main forms of maltreatment to be less than 30%. Lewis, Jahn, and Bishop (cited in Polansky et al., 1981) reported that the intergenerational transmission of neglect was greater than 15% but less than 25%.

SUMMARY

The existing research clearly indicates that children who are physically and emotionally neglected may suffer significant short-term and longer-term cognitive, emotional, and social problems. The negative effects on children's cognitive development appear to begin in infancy and continue to handicap their academic functioning in later years.

The evidence for the effects of neglect on children's socioemotional functioning is more equivocal. The conclusions are based primarily on very small, biased samples of children who have been reported and substantiated for neglect. The available data do not offer clear distinctions in the consequences of different types, severity, or chronicity of the neglect. The connection between neglect and subsequent delinquent or adult criminal activity has not been clearly established; it appears that fewer than 20% of neglected children are arrested for juvenile or adult crimes. Similarly, most instances of neglect have not been found to be intergenerational.

Future research should focus on critical stage-specific developmental tasks of children and domains of adaptive functioning, using an ecological understanding of child development. Most of the research lacks generalizability by reason of small study samples, composed primarily of neglect that has been reported, investigated, and substantiated by CPS or the courts, thus omitting the greater number of children who suffer less severe or societal neglect. Strategies are needed for identifying and obtaining data from this much larger group of neglected children in communities, through schools, child care centers, health care providers, and other agencies.

REFERENCES

Aber, J. L., Allen, J. P., Carlson, V., & Cicchetti, D. (1989). The effects of maltreatment on development during early childhood: Recent studies and their theoretical, clinical, and policy implications. In D. Cicchetti & V. Carlson (Eds.). *Child Maltreatment* (pp. 579-619). New York: Cambridge University Press.

Achenbach, T. M., & Edelbrock, C. (1983). *Manual for the Child Behavior Checklist and Revised Child Behavior Profile.* Burlington, VT: Queen City Printers.

Alfaro, J. D. (1981). Report on the relationship between child abuse and neglect and later socially deviant behavior. In R. J. Hunner & Y. E. Walker (Eds.), *Exploring the relationship between child abuse and delinquency* (pp. 175-219). Montclair, NJ: Allanheld, Osmun.

Allen, R. E., & Oliver, J. M. (1982). The effects of child maltreatment on language development. *Child Abuse & Neglect, 6,* 1299-1305.

Alter, C. F. (1985). Decision-making factors in cases of child neglect. *Child Welfare, 64,* 95-111.

Alwin, D. F., & Thornton, A. (1984). Family origins and the schooling process: Early vs. late influence of parental characteristics. *American Sociological Review, 49,* 784-802.

A nation killing its kids. (1995, April 29). *Atlanta Constitution,* p. A 14.

Anderson, R., Ambrosino, R., Valentine, D., & Lauderdale, M. (1983). Child deaths attributed to abuse and neglect. *Children & Youth Services Review, 5*(1), 75-89.

Ayoub, C. C., & Milner, J. (1985). Failure to thrive: Parental indicators, types, and outcomes. *Child Abuse & Neglect, 9,* 491-499.

Barnett, D., Vondra, J. I., & Shonk, S. M. (1996). Self-perceptions, motivation, and school functioning of low income maltreated and comparison children. *Child Abuse & Neglect, 20,* 397-410.

Belsky, J. (1980). Child maltreatment: An ecological integration. *American Psychologist, 35*(4), 320-335.

Belsky, J. (1993). Etiology of child maltreatment: A developmental-ecological analysis. *Psychological Bulletin, 114*(93), 413-434.

Belsky, J., & Vondra, J. (1989). Lessons for child abuse: The determinants of parenting. In D. Cicchetti & V. Carlson (Eds.), *Child maltreatment: Theory and research on the causes and consequences of child abuse and neglect* (pp. 153-202). Cambridge, UK: Cambridge University Press.

Bousha, D. M., & Twentyman, C. T. (1984). Mother-child interactional style in abuse, neglect, and control groups: Naturalistic observations in the home. *Journal of Abnormal Psychology, 93,* 106-114.

Bronfenbrenner, U. (1979). *The ecology of human development: Experiments by nature and design.* Cambridge, MA: Harvard University Press.

Cicchetti, D., & Rizley, R. (1981). Developmental perspectives on the etiology, intergenerational transmission, and sequelae of child maltreatment. In D. Cicchetti & R. Rizley (Eds.), *Developmental perspectives on child maltreatment* (pp. 31-55). San Francisco: Jossey-Bass.

Crittenden, P. (1988). Family and dyadic patterns of functioning in maltreating families. In K. Browne & P. Stratton (Eds.), *Early prediction and prevention of child abuse* (pp. 161-189). New York: John Wiley.

Crittenden, P. M. (1992). Children's strategies for coping with adverse home environments: An interpretation using attachment theory. *Child Abuse & Neglect, 16,* 329-343.

Crouch, J. L., & Milner, J. S. (1993). Effects of neglect on children. *Criminal Justice and Behavior, 20,* 49-65.

Culp, R. E., Watkins, R. V., Lawrence, H., Letts, D., Kelly, D. J., & Rice, M. L. (1991). Maltreated children's language and speech development: Abused, neglected and abuse and neglected. *First Language, 11,* 377-389.

Davis, S. P., & Fantuzzo, J. W. (1989). The effects of adult and peer social initiations on the social behavior of withdrawn and aggressive maltreated preschool children. *Journal of Family Violence, 4,* 227-248.

Dietrich, K. N., Starr, R. H., & Weisfeld, G. E. (1983). Infant maltreatment: Caretaker-infant interaction and developmental consequences at different levels of parenting failure. *Pediatrics, 72,* 532-540.

Drotar, D., Eckerle, D., Satola, J., Palotta, J., & Wyatt, B. (1990). Maternal interactional behavior with non-organic failure-to-thrive infants: A case comparison study. *Child Abuse and Neglect, 14,* 41-51.

Dubowitz, H., Black, M., Starr, R., & Zuravin, S. (1993). A conceptual definition of neglect. *Criminal Justice and Behavior, 20,* 8-26.

Dunst, C. J. (1993). Implications of risk and opportunity factors for assessment and intervention practices. *Topics in Early Childhood Special Education, 13*(2), 143-153.

Eckenrode, J., Laird, M., & Doris, J. (1993). School performance and disciplinary problems among abused and neglected children. *Developmental Psychology, 29,* 53-62.

Egeland, B. (1991). A longitudinal study of high risk families: Issues and findings. In R. Starr & D. A. Wolfe (Eds.), *The effects of child abuse & neglect* (pp. 33-56). New York: Guilford.

Egeland, B., Sroufe, A., & Erickson, M. (1983). The developmental consequences of different patterns of maltreatment. *Child Abuse and Neglect, 7,* 459-469.

Elmer, E. (1977). A follow-up study of traumatized children. *Pediatrics, 59,* 273-279.

English, D. (1995). Risk assessment: What do we know? Findings from three research studies on children reported to child protective services. In E. Wattenberg (Ed.), *Children in the shadows: The fact of children in neglecting families* (pp. 85-112). Minneapolis: University of Minnesota Press.

Erickson, M., & Egeland, B. (1995). Throwing a spotlight on the developmental outcomes for children: Findings of a seventeen year follow-up study. In E. Wattenberg (Ed.), *Children in the shadows: The fact of children in neglecting families* (pp. 113-126). Minneapolis: University of Minnesota Press.

Erickson, M. F., Egeland, B., & Pianta, R. (1989). The effects of maltreatment on the development of young children. In D. Cicchetti & V. Carlson (Eds.), *Child maltreatment* (pp. 647-684). New York: Cambridge University Press.

Fantuzzo, J. W., Jurecic, L., Stovall, A., Hightower, A. D., & Goins, C. (1988). The effects of adult and peer social initiations on the social behavior of withdrawn maltreated preschool children. *Journal of Consulting and Clinical Psychology, 56,* 34-39.

Farber, E. A., & Egeland, B. (1987). Invulnerability among abused and neglected children. In E. J. Anthony & B. Cohler (Eds.), *The invulnerable child* (pp. 253-288). New York: Guilford.

Fox, L., Long, S. H., & Langlois, A. (1988). Patterns of language comprehension deficit in abused and neglected children. *Journal of Speech and Hearing Disorders, 53,* 239-244.

Garbarino, J. (1982). *Children and families in the social environment.* New York: Aldine.

Gaudin, J. M. (1995). Defining and differentiating child neglect. *APSAC Advisor, 8*(2), 16-19.

Gaudin, J. M., Polansky, N. A., Kilpatrick, A. C., & Shilton, P. (1996). Family functioning in neglectful families. *Child Abuse & Neglect, 20,* 363-377.

George, C., & Main, M. (1979). Social interactions of young, abused children: Approach, avoidance, and aggression. *Child Development, 50,* 306-318.

Giovannoni, J., & Becera, R. (1979). *Defining child abuse.* New York: Free Press.

Giovannoni, J., & Billingsley, A. (1970). Child neglect among the poor: A study of parental adequacy in families of three ethnic groups. *Child Welfare, 49,* 196-204.

Gowan, J. (1993). *Effects of neglect on the early development of children: Final report.* Washington, DC: National Clearinghouse on Child Abuse and Neglect, National Center on Child Abuse and Neglect, Administration for Children & Families.

Herrenkohl, R. C., Herrenkohl, E. C., Egolf, B. P., & Wu, P. (1991). The developmental consequences of child abuse: The Lehigh longitudinal study. In R. H. Starr & D. A. Wolfe (Eds.), *The effects of child abuse and neglect* (pp 57-81). New York: Guilford.

Hess, R. D., & Shipman, V. C. (1984). Early experiences and socialization of cognitive modes in children. *Child Development, 36,* 869-886.

Hoffman-Plotkin, D., & Twentyman, C. (1984). A multimodal assessment of behavioral and cognitive deficits in abused and neglected preschoolers. *Child Development, 55,* 794-802.

Howing, P. T., Wodarski, J. S., Kurtz, P. D., & Gaudin, J. M. (1993). *Maltreatment and the school-age child.* New York: Hayworth.

Kaufman, J., & Zigler, E. (1989). The intergenerational transmission of child abuse. In D. Cicchetti & V. Carlson (Eds.), *Child maltreatment* (pp 129-150). New York: Cambridge University Press.

Kurtz, P. D., Gaudin, J. M., Howing, P. T., & Wodarski, J. S. (1993). Consequences of physical abuse and neglect on the school aged child: Mediating factors. *Children and Youth Services Review, 15,* 85-104.

Leiter, J., Myers, K., & Zingraf, M. (1994). Substantiated and unsubstantiated cases of child maltreatment: Do their consequences differ? *Social Work Research, 18*(2), 67-78.

Lewis, M. L., & Schaffer, S. (1981). Peer behavior and mother-infant interaction. In M. L. Lewis & S. Schaffer (Eds.), *The uncommon child.* New York: Plenum.

Margolin, L. (1990). Fatal child neglect. *Child Welfare, 69*(4), 309-319.

National Committee to Prevent Child Abuse. (1998). Child abuse and neglect statistics. http://www.childabuse.org/facts97.html.

Perez, C. M., & Widom, C. S. (1994). Childhood victimization and long term intellectual and academic outcomes. *Child Abuse and Neglect, 18,* 617-633.

Personal Responsibility and Work Opportunities Act, Pub. L. 104-193, Title I (1996).

Polansky, N. A., Ammons, P., & Weathersby, B. L. (1983). Is there an American standard of child care? *Social Work, 28*(5), 341-346.

Polansky, N. A., Chalmers, M. A., Buttenweiser, E., & Williams, D. P. (1981). *Damaged parents.* Chicago: University of Chicago.

Reidy, T. J. (1977). The aggressive characteristics of abused and neglected children. *Journal of Clinical Psychology, 33,* 1140-1145.

Rivera, B., & Widom, C. S. (1990). Childhood victimization and violent offending. *Violence and Victims, 5,* 19-35.

Rogeness, G. A., Amrung, S. A., Macedo, C. A., Harris, W. R., & Fischer, C. (1986). Psychopathology in abused and neglected children. *Journal of the American Academy of Child Psychiatry, 25,* 659-665.

Schorr, L. B., & Schorr, D. (1988). Within our reach: Breaking the cycle of disadvantage. Garden City, NY: Anchor/Doubleday.

Schweinhart, L. J., & Weikart, D. P. (1989). The High/Scope Perry preschool study: Implications for early childhood care and education. In R. P. Lorian (Ed.), Protecting the children: Strategies for optimizing emotional and behavioral development. *Prevention in Human Services, 7*(1), 109-128.

Sedlak, A. J., & Broadhurst, D. D. (1996). *Third national incidence study of child abuse and neglect: Final report.* Washington, DC: U.S. Department of Health and Human Services, National Center on Child Abuse and Neglect.

Segal, J., & Yahraes, H. (1978). A child's journey: Forces that shape the lives of our young. New York: McGraw-Hill.

Singer, L. (1986). Long term hospitalization of failure-to-thrive infants: Developmental outcomes at three years. *Child Abuse & Neglect, 10,* 479-486.

Starr, R. H., McLean, D. J., & Keating, D. P. (1991). Life span developmental outcomes of child maltreatment. In R. H. Starr & D. A. Wolfe (Eds.), *The effects of child abuse and neglect* (pp. 1-32). New York: Guilford.

Strauss, M. A., Gelles, R. J., & Steinmetz, S. L. (1980). *Behind closed doors: Violence in the American family.* New York: Anchor.

Trickett, P. K., & McBride-Chang, C. (1995). The developmental impact of different forms of child abuse & neglect. *Developmental Review, 15,* 311-337.

U.S. Department of Health and Human Services, National Center on Child Abuse and Neglect. (1996). *Child maltreatment, 1994: Reports from the states to the National Center on Child Abuse and Neglect.* Washington, DC: Government Printing Office.

Wattenberg, E., & Boisen, L. (1995). Testing the community standard on neglect: Are we there yet? In E. Wattenberg (Ed.), *Children in the shadows: The fate of children in neglecting families* (pp. 31-60). Minneapolis: University of Minnesota Press.

Widom, C. S. (1989). The cycle of violence. *Science, 244,* 160-166.

Wodarksi, J. S., Kurtz, P. D., Gaudin, J. M., & Howing, P. T. (1990). Maltreatment and the school-age child: Major academic, socioemotional, and adaptive outcomes. *Social Work, 35,* 506-513.

Zingraff, M., Leiter, J., Johnson, M. C., & Myers, K. A. (1994). The mediating effect of school performance on the maltreatment-delinquency relationship. *Journal of Research in Crime and Delinquency, 31,* 62-91.

Zuravin, S. (1991). Research definitions of child physical abuse and neglect: Current problems. In R. Starr, Jr., & D. Wolfe (Eds.), *The effects of child abuse and neglect: Issues and research.* New York: Guilford.

Neglect of Children's Health Care 6

HOWARD DUBOWITZ

Health care, including physical, mental, and dental health care, is one of the basic needs of children. When children do not receive health care in current times in the United States, it can be construed as a form of neglect. There are several ways this may manifest, and the contributory factors may vary greatly. An understanding of what underlies the problem is crucial for guiding appropriate interventions, but a determination of neglect can be made when the basic need for health care is not adequately met (Dubowitz, Black, Starr, & Zuravin, 1993). This chapter will discuss the definition of neglected health care, its frequency, etiology, major manifestations, and management.

RETHINKING THE DEFINITION OF NEGLECTED HEALTH CARE

In defining neglect, it is important to bear in mind that our main goal is to protect children from harm, actual and potential, not to blame parents. Instead of focusing on omissions in care by parents, our main concern is with the basic needs of children (e.g., adequate food, clothing, protection, health care). Neglect occurs when a basic need is not met, and this can occur for many reasons, including parental omissions in care (Dubowitz et al., 1993). Addressing neglect requires a comprehensive understanding of what is contributing to it and consideration of a broad array of possible interventions. For example, for children exposed to lead, an optimal response includes community resources for lead abatement, policies ensuring compliance by landlords, guidance for parents, and health care for children. This example illustrates the importance of a shared responsibility for meeting children's health care needs.

However, not all health care is equally important. Bross (1982) proposed criteria for legal intervention in medical neglect that offer useful guidance. Neglected health care occurs when

1. *Due to the lack of health care, the child is harmed or at significant risk of harm.* "Significant" is difficult to define; it could refer to a remote possibility of a terrible consequence (e.g., death from untreated meningitis) or the frequent occurrence of a mildly disabling condition (e.g., shortness of breath in an asthmatic without medications). In contrast, missing a follow-up appointment after an ear infection in a well child is probably of little consequence and should not be seen as neglect.

2. *The recommended health care offers a significant net benefit.* This requires weighing the anticipated benefits (e.g., shortened duration of illness) and the possible costs (e.g., the risks of treatment side effects). Again, significance poses a challenge. Is the benefit of medications enabling an asthmatic child to play sports significant? For most children, it probably is. Is the benefit of treating mild lead poisoning significant? Perhaps not, although it depends on the specific treatment being recommended.

These criteria raise the issues of the severity of the condition as well as the likelihood and gravity of the consequences. When considering the consequences, both physical and psychological problems are important, in the short and the long term. The severity of a child's condition and the outcomes, however, cannot be simplistically attributed to the quality of health care. The nature of the problem and other contributory factors must also be considered (e.g., a child's refusal to accept treatment) as well as the adequacy of care.

Should the potential for harm (i.e., endangerment) be grounds for neglect, or must there be actual harm? Most states include potential harm in their definitions of neglect (and abuse). Despite state laws, however, child protective services (CPS) are often overwhelmed and unable to address endangerment, usually viewed as less serious than actual harm. Clinicians interested in prevention should nevertheless respond to instances of endangerment; this often requires interventions other than a CPS report.

Neglect is typically seen as a pattern of omissions in care, not as a solitary or occasional incident. But what if a single incident (e.g., care not obtained for a severely dehydrated infant) seriously harms or endangers a child? Although even a single episode of necessary health care not being received meets the proposed definition of neglect, CPS are unlikely to become involved unless severe consequences (e.g., death) occur. In contrast, some omissions in care may be inconsequential unless they occur repeatedly. For example, 80% adherence to treatment for a streptococcal sore throat appears adequate (Olson, Zimmerman, & Reyes de la Rocha, 1985).

In summary, neglect concerns actual *and* potential harm to a child due to a lack of health care, whatever the reason. Severity is related to the short-term and long-term outcomes, physical and psychological. A pattern of care not being received is particularly worrisome, but rare incidents also warrant attention, especially when serious harm is involved.

THE INCIDENCE AND PREVALENCE OF NEGLECTED HEALTH CARE

It is difficult to estimate the extent of neglected health care. Many instances of neglect are not identified as such by health care providers, and relatively few are reported to CPS. The most recent report from the National Child Abuse and Neglect Data System (NCANDS) on the Detailed Case Data Component indicated that 2% of all maltreatment reports were for medical neglect (U.S. Department of Health and Human Services, 1996). Of the 8,611 children identified, 50% were under 4 years of age; 15% were teenagers. The Third National Incidence Study (NIS-3) was a prospective effort to identify maltreatment in a national sample and not limited to CPS reports (Sedlak & Broadhurst, 1996). Key agencies and professionals were enlisted as so-called sentinels looking out for cases meeting the study definitions of abuse and neglect. "Refusal of health care" was defined as the failure to provide or allow needed care in accordance with recommendations of a competent health care professional for a physical injury, illness, medical condition, or impairment. "Delay in health care" was the failure to seek timely and appropriate medical care for a serious health problem that any reasonable layperson would have recognized as needing professional medical attention. These definitions applied to physical and mental health care.

The general category of physical neglect in NIS-3 included several other types of inadequate care, such as abandonment; inadequate nutrition, clothing, or hygiene; and leaving a young child unattended in a motor vehicle. To date, only the aggregate data for physical neglect have been reported, showing this to be one of the most common forms of maltreatment, with an incidence rate of 19.9 per 1,000 children in the general population per year, a rate double that estimated in 1986. Approximately 25% of the children identified with physical neglect had evidence of harm; the remainder were considered to be endangered.

The foregoing findings are probably gross underestimates. Health care providers consider neglect as egregious omissions in care; less serious cases are unlikely to lead health care providers to apply a highly stigmatizing label and to involve CPS. In addition, neglected health care is often difficult to determine, and there are likely many instances that professionals never know about.

The data on child fatalities due to abuse or neglect reveal that approximately half of the estimated 2,000 deaths each year result from neglect, mostly unsupervised children dying in fires or drowning (U.S. Advisory Board on Child Abuse and Neglect, 1995; see chapter on fatal child neglect, Chapter 8, this volume). Few deaths appear to be due to neglected health care, although sympathy for a grieving family makes it difficult to assess how health care may have prevented a death (e.g., a teen suicide). Between 1975 and 1995, there have also been 172 known deaths of children where medical care was withheld on religious grounds (Asser & Swan, 1998). In most of these cases, it was determined that the prognosis would have been excellent had the children received medical care.

Although U.S. children in general enjoy good physical health, the picture concerning children's mental health care is far more grim. For example, one major study of youth aged 9 through 17 years found that between 38% and 44% of those meeting stringent criteria for a psychiatric disorder in the previous 6 months had a mental-health-related contact in the year prior to the interview (Leaf et al., 1996). Of note, many of the children who had had a professional contact were served in their schools; the study did not discern the qualifications of the professional or the quality or appropriateness of the service. Another study of adolescents with serious emotional disorders also found that only 44% of them received any care during a 2-year period, most of them in their schools (Burns et al., in press). Dental care is also not accessible to many U.S. children: 85% of U.S. schoolchildren have obvious cavities or fillings affecting, on average, more than eight surfaces of their permanent teeth, and their need for treatment is striking, particularly among low-income children (Edelstein & Douglass, 1995). A study of preschoolers found 49% of 4-year-olds had cavities, and fewer than 10% were fully treated (Tang et al., 1997). In sum, neglected health care is not rare. And if access to health care and health insurance are basic needs in the United States, then 10 million children have their health care neglected by our society (Annie E. Casey Foundation, 1997).

THE ETIOLOGY OF MEDICAL NEGLECT

The ecological theory that helps explain physical abuse and neglect is also useful with regard to medical neglect (Belsky, 1980). Etiology is mostly covered in Chapters 2 and 3; the focus here is on medical neglect. Ecological theory posits that there are multiple and interacting contributors to child maltreatment, rather than any single cause, and these factors are at the levels of the individual child and parent, the family, the community, and the society. For example, a parent who has lost his or her job and health insurance and is feeling depressed is at high risk for not ensuring that his or her asthmatic child receives necessary care and medications. There are six major influences on whether children's health care needs are met: (1) context, (2) family, (3) parents, (4) child, (5) the disorder and the treatment, and (6) quality of care.

Context

Context refers to the environment or society, including poverty, culture, and religion. The context shapes the attitude, knowledge, and behavior of parents, as well as the quality of health care children receive. Poverty has been strongly associated with neglect (Sedlak & Broadhurst, 1996). The effects of poverty may result from stress, compromising the functioning of families and parents. Poverty may directly harm children via increased exposure to environmental hazards (e.g., lead, violence) and the risk of malnutrition (Parker, Greer, & Zuckerman, 1988). Poverty is also associated with diminished access to health care, particularly for the "near poor" who do not qualify for Medicaid and lack health insurance. Recent changes in health care reimbursement and for profit-managed care may compromise the health care of children at risk of neglect by pressuring providers to spend less time with clients and to pay less attention to psychosocial problems.

Another crucial part of the context concerns culture and religion. Cultural issues are addressed fully in Chapter 4. Parents may ascribe to religious views that are antithetical to Western medicine, believing in alternative approaches to health and healing. Accordingly, sick children may receive, for example, prayer from a Christian Scientist faith healer. Many illnesses (e.g., colds) are self-limiting, and satisfactory outcomes result, regardless of treatment. Some conditions, however, can lead to serious harm without effective health care. An example is a 2-year-old who had vomited for days and became comatose before dying of a medically untreated bowel obstruction (Skolnick, 1990).

The challenge is to balance an individual's right to freedom of religion, guaranteed by the U.S. Constitution, with the states' rights and duty to protect its younger citizens. The legal doctrine of *parens patria* establishes this role of the states when parents do not adequately care for their children. A contentious debate continues, and most states have "religious exemptions" to their child abuse statutes, stating for example, "a child is not to be deemed abused or neglected merely because he or she is receiving treatment by spiritual means, through prayer according to the tenets of a recognized religion" (American Academy of Pediatrics, 1988, p. 169).

Proponents of the exemptions point to the Constitution for support. Their interpretation has, however, been challenged by court rulings prohibiting parents from martyring their children based on their own beliefs (*Prince v. Massachusetts,* 1944) and from denying them essential medical care (*Jehovah's Witnesses of Washington v. King County Hospital,* 1968). The First Amendment does not sanction harming individuals in the practice of religion.

In summary, poverty and cultural and religious beliefs are aspects of the context influencing children's health care. These factors illustrate the complex underpinnings of child neglect and challenge clinicians to understand these issues and find constructive ways to ensure that children receive adequate health care.

Family

Poor organization of the home has characterized neglectful families (Gaudin & Dubowitz, 1997). (The term *neglectful* refers to parents and families in neglectful situations but does not suggest a stereotype or sole responsibility as perpetrator.) Kadushin (1988) described chaotic families of neglected children with impulsive mothers who repeatedly showed poor planning. Many of the neglectful mothers had negative relationships with the children's fathers, many of whom were incarcerated or had deserted them.

Several studies have found more negative interactions between mothers and their young children in neglectful families (e.g., Crittenden, 1988). Nonorganic failure to thrive might be primarily rooted in a "poor fit" between mother and child. A child's passive, or lively, temperament may displease a parent, for example. In addition, family problems, such as spousal violence or a lack of social support, may contribute to a difficult parent-child relationship and failure to thrive (Giovannoni & Billingsley, 1970; Lyon, this volume, Chapter 12; Polansky, Ammons, & Gaudin, 1985; Wolock & Horowitz, 1979). In contrast, a supportive family can buffer the stressors that impair parenting.

Parents

Many of the characteristics of mothers of neglected children may also contribute to children's health care needs not being met. Most decisions regarding children's health are made by parents, including when to seek professional care. Crittenden's (1993) model helps refine our understanding of parental difficulties by considering four steps: (1) perception of child's problem, (2) interpretation of child's problem, (3) response, and (4) implementation. Difficulties with any of these steps may lead to health care not being obtained.

The parent first needs to perceive the problem. Subtle signs, such as decreased urination or gradually falling grades, may go undetected. Inadequate knowledge about children and health and inappropriate expectations contribute to neglect. For example, parents may not know that a baby with diarrhea risks becoming dehydrated. Parents may not appreciate such needs, particularly if they are cognitively limited (Kadushin, 1988). Twentyman and Plotkin (1982) found that neglectful parents were less accurate than controls in estimating when children should attain developmental milestones. Herrenkohl, Herrenkohl, and Egolf (1983) reported neglect to be associated with limited knowledge about parenting, poor skills, and low motivation to be a good parent. At times, parents may be in denial, an unconscious process, about a child's condition.

Parents may perceive the problem but interpret it incorrectly. For example, based on the parent's prior experience, a child's poor growth may be seen as normal. A lack of knowledge is again an obstacle. A parent may feel moodiness is common in children, unaware that children can be depressed. There are conditions where parents may be unaware treatment exists. Popular or folk interpretations of a symptom, such as an infant crying frequently because he or she is "spoiled," may lead to a problem being missed. Again, parents with limited cognitive abilities may have difficulty interpreting their child's cues, determining the care needed, and understanding and implementing the treatment plan. But children may experience medical neglect, even when no parental cognitive or emotional problems are present. Parents may not appreciate the seriousness of the problem or the importance of the treatment, perhaps due to inadequate communication with health care providers.

After recognizing and interpreting the problem, parents choose their response. Initially, they may hope the problem will resolve spontaneously or with a home remedy. This is often appropriate, but sometimes, the delay in seeking care can have dire consequences. For example, parents may hope a small burn will heal without professional care—not an unreasonable response. If the condition deteriorates, only then may it be clear that medical care is needed. Such delays have been viewed suspiciously, but it is important that reasonable delays be seen as such. In considering neglect, the reasonableness of the situation is key; was care obtained at a point when a reasonable layperson could be expected to have recognized the need for professional help? An inappropriate response may also result from inadequate knowledge, parental distress, as well as cultural or religious beliefs. For example, a depressed youngster may not receive psychotherapy if his or her parents hold such treatment in disdain.

Last, the problem may be with implementing what the parent knows should be done. Many of the already cited reasons may be culprits here. A parent's inaction may be due to being distracted by other priorities (e.g., an eviction notice, obtaining drugs), depression, or difficulty accessing health care.

There are other influences on parents' behavior. Confidence in the remedy or in one's ability to implement the treatment is important. For example, a parent's belief that a medicine works will enhance compliance. Motivation to address a health problem is important and may be influenced by the chronicity of the problem (there may be complacency with long-standing problems) and competing demands. Are there parents who simply do not care or who do not care enough to make sure their children's health care needs are met? Many clinicians sense this, but it is difficult to judge. For all parents and families, there is a need to balance many needs and to prioritize. Paying an electricity bill before filling a prescription may be appropriate, although other ways of obtaining the medication should be sought. We are less likely to be sympathetic, however, to the mother or father who buys cocaine before filling the prescription.

Child

Children may contribute to their health care needs not being met, directly and indirectly. A direct example is an adolescent's denial of his or her diabetes, refusing to adhere to the treatment plan, despite excellent efforts by caring parents. Another child factor is when they give no or few cues that they need help, not revealing the problem. Children's ages may influence perceptions of their vulnerability and neglect, with more concern directed to younger children; almost half of neglect reports are made on children under 4 (U.S. Department of Health and Human Services, 1996). The unmet needs of adolescents may not evoke the same concern.

Belsky and Vondra (1989) described an association between premature, "difficult," and mentally retarded children and the inability of parents to meet their needs. Prematurity may require extended care in a neonatal intensive care unit, which may impair bonding and the attachment between infants and parents. Low birth weight has been found to be a risk factor for neglect in two prospective studies (Brayden, Altemeier, Tucker, Dietrich, & Vietze, 1992; Kotch et al., 1989).

Children with chronic health problems or disabilities have special needs that put them at added risk for those needs not being met. Many parents of such children are wonderfully responsive; others may be deeply disappointed and stressed, unable to provide adequate care. Diamond and Jaudes (1983) found cerebral palsy to be a risk factor for neglect, but another study found no increase in maltreatment among 500 moderately to profoundly retarded children (Benedict, White, Wulff, & Hall, 1990). These families are often involved with multiple professionals, and increased surveillance may bias who is identified as neglected. Overall, it appears that the special needs of children may overwhelm even caring and competent parents, contributing to neglect.

The Disorder and the Treatment

The disorder and the treatment may influence parental behavior. A disorder that is highly visible (e.g., an ugly rash) often evokes a very different response from one that is invisible (e.g., lead poisoning). The severity of the problem makes an understandable difference. Chronic health problems may be accepted, without much alarm. This is mostly a valuable coping strategy, but sometimes, undue complacency may result.

Misgivings about the likely treatment may dissuade a parent from seeking care. Obesity is an example where a parent may recognize the problem but be reluctant to engage in treatment. The cost of treatment may be a deterrent. In addition, simply remembering to give a child medication several times a day may be an obstacle.

Quality of Care

The quality of care includes the relationship between a provider and family. Ideally, there is mutual trust and respect, providing confidence that sound recommendations will be made and that these will be adhered to. Without this, a family might be discouraged from seeking help. Poor communication may be a frequent problem, with the treatment not being clearly conveyed or understood. The goals of treatment may not resonate with a child or family. For example, improving pulmonary function tests may mean little, compared with being able to play sports. Follow-up helps ensure adequate treatment.

THE MAJOR MANIFESTATIONS OF NEGLECTED HEALTH CARE

First, health care might be clearly needed but not obtained, or there may be a harmful delay before care is received. There are also instances where alternative or traditional health care *is* provided, following the beliefs of a subculture or religion, deviant from the U.S. mainstream, and the question of neglect may arise. Second, there is the problem of noncompliance when health care is recommended but not received. Another possible manifestation is failure to thrive, when children do not grow as expected, mostly due to deficiencies in their diet and environment. The prenatal exposure of unborn children to drugs is also a concern (see Chapter 7). In addition, all forms of emotional and physical neglect can impair children's health. A lack of affection and nurturance may harm a child's sense of security, ability to trust, and success in interpersonal relationships. Children who are not adequately supervised and who are exposed to environmental hazards risk being injured or poisoned. Poor sanitation and hygiene can cause or complicate illnesses.

Failure or Delay in Obtaining Health Care

Parents manage most of children's common health problems, such as scrapes and colds, and this usually works well. For more serious problems, parents need to recognize when professional care should be sought. The multiple reasons why necessary health care might not be obtained or be unreasonably delayed were described earlier. A comprehensive understanding of the contributory factors helps guide an appropriate response.

Noncompliance With Health Care Recommendations

Noncompliance with health care appointments and recommendations may be the most common form of medical neglect. Many of the reasons for this were also described earlier. A few special issues should be noted.

It is useful to consider a paradigm shift in thinking about compliance. The traditional view of compliance has been an authoritarian model, whereby the doctor ordered the patient to do something, and if the patient complied, better health was expected. In an ecological model, the many contributors to noncompliance are acknowledged by including contextual and individual factors, aspects of the disorder and its treatment, and the quality of care (Liptak, 1996). In keeping with this understanding of a shared responsibility, the term *noncompliance* should be replaced by *nonadherence* to recommended health care.

Non-adherence is very common. Several studies show overall rates of non-adherence of 30% to 60%, with 20% to 30% for short-term medications, 30% to 40% for preventive regimens, and more than 50% for long-term regimens (Liptak, 1996). For example, one study found that only 25% of parents of hyperactive children adhered to the treatment; fewer than 10% consulted the physician before stopping the medication (Firestone & Witt, 1982). Physicians may also be at fault; their clinical performance has been found to range between 48% and 72% below professional standards (Meichenbaum, 1989). The pervasiveness of non-adherence, however, does not detract from its importance; the results can be fatal.

Health outcomes are related to many factors, including adherence to treatment. One cannot assume that a diabetic teenager whose condition is repeatedly poor is not following the treatment; diabetes can be inherently difficult to control. Another issue is the uncertainty of what constitutes adequate treatment.

Nonorganic Failure to Thrive

Nonorganic failure to thrive (FTT) refers to inadequate growth, usually in infants and young children, where the primary contributors are psychosocial problems rather than medical or organic conditions. Children's growth is routinely tracked on standard growth charts; *failure to thrive* is defined as the weight or height for age falling to below the 5th percentile, or the weight for height falling to below the 10th percentile, or one of these parameters dropping across two major percentiles (e.g., across the 25th and 10th percentiles).

When FTT is diagnosed, a careful history is obtained and a complete examination and screening laboratory tests are conducted to exclude possible medical problems. A comprehensive evaluation should also include an assessment of the primary caregiver, his or her interaction with the child, and the family and home situation. Several of the contributors to neglect identified earlier have also been associated with nonorganic FTT (Zenel, 1997). For example, mothers of FTT infants have been found to be depressed, with impaired psychosocial functioning. A lack of social support has also been identified (Bithoney & Newberger, 1987).

Nonorganic FTT has often been presumed to reflect deficient care (Benoit, Zeanah, & Barton, 1989). However, there are children whose limited growth remains unexplained, even after a comprehensive evaluation.

It therefore is important that neglect be construed only when deficiencies in care are identified, rather than making this diagnosis simply by excluding medical conditions.

EVALUATING POSSIBLE NEGLECTED HEALTH CARE

Is It Neglect?

As proposed earlier, two criteria should be met for determining neglected health care: (1) the lack of or delay in care involving actual or potential harm to the child's health and (2) the child not receiving the recommended care, which would offer a significant net benefit, outweighing the costs, side effects, and risks.

What Is Contributing to the Neglect?

A good understanding of what underlies the neglect is needed to guide appropriate interventions. Relevant information may be available from prior contacts and other professionals. Are there major financial worries? Are there other stressors? What are the strengths and sources of support? Are there particular cultural or religious views? A social worker can help develop this portrait.

There is then the need to probe whether the parent perceives a problem and how it is interpreted. What is their understanding of the disorder and of the child's needs? What has been their response to the problem and why (without being incriminating)? What obstacles have impeded the child receiving necessary care?

There is also a need for examining how the health care provider-family relationship may be contributory. Has communication been clear? Are there reasons (e.g., transportation) that make clinic visits difficult? In addition, aspects of the disorder and treatment should be considered. Does the family appreciate the seriousness of the problem? Can a less costly or simpler treatment (e.g., fewer doses) be offered?

Does the Parental or Professional Behavior Not Meet Reasonable Expectations?

Efforts to identify neglect should be driven by our interest in ensuring children's adequate care, not to blame. Nevertheless, in our current system, the question may be asked as to whether the parental omission in care was unreasonable, a question less often asked of professional behavior. A reasonableness test is whether the desired behavior (e.g., taking a child to a dentist) can reasonably be expected of an average layperson. A child with a very high blood lead level may appear healthy, for example, and one would *not* expect a parent to recognize the problem. Similarly, professionals should not be deemed negligent when unforeseen complications arise. In contrast, parents and professionals contribute to neglect when parents refuse a recommended treatment or when a hurried physician fails to adequately explain the treatment.

Is There a Pattern of Neglect?

It is different if the lapse in health care is a single or rare occurrence rather than a chronic pattern, the latter warranting greater concern. Review of the medical record and discussion with the primary care provider are important. It is similarly important to know whether problems with health care are an exception or associated with other basic needs not being met (i.e., other types of neglect). Health care providers can assess whether a child is receiving adequate medical, mental, and dental health care and adequate nutrition with appropriate growth. The child's clothing and hygiene can be assessed, and providers should have a sense of whether a child's educational needs are being met.

What Is the Severity of Harm and What Is the Risk of Continued Neglect?

The severity of harm, actual and potential, including long-term sequelae, should be estimated. It is more difficult to determine the likely future course and risks to a child's health and safety (see Chapter 5). This assessment is based on a thorough evaluation of the underlying factors, the chronicity of neglect, the co-occurrence of other types of maltreatment, the success of intervention efforts to date, and the willingness and ability of the family to address the problem.

What Efforts or Interventions Have Been Made to Remedy the Neglect and With What Success?

It is important to review prior efforts and their results. If the circumstances are recalcitrant to change, alternative strategies are needed.

MANAGEMENT OF NEGLECTED HEALTH CARE

Neglect of health care presents itself in varied ways and may be due to very different circumstances. This makes it difficult to specify all the measures that may be appropriate. Rather, a number of key principles for approaching neglected health care will be highlighted.

Prevention Is Key

To provide a child optimal health care and to prevent neglect, health care providers need to be familiar with the family structure, beliefs regarding health care, the stresses and strengths, and barriers to care. This understanding requires time and is also an ongoing process; circumstances change. In addition to the child's needs, it is necessary to consider those of the parents and family. It is especially important to identify the family strengths and resources on which to build.

Risk factors for neglect need to be addressed. The section on etiology included risk factors associated with neglect, including maternal depression, cognitive limitations, and substance abuse; families who are stressed and with few supports; and children with chronic disabilities. Families at risk for neglect often require social and mental health services, and health care providers should facilitate referrals. For example, help may be offered in securing health insurance, or a depressed mother may be encouraged to seek treatment. Health care providers can also help by scheduling more frequent visits to provide counseling, support, and monitoring and to anticipate and address barriers to care.

Anticipatory guidance is offered in routine pediatric care when advice is given on potential problems. For example, when physicians explain the natural curiosity of toddlers and recommend safety precautions, they help prevent injuries from inadequate supervision, a form of neglect. For children with identified health problems (e.g., allergies), families should be educated about the condition, what to expect, when to seek help, and what they can do at home.

Convey Concerns to the Family

It is important to forthrightly but kindly state the problem: the concern that the child's health care needs are not being adequately met and how the child is being harmed or at risk of harm. This is the first step before discussing with the family why the problem is occurring and exploring how to improve the child's care. A supportive and constructive stance is key.

Express Interest in Helping

Families where neglect is a problem may be frustrating to work with when change is hard to achieve. It is not a surprise that many health care providers do not enjoy this challenge and harbor negative feelings about such families. It is preferable to recommend another provider or, if one is going to work with the family, to explicitly declare one's interest in helping. This helps develop the rapport and trust on which successful interventions depend.

Begin With the Least Intrusive Approach

The approach needs to fit the underlying problems and risks, but in general, it is advisable to respect the importance of a family's privacy and to start with the least intrusive intervention. For example, when faced with a child failing to thrive, an initial strategy might be to provide counseling on feeding and a suitable diet while closely monitoring the child's growth. Additional measures might include a parenting group and social support. If the problem persists, a home visitor or parent aide may help, and if this still proves inadequate, a referral to CPS may be necessary.

Address Factors Contributing to the Neglect

The sections on the etiology, evaluation, and prevention of neglect included many factors that could underpin the problem of neglect. Identifying and addressing these factors can be a challenge. There are issues that health care providers may feel competent to manage or refer elsewhere.

Provide Extra Support and Monitoring

Recent changes in the reimbursement for health care make it increasingly difficult to provide the more frequent or longer appointments that neglect often requires, posing an ethical dilemma as patients' needs are balanced with corporate dictates for productivity. What do increased support and monitoring entail? This could mean extra time, for example, explaining to parents how to manage a child's condition. It might mean talking to other family members to ensure a shared understanding of and approach to a problem. Monitoring could be to ensure a child's growth is on track or that obesity is diminishing.

Long-Term Intervention May Be Needed

Clinicians may wish to see improvement quickly, so it is frustrating when problems are recalcitrant. We need to come to terms with the reality that many neglectful families need long-term support, akin to those with chronic medical conditions.

Address Continuity and Coordination of Care

For all children, but especially when neglect is a concern, continuity of health care with a single clinic or primary care provider is important. This fosters the relationship and understanding that are key to intervening effectively. Continuity of care also facilitates the coordination of health care when several providers are involved. For primary care providers, there remains an important liaison role between the family and others involved in their care, and managed care usually requires this.

Build on Strengths

Too often, we focus on problems and ignore strengths. This deficit approach does not enable more constructive approaches to working with families. For example, parents' concern for their child's well-being can be used to encourage them to comply with treatment recommendations. We need to build on families' strengths; there are always some.

Consider Informal Supports and Resources

Professionals often think of professionals to provide services to families, overlooking informal help from family and friends and support from religious institutions. Families who are resistant to interventions from a public agency or a mental health professional may accept support from someone they trust and already have a relationship with. Health care providers can encourage a father's involvement in childrearing by inviting him to office visits. Similarly, other kin or supports may be included as we make pediatric care more family focused.

Know the Community Resources

We all need to recognize what we cannot do ourselves and need to refer to others. This requires knowing the resources in the community. Primary care providers are in a good position to encourage reluctant or ambivalent families to accept or try other services.

Know When to Report to CPS

Clinicians often face the dilemma of whether to report a family to CPS. State laws typically mandate that suspected neglect (and abuse) be reported, but there are varying levels of suspicion. Indeed, many CPS agencies are overwhelmed and unable to address situations that do not cross their often high threshold. Two principles help guide the decision on reporting:

(1) Report if the actual or potential harm is serious.
(2) Report if less intrusive interventions have failed and moderate or serious, actual or potential, harm remains a concern.

Other interventions should be attempted for mild or moderate neglect before making a CPS report. For example, an infant may be failing to thrive because the formula is mixed incorrectly. Explaining how to do so and providing further support with a visiting nurse may be an appropriate first strategy. If unsuccessful, CPS may be needed.

Know How to Improve Adherence to (Compliance With) Health Care Recommendations

Identify and Address the Underlying Issues

It is again necessary to consider the individual child and parent as well as the family factors that influence adherence to a treatment plan. A teenager's denial of a chronic disease may warrant counseling, for example. Beliefs concerning the condition or the treatment may impede optimal care and need to be addressed. There may be inadequate skills, such as using inhalers, requiring instruction. Some might be poorly motivated and need encouragement to recognize how their condition can be improved.

Supports and stressors must be recognized. A support group, for example, for families of children with certain health problems can be valuable. Mitigating stressors or enhancing individuals' abilities to cope can help. Including the key persons to be involved in the treatment plan may be useful.

Communicate Well

Good communication is a major determinant of compliance. Communication is clearly more than the language used but incorporates elements of a relationship that is respectful and trusting. Jargon should be avoided. There is a need to prioritize the main take-home messages, to succinctly convey them, and to check that the communication was successful.

It is useful to set clear goals to prevent or remedy a problem, and the goals should be realistic and attainable. For example, visits to an emergency department may be reduced with appropriate treatment. The goals should resonate with the family. For example, numbers for spirometry might mean little in contrast to enabling participation in sport. Last, the goals should be understood and agreed on.

The treatment plan should be in writing to ensure that the plan is remembered and implemented. Possible problems with the plan should be probed. For example, a parent's hesitation about a medication could jeopardize the treatment.

Make Treatment Practicable

It helps to simplify treatment plans and establish priorities. One contributor to non-adherence is a difficult task, such as giving a child four doses of medication a day; if possible, prescribe less frequent dosages. Also, cues help, such as "take this every morning with breakfast." Adherence to recommendations for complex conditions often requires setting priorities.

Follow-Up

Follow-up enables ongoing support, monitoring, and a reminder of the treatment plan. In many situations, a brief telephone call suffices; in more serious situations, a return visit or a home visit by a community nurse is appropriate.

Address Different Cultural or Religious Beliefs

There are ethical issues to consider before judging a cultural or religious practice as neglectful (Dubowitz, 1997). The costs and benefits of advising against one approach and recommending another must be carefully weighed. Most minor conditions resolve spontaneously, and there is much room for flexibility. It is important to first consider whether the alternative approach is harmful and the criteria for neglect are met. If so, clinicians should address the concerns with sensitivity, humility, and flexibility; an acceptable compromise is often possible. For example, children raised on a vegan diet can be adequately nourished, provided there is appropriate attention to all nutrients. Efforts should begin with the least intrusive approach possible, while ensuring that essential health care is not neglected.

At times, compromise is not reached and concerns of neglect persist, requiring the involvement of CPS and perhaps the judicial system. There are also instances when the risks are so serious, such as when death might ensue without urgent treatment, that immediate involvement of the public agencies is needed. In these instances, the court may transfer custody of the child to the state (i.e., CPS) and mandate treatment over the family's objections. Most states, however, have religious exemptions to their child maltreatment statutes, whereby the failure to provide medical care due to religious reasons is not considered abuse or neglect.

If a family holding such beliefs is part of a religious or cultural group, the risks to other children in the group should be considered. Beyond addressing individual cases, it is optimal to discuss one's concerns with leaders of the group. Such an approach may preserve valuable ties group members may have to their community, rather than encouraging them to deviate and risk being ostracized.

Advocacy Is Much Needed

Returning to the context in which neglect occurs, advocacy is needed at different levels: the individual child, parent, family, community, and society. Helping parents improve their children's treatment is advocacy on behalf of the children who are unable to express or meet their own needs. Acknowledging the stress a parent may feel and facilitating help is also advocacy. Efforts to strengthen families and support the development of community resources are also forms of advocacy. Enhancing access to health care illustrates advocacy at the broadest level. Each of these levels of advocacy is valuable in addressing the problems underpinning the neglect of children's health care.

In summary, addressing the neglect of children's health care is a challenge. There are many things health care providers and others can do to improve the health care children receive and to prevent neglect.

REFERENCES

American Academy of Pediatrics, Committee on Bioethics. (1988). Religious exemptions from child abuse statutes, *Pediatrics, 81,* 169-171.

Annie E. Casey Foundation. (1997). *Kids count data book.* Baltimore, MD: Author.

Asser, S., & Swan, R. (1998). Child fatalities from religion-motivated medical neglect. *Pediatrics, 101,* 625-629.

Belsky, J. (1980). Child maltreatment: An ecological integration. *American Psychologist, 35,* 320-335.

Belsky, J., & Vondra, J. (1989). Lessons from child abuse: The determinants of parenting. In D. Cicchetti & V. Carlson (Eds.), *Child maltreatment: Theory and research on the causes and consequences of child abuse and neglect* (pp. 153-202). New York: Cambridge University Press.

Benedict, M. I., White, R. B., Wulff, L. M., & Hall, B. J. (1990). Reported maltreatment in children with multiple disabilities. *Child Abuse & Neglect, 14,* 207-217.

Benoit, D., Zeanah, C. H., & Barton, M. L. (1989). Maternal attachment disturbances in failure to thrive. *Infant Mental Health Journal, 10*(3), 185-203.

Bithoney, W. G., & Newberger, E. H. (1987). Child and family attributes in failure to thrive. *Journal Developmental and Behavioral Pediatrics, 8*(1), 32-36.

Brayden, R., Altemeier, W., Tucker, D., Dietrich, M., & Vietze, P. (1992). Antecedents of child neglect in the first two years of life. *Journal of Pediatrics, 120,* 426-429.

Bross, D. C. (1982). Medical care neglect. *Child Abuse & Neglect, 6,* 375-381.

Burns, B. J., Costello, E. J., Erkanli, A., Tweed, D., Farmer, E., & Angold, A. (in press). Insurance coverage and mental health service use by adolescents with serious emotional disturbance. *Journal of Child and Family Studies.*

Crittenden, P. M. (1988). Relationships at risk. In J. Belsky & T. Nezworski (Eds.), *The clinical implications of attachment* (pp. 136-174). Hillsdale, NJ: Lawrence Erlbaum.

Crittenden, P. M. (1993). An information-processing prospective on the behavior of neglectful parents. *Criminal Justice and Behavior, 20*(1), 27-48.

Diamond, L. J., & Jaudes, P. K. (1983). Child abuse and the cerebral palsied patient. *Developmental Medicine and Child Neurology, 25,* 169-174.

Dubowitz, H. (1997). Ethical issues in professionals' response to child maltreatment. *Child Maltreatment, 2*(4), 348-355.

Dubowitz, H., Black, M., Starr, R., & Zuravin, S. (1993). A conceptual definition of child neglect. *Criminal Justice and Psychology, 20*(1), 8-26.

Edelstein, B., & Douglass, C. (1995). Dispelling the myth that 50% of U.S. school children have never had a cavity. *Public Health Reports, 110,* 522-530.

Firestone, P., & Witt, J. E. (1982). Characteristics of families completing and prematurely discontinuing a behavioral parent-training program. *General Pediatric Psychology, 7,* 209-222.

Gaudin, J., & Dubowitz, H. (1997). Family functioning in neglectful families: Recent research. In J. Duerr Berick & N. Barth (Eds.), *Child welfare research* (Vol. 2). New York: Columbia University Press.

Giovannoni, J. M., & Billingsley, A. (1970). Child neglect among the poor: A study of parental adequacy in families of three ethnic groups. *Child Welfare, 49*(4), 196-204.

Herrenkohl, R., Herrenkohl, E., & Egolf, B. (1983). Circumstances surrounding the occurrence of child maltreatment. *Journal of Consulting and Clinical Psychology, 51,* 424-431.

Jehovah's Witnesses of Washington v. King County Hospital, 278 F. Supp. 488 (Washington, DC, 1967) aff'd per curiam 390 US 598 (1968).

Kadushin, A. (1988). Neglect in families. In E. W. Nunnally, C. S. Chilman, & F. M. Cox (Eds.), *Mental illness, delinquency, addictions, and neglect* (pp. 147-166). Newbury Park, CA: Sage.

Kotch, J., Browne, D., Symons, M., Ringwalt, C., Bentz, W., Evans, G., Rosebloom, L., Glenn, W., Cheng, N., & Park, M. (1989). *Stress, social support, and abuse and neglect in high risk infants.* Springfield, VA: U.S. Department of Commerce, National Technical Information Service.

Leaf, P., Alegria, M., Cohen, P., Goodman, S., McCue Horwitz, S., Hoven, C., Narro, W., Vaden-Kiernan, M., & Regier, D. (1996). Mental health service use in the community and schools: Results from the four-community MACA Study. *Journal of the American Academy of Child Adolescent Psychiatry, 35*(7), 889-897.

Liptak, G. S. (1996). Enhancing patient compliance in pediatrics. *Pediatrics in Review, 17*(4), 128-134.

Meichenbaum, D. (1989). Noncompliance. *Feelings and Their Medical Significance, 31*(2), 4-8.

Olson, R. A., Zimmerman, J., & Reyes de la Rocha, S. (1985). Medical adherence in pediatric populations. In N. Arziener, D. Bendell, & C. E. Walker (Eds.), *Health psychology treatment and research issues.* New York: Plenum.

Parker, S., Greer, S., & Zuckerman, B. (1988). Double jeopardy: The impact of poverty on early child development. *Pediatric Clinics of North America, 35,* 1227-1240.

Polansky, N. A., Ammons, P. W., & Gaudin, J. M., Jr. (1985). Loneliness and isolation in child neglect. *Social Casework, 66*(1), 38-47.

Prince v. Massachusetts, 3/21 U.S. 158 (1944).

Sedlak, A. J., & Broadhurst, D. D. (1996). *Third national incidence study of child abuse and neglect: Final report.* Washington, DC: National Center on Child Abuse and Neglect.

Skolnick, A. (1990). Religious exemptions to child neglect laws, still being passed despite convictions of parents. *Journal of the American Medical Association, 264,* 1226-1233.

Tang, J., Altman, D., Robertson, D., O'Sullivan, D., Douglass, J., & Tinanoff, N. (1997). Dental caries prevalence and treatment levels in Arizona preschool children. *Public Health Reports, 112,* 319-331.

Twentyman, C., & Plotkin, R. (1982). Unrealistic expectations of parents who maltreat their children: An educational deficit that pertains to child development. *Journal of Clinical Psychology, 38,* 497-503.

U.S. Advisory Board on Child Abuse and Neglect. (1995). *A nation's shame: Fatal child abuse and neglect in the United States.* Washington, DC: Government Printing Office.

U.S. Department of Health and Human Services, National Center on Child Abuse and Neglect. (1996). *Child abuse and neglect case-level data 1993: Working paper I.* Washington, DC: Government Printing Office.

Wolock, I., & Horowitz, H. (1979). Child maltreatment and maternal deprivation among AFDC recipient families. *Journal of Orthopsychiatry, 54,* 530-543.

Zenel, J. A. (1997). Failure to thrive: A general pediatrician's perspective. *Pediatrics in Review, 18*(11), 371-378.

7 Prenatal Alcohol and Drug Use and Risk for Child Maltreatment

A Timely Approach to Intervention

IRA J. CHASNOFF
LEE ANN LOWDER

In the past decade, researchers have focused on the effects of substance abuse during pregnancy and its impact on fetal and child development. Many policymakers have latched on to the preliminary findings contained in these studies and have encouraged judges and legislators to employ various criminal and civil sanctions to attempt to deter or punish women who have used illicit drugs and alcohol during pregnancy. However, there has been relatively little research information on which to base such policy recommendations, and although state child abuse and neglect reporting laws across the country are similar in basic content, states have taken divergent approaches to the issue of reporting substance abuse by the pregnant woman. With time, the interplay between maternal substance abuse and child abuse has become more complicated, and the politics of the "War on Drugs" have intruded on medical decision making.

IMPACTS OF PRENATAL DRUG EXPOSURE

The most recent data from the National Institute on Drug Abuse (1994) suggest that up to 221,000 children per year are exposed to illicit substances during gestation. The number of alcohol-exposed children far exceeds this number, placing the total number of infants born each year prenatally exposed to alcohol and illicit drugs at well over 1 million. As intervention strategies and public policy for this large group of children are developed, the importance of understanding the impact of prenatal alcohol and drug exposure on the developing child becomes apparent.

Deficient growth patterns are among the most frequently cited problems occurring among substance-exposed newborns. As a group, average birth weight is significantly reduced in most studies (Chasnoff, Griffith, MacGregor, Dirkes, & Burns, 1989; Eyler, Behnke, Conlon, Woods, & Wobie, 1998; Frank et al., 1990). Although as the child grows older, average weight catches up to normal (Azuma & Chasnoff, 1993; Chasnoff, Griffith, Freier, & Murray, 1992), low birth weight is a significant risk factor for developmental outcome as a child gets older.

Accompanying poor weight gain of the drug-exposed fetus is poor head growth (Chasnoff et al., 1989; Eyler et al., 1998), a reflection of poor intrauterine brain growth. Alcohol, cocaine, and heroin have been shown to be the three drugs most closely associated with poor brain growth. In general, small head circumference at birth is a significant marker of risk for poor developmental outcome.

Because drug-using or alcohol-using women are more likely to smoke cigarettes, have infections complicating their pregnancies, and have inadequate prenatal care and because cocaine in particular has a direct effect on provoking uterine contractions, it is not surprising that there is a high rate of prematurity among prenatally exposed infants (Chasnoff et al., 1989; Eyler et al., 1998; Frank et al., 1990).

The behavior of newborns prenatally exposed to drugs also may be affected, interfering with their ability to interact with their environment, to respond to stimuli as they occur, and to interact appropriately with the mother or other caretaker. Although physical difficulties in prenatally exposed infants occur in only about 25% to 30% of cases, neurobehavioral deficiencies are far more common.

The key areas of neurobehavior affected by prenatal substance exposure appear to be motor behavior (reflexes, motor control, coordination of motor activities), orientation (the infant's ability to respond to visual and auditory stimulation), and state control (the infant's ability to regulate his or her behavior by moving appropriately through the various states of arousal—from sleep to awake to crying and irritable—and to calm himself or herself in response to the demands of the environment) (Chasnoff et al., 1989; Eisen et al., 1991; Lester et al., 1991; Singer, Garber, & Kliegman, 1991; Tronick, Frank, Cabral, Mirochnik, & Zuckerman, 1996).

The motor behaviors of substance-exposed infants can vary widely. The infants may be quite stiff, with rigid posturing and hyperextension of the trunk. They may have difficulty reaching, grabbing, and exploring objects and bringing their hands to the midline, and their reflexes may be hyperactive. On the other hand, quite a few of these infants are very limp and lethargic at birth, with poor response to handling. In either case, the abnormal motor behavior interferes with coordination of the suck-and-swallow response, and feeding difficulties are not uncommon. Alcohol, cocaine, PCP, and heroin have all been shown to affect motor behaviors of newborn infants.

Prenatal substance exposure can affect the newborn's ability to respond to sound and to visual stimuli. Although the infant hears the sound, he or she has difficulty finding where the sound came from or showing attention to the sound. Visual stimuli have the same effect, with the child able to perceive that there is something to see but having difficulty focusing his or her gaze, even briefly, on the object. Children prenatally exposed to cocaine, heroin, or PCP have difficulties with these orientation responses, and prenatal cocaine exposure particularly tends to interfere with visual orientation.

State control in substance-exposed infants often is poorly organized, with the infants spending most of their time in states that shut them off from external stimulation. The infants frequently are very fragile. Their state changes tend to be abrupt and inappropriate, with the child moving from sleeping to crying for no particular reason. Four most frequent patterns of state control problems in drug-exposed infants have been described:

In the first pattern, the infants pull down into a deep self-protective sleep in response to the first stimulation received. These infants remain asleep and in fact enter a deeper sleep as attempts to awaken them increase, indicating they are protecting themselves from what they perceive as negative stimulation.

The second pattern of state control demonstrated by drug-exposed infants is similar to the first, except the infants cannot enter a sufficiently deep sleep to protect themselves from negative stimuli. They have difficulty blocking out negative stimuli, and rather than habituating or getting used to the stimuli, they remain asleep but continue to startle, whimper, change colors, breathe irregularly, and thrash about in response to the stimuli.

The third pattern of state control problems for drug-exposed infants is one in which they vacillate between sleeping and crying. With stimulation, they break into agitated crying, and when the stimulation ceases, they immediately drop back into a deep sleep. The continuous alternations between sleep and crying prevent the child from becoming sufficiently alert to respond adaptively to sound or to visual stimulation.

The final and most common pattern of state control for drug-exposed infants is similar to the third in that these infants use both sleeping and crying to shut themselves off from overstimulation. However, these infants, when managed carefully, are able to reach brief periods of alertness and become responsive to the caretakers. The difficult aspect of this pattern is that the infants require intense but carefully regulated input. This generally requires a more sophisticated degree of parenting than most women with a history of drug abuse are capable of, explaining in large part the increased risk for child maltreatment that occurs in this population.

As the child grows older, many of the acute neurobehavioral difficulties begin to resolve. However, a study of 3-month-old infants who had been prenatally exposed to cocaine found that prenatal cocaine exposure had effects on arousal and attention regulation, although no impact on early cognitive processes was documented (Mayes, Bornstein, Chawarska, & Granger, 1995).

The impact of alcohol on long-term infant growth and development has been examined by Streissguth, Sampson, and Barr (1989) who evaluated the effects of prenatal exposure to alcohol or tobacco or both on IQ scores at 4 years of age. They found a significant relationship between alcohol consumption during pregnancy and low IQ scores of the women's children at age 4 years.

Fried and Watkinson (1990) examined the effects of prenatal exposure to marijuana, tobacco, alcohol, or a combination of these on developmental outcome of exposed children at 36 and 48 months of age. In their white, middle-class sample, the researchers found cigarette smoking to be related to poorer language development and cognitive functioning at both 36 and 48 months of age. Alcohol exposure was related to decreased cognitive abilities at 36 months but not at 48 months of age. Marijuana exposure was not related to cognitive abilities at 36 months but by 48 months was associated with lower scores in the verbal and memory areas.

Early data from the University of California at Los Angeles (Howard, Beckwith, & Rodning, 1989) found that a group of 18-month-old children who had been exposed in utero to cocaine had significantly lower developmental scores than a group of non-drug-exposed infants from similar family and socioeconomic backgrounds. However, it was noted that the mean developmental scores of the exposed group were still within the average range. The researchers further indicated that the drug-exposed children showed striking deficits in the stability and organization of free play. They had less representational play than the control group. The majority of drug-exposed children demonstrated a high rate of scattering, batting, and picking up and putting down toys rather than sustained combining of toys, fantasy play, or curious exploration. This pattern of disruptive and disorganized play appears to be of a similar quality of neurobehavioral regulation as described in newborns affected by intrauterine cocaine exposure.

Several studies have found that prenatal cocaine exposure does not have a direct impact on cognitive development of the child, but environmental factors play a role in predicting global developmental scores (Chasnoff, Anson, & Iaukea, 1998; Hurt et al., 1995; Nulman et al., 1995). Ornoy, Michailevskaya, Lukashov, Bar-Hamburger, and Harel (1994) studied two groups of children born to heroin-dependent mothers, one group who was adopted and the other group raised at home. These researchers concluded that the developmental delays and behavioral problems demonstrated by the heroin-exposed infants were a result of environmental deprivation and the fact that one or both parents in the birth home in which the children were being raised were addicted.

In a prospective study of 4-year-old to 6-year-old children prenatally exposed to cocaine and other drugs, Chasnoff (1997) found that prenatal cocaine or polydrug exposure did not have a direct effect on global cognitive functioning but a strong indirect effect as mediated through the home environment. However, prenatal exposure to cocaine and other drugs did have a significant direct effect on the child's behavior at 4 to 6 years of age, with prenatally exposed children showing higher rates of aggressive behavior, thought problems, impulsivity, and distractibility.

FAMILIES AND SUBSTANCE ABUSE

Drawing firm conclusions from many of these studies is difficult because it is hard to distinguish the purely biological effects of the prenatal exposure from the ongoing environmental problems caused by living in a home with a substance-abusing parent. Systematic consideration of these factors is important in understanding child behavior in general and is particularly relevant to prenatally exposed children and their risk for maltreatment. Child growth and development are dynamic processes involving both social and biological issues, with the biological issues being related to the direct impact of any particular drug on an unborn child's developing brain.

From a psychosocial perspective, the lifestyle of substance-abusing parents is filled with factors that tend to interfere with attempts at parenting, effective childrearing, and participation in the education of their children. These factors are present to some extent in all women who abuse drugs at a high level, regardless of socioeconomic status. Furthermore, the social environment of many addicted women is one of chaos and instability, which has an even greater negative impact on children.

Addicted women frequently have poor family and social support networks; have few positive relationships with other women, and often are dependent on an unreliable, abusive male, thereby increasing their vulnerability to physical and sexual abuse. Children of substance-abusing women are at greater risk for neglect and sexual, physical, and psychological abuse. These difficulties are magnified in children living in poverty, because their mothers frequently lack the social and economic supports that could help lessen some of the social isolation as well as the biological impact of prenatal drug exposure.

Significant psychiatric or psychological problems, such as personality disorders or mood disorders, especially depressive illnesses, are not uncommon in women who use drugs or abuse alcohol. These factors almost invariably impede parenting capabilities further and lessen the chance for a normal developmental course for the child. Even in non-substance-abusing depressed women, there is less involvement with their children, impaired communication among family members, increased friction, lack of affection, and an increase in guilt and resentment toward the child. To further complicate the picture, children of depressed mothers are significantly more likely to show depression than are children of non-depressed mothers. If there is a cyclical relationship between drug use and depression (i.e., drug use leads to depression, which leads to continued drug use), then the probability of transmission of the woman's depressive illness or substance-use problems to her children increases.

THE LINK BETWEEN PERINATAL SUBSTANCE ABUSE AND CHILD ABUSE

There is no question that prenatal substance exposure puts a child at risk, but even more important, it is clear that substance abuse during pregnancy is a marker for familial and environmental factors that place the child at risk for harm. In spite of the need for reliable information that can guide policy development, there are only early research data available regarding risk of subsequent child abuse and neglect in children born to women who use alcohol or illicit drugs during pregnancy. In one study, researchers selected a group of women with a positive urine toxicology at delivery and on follow-up found an incidence of maltreatment in 23% (Kelly, Walsh, & Thompson, 1991). However, focusing on women who already had been selected out for urine toxicology biased the study toward those women who came from a high-risk social situation. In a second study, Kelly (1992) followed a group of children born to cocaine-using women and compared them with a matched group of children whose mothers did not use cocaine. On follow-up, 23% of the cocaine-exposed group compared with 3% in the non-exposed group had substantiated reports of abuse or neglect after discharge from the hospital. The period of time that elapsed between the newborn's discharge from the hospital and the children's age at the point of reporting was not specified. In Illinois, 102 of 513 children (19.9%) who were prenatally exposed to cocaine were subsequently found to have been abused or neglected—a rate 2 to 3 times higher than other children from the same area in Chicago (Illinois Department of Children and Family Services [IDCFS], (1997).

Studies in the past 5 years have begun to document the increased risk for child abuse and neglect that is present in families in which the mother has used alcohol or illicit drugs during pregnancy. The National Committee for Prevention of Child Abuse (1989) estimated that 675,000 children are seriously mistreated annually by an alcoholic or drug-abusing caretaker. In Illinois during fiscal year 1996, under the state's mandated reporting law, 3,436 reports were made to the IDCFS regarding infants born with a positive urine toxicology for an illegal drug, an increase of 3000% since 1985. Of the reported families, 40% had a history of prior IDCFS substantiation of abuse and neglect, and 38% of the mothers had previously given birth to one or more substance-exposed infants, an increase from 26% in fiscal year 1995. These numbers have overwhelmed the child protection system in Cook County and have resulted in growing difficulty in placing the children as well as accessing any services for them.

Unfortunately, when laws have been enacted to mandate reporting of maternal substance abuse during pregnancy, especially the third trimester, the implementation of the laws has resulted in biased selection of minority, poor women (Chasnoff, Landress, & Barrett, 1990). The question of exactly what behaviors during pregnancy should be reported is further clouded by the question of risk associated with the use of legal drugs, such as tobacco, as well as alcohol during pregnancy; continued maternal use of alcohol or illicit drugs after pregnancy; substance abuse by the father or other members of the household; and the general environment of violence in which many addicted people live.

Using data from the National Institute for Mental Health's Epidemiologic Catchment Area survey, researchers found that about half of abusive or neglectful parents have "a lifetime prevalence substance abuse disorder" (Chaffin, Kelleher, & Hollenberg, 1996). When other factors were taken into account, parental substance abuse approximately tripled the risk of maltreatment. Substance-abusing parents were 2.9 times more likely to abuse and 3.24 times more likely to neglect their children than non-substance abusers.

CURRENT APPROACHES TO INTERVENTION

Holding Women Criminally Liable for Harm to the Fetus

In a recent poll, a majority of Americans believed that women who abuse drugs during pregnancy should face criminal prosecution if their children are born impaired (Sherman, 1991). In a poll of people in 15 states, 71% were in favor of criminal sanctions against women whose drug use caused prenatal harm (Hoffman, 1990).

More than 160 women in 24 states have been prosecuted for exposing their children to drugs in utero. Most of the women pled guilty or accepted plea bargains. When the convictions were appealed, however, many were overturned ("Courts side with moms," 1992). Two cases illustrate why most criminal prosecutions have failed. In *State v. Dunn* (1996), the woman was charged with second degree criminal mistreatment of her viable unborn child after she and her newborn tested positive for cocaine. During a prenatal visit, a doctor had advised the woman that her continued cocaine use could damage her child. The woman was scheduled to begin drug treatment but failed to do so. The child, who weighed 4 pounds, 9 ounces at birth, was diagnosed with intrauterine growth retardation and *abruptio placentae* and was blind. In Washington, a parent or guardian is guilty of second degree child endangerment if he or she acts recklessly, and his or her actions create an imminent and substantial risk of death or great bodily harm to a child or dependent, caused by withholding a basic necessity of life. Because no Washington court had ever found that a fetus was a "person" under the criminal statutes and because the woman had not withheld any of the basic necessities of life, the *Dunn* court affirmed the dismissal of criminal charges against her.

The defendant in *Johnson v. Florida* (1992) admitted to a pediatrician that she used cocaine the night before she gave birth in October 1987. In December 1988, while pregnant again, the woman overdosed on crack cocaine. She told paramedics that she had taken $200 worth of crack and was concerned about the effects of the drug on her unborn child. In January 1989, the woman told the obstetrician who was attending the birth of her child that she had used rock cocaine that morning while she was in labor. The day after the baby was born, the mother admitted to a child protection investigator that she had smoked pot and crack cocaine 3 to 4 times every other day throughout her pregnancy and for the previous 3 years.

The Florida Supreme Court was asked to decide whether Florida criminal statutes permitted the prosecution of a mother who ingested a controlled substance prior to giving birth for delivery of a controlled substance to the infant during the 30 to 90 seconds following the infant's birth but before the umbilical cord was severed. The court reasoned that no evidence was presented that the woman timed her cocaine use so that she could transmit cocaine to the baby at birth. If she had taken cocaine a few days earlier, the drug would have been metabolized and eliminated. The court found that

> the legislature never intended for the general drug delivery statute to authorize prosecutions of those mothers who have taken illegal drugs

> close enough in time to childbirth that a doctor could testify that a tiny amount passed from mother to child in the few seconds before the umbilical cord was cut. Criminal prosecution of mothers such as Johnson will undermine Florida's express policy of keeping families intact and could destroy the family by incarcerating the child's mother when alternative measures could protect the child and stabilize the family. (*Johnson v. Florida,* 1992, at 1294)

Some states, however, have successfully prosecuted women who used an illicit substance during pregnancy. In *Commonwealth v. Pellegrini* (1993), the trial court dismissed criminal charges against a woman for possession of cocaine based on a urine test of her newborn. The reviewing court overturned the dismissal, rejecting the mother's claim that the child's medical records were protected by her own right to privacy and allowing the state to proceed with the prosecution.

In *Whitner v. State* (1996), the woman pled guilty to criminal child neglect after she used cocaine in her third trimester of pregnancy, causing her child to be born with cocaine metabolites in his urine. She was sentenced to 8 years in prison. In South Carolina, it is a misdemeanor to endanger the life, health, or comfort of a child by neglecting to provide the child with proper care and attention (South Carolina Code, 1985). The same statute defines a child as a "person under the age of eighteen."

In deciding that the legislature intended this child endangerment statute to protect fetuses, the court noted that South Carolina recognized a civil cause of action for prenatal injury to and wrongful death of a viable fetus and also a criminal cause of action for feticide. The court thought it would be absurd to recognize that a viable fetus was a person under the homicide and wrongful death statutes but not under statutes prohibiting child abuse.

Holding Women Civilly Liable for Harm to the Fetus

The evolution of civil law reflects a progression in the public's perception of the duty of care that third parties, including parents, owe to fetuses. Until 1946, American courts did not recognize any cause of action for fetal injuries, reasoning that the mother and unborn child were one entity, and that only the mother was entitled to recovery *(Dietrich v. Inhabitants of Northampton,* 1884). Now, all states permit causes of action for prenatal injury, based on the premise that the fetus has a right to begin life with a sound mind and body. About one third of states permit such recovery even when the fetus was not viable at the time of the injury (Garcia, 1992).

Some courts have been reluctant to apply this duty of care to parents. In *Stallman v. Youngquist* (1988), the Illinois Supreme Court held that a child cannot sue his or her mother for prenatal injuries that resulted from the mother's negligent driving. The *Stallman* court explained that its decision was based on the unique relationship between a pregnant woman and the fetus she is carrying, which it described as "unlike the relationship between any other plaintiff and defendant" (at 355).

The Michigan Court of Appeals reached the opposite result, allowing a child to sue her mother for negligently taking tetracycline during pregnancy, causing the child's teeth to be discolored (*Grodin v. Grodin,* 1980). The court reasoned that the "mother would bear the same liability as a third person for injurious, negligent conduct that interfered with the child's 'legal right to begin life with a sound mind and body' " (at 870).

Asserting Jurisdiction Over Fetuses

A few courts have been asked to exercise jurisdiction to protect fetuses. Two courts have ordered women to undergo cesarean sections to benefit their fetuses—the Supreme Court of Georgia, in *Jefferson v. Griffin Spalding County Hospital Authority* (1981), and the Superior Court of the District of Columbia, in *In re Madyun* (1986). An Illinois appellate court refused to order a woman to submit to a cesarean section: *Doe v. Doe* (1994) held that Illinois courts should not balance the rights of a viable, near-term fetus, whom doctors believed would be born dead or severely retarded if vaginally delivered, against the right of the mother to refuse medical treatment as invasive as a cesarean section.

Other courts have ordered pregnant women to submit to blood transfusions, which violated their religious beliefs, to save their lives and the lives of their fetuses (*Raleigh Fitkin-Paul Morgan Memorial Hospital v. Anderson,* 1964); *In the Interest of Fetus Brown,* 1996).[1] In the successful blood transfusion and cesarean section cases, courts have subordinated pregnant women's rights to fetal rights.

The Wisconsin Supreme Court overturned the decisions of a trial court and appellate court to exercise juvenile court jurisdiction over a fetus in *Angela M. W. v. Kruzicki* (1995). This case was initiated by an obstetrician, who determined through drug screening that his patient was using cocaine and other drugs during her second and third trimesters of pregnancy. The obstetrician counseled the woman to seek voluntary inpatient treatment. When she refused, the doctor made a report of child abuse, and the state petitioned for protective custody of the fetus.

The petition included the doctor's affidavit that the woman's active cocaine use presented a real and immediate danger to the health, safety, and continued viability of the unborn child. In the doctor's opinion, if the woman were not compelled to stop using drugs, she would continue to do so, with the following likely effects on her child: "low weight gain, abruptio placenta, increased infectious diseases, hypertension and tachycardia, preterm labor and delivery, possible precipitous delivery, and increased risks for pregnancy loss, including spontaneous abortion and still birth, SIDS, congenital malformations, intraventricular hemorrhage and precipitous labor" (*Angela M. W. v. Kruzicki,* 1995, at 485). Before the order was executed, the woman volunteered for inpatient treatment. The order was amended to provide that the fetus was to be held in protective custody at the treatment facility of the woman's choice. If the woman left treatment, the fetus was to be held in protective custody at a designated hospital (at 486).

Under the Wisconsin juvenile code, a child is "a person who is less than 18 years of age" (Wisconsin Statutes, 1985). The appellate court gave three reasons for ruling that a viable fetus is a person for purposes of the Wisconsin child protection statute. The court first pointed to the United States Supreme Court's recognition in *Roe v. Wade* (1973) that states have a legitimate interest in protecting potential life at the point of viability. The court reasoned that the goals of the child protection statute could not be vindicated if the potential life of a viable fetus was not "provided a safe environment in the womb of its mother" (*Angela M. W. v. Kruzicki,* 1995, at 489). The court stated,

> By recognizing that a state may intervene in an abortion decision after viability, *Roe* necessarily recognizes the right of the state to protect the potential life of the fetus over the wishes of the mother to terminate the pregnancy. Why then cannot the state also protect the viable fetus from maternal conduct that functionally presents the same risk and portends the same result—the death of the viable fetus? (at 489)

In support of its reasoning, the court pointed to the Wisconsin feticide statute, which makes it illegal for any person other than the mother to intentionally destroy an unborn child (Wisconsin Statutes, 1997). The court also noted that it would not be logical to grant property rights to an unborn child and to allow a cause of action for its wrongful death but then to prohibit the state from intervening to preserve its life and health in the first place.

In response to the woman's challenge that the juvenile court had no jurisdiction over her, as an adult, the appellate court engaged in novel reasoning. It explained that the trial court had not asserted any jurisdiction over the woman nor ordered her into involuntary treatment. The court insisted that the order was directed to the fetus, not the woman (*Angela M. W. v. Kruzicki,* 1995, at 494).

In determining that the state has a compelling interest in protecting viable fetuses, the court cited statistics from Milwaukee County that 10% to 15% of babies are born to mothers who used cocaine while they were pregnant (*Angela M. W. v. Kruzicki,* 1995, at 495). The court rejected the argument that confinement of pregnant women would not be productive because it might discourage them from receiving prenatal care or substance abuse treatment or encourage them to deliver at home. The court emphasized that the obstetrician in this case had encouraged the woman to obtain treatment voluntarily and had reported her continued drug use only when she refused to obtain it.

The dissenting justice argued that the majority's decision to include a fetus in the statutory category of "a person less than 18 years of age" defied common sense. He explained,

> In everyday affairs, age is measured from the time of birth, not conception, not quickening and not viability, and one cannot be a "child" by definition until he or she has been born and his or her age has begun to accrue. (*Angela M. W. v. Kruzicki,* 1995, at 498)

The dissent cited concerns of the American Medical Association's (AMA) Board of Trustees that an adversary relationship between the woman and fetus would discourage a healthy relationship between the mother and her future child, would foster distrust of doctors, and would discourage women from seeking prenatal care and from providing accurate information to their doctors. The dissent emphasized the AMA's concern that pregnant women from minority groups and poor women would be unfairly affected by such intervention. The AMA reviewed a recent study that demonstrated the severe stresses that may contribute to substance abuse:

> Compared to nonabusers, female substance abusers have more dysfunction in their families, suffer from higher levels of depression, anxiety, sense of powerlessness, and have low levels of self-esteem and self-confidence. Seventy percent were sexually abused as children; 83% had chemically dependent parents; 70% reported being beaten and 10% were homeless. (AMA Board of Trustees, 1990)

On April 22, 1997, the Supreme Court of Wisconsin reversed the appellate court's decision, finding that the legislature did not intend to include fetuses within the definition of children for purposes of the child protection statute (*Angela M. W. v. Kruzicki*, 1997). The Supreme Court noted,

> The confinement of a pregnant woman for the benefit of her fetus is a decision bristling with important social policy issues. We determine that the legislature is in a better position than the courts to gather, weigh and reconcile the competing policy proposals addressed to this sensitive area of the law. (at 29.46)

An appellate court in Ohio also refused to uphold juvenile jurisdiction over a pregnant woman. In *Cox v. Court of Common Pleas* (1988), the woman, who was 7 months pregnant, had used cocaine and opiates throughout her pregnancy, failing 23 drug screenings. At the time of the hearing, she had begun a methadone maintenance treatment program. However, she had refused to obtain prenatal care. The trial court asserted juvenile court jurisdiction over the woman and ordered her to stop using illegal drugs and to submit to a medical examination. When the woman failed to comply with the court order, the prosecutor asked the court to hold her in contempt and to place her in a secure drug treatment facility to prevent further injury to the fetus. The reviewing court held that the juvenile court could not "compel a pregnant woman to take action for the alleged benefit of her unborn child" (at 725).

Involuntary Civil Commitment of Pregnant Women

Thirty-seven states allow drug-dependent persons to be involuntarily committed for treatment (Garcia, 1992). Some commentators have suggested that these civil commitment statutes should be used to protect fetuses from intrauterine drug exposure (Garcia & Keilitz, 1991; Wilton, 1991).

Minnesota includes any pregnant woman "who has engaged during pregnancy in habitual or excessive use, for nonmedical purposes, of any of the following controlled substances or their derivatives: cocaine, heroin, phencyclidine, methamphetamine or amphetamine" in its definition of chemically dependent people who are subject to civil commitment (Minnesota Statutes, 1991, § 243B.02[2]). The local child welfare agency is mandated to seek emergency commitment of pregnant substance abusers who refuse recommended voluntary services or fail recommended treatment (Minnesota Statutes, 1990).

In Hillsborough County, Florida, pregnant women can be civilly committed to drug treatment by an Involuntary Drug Court. If they continue to use drugs or refuse to obtain treatment, they can be held in contempt of court. They can be sentenced to 5 months and 29 days in jail, where they will also receive drug treatment (Garcia, 1992).

Voluntary Treatment Approaches

Several approaches to treatment of substance-abusing pregnant women have been attempted. Most research shows that the core ingredient for success relies on recognition of the gender-specific requirements of women and mothers. A gender-specific approach grounded in women's experiences (Finkelstein, Kennedy, Thomas, & Kearns, 1997) suggests the central importance of the following four factors in women's use and abuse of substances:

1. Men frequently play a major role in women's initiation and maintenance of substance use and abuse.
2. A woman's connections to her children are important in prevention, treatment, and recovery.
3. Connections can be both positive and negative. Members of a support network can and do provide nurturance; however, sometimes they do this in detrimental ways, such as in condoning negative and harmful behavior.
4. Social support and positive relationships are important in increasing a woman's self-efficacy and self-esteem and therefore in preventing misuse of substances and aiding in recovery.

Defining Prenatal Substance Abuse as Child Abuse or Neglect

A few states have enacted legislation that defines the mother's prenatal substance abuse as child abuse. In Florida (Florida Statutes, 1991, 415.503[9]), a newborn's drug dependency is a ground for suspicion of child abuse and neglect. However, no parent of a drug-dependent newborn shall be subject to criminal investigation solely on the basis of the infant's drug dependency (Florida Statutes, 1991, 415.503[7]). In Illinois, any newborn whose blood or urine contains any amount of a controlled substance is defined as an abused or neglected child (Smith Hurd Annotated, 1989). In Indiana, a child in need of services includes one who is born with fetal alcohol syndrome or drug addiction or a child injured or not developing normally because of the mother's substance abuse and not receiving or unlikely to receive proper care without court intervention (Indiana Code, 1989). Massachusetts defines newborns who are addicted to drugs as abused (Massachusetts General Laws, 1990). In Minnesota, child neglect includes prenatal exposure to a controlled substance used by the mother for other than medicinal purposes (Minnesota Statutes, 1989). Oklahoma defines a deprived child as one

> who is in need of special care and treatment because of his physical or mental condition including a child born in a condition of dependence on a controlled dangerous substance, and his parent . . . is unable or willfully fails to provide such special care and treatment. (Oklahoma Statutes, 1990)

In several states that do not have specific statutory provisions defining intrauterine exposure to drugs and alcohol as child abuse, courts have nevertheless found that the mother's drug use during pregnancy was abusive or neglectful. The child in *In re Smith* (1985) was born prematurely, weighing just above the fifth percentile for 35 weeks' gestation. She was "jittery, irritable, and was found to have a small philtrum, increased facial hirsutism, and a thin upper lip" (at 332). When the mother gave birth to this child's older sibling, she had been ordered to complete inpatient alcohol treatment and to abstain from abusing alcohol.

The woman had had a drinking problem since age 15. She admitted to hospital staff that she drank about 10 alcoholic drinks 3 to 4 days a week. Although she was encouraged to obtain prenatal care and substance abuse treatment, the woman attended only one prenatal appointment—2 days before the second child was born. The court held that the woman's abuse of alcohol during pregnancy and her inadequate prenatal care created an imminent danger, a sufficient basis for finding her child to be neglected.

The woman in *In re Ruiz* (1986) was an addict who had injected heroin intravenously in the 2 weeks prior to her child's birth. The newborn tested positive for cocaine and heroin, and some of his withdrawal symptoms lasted more than 10 days, including hypertonicity, jitteriness, diarrhea, and feeding difficulty. Although the Ohio statute contained no specific language on prenatal substance abuse, the court reasoned that a child has the right to begin life with a sound mind and body and held that a viable fetus is a child for purposes of the Ohio child protection statute.

Termination of Parental Rights

Courts have split on the issue of whether a mother's drug use renders her unfit, for purposes of terminating her parental rights. The defendant in *In the Interest of Guillory* (1981) was on probation for possession of heroin at the time her child was born. She continued to use drugs thereafter. The court found evidence that the mother engaged in conduct, before and after the child's birth, that endangered the child's physical and emotional well-being and was sufficient to terminate her parental rights.

The mother in *In re Chan-Charay T.* (1996) had six children, two of whom were born testing positive for controlled substances. The mother's rights to her three oldest children had been terminated due to her chronic neglect, substance abuse, and abandonment of the children. The court found that the mother was unlikely to successfully complete a long-term drug program, emphasizing that "[a]t no time during the past eight years has she been able to sustain her sobriety for any period outside of a correctional center or a drug abuse program" (at 5). The court noted that the mother "had very poor attendance in substance abuse programs and has been prematurely discharged from over four treatment centers due to noncompliance and threatening behavior, as well as poor attendance" (at 5). The court terminated the woman's rights to her three younger children, finding it would be unfair to make them wait to see if their mother would succeed in drug treatment in the future.

An Arizona court of appeals reached the opposite result in *Appeal in Pima County Juvenile Severance Action* (1995). The State sought to terminate the parental rights of a mother who gave birth to twins, one of whom suffered fetal alcohol syndrome, the other, fetal alcohol effects. The court held that the mother's ingestion of alcohol during pregnancy could not be the basis for terminating her parental rights. The court stated that "chronic substance abuse during pregnancy in and of itself does not reflect an inability to parent that would justify severance of a parent's fundamental rights" (at 558).

SUBSTANCE ABUSE AND CHILD ABUSE: A PROPOSED INTERVENTION STRATEGY

Based on the documented risk of child abuse and neglect in families in which the mother used alcohol or illicit drugs during pregnancy, we propose that interventions should occur as soon as it is determined that a newborn was exposed to illegal drugs or alcohol in utero. The prosecution and treatment of people who drive under the influence of alcohol or illegal drugs is one model to consider applying in such cases.

In Illinois, a person who drives under the influence of alcohol or illegal drugs is guilty of a Class A misdemeanor (Smith Hurd Annotated, 1996). On a DUI (driving under the influence) conviction, the Secretary of State suspends the driver's license. Depending on the amount of alcohol in the driver's blood, the court can order 8 to 30 hours of remedial education and counseling or immediate treatment.

After a DUI conviction but prior to sentencing, the driver must submit to and pay for a professional substance abuse evaluation, to determine the extent of the problem. For a second DUI conviction within 5 years, the driver receives a mandatory sentence of 49 consecutive hours of imprisonment or 100 hours of community service. If the driver convicted of a second DUI was transporting a child under age 16, he or she must pay a minimum fine of $500 and participate in 5 days of community service in a program benefiting children.

It is instructive to compare the legal treatment of people who are convicted of DUI with the legal treatment of women who give birth to more than one substance-exposed newborn. In Chicago, the IDCFS does not bring a mother's first drug-exposed newborn to the attention of the Juvenile Court. Instead, the agency refers the mother to a drug treatment program. Because IDCFS does not seek court intervention for the first drug-exposed newborn, the most common case in the Child Protection Division of the Cook County Juvenile Court is that of a mother's second or third baby who tests positive for prenatal drug exposure. The reality is that many women who have given birth to drug-exposed children continue to use drugs, fail to obtain treatment, and give birth to subsequent drug-exposed children.

In Illinois, drivers with first-time DUI convictions lose their licenses. They are ordered to submit to alcohol or drug (or both) assessments and to attend substance abuse treatment and education. In Chicago, mothers who expose their first child to illegal drugs in utero are not brought to the attention of the court nor do they receive mandatory education or treatment. Based on the significant connection between substance abuse and child abuse and neglect, it appears that mothers who give birth to substance-exposed children and do not obtain treatment pose a significant threat to their children's health.

There is no simple solution to this problem. However, given these circumstances, we propose that a structure for intervention based on DUI laws be initiated:

1. Every pregnant woman should be evaluated by the primary prenatal care provider with a standardized risk assessment instrument for substance abuse at each prenatal visit. The purpose of this step is not to turn the primary prenatal care provider into a watchdog but to identify those women at risk for substance use during pregnancy and to refer the identified women for further assessment. A successful approach to screening in a prenatal-care setting serves a first-level function: to identify the presence or absence of risk for substance use. In the primary health care setting, the "4-P's" (a four-question screening instrument that focuses on four specific domains for risk of substance abuse: family history of substance abuse, substance abuse by the woman's current partner, and substance use by the woman prior to and during pregnancy) has been used successfully to identify high-risk women (*Maternal Substance Use Assessment,* U.S. Department of Health and Human Services, 1993). This approach can also be used postpartum for the woman with no prenatal care.

2. Any pregnant woman or postpartum woman with a positive initial screen for substance use should be further assessed for substance abuse that can affect the outcome of the unborn child. Any woman found to be using alcohol or illicit drugs should then be referred to treatment. If the

woman refuses treatment, prenatal care should continue, and at each visit, the prenatal care provider should continue to address the woman's substance abuse within a health care context.

3. On the birth of the first child of a woman who has used drugs or alcohol during pregnancy, as evidenced by positive history or by positive urine toxicologies in the mother at any time during gestation or in the child at birth, child protective services (CPS) should be notified. For a first report, the woman should be fully evaluated and referred to a structured educational or treatment program. If the woman does not participate fully in treatment, CPS should initiate proceedings to evaluate the home and to ensure the safety of the children.

4. If the woman continues to use drugs or alcohol, although she has been offered treatment, and gives birth to another child who tests positive for drugs or alcohol, her parental rights should be reviewed and, when appropriate, terminated. With regard to illicit substances, this approach became the law in Illinois on January 1, 1998 (Illinois Public Act, 1998).[2]

For this approach to work, several issues must be addressed head-on:

1. Screening for alcohol and drug use during pregnancy should be implemented for every pregnant woman, regardless of race, income, or social class. Such screening should not depend on urine toxicologies but on the use of a standardized screening instrument, such as the 4P's, administered by the health care professional or self-administered.

2. Concerns about driving pregnant women out of the health care system must be addressed. Most studies that have found this to be the case have been conducted in communities or hospitals where only selected women were given urine toxicologies and then reported to the police if the toxicology was positive. The use of a standardized screening with all pregnant women should minimize race and class bias.

3. Adequate treatment programs, both in numbers and quality, must be available to all pregnant or parenting women who need treatment. If a woman fails to comply with mandated treatment due to the lack of adequate treatment facilities, this mitigating factor should be considered in any court proceeding that affects her parental rights.

4. Decisions to reunite a woman with her child should be based on the woman's adherence to and progress toward clearly stated treatment goals. These goals should be established collaboratively by the woman, the treatment program, the CPS team, and the health care provider.

Substance abuse in pregnancy will continue to be a major factor in child neglect and abuse cases. Based on emerging data from long-term studies of children prenatally exposed to alcohol, cocaine, and other drugs, prenatal exposure places children at high risk of behavioral problems: impulsivity, poor social interaction, aggressive behavior, depression, anxiety, distractibility. These behavior problems may make the child more difficult to care for and more apt to be abused by a parent out of control because of his or her addiction to alcohol or illicit drugs. These also are the same behavioral characteristics that have been found in 6-year-olds and 7-year-olds to be predictive of adolescent substance abuse. To interrupt the intergenerational cycle of substance abuse and child abuse, new policies must be undertaken that will serve the best interests of the child and of the family.

NOTES

1. The trial court's order was reversed on appeal: *In re Fetus Brown,* Ill. App. 1st Dist. No. 1-96-2316, December 31, 1997, slip op.

2. Illinois Public Act 90-13, adding 750 ILCS 50/1(D)(r), which defines parental unfitness, for the purpose of terminating parental rights, as:

> a finding that at birth the child's blood, urine, or meconium contained any amount of a controlled substance . . . or a metabolite of a controlled substance, with the exception of controlled substances or metabolites of such substances, the presence of which in the newborn infant was the result of medical treatment administered to the mother or the newborn infant, and that the biological mother of this child is the biological mother of at least one other child who was adjudicated a neglected minor . . . under the Juvenile Court Act . . . after which the biological mother had the opportunity to enroll in and participate in a clinically appropriate substance abuse counseling, treatment, and rehabilitation program.

REFERENCES

American Medical Association Board of Trustees. (1990). Legal interventions during pregnancy: Court-ordered medical treatments and legal penalties for potentially harmful behavior by pregnant women. *Journal of the American Medical Association, 264,* 2663-2668.

Angela M. W. v. Kruzicki, 197 Wis. 2d 532, 541 N.W.2d 482 (Ct. App. 1995), *rev'd* 209 Wis. 2d 112, 561 N.W.2d 729 (1997).

Appeal in Pima County Juvenile Severance Action, 183 Ariz. 546, 905 P.2d 444 (Ariz. Ct. App. 1995).

Azuma, S. D., & Chasnoff, I. J. (1993). Outcome of children prenatally exposed to cocaine and other drugs: A path analysis of three-year data. *Pediatrics, 92,* 396-402.

Chaffin, M., Kelleher, K., & Hollenberg, J. (1996). Onset of physical abuse and neglect: Psychiatric, substance abuse and social risk factors from prospective community data. *Child Abuse & Neglect, 20,* 191-200.

Chasnoff, I. J. (1997). Prenatal exposure to cocaine and other drugs: Is there a profile? In P. J. Accardo, B. K. Shapiro, & A. J. Capute (Eds.), *Behavior belongs in the brain.* Baltimore, MD: York.

Chasnoff, I. J., Anson, A., & Iaukea, K. M. (1998). *Understanding the drug exposed child: Approaches to behavior and learning.* Chicago: Imprint Publications.

Chasnoff, I. J., Griffith, D. R., Freier, C., & Murray, J. (1992). Cocaine/polydrug use in pregnancy: Two year follow-up. *Pediatrics, 89,* 284-289.

Chasnoff, I. J., Griffith, D. R., MacGregor, S., Dirkes, K., & Burns, K. A. (1989). Temporal patterns of cocaine use in pregnancy. *Journal of the American Medical Association, 161,* 1741-1744.

Chasnoff, I. J., Landress, H. J., & Barrett, M. E. (1990). The prevalence of drug or alcohol use during pregnancy and discrepancies in mandatory reporting in Pinellas County, Florida. *New England Journal of Medicine, 322,* 1202-1206.

Commonwealth v. Pellegrini, 608 N.E.2d 717 (S. Jd. Ct. Mass. 1993).

Courts side with moms in drug cases: Florida woman's conviction overturned for delivering cocaine via umbilical cord. (1992). *ABA Journal, 78,* 18.

Cox v. Court of Common Please, 42 Ohio App. 3d 171, 537 N.E.2d 721 (1988).

Dietrich v. Inhabitants of Northampton, 138 Mass. 14 (1884).

Doe v. Doe, 632 N.E.2d 326 (Ill. App. 1st Dist. 1994).

Eisen, L. N., Field, T. M., Bandstra, E. S., Roberts, J. P., Morrow, C., Larson, S. K., & Steele, B. M. (1991). Perinatal cocaine effects on neonatal stress behavior and performance on the Brazelton Scale. *Pediatrics, 88,* 477-480.

Eyler, F. D., Behnke, M., Conlon, M., Woods, N. S., & Wobie, K. (1998). Birth outcome from a prospective, matched study of prenatal crack/cocaine use: I. Interactive and dose effects on health and growth. *Pediatrics, 101,* 229-237.

Finkelstein, N., Kennedy, C., Thomas, K., & Kearns, M. (1997). *Gender-specific substance abuse treatment.* Alexandria, VA: National Women's Resource Center for the Prevention and Treatment of Alcohol, Tobacco and Other Drug Abuse and Mental Illness.

Florida Statutes, ch. 415.503(9)(a)(2) (1991).

Frank, D. A., Bauchner, H., Parker, S., Huber, A. M., Kyei-Aboagye, K., Cabral, H., & Zuckerman, B. (1990). Neonatal body proportionality and body composition after in-utero exposure to cocaine and marijuana. *Journal of Pediatrics, 117,* 622-626.

Fried, P. A., & Watkinson, B. (1990). 36-and 48-month neurobehavioral follow-up of children prenatally exposed to marijuana, cigarettes, and alcohol. *Developmental and Behavioral Pediatrics, 11,* 49-58.

Garcia, J., & Keilitz, I. (1991). Involuntary civil commitment of drug-dependent persons with special reference to pregnant women. *Mental and Physical Disability Legal Report, 15,* 418.

Garcia, S. (1992). Drug addiction and mother/child welfare. *Journal of Legal Medicine, 13,* 129-161.

Grodin v. Grodin, 301 N.W.2d 869 (Mich. Ct. App., 1980).

Hoffman, J. (1990, August 19). Pregnant, addicted—and guilty? *New York Times,* sec. 6, p. 34.

Howard, J., Beckwith, L., & Rodning, C. (1989). The development of young children of substance-abusing parents: Insights from seven years of intervention and research. *Zero to Three, 9,* 8-12.

Hurt, H., Brodsky, N. L., Betancourt, L., Braitman, L. E., Malmud, E., & Giannetta, J. (1995). Cocaine-exposed children: Follow-up through 30 months. *Journal of Substance Abuse, 7,* 267-280.

Illinois Department of Children and Family Services, Office of the Inspector General. (1997). *Recommendations for improving the state's child welfare response to families affected by parental substance abuse.* Springfield, IL: Illinois Department of Children and Family Services.

Illinois Public Act 90-13, 750 ILCS 50/1(D)(r) (1998).

Indiana Code, Ann. § 31-6-4-3.1 (West 1989 Cum. Supp.).

In re Chan-Charay T., 1996 WL 689930 (Conn. Super., November 20, 1996).

In re Fetus Brown, Ill. App. 1st Dist. No. 1-96-2316, December 31, 1997 slip op.

In re Madyun, 114 Daily Wash. L. Rptr. 2233 (1986).

In re Ruiz, 27 Ohio Misc.2d 31, 500 N.E.2d 935 (Ohio Ct. Comm. Please, 1986).

In re Smith, 128 Misc.2d 976, 492 N.Y.S.2d 331 (N.Y. Fm. Ct., 1985).

In the Interest of Fetus Brown, Cook County, Ill., Child Protection Division, June 28, 1996.

In the Interest of Guillory, 618 S.W.2d 948 (Ct. Civ. App. Tex. 1981).

Jefferson v. Griffin Spalding County Hospital Authority, 247 Ga. 86, 274 S.E.2d 457 (1981).

Johnson v. Florida, 602 So.2d 1288 (1992).

Kelly, S. J. (1992). Parenting stress and child maltreatment in drug-exposed children. *Child Abuse & Neglect, 16,* 317-328.

Kelly, S. J., Walsh, J. H., & Thompson, K. (1991). Prenatal exposure to cocaine: Birth outcomes, health problems and child neglect. *Pediatric Nursing, 17,* 130-135.

Lester, B. M., Corwin, M. J., Sepkoski, C., Seifer, R., Peucher, M., McLaughlin, S., & Golum, H. L. (1991). Neurobehavioral syndromes in cocaine-exposed newborn infants. *Child Development, 62,* 694-705.

Massachusetts General Laws, c. 119, § 51A (1990 ed.).

Mayes, L. C., Bornstein, M. H., Chawarska, K., & Granger, R. H. (1995). Information processing and developmental assessments in 3-month-old infants exposed prenatally to cocaine. *Pediatrics, 95,* 539-545.

Minnesota Statutes, § 626.556 (Supp. 1989).

Minnesota Statutes, Ann. § 626.5561 (West 1990 Cum Supp.).

Minnesota Statutes, Ann. § 243B.02(2) (West 1991).

National Committee for Prevention of Child Abuse. (1989). *Substance Abuse and Child Abuse Fact Sheet.* Chicago: Author.

National Institute on Drug Abuse. (1994). *National pregnancy and health survey.* Rockville, MD: U.S. Department of Health and Human Services.

Nulman, I., Rovet, J., Altmann, D., Bradley, C., Einarson, T., & Koren, G. (1995). Neurodevelopment of adopted children exposed in utero to cocaine: Comments. *Journal of Development and Behavioral Pediatrics, 16,* 418-30.

Oklahoma Statutes, Ann. Title X, § 1101(4) (West 1990 Cum. Supp.).

Ornoy, A., Michailevskaya, V., Lukashov, I., Bar-Hamburger, R., & Harel, S. (1994). The developmental outcome of children born to heroin-dependent mothers, raised at home or adopted. *Canadian Medical Association Journal of Medicine, 151,* 1591-1597.

Raleigh Fitkin-Paul Morgan Memorial Hospital v. Anderson, 42 N.J. 421, 201 A.2d 537 (N.J. 1964).

Roe v. Wade, 410 U.S. 113 (1973).

Sherman, R. (1991). Courts disagree on mother's liability. *National Law Journal,* p. 30.

Singer, L. T., Garber, R., & Kliegman,R. (1991). Neurobehavioral sequelae of fetal cocaine exposure. *Journal of Pediatrics, 119,* 667-672.

Smith Hurd Ann., 705 ILCS 405/2-3 (1989).

Smith Hurd Ann., 625 ILCS 5/11-501 (West 1996).

South Carolina Code, Ann. § 20-7-50 (1985).

Stallman v. Youngquist, 125 Ill. 2d 267, 531 N.E.2d 355 (1988).

State v. Dunn, Wash. App. 122, 916 P.2d 952 (Ct. App. Wash. 1996).

Streissguth, A., Sampson, P., & Barr, H. (1989). Neurobehavioral dose-response effects of prenatal alcohol exposure in humans from infancy to adulthood. *Annals of the New York Academy of Sciences, 562,* 145-158.

Tronick, E. Z., Frank, D. A., Cabral, H., Mirochnik, M., & Zuckerman, B. (1996). Late dose response effects of prenatal cocaine exposure on newborn neurobehavioral performance. *Pediatrics, 98,* 76-83.

U.S. Department of Health and Human Services, Center for Substance Abuse Prevention. (1993). *Maternal Substance Use Assessment Methods Reference Manual* (U.S.DHHS Publication No. (SMA)93-2059). Rockville, MD: Author.

Whitner v. State, 1996 WL 393164 (S.C., July 15, 1996).

Wilton, J. (1991). Compelled hospitalization and treatment during pregnancy: Mental health statutes as models for legislation to protect children from prenatal drug and alcohol exposure. *Family Law Quarterly, 25,* 149.

Wisconsin Statutes, § 48.02(2) (1985).

Wisconsin Statutes, § 940.04(2)(a) (1997).

Fatal Child Neglect

BARBARA L. BONNER
SHEILA M. CROW
MARY BETH LOGUE

A 4-month-old infant died from massive trauma after being ejected from the front seat of a car in a traffic collision. The child was not secured in an infant car seat.

An 18-month-old toddler fell from a second-story window and suffered fatal head injuries. The window had no window guards, and the child had climbed onto the windowsill when his mother thought he was asleep in the room.

A 6-month-old infant was found dead, covered with roach bites, in substandard housing. The medical examiner found no anatomical cause of death and ruled the child died from sudden infant death syndrome.

An 8-year-old boy drowned in a neighbor's covered above-ground pool after he became trapped under the cover to retrieve a toy he dropped in the pool. There was no fence around the pool.

A 6-year-old boy fatally shot his 4-year-old brother with a handgun he found in the pocket of a coat hanging in the closet. The parents were in the next room watching television.

A parent failed to follow through with recommended treatment for her child's asthma. The child died during an acute asthma attack.

Children die each year as a result of neglect on the part of their parents, other caregivers, and the community. To date, the focus on child deaths resulting from maltreatment has been on abuse-related deaths, such as death due to head trauma or internal injuries following a beating. These deaths often have dramatically apparent medical findings that indicate the cause of death, although determining who inflicted the injuries can be highly problematic for investigators. In contrast, deaths from neglect can occur as a result of inadequacies in physical protection, supervision, nutrition, or health care. These deaths may leave less obvious clues to the etiology, and ultimately, the responsibility of parents, caregivers, or the community. Thus, deaths due to child neglect can be more difficult to investigate and prosecute and can result in a lack of protection for siblings, other children in the household, and children in the general population.

The distinction between deaths due to neglect and deaths due to abuse is whether or not the cause of death was an error of omission (neglect) or an act of commission (abuse) (Erickson & Egeland, 1995). Although there are numerous case reports and studies that describe child deaths due to neglect, there continues to be considerable controversy about how fatal neglect is defined, how cases are established, and therefore how fatal child neglect is assessed, described, and prevented. Nevertheless, child deaths due to neglect are an increasingly important area for professional attention (Lung & Daro, 1996).

This chapter will present a broad overview of what is known about fatal child neglect, including definition, incidence, etiology, investigation, and the current professional and societal responses to this issue.

DEFINING FATAL NEGLECT

Fatal neglect is narrowly defined as death due to parental (or caregiver) failure to provide a reasonable standard of care. Rosenberg (1994) identified three primary parental responsibilities, with the understanding that if these are not fulfilled, the result may be fatal child neglect. In general, parents or the primary caretakers have a responsibility to provide for the needs of the child, supervise the child adequately, and intervene appropriately to prevent harm. What constitutes reasonable provision, supervision, and intervention will largely depend on the collective views of physicians, lawyers, schools, social services, and others within that community (Rosenberg, 1994).

There is no standard definition of death due to neglect across disciplines or, for that matter, within disciplines. Legal definitions of neglect, for example, vary widely among jurisdictions but may contain similar underlying principles (Bulkley, Feller, Stern, & Roe, 1996). The same is true among the medical and social services professions. For example, a physician may view the death as accidental and a child protective service (CPS) worker may view the death as an accident that was neglect related. A death attributed to neglect by law enforcement may lead to prosecution, whereas death attributed to an accident that was neglect related by CPS personnel may lead only to parent education and increased prevention services for the protection of other children in the home. In the examples provided at the beginning of the chapter, whether or not the death is attributed to neglect likely depends as much on who is evaluating the case and for what purpose as it does on the circumstances of the death itself.

Fatal child neglect may also be broadly defined as a multidimensional problem that requires a focus on all possible determinants of the death: the risk of actual versus potential harm, the severity of the likely harm to the child, and the frequency and chronicity of the situation or the circumstances in which the neglect occurred. Rather than focusing on unidimensional causes (e.g., parental failure), Dubowitz and Black (1996) advocate a focus on all elements of the system in which a neglected child lives. Parents have the ultimate responsibility of protecting and providing for their children, but society has a responsibility as well. A public health approach to child neglect deaths includes attention to the assessment of risk that goes beyond the individual child and caregiver and includes other individuals in the community as well as law enforcement, CPS, community groups or agencies, schools and legislative bodies. Community standards of care (e.g., housing regulations on fencing pools) and tolerance of hazards to children (e.g., acceptance of unsecured handguns in the home or violence in the neighborhood) are important factors implicated in child neglect and the deaths that may result. Such a broad focus in defining fatal neglect invites an equally broad range of targets for prevention. However, not all purposes are well served by broad definitions. For example, attorneys and judges interested in criminal prosecution are more interested in a narrow definition focused on responsibility and blame of individuals rather than of groups or conventions in society.

In summary, fatal child neglect is usually defined as the death of a child due to parental failure to provide for a child's needs adequately, supervise a child, or intervene to protect a child from harm. The responsibility to meet these needs falls primarily on parents, although other caregivers, community members, and society as a whole share in this responsibility. Despite the apparent simplicity of this definition, when applied to real-life circumstances, defining neglect and assessing responsibility are complex issues. A more complete discussion of these complexities and controversies is presented in the following sections.

Incidence

The U.S. Advisory Board on Child Abuse and Neglect (1995) estimated conservatively that each year, nearly 2,000 children under the age of 18 die from child maltreatment. The major causes of death for all children included natural causes (diseases or medical problems), non-inflicted (i.e., accidental) injuries, homicide, and suicide. Deaths due to neglect can be found in all of these categories. Diseases or medical problems include such things as congenital heart disease, ingestion of toxins or poisons, pneumonia, and meningitis. Neglect may be implicated in any of these conditions in the failure to seek or follow through with medical attention in a timely manner. Non-inflicted injuries include drowning, burns, falls, gunshot wounds, and motor vehicle crashes, among other causes. Neglect in deaths due to injury or poisoning may involve a failure to supervise children, secure hazardous materials, or to protect children from dangerous situations. Homicide deaths include those in which the child was abused as well as those in which a child was the intended or unintended victim of other crime. In these instances, neglect may be a failure to protect children from dangerous situations. In suicide deaths of children, the failure to secure adequate mental health services may be a form of neglect.

A frequently used source of national mortality data is the National Center for Health Statistics (NCHS), a division of the Centers for Disease Control and Prevention. According to the most recent data, 59,661 children, 0 through 19 years of age, died in 1995 in the United States (Anderson, Kochanek, & Murphy, 1997). Of these, 13,234 (22%) deaths are attributed to unintentional ("accidental") injuries,[1] making it the leading cause of death in children older than 1 year of age. Within the unintentional-injuries category, fatal traffic accidents accounted for the deaths of 8,227 children (62%), drowning for 1,502 deaths (11%), fire and burn injuries for 877 deaths (7%), suffocation for 739 deaths (6%), falls and poisoning for 476 deaths (3%), and other causes, 1,413 (11%). The extent to which neglect was a factor in these deaths depends on the definition of neglect used by the professionals investigating the deaths.

Anderson et al. (1997) reported that suicide accounted for the deaths of 2,227 children ages 0 through 19. Of these children, 85% were 15 through 19 years of age. Homicide accounted for the deaths of 4,586 children ages 0 through 19, with 71% of those children being between the ages 15 through 19. Three hundred and eleven (7%) of the children were under 1 year of age; 452 (10%) were aged 1 through 4; 157 (3%) were aged 5 through 9; and 404 (9%) were aged 10 through 14. Firearms were the most frequently used weapon in both homicide and suicide deaths. Although homicide deaths result from acts of commission, neglect may be a factor that increases a child's risk of death in some homicide cases. One example is when a gun is left unsecured in a home and a child shoots another child while playing with the weapon (Wintemute, Teret, Kraus, Wright, & Bradfield, 1987). The report also identified 127 children less than 1 year of age who died as a result of abuse or other type of maltreatment (Anderson et al., 1997).

Through annual review of states' CPS data, the National Committee to Prevent Child Abuse has identified a steady increase in the number of child maltreatment fatalities over the past 8 years (Lung & Daro, 1996). They estimated that in 1995, there were 1,248 child deaths in the United States and the District of Columbia—a figure 4 times higher than the NCHS data for that same year. From 1993 to 1995, for the 26 states that identified the type of maltreatment causing the death, Lung and Daro estimated that 37% of the deaths were determined to be neglect related, 48% were abuse related, and 15% were the result of both types of maltreatment. Thus, approximately 650 deaths in 1995 were attributed to neglect.

There are several problems in estimating the number of fatalities due to neglect or child maltreatment in general. First, complete and accurate information about the numbers and circumstances of deaths is often unavailable (Anderson et al., 1991). For example, if two young children are left alone at night and die in a house fire but information about the supervision of the children is not recorded, the deaths may be attributed to an accident without indicating that neglect was involved. Second, the current classification system (International Classification of Diseases, 9th edition [ICD-9; World Health Organization, 1977]) for specifying child maltreatment deaths is "based on an outmoded approach that narrowly focuses on the Battered Child Syndrome" (U.S. Advisory Board on Child Abuse and Neglect, 1995, p. 23). Thus, even if the children's deaths in the previous example were determined to be neglect related, the death certificates would still list the cause of death as accidental, and the current vital statistics system would not record parental neglect as a contributing cause. Many professionals would concur that in these cases, the death certificates' causes of death were not accurate or complete.

One study (McClain, Sacks, Froehlke, & Ewigman, 1993) found that the magnitude of abuse and neglect fatalities could be estimated by using death certificate data and statistical estimation models that account for the limitations of current attributions of cause of death. They estimated that about 85% of child maltreatment deaths are not recorded as such on death certificates. This miscoding on death certificates may be the result of limitations in the ICD-9, a failure to recognize child maltreatment, definitional inconsistencies, or a reluctance to add blame or stigma to grieving parents.

In summary, the actual number of children who die as a result of neglect each year is not known. Inaccurate and incomplete information, coupled with an outdated death classification system and miscoding of neglect-related deaths on death certificates, contributes to the uncertainty of the number of child-neglect-related deaths.

ETIOLOGY OF NEGLECT FATALITIES

When a child dies from neglect, the parents are typically viewed as being involved or having caused the death. However, in some cases, this is likely an oversimplification of a problem with multiple causes. Ultimately, parents are responsible for their children's safety, but there are numerous environmental factors that can affect parents' ability to protect their children. Dubowitz and Black (1996) advocate for a comprehensive approach to the problem of fatal child neglect and recommend assessment of multiple and interacting factors, including individual characteristics (of both child and caregiver), family characteristics, the community within which the child lived, and broader society.

Little research has been done in the identification of factors that differentiate parents who neglect their children and parents who fatally neglect their children. Rarely are parents available for evaluation to examine risk factors that may differentiate these two groups. Korbin (1994) has identified several risk factors associated with fatally maltreating parents: poverty, stressful life circumstances, history of childhood abuse, substance abuse, domestic violence, and so forth. Many parents, however, may have one or all of these risk factors and still do not abuse or neglect their children. Thus, no clear statements about parental factors associated with fatal neglect can be made at this time.

In the following section, we describe several types of fatalities that can be attributed to neglect, with a discussion of how these contributory factors may be implicated. The types of fatalities described include those due to inadequate supervision or exposure to hazards and lack of medical or mental health care. There are other types of neglect-related deaths (e.g., abandonment, lack of protection in motor vehicles). Those described here represent what we believe are the most common forms of neglect-related death.

Inadequate Supervision-Hazard Exposure

Recently, there has been a trend to distinguish between fatalities that are a result of lack of supervision and those that are a result of chronic neglect (Ewigman, Kivlahan, & Land, 1993; Zuravin, 1991). Supervisory neglect involves a clear absence of parental or adult supervision that places a child at significant risk or harm. Consider the example of a parent who leaves two children, ages 4 and 6, alone for several hours. If exposed to a significant, dangerous hazard during that time (e.g., falling into a swimming pool or setting a fire), the children could die as a result of a single instance of supervisory neglect. Chronic neglect fatalities are characterized by a long-standing pattern of neglect that results in a child's death. For example, a child may die of malnutrition after a parent consistently fails to recognize and respond to a child's nutritional needs.

Failure to supervise children around potentially dangerous environments (e.g., bodies of water) or a lack of supervision that allows children to create hazards (e.g., leaving matches or cigarette lighters available to a curious child) can be a critical factor in child deaths due to neglect. It is also likely that the role of neglect may be underreported in these types of deaths. Two of the most common types of such deaths are those due to smoke inhalation from fires set by children and those due to drowning.

Smoke Inhalation

It is estimated that in 1995, approximately 877 children less than 19 years of age (more than 500 were less than 5 years of age) died as a result of unintentional residential fires (NCHS, 1997).

Most fires in which children die are set by children, the result of children playing with fire rather than arson (Federal Emergency Management Agency [FEMA], 1993). Children typically die from smoke inhalation because they are unable to escape or become confused and attempt to hide from the fire. The major contributors to deaths from fires set by children are the ready availability of combustibles, inadequate supervision, and the lack of working smoke detectors (FEMA, 1993).

A 10-year study of Scottish house fires found that in nearly 30% of the cases involving the deaths of children, alcohol was an important factor. Of these cases, the majority involved a parent who was intoxicated at the time of the fire (Squires & Busuttil, 1995). The authors further state that child fatalities as a result of house fires can frequently be attributed to negligent parental behavior. Even though a parent cannot be expected to provide immediate supervision of a child 24 hours a day, it can be expected that a parent would secure combustibles from children's access, provide appropriate fire safety information and training, and be in the vicinity to assist in an escape or to extinguish a fire.

Case History

M. A. and S. W., half-siblings aged 15 months and 24 months, perished in a house fire. The fire scene investigation report indicated that at the time of the fire, six children under 5 years of age were playing in the house while the parents slept. The children ignited curtains with a cigarette lighter. They threw blankets, toys, shoes, and other items on the fire to try to extinguish the flames. Once the fire started across the ceiling, four of the children left the bedroom, shut themselves in the bathroom, and began crying for help. M. A. and S. W. would not go into the bathroom and ran to other parts of the house. The father rescued the four children in the bathroom but was unable to rescue the other two children. The father was severely burned, but the mother escaped without injury.

The oldest child was interviewed and stated that the children never thought about waking up their parents. He told the fire investigator that he had been responsible for starting another house fire 2 years earlier because he was cold and "mommy would not wake up to get the house warm." He further reported he did not like starting fires, but he liked putting them out. Three months before the fire, a report for neglect of S. W. and another sibling was ruled uncertain by CPS.

The State Fire Marshall's Office determined that the fire fatalities were a result of negligence by the landlord and the parents. The landlord had failed to install a smoke detector in the rental property as required by law, and the parents were aware that the oldest child enjoyed playing with fire and posed a safety threat. The cause of the fire was determined to be accidental. The failure to provide a smoke detector in a residential dwelling and the failure to show the tenant how to use and maintain the smoke detector resulted in a misdemeanor charge being filed on the landlord—a fine not less than $50 and not more than $100.

This case is an excellent example of the combination of parental and environmental neglect factors that can lead to a child's death. The parents were seen by CPS as neglectful due to lack of supervision, and the landlord was held responsible for not properly installing a smoke detector.

Drowning

In 1995, there were 1,567 deaths of children less than 18 years of age due to drowning (NCHS, 1997). More than a third of those cases were children under 5 years. Children can drown in any body of water (i.e., swimming pools, bathtubs, hot tubs, buckets, ponds, lakes, rivers, or drainage ditches). There are several studies that examine or discuss childhood drowning and the possibility of neglect (Budnick & Ross, 1985; Feldman, Monastersky, & Feldman, 1993; Griest & Zumwalt, 1989; Lavelle, Shaw, Seidl, & Ludwig, 1995; Schmidt & Madea, 1995; Wintemute, 1992). These studies indicated that most drowning deaths due to neglect occur in the bathtub (especially for children under 5 years of age) and around swimming pools.

Bathtub drowning or near-drowning from neglect results from inadequate supervision, including supervision by an older child (Budnick & Ross, 1985). A 10-year retrospective review of 21 cases of pediatric bathtub near-drowning found 67% to be suspicious for abuse or neglect (Lavelle et al., 1995). The children ranged in age from 4 months to 6 years, with

75% under age 2 and 48% under age 1. Griest and Zumwalt (1989) suggested that maltreatment deaths due to bathtub drowning may be underreported because of a lack of definitive physical evidence of abuse or neglect and the reliance on histories provided by caregivers to establish the cause of death. Gillenwater, Quan, and Feldman (1996) recommended attention be paid to factors that might be indicators of abuse or neglect in the investigation of child drowning. These include a history that is inconsistent with physical findings or reports of other witnesses, prior history of abuse or neglect, delay in seeking medical care, or a lack of adequate supervision.

Private swimming pools are another site of child deaths due to neglect. A recent review of research on swimming pool deaths found that two thirds of the children were being supervised by a parent, with a momentary lapse in supervision immediately preceding the drowning (Wintemute, 1992). Although acknowledging the brief lack of supervision as a contributing factor, Wintemute (1992) stated that complete pool fencing, as is required by law in some localities, is the most promising prevention strategy and could, in fact, reduce drowning and near-drowning by 50% to 80%.

A report from the United Kingdom argues for increased supervision of children in bathtubs and around recreational water sites (Kemp & Sibert, 1992). These authors further suggested that increased water safety education for children, more lifeguards at public pools and beaches, and enforcement of life jacket laws could reduce child deaths due to drowning.

These recommendations for broader community interventions are consistent with the notion that drowning deaths are due not only to a caretaker's failure to supervise but also to society's negligence in providing adequate safeguards.

Case History

B. V., a 2-year-old male, was found lying face down in the bathtub by an 8-year-old sent to check on him. He had been placed in the bathtub by his mother, who then went to the kitchen and was absent for approximately 10 minutes. B. V. was transported by ambulance to a local hospital. He was unresponsive and had a rectal temperature of 90 degrees Fahrenheit. After medical treatment, the child's breathing resumed, and he was transported to a tertiary care hospital. B. V. remained in the pediatric intensive care unit for 9 days with minimal brain function and no response to any stimuli. He was then transferred to a standard hospital room where he died 2 days later. The mother refused to have an autopsy performed. Subsequently, the death certificate was signed by an attending physician, and the cause of death was pneumonia with anoxic brain injury as a result of near-drowning. The CPS worker advised B. V's mother that 10 minutes was too long to leave a 2-year-old in the bathtub unsupervised. B. V.'s mother replied that she had done it many times before and that nothing had happened.

Further examination of the medical chart revealed that prior to B. V.'s death, he had a sibling who had experienced an apparent life-threatening event (previously termed "near miss" sudden infant death syndrome). The sibling was placed on cardiac and apnea (breathing) monitors for 7 to 8 months. In addition, B. V. had been to the children's hospital approximately 2 weeks prior for a major injury to his big toe. B. V.'s toe had been severed and required numerous stitches. The mother stated that this incident was a result of the 4-year-old brother slamming the door on B. V.'s foot. Furthermore, B. V. had been seen in a different local hospital for a finger fracture the month before his death. None of the available reports indicated the mother's history of how the finger fracture occurred.

No charges were filed in the death of B. V.

This case illustrates chronic supervisory neglect but also shows that a child's death can occur in a short period of time. The mother's self-reported practice of leaving the children in the bathtub unsupervised is an example of a pattern of chronic failure to supervise in a manner appropriate for the age and development of the child. Also note that the series of suspicious events that preceded the death did not result in protective or preventive services for the family.

Other types of deaths include falls from unprotected windows (e.g., from high-rise apartments) or from baby walkers that contribute to toddlers tumbling down stairs. If such incidents suggest inadequate protection or supervision of the child, they should be evaluated for the possibility of neglect to protect other children in the home.

Medical Neglect

Medical neglect has various forms that could place a child at significant risk of death or actually result in the death of a child. Medical neglect occurs when a parent does not comply with medical recommendations (e.g., not filling prescriptions or not administering the medications), fails to seek or delays seeking appropriate health care (e.g., not having a child evaluated immediately for burns or other injuries), fails to recognize medical problems (e.g., serious signs or symptoms of illness are not seen to be significant), refuses treatment because of religious commitment or affiliation (e.g., refusing blood transfusions or procedures that could be lifesaving, relying on religious healers and rejecting medical treatment), or prenatally exposes a child to drugs (e.g., cocaine or alcohol). The Centers for Disease Control and Prevention do not maintain statistics specifically for deaths related to medical neglect, thus the actual numbers of deaths are unknown.

Assessment and intervention in medical neglect require that health care providers and child welfare workers take into account the caregiver's ability to recognize the importance of treatment and his or her ability to comply with medical recommendations. A parent's ability to comply involves access to medical services; available transportation; and funds to pay for services, medications, and supplies. Interventions may involve education, home health follow-up, and financial and transportation assistance.

Case History

R. S., a 7-month-old infant with respiratory problems, was brought to a local emergency room. The parents left the hospital after police were called to intervene in a fight between the parents. The family returned to the hospital later that day but again left the hospital during a fight before the infant was seen by medical staff. The infant was brought to the hospital the next day by a maternal grandfather. R. S. was hospitalized and treated for severe respiratory distress and malnutrition. The physician noted that the child was the size of a newborn infant.

The CPS record stated that both parents currently abused drugs and alcohol and that the mother reported using crack, marijuana, and alcohol during her pregnancy. Both parents had outstanding warrants for their arrest, and both had served time in prison.

R. S. died of multiple organ dysfunction and pneumonia after 5 days in the hospital. The medical examiner ruled the death as due to natural causes. However, CPS workers determined that the death was due to medical neglect. R. S.'s sibling was removed from the home and placed in protective custody. No criminal investigation was conducted because of the medical examiner's opinion.

Although it is a rare event and one not heretofore discussed in the fatal-neglect literature, suicide accounts for a significant number of child deaths each year. The NCHS reported 2,227 suicides in 1995 in children under 19 years of age (NCHS, 1997). Of these, 15% were under 15 years of age. These deaths may be neglect related if parents fail to follow through with treatment recommendations (e.g., opting for outpatient counseling rather than the recommended inpatient treatment following a suicide attempt) or if parents fail to recognize signs and symptoms indicative of serious mental health problems. In addition to the parent's role in suicide deaths, societal and economic factors (including the relative unavailability of adequate insurance coverage for mental health problems, long waiting lists for appropriate care, and the stigma that mental health problems and treatment carries) also contribute to suicide deaths.

Other Fatal Injuries

Child deaths can result from other injuries, such as suffocation (679 deaths), poisoning (258 deaths), and falls (219 deaths) (NCHS, 1997). These deaths may also be the result of neglect. Failure to secure hazards (e.g., tying drapery cords up out of the reach of children; storing poisons in locked, inaccessible cabinets; installing window guards) and failure to provide adequate, age-appropriate supervision can result in injury or death.

EVALUATION, INTERVENTION, AND PROTECTION

If the definition of fatal neglect is expanded to involve multiple levels of the system in which a child lives, then evaluation and intervention efforts should address these levels. A comprehensive evaluation of a child's death would include assessment of the potential contributory factors, including parental, community, and societal factors. At the parental level, a thorough review of the circumstances in which the death occurred should be conducted by trained law enforcement, health care, and CPS personnel. This should include evaluation of the cause of death, the degree to which the parent's explanation of how the injury or death occurred matches the medical findings, previous reports for maltreatment of the child or siblings, and any delay in seeking medical care. A thorough evaluation of the site of injury or death ("death scene") is essential.

The nature of intervention and the approach for working with families depends on many factors, including their receptivity to assistance. In cases in which a death was determined to be accidental or from natural causes and the parents were not seen as responsible, the family may have friends, other family members, or religious ties that provide support and assistance. In other cases, where there are suspicions that the parents were negligent but the findings are unsubstantiated, the family may be highly resentful of the intrusion by law enforcement, CPS, and other agencies, and they may refuse any services.

Other cases may result in a determination that the parents were neglectful, and although criminal charges are not filed, a service plan is developed by CPS, perhaps monitored by the court. For example, if there are other children in the family that could be at risk for maltreatment, a family may be required to make necessary repairs to the home or to move to a safer home. Parents may be required to attend safety education or parenting classes, and additional services, such as an in-home parent aid, may be assigned to the family. A CPS case worker will work with the family to ensure that the service plan is completed.

Some factors guiding the intervention include the severity of the neglect and the resultant harm to the child, the probability that injury would occur as a result of this kind of neglect, the parent's capacity for judgment, and the community's standard of reasonable care. For example, two children were killed when they were hit by an oncoming train while trying to cross a train trestle with their father. Crossing train trestles is a rare event, and education about train safety and danger might be sufficient to prevent such deaths. However, the likelihood of survival after being hit by a train is very small, thus rendering this situation very dangerous. In another example, a depressed parent might be chronically unaware of increasing complications (e.g., mild pain crises) of a child's sickle cell disease. This initially results in low-grade but long-term discomfort for the child but places him or her at greater risk for other more serious medical complications (e.g., stroke). In this instance, appropriate intervention might be increasing supervision of the parent regarding medical issues, arranging for evaluation and treatment of the parent's depression, and securing reliable transportation and telephone access so the parent can maintain contact with medical professionals.

Prosecution of the parent or caregiver is sometimes sought as an intervention after other children in the household have been protected. It can be argued that prosecution serves only to intervene at the level of the parent or caregiver, with little or no effect on the other systemic factors that play roles in fatal child neglect. However, as case law accumulates, precedent is set and community standards for definitions of neglect evolve. Thus, in addition to punishing neglecting parents and protecting other children in the home, prosecution plays an important role at the societal level in addressing issues of neglect. Rosenberg (1994) suggested that the following criteria be used in making a decision about prosecuting a parent for supervisory neglect. These same standards can also inform decisions about prosecution of other types of neglect (failure to provide, failure to intervene). She suggested that any decision about prosecution take into account the following factors: (a) age and developmental stage of the child, (b) length of time child was unsupervised, (c) circumstances of the lack of supervision, (d) parent's mental and physical capacities, (e) history of supervision, (f) ethnic-cultural view of parental care, and (g) the extent to which the neglect is income related.

Prevention

A public health approach to fatal child neglect targets three populations for prevention efforts. *Primary* prevention efforts are directed at the general population and include such issues as bicycle and helmet use, infant car seats, life jacket laws, and immunizations. *Secondary* prevention interventions are targeted to a group of people thought to be at increased risk for fatal neglect. For example, people with children who live in high-rise apartment buildings might be warned to install window guards, communities with older buildings with lead-based paint might enact laws on lead abatement, and neighborhoods with swimming pools might have ordinances about pool fencing to prevent accidental drowning. *Tertiary* prevention measures are applied to those who have already experienced a child fatality. These take the form of intervening with and protecting other children in the home. This is the most difficult level of prevention for service providers but often has a galvanizing effect on many people. For example, after the death of a child who had been returned to his abusing parents, the state of Oklahoma enacted sweeping changes in child protection laws.

Fatality Review Teams

One response to the problem of child maltreatment fatalities has been the establishment of child death review teams (CDRTs) at the state and local levels. Currently, all 50 states have state or local (or both) child death review boards or teams that review child deaths (M. Durfee, personal communication, September 5, 1997). CDRTs are multidisciplinary groups, with membership that varies across jurisdictions. Typically, membership consists of medical examiners, CPS personnel, pediatricians, law enforcement, and public health professionals. Some teams are legislatively mandated, with mandates that specify those agencies required to provide the team with case information (e.g., medical examiner reports, law enforcement records). In other states, interagency agreements allow for the exchange of records and information. CDRT reviews typically examine abuse-related or neglect-related deaths as certified by the medical examiner or coroner, but over time, teams tend to expand their purview to include all types of child deaths. Review of deaths by these teams sometimes changes the official attribution of the cause of death. For example, a death initially attributed to accidental drowning may be attributed to homicide following the CDRT review. The number of cases reviewed varies widely from state to state by number of deaths, size of state, and jurisdiction of the team. CDRTs are seen as playing an important role in addressing the problems of fatal child neglect. By evaluating patterns seen in cases reviewed, CDRTs can draw attention to educational needs of professionals who investigate child deaths, and they can make recommendations for policies to improve prevention efforts.

CONCLUSIONS AND RECOMMENDATIONS

This chapter provided an overview of fatal child neglect. Although there is a growing recognition of the role that neglect plays in child fatalities, research and prevention efforts are hampered by the lack of a clear definition of fatal neglect.

The best estimates suggest that there are approximately 650 neglect-related deaths per year in the United States, although the incidence of fatal neglect depends on how neglect is defined. Estimation is also hampered by incomplete information on the circumstances of deaths, a death classification system that misattributes neglect-related deaths, and a lack of expertise in child maltreatment on the part of those who investigate child deaths. The investigation and evaluation of child deaths should include a comprehensive assessment of all factors involved in the death, not just parental responsibility. This evaluation may lead to primary, secondary, and tertiary prevention measures.

Our ability to count and prevent deaths due to neglect would be greatly enhanced by standardization of definitions and data collection and increased training for those investigating and intervening with fatal child neglect (CPS workers, law enforcement, courts, medical examiners, and other health professionals). With increased attention to this matter, more effective efforts can be directed to reducing the number of child deaths due to neglect.

NOTE

1. The concept of intentionality as it relates to neglect is controversial. It can be argued that parents rarely intend to or plan to fail to protect, supervise, or provide for their children. Nevertheless, children suffer maltreatment and die as a result of unintentional but reasonably preventable neglect. The CDC report classifies deaths as intentional or unintentional, although this distinction may have little use in assessing the extent to which neglect was a factor in an injury.

REFERENCES

Anderson, R. N., Kochanek, K. D., & Murphy, S. L. (1997). Report of final mortality statistics, 1995. *Monthly Vital Statistics Report, 45*(Suppl 2). Washington, DC: National Center for Health Statistics.

Anderson, T. L., Wells, S. J., Durfee, M., Ewigman, B., Froehlke, R., Kivlahan, C., & McClain, P. (1991). *Data collection for child fatalities: Existing efforts and proposed guidelines.* Chicago: American Bar Association.

Budnick, L. D., & Ross, D. A. (1985). Bathtub-related drownings in the United States. *American Journal of Public Health, 75*(6), 630-633.

Bulkley, J. A., Feller, J. N., Stern, P., & Roe, R. (1996). Child abuse and neglect laws and legal proceedings. In J. Briere, L. Berliner, J. A. Bulkley, C. Jenny, & T. Reid (Eds.), *The APSAC handbook on child maltreatment* (pp. 271-296). Thousand Oaks, CA: Sage.

Dubowitz, H., & Black, M. (1996). Medical neglect. In J. Briere, L. Berliner, J. A. Bulkley, C. Jenny, & T. Reid (Eds.), *The APSAC handbook on child maltreatment* (pp. 227-241). Thousand Oaks, CA: Sage.

Erickson, M. F., & Egeland, B. (1995). Child neglect. In J. Briere, L. Berliner, J. A. Bulkley, C. Jenny, & T. Reid (Eds.), *The APSAC handbook on child maltreatment* (pp. 4-20). Thousand Oaks, CA: Sage.

Ewigman, B., Kivlahan, C., & Land, G. (1993). The Missouri child fatality study: Underreporting of maltreatment fatalities among children younger than five years of age, 1983 through 1986. *Pediatrics, 91,* 330-337.

Federal Emergency Management Agency. (1993). *Fire in the United States, 1983-1990* (Publication no. USFA/FA-140). Washington, DC: U.S. Fire Administration.

Feldman, K. W., Monastersky, C., & Feldman, G. K. (1993). When is childhood drowning neglect? *Child Abuse and Neglect, 17,* 329-336.

Gillenwater, J. M., Quan, L., & Feldman, K. W. (1996). Inflicted submersion in childhood. *Archives of Pediatric and Adolescent Medicine, 150,* 298-303.

Griest, K. J., & Zumwalt, R. E. (1989). Child abuse by drowning. *Pediatrics, 86,* 41-46.

Kemp, A., & Sibert, J. R. (1992). Drowning and near drowning in children in the United Kingdom: Lessons for prevention. *British Medical Journal, 304,* 1143-1146.

Korbin, J. E. (1994). Perpetrators of fatal child maltreatment. *The APSAC Advisor, 7,* 45-46.

Lavelle, J. M., Shaw, K. N., Seidl, T., & Ludwig, S. (1995). Ten-year review of pediatric bathtub near-drownings: Evaluation for child abuse and neglect. *Annals of Emergency Medicine, 25*(3), 344-348.

Lung, C. T., & Daro, D. (1996). *Current trends in child abuse reporting and fatalities: The results of the 1995 annual fifty-state survey.* Chicago: National Committee to Prevent Child Abuse.

McClain, P. W., Sacks, J. J., Froehlke, R. G., & Ewigman, B. G. (1993). Estimates of fatal child abuse and neglect, United States, 1979 through 1988. *Pediatrics, 91,* 338-343.

National Center for Health Statistics. (1997). *U.S. injury mortality statistics.* [On-line]. Available: http://www.cdc.gov/ncipc/osp/usmort.htm

Rosenberg, D. (1994). Fatal neglect. *The APSAC Advisor, 7*(4), 38-40.

Schmidt, P., & Madea, B. (1995). Death in the bathtub involving children. *Forensic Science International, 72,* 147-155.

Squires, T., & Busuttil, A. (1995). Child fatalities in Scottish house fires 1980-1990: A case of child neglect? *Child Abuse & Neglect, 19,* 865 873.

U.S. Advisory Board on Child Abuse and Neglect. (1995). *A nation's shame: Fatal child abuse and neglect in the United States.* Washington, DC: U.S. Department of Health and Human Services.

Wintemute, G. J., Draus, J. F., Teret, S. P., & Wright, M. (1987). Drowning in childhood and adolescence: A population-based study. *American Journal of Public Health, 77,* 830-832.

Wintemute, G. J., Teret, S. P., Kraus, J. F., Wright, M. A., & Bradfield, G. (1987). When children shoot children: 88 unintended deaths in California. *Journal of the American Medical Association, 257*(22), 3107-3109.

World Health Organization. (1977). *Manual of the international classification of disease, injuries, and causes of death.* Geneva, Switzerland: Author.

Zuravin, S. (1991). Research definitions of child abuse and neglect: Current problems. In R. Starr & D. Wolfe (Eds.), *The effects of child abuse and neglect: Issues and research* (pp 100-128). New York: Guilford.

9 The Prevention of Child Neglect

E. Wayne Holden
Laura Nabors

The high incidence rate and negative long-term consequences associated with child maltreatment (Starr & Wolfe, 1991) have resulted in substantial interest in prevention over the past two decades. Attention has been devoted to applying the public health model to prevent child maltreatment. Risk and protective factors have been identified, etiological models have been developed, and preventive strategies have been tested, both in small clinical trials and in larger dissemination projects. This information has significantly affected public policy and program development, with community-based programs now offering some preventive services, primarily for high-risk families. As prevention science in the area of general behavioral-mental health disorders moves into the next century (Munoz, Mrazek, & Haggerty, 1996), one can argue that significant gains in reducing the incidence and negative sequelae of child maltreatment can occur, with appropriate financial support.

Progress in the area of child maltreatment prevention, however, has been difficult to achieve due to the wide range of nonspecific risk factors involved, the complexity of etiological models, and difficulty with defining and measuring outcomes. This can be contrasted with other areas of disease prevention where fewer and perhaps more salient risk factors (e.g., exposure to hazardous materials, such as asbestos) can be targeted and structural-passive preventive intervention strategies (e.g., removal of asbestos from buildings) can be implemented that do not require complex behavioral change by multiple individuals. Furthermore, difficulties with defining and accurately measuring both proximal and distal outcomes have complicated work in child maltreatment prevention. The target for change in this area is clearly an interpersonal process rather than a traditionally defined individual outcome. Even though child mortality is an important outcome, for the most part, interventions are designed to enhance functioning that decreases maladaptive parent-child interactions and subsequent child morbidity. In addition, dissemination efforts have been hampered by complexities in the political process that limit the full implementation of soundly grounded policy initiatives and promising demonstration programs.

This chapter will focus specifically on the prevention of child neglect, the most prevalent form of child maltreatment (Gaudin, 1993). One paradox that is important to underscore is that even though neglect is the most prevalent form of child maltreatment, it has infrequently been targeted for preventive intervention (Dubowitz, 1994). This has occurred for a number of reasons, which we will attempt to address throughout this chapter. The first portion of the chapter will discuss definitional issues both with respect to child neglect and the application of prevention strategies. We will then briefly review successful prevention programs to highlight their specific applicability to the area of neglect. Afterwards, the implications of our current knowledge of the prevention of neglect for public policy and dissemination will be addressed. The chapter will conclude with specific recommendations for research, practice, and policy as we look ahead.

DEFINITIONS OF NEGLECT AND PREVENTIVE APPROACHES

Definitions of Neglect

As Zuravin has discussed in depth in Chapter 2, this volume, child neglect is difficult to define separately from other forms of child maltreatment. Broadly defined, child maltreatment refers to "any active or passive behavior denying a child his or her full potential to grow and develop" (Thyen, Thiessen, & Heinsohn-Krug, 1995, p. 1343). The recently reauthorized Child Abuse Prevention and Treatment Act (CAPTA; 1996) offered a specific definition:

> At a minimum, [child neglect is] any recent act or failure to act on the part of a parent or caretaker, which results in death or serious physical and emotional harm, or sexual abuse or exploitation, or presents an imminent risk of serious harm. (Sec. 110).

This definition narrows the targets for intervention and prevention efforts to *recent* cases involving *serious* or imminent harm. Families experiencing mild or moderate risk for child maltreatment may be more responsive to intervention efforts yet less likely to be targeted, based on this definition (Kowal et al., 1989; Willett, Ayoub, & Robinson, 1991), which offers a minimal standard that states may expand on.

As Korbin and Spilsbury discuss in Chapter 4, cultural contexts must also be taken into consideration when defining neglect. Considering contexts of neglect within an ecological model may be the optimal framework for defining and explaining (Belsky, 1991, 1993; Belsky & Vondra, 1990) neglect. An ecological approach in which child neglect is viewed as a product of parent, family, community, and societal factors is consistent with a broader view of the causes of neglect. Furthermore, an ecological approach to understanding neglect encourages the development of multicomponent prevention strategies.

Defining Prevention Strategies

Prevention strategies may be conceptualized as universal, selected, and indicated (see Daro, 1996; Daro & McCurdy, 1994; Leventhal, 1996; MacMillan, MacMillan, Offord, Griffith, & MacMillan, 1994). *Universal* strategies are primary prevention efforts directed at a whole population. These types of strategies are implemented to decrease neglect in all types of environments (Thyen et al., 1995). Although multidimensional approaches that simultaneously address multiple risk factors may be optimal, more limited prevention strategies (e.g., treating a mother's depression) may be sufficient to prevent neglect.

Ideal universal prevention efforts would encompass "all aspects of human and social behavior that place children at risk" (Daro & McCurdy,

1994, p. 106). Examples of universal strategies include programs that aim to ameliorate community neglect by attempting to reduce violence, poverty, and family isolation. Media programs that aim to increase parent knowledge of developmentally appropriate childrearing practices or to decrease parent stress and isolation are another type of universal preventive intervention that has not received significant attention. Child empowerment programs in a school district, such as those designed to prevent child sexual abuse and educate children about conflict resolution, are also examples of universal prevention strategies. Although universal strategies remain the so-called first-strike intervention in decreasing neglect, efforts to examine the efficacy of these interventions in reducing maltreatment have yielded equivocal results and are plagued with methodological problems (Daro & McCurdy, 1994). Large numbers of families that participate in universal preventive interventions need to be followed across long periods of time to provide evidence for effectiveness.

Selected intervention strategies often are equated with secondary prevention efforts. Smaller, high-risk groups of the population are targeted for preventive intervention. The objectives of selected intervention strategies are to minimize the effects of high-risk situations and to prevent episodes of child neglect. Vulnerable families or those considered to be at moderate risk, who experience stress related to poor housing conditions, inadequate transportation, financial difficulties, or poor family communication, are typically identified for selected interventions (Thyen et al., 1995). These interventions also include strategies designed to treat families with children who show mild signs of or are in the early stages of neglect (e.g., children with poor hygiene and nutrition). Selected preventive interventions typically are more comprehensive and intensive than universal interventions. For instance, nurse home visiting programs have been successful selected strategies to prevent child maltreatment (Olds et al., 1997; Olds, Henderson, Chamberlin, & Tatelbaum, 1986; Olds & Kitzman, 1993).

Indicated preventive interventions are similar to tertiary prevention efforts or treatment strategies, implemented after a problem or psychopathology has been identified. Indicated strategies aim to minimize the effects of neglect and to prevent further neglect (Thyen et al., 1995). Examples of indicated interventions include referral of a parent or a child (or both) for therapy after neglect has been confirmed. Selected and indicated interventions may provide similar services to families but target different populations (e.g., at risk vs. after the occurrence of neglect). As mentioned earlier, the cycle of maltreatment is often long-term, for both neglect and abuse (Levy, Markovic, Chaudry, Ahart, & Torres, 1995). Therefore, effective indicated interventions should be comprehensive and include follow-up to reduce the recurrence of maltreatment.

Conceptual and Theoretical Models of Neglect

Sound theoretical and empirical models of the etiology of neglect are critical as guides for developing, testing, and implementing preventive interventions. Bowlby (1988) suggested that a secure attachment bond between infants and caregivers is necessary for the infant's survival and normal development. He asserted that maltreatment, including neglectful behavior by the parent, negatively affected the quality of the infant-caregiver attachment relationship by compromising the infant's view of self and others. The attachment of a young child or infant to his or her caregiver is typically assessed using the Ainsworth "Strange Situation" paradigm (Ainsworth & Wittig, 1969), where the strength and quality of attachment is assessed by studying the child's responses to separation and reunion episodes with the caregiver and a stranger. Ainsworth and others have found that maternal unresponsiveness or insensitivity is related to child anxiety (Ainsworth, 1989; Crittenden, 1985). An anxious or insecure attachment style often is a trait displayed by young children who have experienced neglect (Crittenden & Ainsworth, 1989). Secure attachment appears to be the foundation for trust and later interpersonal relationships.

Mothers of neglected children interact with their children in a manner that has been described as withdrawn, insensitive to the child's cues and needs, understimulating, and passive (Carlson, Cicchetti, Barnett, & Braunwald, 1989; Crittenden, 1985; Crittenden & Ainsworth, 1989). Crittenden (1985) suggested that neglecting mothers exhibit a "helpless" mentality. Their affect typically is depressed or sad, and they do not see themselves as able to elicit needed help from others and do not perceive others as willing to provide needed assistance to them. This type of attitude results in a lack of parenting, and this abdication of the parental role results in neglect of children. Studying the attachment relationship between caregiver and child is a focus for research on child neglect.

Ecologically based theories, however, offer a broadly based conceptualization of the causes of neglect (Belsky, 1993; Garbarino, 1977). These theories more adequately explain the complicated interactions among individual, parental, family, community, and cultural risk factors and the occurrence of neglect. Belsky (1981, 1993) proposed an ecologically based model integrating different contributing factors to child maltreatment, such as cultural tolerance of abuse, parental history of abuse, dysfunctional parent-child interactions, and societal factors (e.g., poverty, single-parent family). He suggested that child neglect and abuse are determined by multiple, nested factors found within the child, parent, family, community, and culture.

The model developed by Belsky (1981, 1993) is a useful conceptual framework for understanding the etiology of child neglect, because this model emphasizes the importance of the *interaction* of multiple factors across individual, family, community, and cultural contexts as determinants of neglect and other forms of maltreatment. Issues related to maltreatment differ based on the child's developmental level and level of maturity (Finkelhor, 1995; Garbarino, 1992). Therefore, it is important to consider the relations among development, maturity, and ecological factors when developing, evaluating, or disseminating preventive interventions for neglect. For example, the prenatal-perinatal developmental period may be a particularly salient time for instituting preventive interventions on a family level, yet the ultimate impact of these interventions may not be apparent until later in life. Ecological and developmental frameworks for conceptualizing neglect integrate aspects of psychodynamic, behavioral, and social learning theories and remind policymakers that prevention efforts must address the most significant etiological factors (Daro & McCurdy, 1994; Willis, Holden, & Rosenberg, 1992). Effectiveness can be greatly enhanced by basing the development of preventive interventions on the best available knowledge and theoretical models of neglect.

MODEL CHILD MALTREATMENT PREVENTION PROGRAMS

As previously noted, child neglect has not been the focus of many of the preventive interventions that have been tested in the area of child maltreatment. This is due to the fact that neglect frequently co-occurs with abuse (Levy et al., 1995). In addition, etiological models specific to neglect and independent from other forms of child maltreatment are currently limited. Although some risk factors differentiating abuse from neglect have been identified, outcome variables in child maltreatment prevention programs have focused on generic proximal outcomes that are related to the occurrence of abuse or neglect (e.g., parenting skills, social support). Given the relationships of neglect to nonspecific factors that generally increase family distress, it may be important to view neglect as one of many targets for preventive intervention and to include other important aspects of family functioning. A number of excellent comprehensive reviews are currently available of the wide range of programs that have been implemented to prevent child maltreatment (Guterman, 1997; Hay & Jones, 1994; Leventhal, 1996; Olsen & Spatz-Widom, 1993; Willis et al., 1992; Wolfe, Reppucci, & Hart, 1995). These reviews generally conclude that evidence is available to support the implementation of specific strategies for preventing child maltreatment, although more work is needed to appropriately contextualize these programs and to construct better-informed developmental models of child maltreatment. The following review of two of the most frequently cited child maltreatment prevention programs will highlight their relevance to preventing neglect.

The most widely cited and methodologically elegant preventive intervention trial in the area of child maltreatment was conducted in Elmira, New York, by Olds and associates (Olds et al., 1986; Olds, Henderson, Phelps, Kitzman, & Hanks, 1993; Olds, Henderson, Tatelbaum, & Chamberlin, 1988). This randomized clinical trial evaluated the efficacy of intensive nurse home visitation during pregnancy and the first 2 years of a child's life. A wide range of proximal and distal outcomes associated with child maltreatment as well as rates of child protective service (CPS) reports to child protective services were evaluated. Early reports from this trial (Olds et al., 1986) indicated lower rates of child maltreatment in the highest risk group (e.g., teenage, single, low socioeconomic status parents) that received the most comprehensive intervention (e.g., intensive nurse home visitation services both prenatally and postnatally) with accompanying positive effects on the children's development (Olds & Henderson, 1989). However, later evaluations of outcomes indicated that the early benefits of intervention may have washed out across time, as both parents and children appeared to be functioning similarly across intervention and control groups at follow-up when children were entering the school-age years (Olds et al., 1994). Analyses of a 15-year follow-up of families participating in this project (Olds et al., 1997), however, are encouraging and suggest that families receiving nurse home visitation continued to display significantly lower rates of reported child maltreatment than control families.

Despite the fact that this clinical trial did not specifically target child neglect, the implications of its results for programs to prevent neglect are many. First, this project documented that providing appropriate professional support during difficult transition periods (e.g., prenatal-perinatal and infancy) for high-risk families is an effective strategy for developing parent and child strengths and preventing negative outcomes. Such strategies have become the cornerstone of recommendations for widespread dissemination of child maltreatment prevention programs on a national level (Leventhal, 1996). The generalization of nurse home visitation to the specific prevention of child neglect makes theoretical and intuitive sense. Second, long-term follow-up in this project indicates that the effectiveness of nurse home visitation varied across time. Extended follow-up periods are needed that track interventions whose impact may differ at different developmental stages in individual children and families. The immediate implication for programs designed to target neglect is that ideally they should follow families for long periods of time to measure varying outcomes. Programs may need to tailor interventions for specific developmental periods. Third, positive effects were detected in the highest-risk families, suggesting resources should be allocated to intensive selected interventions for at-risk populations rather than allocated to less intensive universal interventions aimed at whole populations. Greater attention needs to be devoted to measuring risk for child neglect and targeting families who are at high risk if we are to be successful in these efforts. Risk assessment is fraught with a number of problems, however. For example, many risk factors are not specific to child maltreatment but instead are predictive of many negative outcomes for children. This decreases the sensitivity and specificity of any one or set of risk factors for child maltreatment. Fourth, the preventive intervention tested in this clinical trial required substantial personnel resources across a relatively long period of time. This suggests that effective preventive interventions with high-risk families will be labor- and time-intensive with costs approximating those needed to detect and monitor families after maltreatment has occurred.

Although this nurse home visitation prevention program represents the most well-researched and documented clinical trial conducted to date in child maltreatment prevention, the most impressive demonstration project was the Healthy Start program conducted in Hawaii (Breakey &

Pratt, 1991). This project was conducted on a populationwide basis with a large percentage of all families screened at birth to identify those at high risk. Targeted families received preventive services to enhance family functioning and child development. This multidimensional prevention program included screening, nurse home visitation, coordination with other community services, and long-term follow-up until the child reached age 5.

Initial outcome evaluations of Healthy Start revealed significantly lower rates of child maltreatment compared with high-risk families who were not enrolled in the program (Fuddy, 1992). Physical abuse and neglect were prevented in approximately 99% of the families that participated in the program (Wallach & Lister, 1995). Positive developmental outcomes and improved health status were also reported for children at age 2, relative to controls. The specific intervention strategies as well as the provision of social support were likely responsible for the program's positive effects on overall rates of maltreatment. A home visitation model was used that employed closely supervised paraprofessionals as intervention agents. Paraprofessionals developed ongoing relationships with families to provide support and assist parents with skill development as well as serving as a liaison to community services (Wallach & Lister, 1995). The success of this demonstration project resulted in the Healthy Start model of family engagement and service provision being adopted by the National Committee to Prevent Child Abuse and Neglect on a national level and disseminated as Healthy Families America (Wallach & Lister, 1995).

The success of this program on a populationwide basis coupled with the results of Olds et al.'s (1986) clinical trial has prompted others to adopt similar approaches to the prevention of maltreatment. In many communities, nurse and paraprofessional home visitation programs are now available to high-risk families to enhance family functioning and child development. However, as noted by Leventhal (1996), these programs have not proliferated at the rate expected, given the evidence for their efficacy and effectiveness. *Efficacy* refers to the impact of an intervention under ideal circumstances, such as a randomized clinical trial, whereas *effectiveness* refers to the impact of an intervention under real-world conditions, such as within a community-based demonstration project.

The initial costs of such programs during times of overall fiscal constraint may be responsible for the limits placed on their generalization. Evidence for initial cost effectiveness of the Olds, Henderson, Chamberlin, et al. (1986) and the Olds, Henderson, Tatelbaum, et al. (1988) randomized clinical trials, however, has been reported (Olds et al., 1993). Savings recouped from other social service programs reduced the overall costs of providing intervention services to families in half. Savings were even higher for low-income families, with an average dividend of $180 reported. The data that are currently available regarding the short-term outcome of intensive, selected child maltreatment programs coupled with the encouraging results of this cost effectiveness analysis argue strongly that long-term cost effectiveness is likely to be found as participants in these programs are tracked longitudinally. The current absence of long-term cost effectiveness data should not deter policymakers and program developers from providing sufficient resources to support their dissemination.

As noted earlier, this brief review of exemplary prevention programs is not intended to be comprehensive but rather to underscore a number of issues important to the prevention of neglect. Given the strong association of neglect with poverty and the multitude of risk factors, independent of maltreatment, for negative child health and mental health outcomes in impoverished families, it is our contention that intensive, selected interventions for high- and moderate-risk families should be pursued as the most appropriate approach for addressing the prevention of neglect. These multimodal approaches should provide social support, parenting education, and liaison with other community social welfare, mental health, and health programs. The development of etiological models specific to child neglect is critical to the successful identification of candidate families who are likely to benefit most from specific prevention efforts. Models that assist in identifying and clarifying risk factors and developing preventive approaches at other family developmental stages beyond prenatal-perinatal or infancy are also clearly needed. For example, families with young school-age children are important targets for neglect prevention approaches.

Effective prevention services should be both general services that support families and targeted services that aim to prevent neglect (Leventhal, 1996). General services include high-quality child care, job training programs, family resource centers, programs to promote family and economic self-sufficiency, and welfare reform (Hay & Jones, 1994; Kaufman & Zigler, 1992; Leventhal, 1996). In general, prevention efforts should aim to effect positive changes in community and societal-level risk factors, such as neighborhood violence and drug trafficking, poor health care, family and community isolation, and poverty, to reduce the impact of risk factors that often lead to neglect (Hay & Jones, 1994). Viewing the prevention of neglect from a systems perspective constantly reminds us that all successful community service programs designed to support families and child development across the health, educational, and social services systems will prevent the occurrence of a range of negative outcomes for children, including neglect. Many opportunities exist for integrating strategies across systems to promote positive child development. The future success of the prevention of neglect on a communitywide basis is dependent on our ability to integrate the service systems so that families can be appropriately supported and nurtured across their developmental life span.

PUBLIC POLICY AND PREVENTION OF NEGLECT

To successfully implement prevention programs, it will be important to consider the ecological model (Belsky, 1993; Belsky & Vondra, 1990; Garbarino, 1977) of neglect. If the definition proposed in the reauthorized CAPTA (1996) is adopted by the states, prevention efforts will be aimed primarily at very high risk families, who will require intensive, selected interventions as opposed to other families at lower risk who may respond to less intensive, universal approaches (Kowal et al., 1989; Willett et al., 1991). Prevention efforts will need to be culturally sensitive, because neglect is a phenomenon embedded in sociocultural differences (Zuravin & Shay, 1991). Furthermore, to successfully implement prevention programs, policymakers; mental health, social work, and medical personnel; as well as the media will need to advocate for a change in cultural norms and public laws that portray family matters as private and children's rights as secondary to the parental right to privacy in childrearing matters (Daro, 1996; Melton, 1996). Although the effects of public education campaigns are difficult to measure, efforts to change cultural norms by affecting a societywide basis are critical to sustaining communitywide prevention efforts for families.

Policy should be based on knowledge about the incidence and causes of neglect. The field is not currently at this stage due to the difficulties in determining cause-and-effect relationships for many contributory factors (Olsen & Spatz-Widom, 1993). It has also been difficult to clarify the impact of interactions among these factors (e.g., poverty, single-parent household, and parental feelings of helplessness). In addition, neglect is a multidimensional phenomenon composed of physical, medical, psychological, and other outcomes. Effective public policy regarding the prevention of neglect should be guided by the development, support, and stimulation of research projects that address these issues. However, some factors, such as poverty, are strongly associated with neglect. The prevention of neglect should thus include efforts to address the problem of poverty.

Multidisciplinary efforts will be necessary to develop protocols with multiple outcome measures to evaluate interventions. Multiple outcome measures are important, because interventions may effect outcomes in different ways (i.e., interventions may influence some outcomes but not others) (Brunk, Henggeler, & Whelan, 1987; Drotar, 1992). Researchers need to assess the relationship between the level of training and skill of care providers (e.g., paraprofessionals, nurses, pediatricians) and outcomes. Different types of care providers may be more or less effective in working with parents for specific types of intervention programs. For example, paraprofessionals may have a greater impact for programs delivered in communities than doctors, whereas nurses or social workers may be more effective in delivering school-based prevention programs than paraprofessionals. This field is a relatively new area of investigation and therefore prospective, longitudinal studies are needed to further advance our knowledge (Daro, 1996; Peterson & Brown, 1994).

Demonstration projects need to be combined with policy and research efforts. These projects should be designed to ameliorate or reduce risk factors at multiple levels: child, parent, family, community, and cultures. Identification of additional risk factors and examination of the interactive effects of risk factors require research on interventions conducted within relatively large-scale demonstration projects. For example, the information derived from the Hawaii Healthy Start project has greatly aided our understanding of the prevention of child maltreatment despite the fact that this program was not conducted as a randomized clinical trial. Demonstration projects should be designed to gather information about understudied factors, such as the role of fathers (Zuravin & Shay, 1991), and to reduce the impact of risk factors, such as parental history of abuse (Egeland, Jacobvitz, & Sroufe, 1988; Gaudin, 1993) or feelings of helplessness (Crittenden, 1985; Crittenden & Ainsworth, 1989), poor community standards for child supervision (Peterson & Brown, 1994), and societal tolerance of violence toward children (Belsky, 1981; Garbarino, 1996). It also will be important to consider the developmental level and maturity of the child when designing prevention programs (Finkelhor, 1995; Olsen & Spatz-Widom, 1993). There is a need to understand the relations among risk factors and child developmental levels and to identify new risk factors through applied research evaluating demonstration projects; this will inform policy and programming decisions. Demonstration programs may be most effective when interventions are intensive (frequent contacts), comprehensive, long-term (carried out over years), and provide parent training as well as methods for linking families to support services (Guterman, 1997).

Prevention efforts will be more successful as we better understand what underpins the problem. Reiss and Price (1996) suggested that research on prevention programs should aim to reduce risk, enhance protective factors, identify preclinical cases, and prevent the development of full-blown cases. Such knowledge should help in the early identification of families at risk. Ultimately, however, continued progress in this area will depend on the commitment of resources to expand prevention services based on currently available knowledge, which is sufficient to prevent neglect.

One of the primary goals of the CPS system is to reduce the incidence of child maltreatment, including neglect. A recent national report, however, underscored the emergency nature of child maltreatment in the United States and the inadequacies in the current child protection system (U.S. Advisory Board on Child Abuse and Neglect, 1993). In most communities, early identification and intervention are laudable goals of this system, yet these goals are often not achieved due to overwhelming caseloads as well as limited resources for expanding services into the prevention realm. This is particularly problematic for neglect because at-risk cases without actual physical harm may receive little attention from an overextended child protection system. Child protection laws are designed not only to deter potentially abusive or neglectful adults but also to assist families to overcome the barriers that may interfere with the adequate nurturing and rearing of their children. Community-based approaches that actively involve natural support systems, neighborhoods, and community members to assist all families, but especially those in need, may be more effective in preventing child neglect. This seems preferable to relying on an already overburdened CPS system or expecting that an added component to this system will work effectively.

CONCLUSIONS

This chapter has addressed the prevention of child neglect from a multidimensional perspective in an attempt to highlight a number of issues that have relevance for this area. We began with an optimistic tone regarding the progress that has been made in the prevention of child maltreatment over the past two decades and the possibility of further significant progress as we move into the future. Clearly, the foundations for making substantial progress in the prevention of neglect have been forged. Continued progress will depend on further articulation and empirical support for etiological models, the application of a developmental perspective within the context of longitudinal follow-up, integration of outcomes research into community programs, and the development of neighborhood-based support systems that facilitate positive outcomes for children and families. Future progress will require policymakers to recognize the importance of investing in the support of at-risk families and to recognize that cost offsets may not occur immediately. Effective policy in this area should be guided by assessing multiple outcomes longitudinally to understand the ultimate effectiveness of programs designed to enhance health and safety and physical and mental health outcomes in children.

On a more global level, the progress that our society makes in supporting and nurturing family development across multiple contexts is intimately connected to the prevention of neglect. Reducing poverty, controlling substance abuse, decreasing interpersonal violence, and promoting mental health within all individuals will prevent the occurrence of negative outcomes for children, including child maltreatment. The interconnections that are apparent between multiple societal problems offer the opportunity that most interventions designed to ameliorate or prevent each of these problems will have a positive, cascading effect on related concerns. The greatest public health challenges that lie ahead are to develop a more informed understanding of this social interconnectedness and how we might intervene with optimal results. With this understanding, we may be able to more efficiently allocate our limited resources to obtain the greatest gains in promoting healthy outcomes for all children, adults, and families in the next century.

REFERENCES

Ainsworth, M. D. S., & Wittig, B. A. (1969). Attachment and exploratory behavior of one-year-olds in a strange situation. In B. M. Foss (Ed.), *Determinants of infant behavior—IV.* London: Metheun.

Ainsworth, M. S. (1989). Attachments beyond infancy. *American Psychologist, 44,* 709-716.

Belsky, J. (1981). Child maltreatment: An ecological integration. *Annual Progress in Child Psychiatry and Child Development,* 637-665.

Belsky, J. (1991). Psychological maltreatment: Definitional limitations and unstated assumptions. *Development and Psychopathology, 3,* 31-36.

Belsky, J. (1993). Etiology of child maltreatment: A developmental-ecological analysis. *Psychological Bulletin, 114,* 413-434.

Belsky, J., & Vondra, J. (1990). Lessons for child abuse: The determinants of parenting. In D. Cicchetti & V. Carlson (Eds.), *Child maltreatment: Theory and research on the causes and consequences of child abuse and neglect* (pp. 153-202). Cambridge, UK: Cambridge University Press.

Bowlby, J. (1988). *A secure base: Parent-child attachment and healthy human development.* New York: Basic Books.

Breakey, G., & Pratt, B. (1991). Healthy growth for Hawaii's "Healthy Start:" Toward a systematic statewide approach to the prevention of child abuse and neglect. *Zero to Three, 11,* 16-22.

Brunk, M., Henggeler, S. W., & Whelan, J. P. (1987). Comparison of multisystemic therapy and parent training in the brief treatment of child abuse and neglect. *Journal of Consulting and Clinical Psychology, 55,* 171-178.

Carlson, V., Cicchetti, D., Barnett, D., & Braunwald, K. (1989). Finding order in disorganization: Lessons from research on maltreated infants' attachment to their caregivers. In D. Cicchetti & V. Carlson (Eds.), *Child maltreatment: Theory and research on the causes and consequences of child abuse and neglect* (pp. 494-528). New York: Cambridge University Press.

Child Abuse Prevention and Treatment Act, Pub. L. 93-247, 42 U.S.C. 5101 (as revised in 1996).

Crittenden, P. M. (1985). Maltreated infants: Vulnerability and resilience. *Journal of Child Psychology and Psychiatry and Allied Disciplines, 26,* 85-96.

Crittenden, P. M., & Ainsworth, M. D. S. (1989). Child maltreatment and attachment theory. In D. Cicchetti & V. Carlson, (Eds.), *Child maltreatment: Theory and research on the causes and consequences of child abuse and neglect* (pp. 432-463). New York: Cambridge University Press.

Daro, D. (1996). Preventing child abuse and neglect. In J. Briere, L. Berliner, J. A. Bulkley, C. Jenny, & T. Reid (Eds.), *The APSAC handbook on child maltreatment* (pp. 343-358), Thousand Oaks, CA: Sage.

Daro, D., & McCurdy, K. (1994). Preventing child abuse and neglect: Programmatic interventions. *Child Welfare, 73,* 405-430.

Drotar, D. (1992). Prevention of neglect and nonorganic failure to thrive. In D. J. Willis, E. W. Holden, & M. Rosenberg (Eds.), *Prevention of child maltreatment: Developmental and ecological perspectives* (pp. 115-149). New York: John Wiley.

Dubowitz, H. (1994). Neglecting the neglect of neglect. *Journal of Interpersonal Violence, 9,* 556-560.

Egeland, B., Jacobvitz, D., & Sroufe, L. A. (1988). Breaking the cycle of abuse. *Child Development, 59,* 1080-1088.

Finkelhor, D. (1995). The victimization of children: A developmental perspective. *American Journal of Orthopsychiatry, 65,* 177-193.

Fuddy, L. (1992). *Hawaii's Healthy Start's success.* Paper presented at the Ninth International Congress on Child Abuse and Neglect, Chicago, Illinois.

Garbarino, J. (1977). The human ecology of child maltreatment: A conceptual model for research. *Journal of Marriage and the Family, 39,* 721-735.

Garbarino, J. (1992). Preventing adolescent maltreatment. In D. J. Willis, E. W. Holden, & M. Rosenberg (Eds.), *Prevention of child maltreatment: Developmental and ecological perspectives* (pp. 94-114). New York: John Wiley.

Garbarino, J. (1996). Can reflections on 20 years of searching. *Child Abuse and Neglect, 20,* 157-160.

Gaudin, J. M. (1993). *Child neglect: A guide for intervention.* Washington, DC: U.S. Department of Health and Human Services.

Guterman, N. B. (1997). Early prevention of physical child abuse and neglect: Existing evidence and future directions. *Child Maltreatment, 2,* 12-34.

Hay, T., & Jones, L. (1994). Societal interventions to prevent child abuse and neglect. *Child Welfare, 73,* 379-403.

Kaufman, J., & Zigler, E. (1992). The prevention of child maltreatment: Programming, research and policy. In D. J. Willis, E. W. Holden, & M. Rosenberg (Eds.), *Prevention of child maltreatment: Developmental and ecological perspectives* (pp. 269-295). New York: John Wiley.

Kowal, L. W., Kottmeier, C. P., Ayoub, C. C., Komives, J. A., Robinson, D. S., & Allen, J. P. (1989). Characteristics of families at risk of problems in parenting: Findings from a home-based secondary prevention program. *Child Welfare, 68,* 529-538.

Leventhal, J. M. (1996). Twenty years later: We do know how to prevent child abuse and neglect. *Child Abuse and Neglect, 20,* 647-653.

Levy, H. B., Markovic, J., Chaudry, U., Ahart, S., & Torres, H. (1995). Reabuse rates in a sample of children followed for 5 years after discharge from a child abuse inpatient assessment program. *Child Abuse and Neglect, 11,* 1363-1377.

MacMillan, H. L., MacMillan, J. H., Offord, D. R., Griffith, L., & MacMillan, A. (1994). Primary prevention of child physical abuse and neglect: A critical review: I. *Journal of Child Psychology and Psychiatry and Allied Disciplines, 35,* 835-856.

Melton, G. B. (1996). The child's right to a family environment: Why children's rights and family values are compatible. *American Psychologist, 51,* 1234-1238.

Munoz, R. F., Mrazek, P. J., & Haggerty, R. J. (1996). Institute of medicine report on prevention of mental disorders. *American Psychologist, 51,* 1116-1122.

Olds, D. L., Eckenrode, J., Henderson, C. R., Kitzman, H., Powers, J., Cole, R., Sidora, K., Morris, P., Pettitt, L., & Luckey, D. (1997). Long-term effects of home visitation on maternal life course and child abuse and neglect. *Journal of the American Medical Association, 278*(8), 637-642.

Olds, D. L., & Henderson, C. R. (1989). The prevention of maltreatment. In D. Cicchetti & V. Carlson (Eds.), *Child maltreatment: Theory and research on the causes and consequences of child abuse and neglect* (722-763). New York: Cambridge University Press.

Olds, D. L., Henderson, C. R., Chamberlin, R., & Tatelbaum, R. (1986). Preventing child abuse and neglect: A randomized trial of home nurse visitation. *Pediatrics, 78,* 65-78.

Olds, D. L., Henderson, C. R., Phelps, C., Kitzman, H., & Hanks, C. (1993). Effect of prenatal and nurse home visitation on government spending. *Medical Care, 31,* 155-174.

Olds, D. L., Henderson, C. R., Tatelbaum, R., & Chamberlin, R. (1988). Improving the life-course development of socially disadvantaged mothers: A randomized trial of nurse home visitation. *American Journal of Public Health, 78,* 1436-1445.

Olds, D. L., & Kitzman, H. (1993). Review of research on home visiting for pregnant women and parents of young children. *The Future of Children, 3,* 53-92.

Olsen, J. L., & Spatz-Widom, C. (1993). Prevention of child abuse and neglect. *Applied and Preventive Psychology, 2,* 217-229.

Peterson, L., & Brown, D. (1994). Integrating child injury and abuse-neglect research: Common histories, etiologies, and solutions. *Psychological Bulletin, 116,* 293-315.

Reiss, D., & Price, R. H. (1996). National research agenda for prevention research: The National Institute of Mental Health Report. *American Psychologist, 51,* 1109-1115.

Starr, R. H., & Wolfe, D. A. (Eds.). (1991). *The effects of child abuse and neglect.* New York: Guilford.

Thyen, U., Thiessen, R., Heinsohn-Krug, M. (1995). Secondary prevention—Serving families at risk. *Child Abuse and Neglect, 19,* 1337-1347.

U.S. Advisory Board on Child Abuse and Neglect. (1993). *The continuing child protection emergency: A challenge to the nation.* Washington, DC: Government Printing Office.

Wallach, V. A., & Lister, L. (1995). Stages in the delivery of home-based services to parents at risk of child abuse: A Healthy Start experience. *Scholarly Inquiry for Nursing Practice: An International Journal, 9,* 159-173.

Willett, J. B., Ayoub, C. C., & Robinson, D. (1991). Using growth modeling to examine systematic differences in growth: An example of change in the functioning of families at risk of maladaptive parenting, child abuse, or neglect. *Journal of Consulting and Clinical Psychology, 59,* 38-47.

Willis, D. J., Holden, E. W., & Rosenberg, M. (1992). Child maltreatment and prevention: Introduction and historical overview. In D. J. Willis, E. W. Holden, & M. Rosenberg (Eds.), *Prevention of child maltreatment: Developmental and ecological perspectives* (pp. 1-14). New York: John Wiley.

Wolfe, D. A., Reppucci, N. D., & Hart, S. (1995). Child abuse prevention: Knowledge and priorities. *Journal of Clinical Child Psychology, 24*(Suppl.), 5-22.

Zuravin, S. J., & Shay, S. (1991). Preventing child neglect. In D. DePanfilis & T. Birch (Eds.), *National Child Maltreatment Prevention Symposium.* Washington, DC: National Center on Child Abuse and Neglect.

10 Evaluation and Risk Assessment of Child Neglect in Public Child Protection Services

DIANA J. ENGLISH

Most public child protective service agencies (CPS) would agree that the primary mission of CPS is the protection of children. However, there are often misconceptions about the actual operation of CPS and the scope of the CPS mission. The CPS mandate is governed by federal and state laws as well as local agency policies and regulations. The ability to carry out child protection laws, policies, and regulations is affected by resources available to individual agencies. At the local level, operational definitions may or may not be clearly delineated, may or may not be understood and agreed on by the community, and may or may not be actually implemented due to inadequate resources and appropriate services for families referred to CPS.

This chapter reviews the role of child protective services in the protection of children, reviews factors that influence its scope, and describes the methods used by CPS to carry out their mandate. Last, this chapter discusses risk assessment in child protection, its general application, and how risk assessment relates to and affects CPS services provided to child-neglecting families.

References to the maltreatment of children can be traced throughout recorded history; however, an organized social response on a national level did not occur until the mid-20th century. The 1974 Child Abuse Prevention and Treatment Act (CAPTA; 1974) established a minimum standard definition of child maltreatment and guidelines for the development of state child protection systems. Before the passage of the 1974 CAPTA, there was intense debate about the parameters of maltreating behavior to be included in a national definition of child maltreatment. There was strong opposition to the inclusion of emotional and physical neglect in the definition, based on a belief that government should intrude in family privacy only when there was an issue of "demonstrable" harm to the child (Wald, 1987).

Despite the opposition, advocates for a broad definition of maltreatment prevailed. Emotional and physical neglect were included in the 1974 CAPTA definition of maltreatment, and each state incorporated these definitions within their child protection systems. Although the federal government established guidelines for the development of CPS systems, individual states were free to develop local systems within these broad guidelines. Some states adopted CPS programs that operated on a statewide basis; others adopted local or county-based programs that included broad oversight functions at the state level. Regardless of organization, CPS programs established similar functions or decision points to govern the operation of the child protection program.

CPS INTERVENTION

CPS intervention is initiated when child maltreatment is reported to a CPS agency. CPS programs have an intake process for screening allegations of child maltreatment. CPS programs have an investigation function, guidelines for substantiating maltreatment allegations, and rules regarding service provision to families referred to or substantiated for maltreatment. The referent alleges an act of maltreatment has occurred or that a child is at risk of maltreatment by a parent or caregiver. Allegations are made by the community at large and by professionals. In some states, all citizens are mandated reporters; in others, specific professional groups are designated. Mandated reporters must report the concern to CPS.

Once a referral has been made, a decision must be made as to whether the referral is accepted by the CPS program. Typically, a referral is "screened in" if there is a specific allegation of maltreatment or if the acts alleged indicate the child(ren) to be at imminent risk. The specific allegation of maltreatment should involve an alleged act of omission or commission that meets the state's definition of maltreatment. If not, the case may be classified as "information only" and screened out. Once accepted for investigation, allegations are prioritized in terms of immediacy of response and level of investigation. "Immediate" usually means an investigation within 24 to 72 hours. Cases not assessed as immediate may not, in some states, be investigated for up to 10 days. Even if accepted as a legitimate CPS referral, investigation may consist only of a record check or collateral phone call. This low level of investigation, however, usually applies to cases considered "low risk" based on the intake information.

An investigation usually includes a review of agency records for prior reports, contact with others who may have relevant information, and face-to-face contact with the child and caregiver. States vary on whether the focus of the investigation is on making a finding of maltreatment, making a determination of whether the child is at risk of maltreatment, or both. If the agency is maltreatment focused, and it is determined that maltreatment has not occurred, then no further action is taken. If it is determined that maltreatment has occurred, a decision is made as to whether the agency will intervene and if so, in what way. Sometimes, a determination of maltreatment is made, but CPS takes no further action. For example, CPS may choose not to act in a situation where abuse has occurred, but it is assessed as a one-time occurrence that seems unlikely to recur in the future. In this instance, the case would be substantiated, but the agency would not open the case for services, although the family may be referred to other services. If a referral is substantiated and the CPS worker determines the child remains at risk, the case should be opened for services. In some situations, there may be a substantiated report, the child is determined to be at risk, but the family is not cooperative and refuses to participate in services. In this situation, if there is insufficient evidence to obtain court jurisdiction to require a family's participation in services, the case may still be closed.

Some states offer services to families even if maltreatment is not substantiated. These states operate under a "risk" (of maltreatment)-focused system. In risk-focused CPS programs, services can be offered on a voluntary basis. If, however, the family does not wish to accept services and there is insufficient evidence to take the case to court, the case may be closed, even if the child is believed to be at risk.

Although there is a national definition of child maltreatment that sets a minimum standard, definitions adopted at state and local levels determine who enters the CPS system. Furthermore, policies established within individual CPS systems shape how referrals are processed and what happens to families. During the past three decades that states have been managing child protection services, they have developed and refined their systems as local conditions have changed. During this period, on a national level, Congress continued to expand the definition of child maltreatment in the reauthorization of CAPTA legislation in 1978, 1984, 1987, 1989, 1992, and 1996. For example, in 1984, medical neglect was added as a new category of child maltreatment, and in 1992, the associations between different types of family violence were recognized.

Potentially significant changes in national definitions of child maltreatment occurred during the 1996 CAPTA reauthorization (U.S.DHHS, 1996). The debate on the appropriate scope of CPS intervention was reopened, centered on whether the CPS mandate should be restricted to allegations where there was demonstrable harm to children or whether it should include endangerment or potential harm. Limiting CPS to cases with demonstrable harm excludes many cases where children are at risk of significant harm. There is also the issue of cumulative harm for acts of commission or omission that result in harm to children over a period of time, as well as long-term effects that may become apparent only much later (DiLeonardi, 1993). This is particularly a concern with neglect. Research indicates that the long-term harm to children may be as or more harmful than other types of maltreatment (Crouch & Milner, 1993). Despite these concerns, advocates for a narrow CPS definition prevailed, and the 1996 CAPTA restricted the definition to, at a minimum, any recent act or failure to act on the part of a parent or caregiver, which results in death or serious physical or emotional harm, or sexual abuse or exploitation, or presents an imminent risk of serious harm. This definition may lead states to narrow their definitions and to the exclusion of many high-risk cases.

However, CAPTA set only a minimum standard; states can choose a broader definition.

The outcome of this debate and subsequent interpretation of the CPS mandate may have a significant impact on who will be served by CPS, especially as it relates to child neglect. Operational definitions for "recent" and "serious" adopted by state CPS systems may seriously limit the kinds of neglect referrals accepted, investigated, and served by CPS. It is relatively easy to conclude that a parent who molests a child has committed abuse, even if there is no observable physical injury or if the child is asymptomatic and does not demonstrate immediate harm. What about a 4-year-old child whose mother lives in a house with broken glass on the floor, rotten food in the refrigerator and cupboards, or used needles on the floor? The child has not been cut, does not have food poisoning, or has not been pricked by the needle; in fact, the child has not experienced actual physical, observable harm. Is this child at risk, and does this child warrant CPS involvement? Although terms such as "demonstrable" harm seem simple, they are not. There is wide variability in how these terms are interpreted and applied in actual practice. Furthermore, some CPS systems already screen out all but the most serious CPS allegations, especially those for neglect.

SCOPE OF THE PROBLEM

Data on the incidence of maltreatment from all sources indicate a significant increase in the number of children reported to CPS. In 1984, 1,727,000 were reported to CPS (American Association for the Protection of Children, 1986); by 1994, 2.9 million children were reported to CPS nationwide, and 1 million of these cases were substantiated. Data from the 1994 National Child Abuse and Neglect Data System indicate that child neglect is reported at twice the rate of physical abuse and nearly four times the rate of sexual abuse. Typically, in neglect referrals, especially for failure to provide basic needs, it is assumed that all the children in the family are victims. Official estimates based on reported cases are clearly low; the Third National Incidence Study indicates that professionals do not report as much as 40% of the maltreatment that they identify (Sedlak & Broadhurst, 1996).

CPS SYSTEM RESPONSES TO INCREASED REFERRALS

During the past decade, public child protection programs have been unable to keep pace with the increasing volume and increased severity of child maltreatment referrals (Sedlak & Broadhurst, 1996). In addition, there has been a corresponding increase in both knowledge and understanding regarding the effects of child maltreatment with short-term and long-term consequences for children's physical, social, and psychological health and well-being. Although available information indicates that the mandate for CPS intervention should be broadened, the scope is being narrowed.

In the late 1980s, in response to increasing referrals and decreasing resources, CPS agencies began to develop risk assessment models, partly to help manage their workloads. The major motivation was to improve the quality and consistency of decisions. Since 1985, more than 40 states nationwide have adopted a form of risk assessment to promote more comprehensive assessments and to help prioritize services (Berkowitz, 1991; English & Pecora, 1994). How states approach risk assessment parallels their philosophies regarding child protection. A number of different approaches to risk assessment have been developed; however, two primary models have been adopted in most states. Before discussing these two predominant approaches, it is important to understand the different philosophical approaches to child protection that have emerged during the last decade and to understand the theoretical underpinnings for child maltreatment assessment and intervention.

Approaches to Child Protection

Most CPS programs are maltreatment focused, which means that CPS does not intervene unless abuse or neglect has been substantiated. Even if the family presents significant risk factors, if the allegation that brought the family into the CPS system is not substantiated, the family will not be offered services from the CPS agency. The other approach is a risk-focused system, in which a CPS worker assesses risk at the same time he or she is assessing whether or not a particular incident occurred. In risk-focused systems, families can be offered services on a voluntary basis even if maltreatment is not substantiated, and in some situations, the court may even be petitioned if the child is considered at risk and the caregiver is not protecting the child.

Some argue that CPS is too intrusive in family life and that intervention should be restricted to substantiated cases. Others argue against a system based on substantiation. Research indicates bias in who and what types of cases are substantiated (English, 1997). Factors influencing the likelihood of substantiation include child and caregiver characteristics, characteristics of referents, presence of physical evidence, availability of a credible witness or child credibility, time spent on the investigation, the time of day the referral was made, and resources available in the community (Eckenrode, Powers, Doris, Munsch, & Bogler, 1988; Groenveld & Giovannoni, 1977; Scheurman, Stagner, Johnsen, & Mullen, 1989). Clearly, failure to substantiate a specific allegation of maltreatment does not mean the child has not been maltreated or has not experienced harm. For a review of these issues, see Drake (1996). Factors such as resource availability or the type of referent have little to do with the presence of maltreatment. Although a finding of maltreatment should be a necessary prerequisite for intrusive governmental interventions, such as dependencies or criminal proceedings, few CPS referrals are subject to this level of intrusion. Even if unable to substantiate a particular incident, if a significant risk of maltreatment is present and the family wishes to participate in services, they should have the opportunity.

Theories of Maltreatment

How risk for maltreatment is defined depends in part on underlying beliefs about factors related to the healthy growth and development of children and beliefs about why parents or caregivers maltreat children. Conceptual models explaining child maltreatment have been evolving. In the early 1960s, single-factor models hypothesized psychopathology of the parent as the key factor in explaining maltreating behavior (Kempe, Silverman, Steele, Droegmueller, & Silver, 1962; Spinetta & Rigler, 1972). In the 1970s, sociocultural models included broader community and societal factors (Gelles, 1973; Gil, 1971). More recently, multifactorial ecological and transitional models have influenced CPS risk assessment (Belsky, 1980; Parke & Collmer, 1975; Wolfe, 1987).

The more complex etiologic models (ecological, transactional) hypothesize that multiple and interactive factors contribute to maltreatment, including factors related to the individual child, the parent, the family, the neighborhood and community, and society at large. Factors within or between any of these levels may interact to raise or lower the likelihood of maltreatment in an individual family. Some factors, such as substance abuse or domestic violence, increase the likelihood of maltreatment. Other factors, such as social support, might balance or compensate for risks to reduce the likelihood of harm. Some risk factors might be fixed or enduring, whereas others might be more transient. Last, according to the transactional model, changing circumstances can alter a family's risk of maltreatment (Wolfe, 1987). In other words, families might move in and out of a risk continuum based on changing circumstances in their lives. To conduct a comprehensive assessment of risk, interactions between different areas must be considered.

To further complicate the assessment of risk for maltreatment, there has emerged an increased emphasis on the importance of a developmental perspective in terms of understanding child maltreatment (Cicchetti, 1992; Crouch & Milner, 1993; Dubowitz, Black, Starr, & Zuravin, 1993). Developmental tasks for a child vary depending on age and ability. The impact and experience of specific types of abuse at one developmental stage may be different than at other stages. Furthermore, maltreatment experienced at one developmental age may not manifest until later. This developmental perspective is particularly important when assessing the consequences of child neglect and should influence the consideration of serious harm. To date, most CPS programs assess risk in the short term (6 months). These risk protocols do not take a long-term view of harm that may accumulate or become apparent over time. There is an emerging sentiment that risk assessment in child protection should include a constellation of contributing factors known to contribute to the likelihood of child maltreatment (Ammerman, 1990; Ammerman & Platz, 1996; Cicchetti, 1992; English & Pecora, 1994; National Research Council, 1993; Wolfe, 1987). This constellation of risk (and protective) factors includes child, incident, caregiver, family, community, and cultural factors. Although many risk factors may apply across maltreatment types, it is possible that there are different risk factors for different types of maltreatment. There is also a question as to whether children who are maltreated experience only one type of maltreatment or whether, in most instances, children experience multiple forms of maltreatment (English, Marshall, Brummel, & Coghlan, 1998).

Models of Risk Assessment

Although the foregoing debate has influenced the development of different risk assessment models in CPS, there has also been some confusion over the purpose and role of risk assessment in child protection. What is being assessed? The answer depends on the risk assessment model and the structure of the CPS system within which the model is used. Within the CPS community, there are four basic approaches to the development of risk assessment models (see English & Pecora, 1994). These models are known as consensus-based models, actuarial models, risk checklists or scales, and risk influence models. The actuarial and consensus-based models are the two that have been most widely adopted, and they are described here.

The actuarial model of risk assessment is basically atheoretical in that no underlying theory of the etiology of child maltreatment influences what factors are included in the actuarial risk scales. Risk factors in actuarial models are derived from a cross-sectional, point-in-time analysis of previously closed, substantiated CPS referrals in a particular jurisdiction. Information available in closed CPS case files may be analyzed, and factors found to be statistically associated with the likelihood of a case being re-referred and substantiated are identified. These factors are given numerical weights and combined into a risk matrix. Typically, there are separate matrices for physical or sexual abuse and neglect. Each risk factor is scored, and a total risk score is derived by adding the individual risk factor weights. Factors that have been associated with previously substantiated cases are used to weigh the likelihood of a substantiated new referral. Cases that are highly likely to be re-referred and substantiated are given higher risk scores and prioritized for services. After a case has been substantiated, a needs assessment is conducted to determine what services will be offered to the family.

Each jurisdiction that has adopted an actuarial risk model has identified its own risk factors based on the associations between risk factors and substantiation in their own jurisdiction. In actuarial risk systems, risk is not assessed until a CPS referral has been substantiated. The actuarial model does not account for interactions among risk factors in assessing the overall level of risk.

Consensus-based risk models are based on the ecological theory of maltreatment and include risk factors across several domains, including child, caregiver, caregiver-child interaction, and environment. These models have been developed based on a review of the maltreatment literature, incorporating risk factors that have been associated with maltreatment. In addition, risk factors identified by CPS workers considered to be predictive of maltreatment are included. The consensus-based risk models were primarily designed as guidelines for structured decision making that would help ensure more systematic and comprehensive CPS assessments. Consensus-model decision points include when to accept a CPS referral for investigation, when to substantiate a report, and when to open a case for services. The goal is to conduct a comprehensive assessment of risk. Like actuarial models, the risk being assessed is the likelihood of recurrence of child maltreatment, absent intervention. A related risk being assessed is the likely severity of the recurrence.

In consensus-based systems, risk is assessed during the investigation phase of a case as part of the decision-making process as to whether to open a case for service. The focus of the investigation is not limited to substantiation, although that decision is made as part of the investigation. Instead, the primary emphasis is on a comprehensive assessment of risk for maltreatment. Overall risk is assigned by a CPS worker, based on an assessment of the risk factors present as well as the interactions between risk factors. Absent substantiation, CPS authority to intervene after a 30- to 90-day investigation period is limited to a family's willingness to cooperate with services on a voluntary basis or the ability of the CPS agency to obtain court jurisdiction to continue to intervene. Consensus-based risk models generally incorporate risk factors associated with different types of maltreatment in one matrix. Like actuarial models, individual risk factors are scored on severity and scaled from low to high risk; however, there is no overall score derived from adding individual risk factor scores.

QUESTIONS CONCERNING RISK ASSESSMENT MODELS

Questions remain about the reliability and validity of risk assessment models. Research in this area has been in existence only for about 10 years, and resources have not been adequate. English and Pecora (1994) reviewed risk assessment research conducted from 1987 to 1992 and found comparative studies of different models, research on the accuracy of screening criteria, classification and model-building implementation, and cultural sensitivity. These studies found that although there are common risk factors, there is no one outstanding model of risk assessment. Findings across studies were not easy to compare. There are serious questions about the implementation of risk models in practice, with the more subjective and probably most important risk factors for decision making being the least reliably rated across workers (English, Marshall, et al., 1998). Classification (actuarial models) and prediction research are hindered by reliance on a questionable outcome—substantiation (English, Brummel, Coghlan, Novicky, & Marshall, 1998; English, Marshall, et al., 1998). Although preliminary work on important questions has been done, many questions remain. For example, little is known about whether there are different risk factors for specific types of maltreatment, whether the presence of one risk factor raises or lowers the importance of other risk factors, or how protective factors interact with risk factors. These and other questions need to be explored before questions about the validity and reliability of risk assessment models can be answered.

In their review of risk instrument performance, Lyons, Doueck, and Wodarski (1996) concluded that many of the risk models do have acceptable psychometric properties, including internal consistency, interrater reliability, and concurrent validity. It was also concluded that until further research is conducted, these models should not be relied on for case decision making (Lyons et al., 1996, p. 153). However, it is appropriate to use risk models as guidelines for comprehensive assessments.

The limited research data on risk assessment are only partially related to inadequate funding. Other obstacles to research on risk assessment have been identified. For example, research on the questions listed earlier require very large samples. Until recently, research on risk assessment has been limited by small samples and missing and incomplete data. With the initiation of electronic case management systems, this problem should be remedied. Easily accessible, large data sets will enable researchers to examine risk factors associated with different types and subtypes of maltreatment.

Last, some assert that inappropriate statistical techniques have been used in the research conducted to date. Camasso and Jagannathan (1995), in reviewing risk assessment research, concluded that the dependence of sensitivity and specificity rates on the diagnostic criterion selected does not appear to be well understood (p. 176). They state that the limits of point estimates in the evaluation of diagnostic test accuracy are well-known in other fields and should be applied to risk assessment research. Unfortunately, these techniques have not been adequately used, raising questions regarding the predictive validity of research conducted thus far.

Despite shortcomings in the research on risk assessment in child protection, the reality is that decisions about risk are made every day. At a minimum, risk models offer criteria to be evaluated for decision making. Whether the factors used in individual models are the "right" ones is an open question. Risk models do not claim to predict future abuse and neglect. They are used to promote more consistent and comprehensive assessments of risk, based on the best available knowledge. These models may indeed be found to be predictive, but that remains uncertain. In the meantime, CPS must be able to explicate the basis for decisions that affect families' lives and children's protection. Structured risk assessment models, appropriately implemented, can provide this rationale.

What Is Currently Known About Risk for Neglect?

Many risk factors associated with families referred to CPS for neglect are also found in distressed, non-maltreating families. Families characterized by poverty are also characterized by stress and social isolation, but these families may not maltreat their children. The key to evaluating risk for neglect is to separate out those characteristics that may be common to many families and identify those who omit appropriate care for their children for reasons other than poverty. This discussion focuses on risk factors associated with CPS referral.

Child Characteristics

Young children are referred more frequently for neglect than older children; however, the true extent of neglect across age groups is unknown. The peak age for neglect allegations by professionals is ages 6 to 8 years (Sedlak & Broadhurst, 1996); however, this finding is influenced by increased surveillance of children in school. Gender has not been found to be associated with neglect; however, there appears to be an association between developmental delay and neglect (Ammerman, 1990; Jaudes & Diamond, 1985; Starr, 1988).

Caregiver Characteristics

There is contradictory evidence on the relationship between caregiver characteristics, such as intelligence and ethnicity, and child maltreatment (Wolfe, 1987). However, there is evidence that neglect is more likely to be associated with single-parent, female head of household; low socioeconomic status; household crowding; caregiver educational level; and family size (Paget, Phillip, & Abramczyk, 1993; Zuravin, Orme, & Hegar, 1994). However, Nelson, Saunders, and Landsmann (1990) and DiLeonardi (1993) found that lower socioeconomic status was most often associated with chronic rather than situational neglect. Zuravin (1991) and Wolock and Horowitz (1979) found differences between neglecting and non-neglecting mothers over and above poverty. These included poor problem-solving abilities, poor management skills, and low self-esteem. Neglecting families have also been found to be lonely and isolated, with personal histories of maltreatment as children, domestic violence, and depression (Belsky, 1993; Giovannoni & Billingsley, 1970; Polansky, Ammons, & Gaudin, 1985; Wolfe, 1987; Wolock & Horowitz, 1979; Zuravin & Grief, 1989). Last, neglecting caregivers have been found to have problems with substance abuse, inadequate parenting skills, unrealistic expectations of their children, and dysfunctional attachment to their children (Paget et al., 1993; Zeanah & Zeanah, 1989; Zuravin & Grief, 1989). In addition, a lack of social support and stress has been associated with neglecting behaviors by caregivers toward their children (Avison, Turner, & Noh, 1986; Azar, 1991; Belsky, 1993; Wolfe, 1987; Zuravin & Taylor, 1987).

PRACTICE DILEMMAS

The presence or absence of any one of the risk factors in and of themselves do not mark a neglecting family; however, it is believed that their presence and the interactions between them increase the likelihood of maltreatment (Azar, 1991; Belsky, 1980, 1993; English, Aubin, Fine, & Pecora, 1993).

Unfortunately, there is little research on how these risk factors interact or on the influence protective factors might have on overall assessment of risk. For example, it is unknown whether specific family strengths cancel out the effect of a particular risk or whether risk and protective factors are unrelated to each other. Despite the lack of definitive answers, CPS workers must make decisions on what cases to screen in, to investigate, to substantiate, to keep open for services, and to initiate court action on and whether children should be placed out of the home. Although these decisions may be different for each type of maltreatment, they are particularly troublesome for neglect. Most neglect cases do not result in observable injuries, and there is uncertainty about what composes appropriate childrearing practice, which is complicated by cultural differences. What constitutes dangerous or unacceptable care of a child is influenced by laws, agency practice, and community standards. How CPS responds to dangerous and unacceptable care of a child is also related to resources. Many state laws on neglect are similar, but agency practice may vary widely. Several studies on community standards related to neglect in different jurisdictions have produced remarkably similar results. Polansky, Chalmers, Buttenweiser, & Williams (1978) and Giovannoni (1990) found that views on behavior seen as neglectful were similar across different socioeconomic groups. However, Wolock (1982) and Wells (1987) found that community demographics can affect the interpretation of severity.

It is interesting that there appears to be less consistency across professional groups regarding the basis for state intervention in cases of maltreatment (Besharov, 1985; Wald, 1987). Boisen (1994) found that community-based and CPS workers had markedly different assessments of risk when children were exposed to drug or alcohol abuse and there were allegations of neglect. There was greater agreement between these two groups regarding supervision of a child. Rose and Meezan (1995) also found that CPS workers viewed neglect more seriously than foster care workers. Both groups rated neglecting behaviors less seriously than did laypersons from the community at large. Individuals in the community in general viewed maltreating behaviors more seriously, especially neglect behaviors associated with failure to provide basic needs and supervision, than did CPS professionals. This difference may partially be explained by the perceived seriousness of CPS cases of physical and sexual abuse compared with the less obvious or cumulative harm of neglect. In addition, CPS workers accustomed to high-risk situations have a different context for judging the vignettes in these studies.

Systems Issues

There is growing evidence that CPS is narrowing the gateway to its services (Wells, Downing, & Fluke, 1990). The American Association for the Protection of Children (1986) found that acceptance of a CPS referral was related to the availability of resources, and Eckenrode et al. (1988) found that CPS screen-out rates increased with the increase in referrals. The nature of the incident and the type of referent also influenced who entered the CPS system, especially as related to neglect (Hutchinson, 1989). English and Aubin (1991) found that neglect reports from the community were more likely to be classified as low risk and diverted from the CPS system compared to reports from professionals. CPS referrals have also been more likely to be substantiated if the referral was from a professional compared to a layperson (Eckenrode et al., 1988; Groenveld & Giovannoni, 1977).

Even if neglect cases are screened in, there are system factors that influence the likelihood of investigation and of substantiation. In one study, English et al. (1997) found that physical neglect referrals were less likely to be responded to by CPS on an emergent basis, were assessed at intake as lower risk than any other type of maltreatment, and were less likely to be investigated. Several studies have found that increased worker contacts and the amount of time spent on the investigation influenced the likelihood of substantiating maltreatment (Eckenrode, Powers, Doris, Munsch, & Bolger, 1987; Giovannoni, 1989; Wells, 1987; Winefield & Bradley, 1992).

CPS referrals are more likely to be substantiated if the parental behavior is assessed as intentional (Alter, 1985), although neglecting behaviors are not typically considered intentional. Despite the general influence of prior reports increasing the likelihood of substantiating subsequent reports, neglect reports with priors are less likely to be substantiated than other types of maltreatment (English, Brummel, et al., 1998). Last, Scheurman et al. (1989) found that the presence of physical evidence, whether a caregiver admits to maltreatment, the credibility of the child, and confirmation of maltreatment by a collateral all increase the likelihood of CPS substantiation. Although inconclusive, these studies pose troubling questions about the fate of neglect referrals in the public child protection system as it currently operates.

SUMMARY AND CONCLUSION

Allegations of neglect are the least likely maltreatment reports to meet the threshold for CPS intervention. If a severe case of neglect does enter the CPS system, the child is more likely to be separated from parental custody compared with other types of abuse. However, when CPS resources fail to keep pace with the increase in and the seriousness of referrals, it is likely that more neglect referrals will be excluded. Resource deficits in CPS raise the question of whether CPS is the right resource for neglecting families. Although neglect is strongly associated with poverty, it is also associated with inadequate parenting skills and knowledge and other caregiver deficits. Community-based support services may be the most appropriate intervention for lower-risk, non-chronic neglect situations. In-home specialists, such as home health nurses who can model parenting behaviors, may be more effective than other types of services routinely offered by CPS workers. Higher-risk neglect cases, where substance abuse, domestic violence, or other high-risk factors are present, may be more appropriately served by a more intrusive service that can invoke legal interventions, if necessary, to protect the child.

One issue that clearly needs to be addressed is the definition of neglect and the interpretation of serious harm. Research on the effects of neglect indicates that children whose caregivers omit basic parenting and fail to provide basic needs can experience serious delays to their physical, emotional-cognitive, and social development. If we value child well-being and the right of our most vulnerable children to an environment that promotes healthy growth and development, then we must address potential as well as actual harm. Based on the types of referrals from the community at large as well as professionals, it is clear that there is a community perception that children who experience deprivation of basic needs are being maltreated.

In the 1990s, CPS systems' primary response has been investigation and intervention if the child is at imminent risk. A family may voluntarily participate in services, or CPS may seek legal authority to intervene if the child is in need of protection. However, children who are not at risk of immediate harm are classified at lower risk, either at intake or after investigation, and are not generally served by CPS. At most, some services are offered as part of the investigation phase of service delivery, but there is little or no follow-up by CPS to determine if the services were appropriate or effective.

As alternative response systems are developed in the community, it may be an appropriate CPS role to act as a conduit for service referral to less intrusive but appropriate services for neglecting families. This requires that community-based agencies have effective interventions for neglecting families. Also important is the accuracy of risk assessment in differentiating serious or chronic neglect from less severe cases. The key to successful assessment is for CPS programs to take a larger view of the concept of serious harm and to consider long-term and cumulative harm to children. More emphasis should be made on child development and prior history and referrals, substantiated or not. Chronically neglecting families frequently have long histories of referral to CPS. If CPS focuses only on the immediate allegation before them and not the pattern reflected in multiple referrals, then many neglected children will continue to be inappropriately excluded from the CPS system.

Based on research conducted during recent decades, we know a lot more now about the detrimental effects on children of inadequate or abusive caregiving. We also know these effects are not necessarily short-term or transitory. Indeed, there is evidence that neglect may cause as much harm as other types of maltreatment.

Communicating the serious outcomes of child neglect is an important task for all involved in the care and protection of children. We have guidance from research concerning risk assessment and effective interventions. We need to integrate this knowledge and use it when developing our response to this serious problem.

REFERENCES

Alter, C. F. (1985). Decision making factors in cases of child neglect. *Child Welfare, 2*(2), 99-111.

American Association for the Protection of Children. (1986). *Highlights of official child neglect and abuse reporting, 1984*. Denver, CO: American Humane Association.

Ammerman, R. T. (1990). Etiological models of child maltreatment: A behavioral perspective. *Behavior Modification, 14*(3), 230-254.

Ammerman, R. T., & Platz, R. J. (1996). Determinants of child abuse potential: Contribution of parent and child factors. *Journal of Clinical Child Psychology, 25*(3), 300-307.

Avison, W. R., Turner, R., & Noh, S. (1986). Screening for problem parenting: Preliminary evidence on a promising instrument. *Child Abuse and Neglect, 10,* 157-168.

Azar, S. T., (1991). Models of child abuse: A theoretical analysis. *Criminal Justice and Behavior, 18*(1), 30-46.

Belsky, J. (1980). Child maltreatment: An ecological integration. *American Psychologist, 35,* 320-335.

Belsky, J. (1993). Etiology of child maltreatment: A developmental ecological analysis. *Psychological Bulletin, 114,* 413-434.

Berkowitz, S. (1991). *Key findings from the state survey: Component of the study of high risk child abuse and neglect groups.* Rockville, MD: Westat.

Besharov, D. J. (1985). Right vs. rights: The dilemma of child protection. *Public Welfare, 43*(2), 19-27.

Boisen, L. (1994). Testing the community standard on neglect: Are we there yet? In E. Wattenburg (Ed.), *Children in the shadows: The fate of children of neglecting families.* Minneapolis: University of Minnesota Press.

Camasso, J. J., & Jagannathan, R. (1995). Prediction accuracy of the Washington and Illinois risk assessment instruments: An application of receiver operating characteristic curve analysis. *Social Work Research, 19*(3), 174-182.

Child Abuse Prevention and Treatment Act, Pub. L. 93-247, 42 U.S.C. 5101, § 3 (1974).

Child Abuse Prevention and Treatment Act, Pub. L. 93-247, 42 U.S.C. 5101 (as revised in 1996).

Cicchetti, D. (1992). *Development and psychopathology* (B. Nurcombe, Dep. Ed.). Cambridge, UK: Cambridge University Press.

Crouch, L., & Milner, J. S. (1993). Effects of child neglect on children. *Criminal Justice and Behavior, 20,* 49-65.

DiLeonardi, J. W. (1993, November). Families in poverty and chronic neglect of children. *Families in Society: The Journal of Contemporary Human Services,* 557-562.

Drake, B. (1996). Unraveling "unsubstantiated." *Child Maltreatment, 1*(3), 261-271.

Dubowitz, H., Black, M., Starr, R. H., & Zuravin, S. (1993). A conceptual definition of child neglect. *Criminal Justice and Behavior, 20*(1), 8-26.

Eckenrode, J., Powers, J., Doris, J., Munsch, J., & Bolger, N. (1988). Substantiation of child abuse and neglect reports. *Journal of Consulting and Clinical Psychology, 56*(1), 9-16.

English, D. J. (1997). Current knowledge about CPS decision-making. In T. D. Morton & W. Holder (Eds.), *Decision-making in children's protective services: Advancing the state of the art* (pp. 56-74). Atlanta, GA: Child Welfare Institute.

English, D. J., & Aubin, S. W. (1991). *Impact of investigations: Outcome for CPS cases receiving differential levels of service: Final report* (Grant # 90-CA-1366/01). Washington, DC: National Center on Child Abuse and Neglect.

English, D. J., Aubin, S. W., Fine, D., & Pecora, P. J. (1993). *Risk assessment as a practice method in child protective services* (Grant Nos. 90-CA-1456/01 & 02). Washington, DC: National Center on Child Abuse and Neglect.

English, D. J., Brummel, S., Coghlan, L. K., Novicky, R. S., & Marshall, D. B. (1998). *Decision-making in child protective services: A study of effectiveness. Final report, Phase II: Social worker interviews.* Olympia, WA: Department of Social and Health Services, Children's Administration, Management Services Division, Office of Children's Administration Research.

English, D. J., Marshal, D. B., Brummel, S., & Coghlan, L. K. (1998). *Decision-making in child protective services: A study of effectiveness. Final report, Phase I: Quantitative analysis.* Olympia, WA: Department of Social and Health Services, Children's Administration, Management Services Division, Office of Children's Administration Research.

English, D. J., & Pecora, P. J. (1994). Risk assessment as a practice method in child protective services. *Child Welfare, 73*(5), 451-473.

Gelles, R. (1973). Child abuse as psychopathology: A sociological critique and reformulation. *American Journal of Orthopsychiatry, 43,* 611-621.

Gil, D. (1971). A sociocultural perspective on physical child abuse. *Child Welfare, 50,* 389-395.

Giovannoni, J. (1989). Substantiated and unsubstantiated reports of child maltreatment. *Children and Youth Services Review, 11,* 299-318.

Giovannoni, J. (1990). Unsubstantiated reports: Perspectives of child protection workers. *Child and Youth Services, 15,* 51-62.

Giovannoni, J. M., & Billingsley, A. (1970). Child neglect among the poor: A study of parental adequacy in families of three ethnic groups. *Child Welfare, 49,* 196-204.

Groenveld, L. P., & Giovannoni, J. M. (1977, Summer). Disposition of child abuse and neglect cases. *Social Work Research and Abstracts, 10*(2), 24-30.

Hutchinson, E. D. (1989). Child protective screening decisions: An analysis of predictive factors. *Social Work Research and Abstracts, 24,* 9-15.

Jaudes, P. K., & Diamond, L. J. (1985). The handicapped child and child abuse. *Child Abuse and Neglect, 9,* 341-347.

Kempe, C. H., Silverman, F. N., Steele, B. R., Droegmueller, N., & Silver, H. K. (1962, July). The battered child syndrome. *Journal of the American Medical Association, 181,* 17-124.

Lyons, P., Doueck, H., & Wodarski, J. S. (1996). Risk assessment for child protective services: A review of the empirical literature on instrumental performance. *Social Work Review, 20*(3), 143-155.

National Research Council. (1993). *Understanding child abuse and neglect.* Washington, DC: National Academy Press.

Nelson, K., Saunders, E., & Landsmann, M. (1990). *Chronic neglect in perspective: A study of chronically neglecting families in a large metropolitan county* (Grant # 90CJ0102/02). Washington, DC: U.S. Department of Health & Human Services.

Paget, K. D., Phillip, J. D., & Abramczyk, L. W (1993). Recent developments in child neglect. *Advances in Clinical Child Psychology, 15,* 121-175.

Parke, R., & Collmer, C. W. (1975). Child abuse: An interdisciplinary analysis. In E. M. Hetherington (Ed.), *Review of child development research: Vol. 5.* Chicago: University of Chicago Press.

Polansky, N. A., Ammons, P. W., & Gaudin, J. M., Jr. (1985). Loneliness and isolation in child neglect. *Social Casework, 66,* 38-47.

Polansky, N., Chalmers, M. A., Buttenweiser, E., & Williams, D. (1978). Assessing adequacy of child caring: An urban scale. *Child Welfare, 57,* 439-499.

Rose, S. J., & Meezan, W. (1995). Variations in perception of child neglect. *Child Welfare, 75*(2), 139-160.

Scheurman, J. R., Stagner, M., Johnson, P., & Mullen. E. (1989). Child abuse and neglect decision making in Cook County. Chicago: University of Chicago, Chapin Hall Center for Children.

Sedlak, A. J., & Broadhurst, D. D. (1996). *Third national incidence study of child abuse and neglect: Final report.* Washington, DC: U.S. Department of Health and Human Services, National Center on Child Abuse and Neglect.

Spinetta, J. J., & Rigler, D. (1972). The child abusing parent: A psychological review. *Psychological Bulletin, 77*(4), 296-304.

U.S. Department of Health and Human Services, National Center on Child Abuse and Neglect. (1996). *Child maltreatment, 1994: Reports from the states to the National Center on Child Abuse and Neglect.* Washington, DC: Government Printing Office.

Wald, M. (1987). State intervention on behalf of neglected children: A search for realistic standards. *Stanford Law Review, 27,* 985-1040.

Wells, S. J. (1987). Screening practices in child protective services. In *Proceedings of the Invitational Policy Conference on Definitional Issues: May 29, 1987, Arlington, Virginia.* Washington, DC: American Bar Association, National Legal Resource Center for Child Advocacy and Protection.

Wells, S. J., Downing, J. D., & Fluke, J. (1990). Gatekeeping in child protective services: A survey of screening policies. *Child Welfare, 64*(4), 357-369.

Winefield, H. R., & Bradley, P. W. (1992). Substantiation of reported child abuse or neglect: Predictors and implications. *Child Abuse and Neglect, 16,* 661-671.

Wolfe, D. A. (1987). *Child abuse: Implications for child development and psychopathology.* Newbury Park, CA: Sage.

Wolock, I. (1982). Community characteristics and staff judgments in child abuse and neglect cases. *Social Work in Research and Abstracts, 18*(2), 9-15.

Wolock, I., & Horowitz, B. (1979). Child maltreatment and material deprivation among AFDC-recipient families. *Social Services Review, 53*(2), 174-194.

Zeanah, C. H., & Zeanah, P. D. (1989). Intergenerational transmission of maltreatment: Insights from attachment theory and research. *Psychiatry, 52*(2), 177-196.

Zuravin, S. J. (1991). Research definitions of child abuse and neglect: Current problems. In R. H. Starr, Jr., & D. A. Wolfe (Eds.), *The effects of child abuse and neglect: Issues and research* (pp. 100-128). New York: Guilford.

Zuravin, S., & Grief, J. L. (1989). Normative and child maltreating DC mothers. *Social Casework, 70,* 76-84.

Zuravin, S. J., Orme, J. G., & Hegar, R. L. (1994). *Factors predicting severity of child abuse injury: An empirical investigation using ordinal probit regression.* Baltimore: The University of Maryland-Baltimore, School of Social Work.

Zuravin, S. J., & Taylor, R. (1987). The ecology of child maltreatment identifying and characterizing high-risk neighborhoods. *Child Welfare, 66*(4), 497-506.

11 Intervening With Families When Children Are Neglected

DIANE DEPANFILIS

Child neglect is the most common and the least understood form of child maltreatment. The purpose of this chapter is to synthesize what we know about promising approaches to help families meet the basic needs of their children. This is not to suggest that neglect is only the result of omissions by caregivers but acknowledges the primary role of the family in nurturing children. This paper will integrate knowledge that has been previously generated through recent efforts to review the limited research on effective interventions (DePanfilis, 1996; Gaudin, 1988, 1993b; Gaudin, Wodarski, Arkinson, & Avery, 1990/91; Howing, Wodarski, Gaudin, & Kurtz, 1989; Smokowski & Wodarski, 1996) and propose intervention strategies based on the field's best collective knowledge and experience.

DEFINITIONS

For the purposes of this paper, neglect (1) refers to acts of omission of care to meet a child's basic needs that (2) result in harm or a threat of harm to children (Dubowitz, Black, Starr, & Zuravin, 1993). This definition infers that neglectful conditions are not always due to omissions by caregivers alone but may also be due to other factors beyond the control of impoverished families. This author concurs with a very early paper (Lewis, 1969) that underscored the importance of the social context of neglect. Lewis defined *parental neglect* as insufficient child care and guidance by a responsible adult and *community neglect* as insufficient provision of resources to support parents in their efforts to provide children with adequate care and guidance. In both instances, the responsible persons (parents or community authorities) are not likely to provide adequate care without outside intervention.

Going beyond this definition, a child's basic needs may not be met in many different ways. Using a combination of definitions (American Professional Society on the Abuse of Children [APSAC], 1995; Magura & Moses, 1986; U.S. Department of Health and Human Services [U.S.DHHS], 1988; Zuravin & DePanfilis, 1996), intervention may need to address the following circumstances when children's basic needs are not met: inadequate supervision, inappropriate substitute child care, abandonment, instability of living arrangements, failure to receive needed health care, inattention to personal hygiene, inattention to household sanitary conditions, inattention to household safety, presence of hazardous physical conditions in the home, inattention to nutritional needs, inadequacy of clothing, witnessing violence, permitting drug or alcohol use (or both), permitting other maladaptive behavior, inadequate nurturance or affection, isolation, inattention to mental health care needs, and inattention to educational needs.

PRINCIPLES FOR EFFECTIVE INTERVENTION

Considering the multiple pathways that can lead to neglect (see Crittenden, Chapter 3, this volume) and the many ways in which a child's basic needs may not be met, it is not surprising that there is little empirical research that provides clear support for one intervention approach versus another. However, although there may be much more that we need to learn, findings from recent reviews (DePanfilis, 1996; Gaudin, 1988, 1993b; Gaudin et al., 1990/91; Howing et al., 1989; Smokowski & Wodarski, 1996) do suggest some basic principles for practitioners who intervene with families when children's basic needs are not met.

Ecological-Developmental Framework

Intervention is more likely to be effective if it operates from a conceptual framework that views neglect within a system of risk and protective factors interacting across four levels: (1) the individual or ontogenic level, (2) the family microsystems, (3) the exosystem, and (4) the social macro system (Belsky, 1980). The National Research Council (1993) succinctly describes this model as follows:

> The ontogenic level involves individual characteristics and the changing developmental status of family members. The family microsystem includes the family environment, parenting styles, and interactions among family members. The exosystem consists of the community in which the family lives, the work place of the parents, school and peer groups of the family members, formal and informal social supports and services available to the family, and other factors such as family income, employment, and job availability. Finally, the social macro system consists of the overarching values and beliefs of the culture. (p. 110)

To be most effective, intervention should be directed at multiple levels (ontogenic, family microsystem, and exosystem) depending on the specific needs of the family. In addition, over the long term, programs should consider strategies to also address the social macrosystem. Policy initiatives must be targeted at social conditions that continue to oppress large segments of the population, especially the poorest of the poor, including families who are unable to provide minimally adequate care for their children (Nelson, Saunders, & Landsman, 1993). Examples suggested by Nelson and colleagues include the availability of affordable child care, increased education and employment opportunities, adequate low-income housing and rent subsidies, and large-scale drug prevention and treatment initiatives. Policies further need to ensure that both family preservation and support services are integrated into community institutions, such as schools, churches, and recreational organizations serving families (Thomlison, 1997). Thomlison suggests that risk-focused programing should prevent the accumulation of risk factors; establish and maintain prosocial situations and opportunities; focus on resilience and adaptation; facilitate active involvement of parents, children, and others in planning; ensure that services to at-risk populations are both necessary and sufficient; provide timely, careful, and expert evaluation, assessment, and follow-up services throughout the formative childhood years; and build safe, stable environments to permit families to establish structure, routines, rituals, and organization. Because this chapter is geared to intervention with families, the reader is encouraged to refer to the chapter by Gelles (Chapter 14, this volume) for further discussion of these and other macro-level interventions.

Importance of Outreach and Community

Families with children whose basic needs may not be met are typically poor and lack access to resources (Gaudin, 1993b; Smale, 1995). Furthermore, these families are more likely to be socially isolated, experience loneliness, and lack social support in both rural and urban areas than non-neglecting comparison groups (DePanfilis, 1996). Last, traditional, in-office, one-to-one counseling by professionals has proven to be ineffective with neglect (Cohn & Daro, 1987). Intervention therefore must include aggressive outreach and advocacy and be designed to mobilize concrete formal and informal helping resources.

Services provided in the home and within the neighborhood and community are therefore essential. The helper is in a much better position to understand the family in their daily environment and to break down and manage the natural resistance of the family to change (Anderson & Stewart, 1983). To be most effective, interventions must be a collaborative process between the family and the community. Strategies should encourage an inclusive process that allows people from schools, churches, health centers, businesses, child care facilities, and other sectors to come together to plan and carry out goals for strengthening their neighborhood (Zuravin & Shay, 1992). In turn, people will be linked to people, and informal helping relationships will be built.

Importance of Family Assessment

Effective intervention to remedy child neglect must be based on a comprehensive assessment of the family, with attention to the *type* of neglect that may be apparent and to the *specific contributing causes* at the individual, family, neighborhood, and community levels (Gaudin, 1988,

1993b). When available, this assessment should be undertaken in conjunction with other service providers to form a comprehensive picture of the individual, interpersonal, and societal pressures on the family members—individually and as a group. For both practice accountability and usefulness, practitioners should consider using standardized clinical measures of risk and protective factors as well as parenting attitudes, knowledge, and skills for assessment and recording information (Smokowski & Wodarski, 1996). Examples of clinical measures and recording formats that may be useful are provided in several texts (Bloom, Fischer, & Orme, 1995; Dunst, Trivette, & Deal, 1988; Fischer & Corcoran, 1994a, 1994b; Hudson, 1982; Karls & Wandrei, 1994; Magura & Moses, 1986; Magura, Moses, & Jones, 1987; McCubbin, Thompson, & McCubbin, 1996; Walmyr Publishing Co., 1990, 1992).

Because each family is unique and families with neglect problems are heterogeneous, no single intervention will be effective in all situations (National Research Council, 1993; Wolfe, 1993). Interventions must be tailored to the specific needs of individual families, and programs must be flexible to accommodate differences. There are significant differences between families who have experienced chronic multiple problems that led to neglect compared with families who may have experienced a recent crisis—for example, homelessness or unemployment—that has led to a child's basic needs being unmet (Nelson et al., 1993). Furthermore, because of the many different types of family systems, it is important that intervention be geared to the family's own definition of family and to culturally based differences and strengths (Lloyd & Sallee, 1994). In the past, mainstream efforts with families have focused too heavily on mothers without enough attention to fathers and other primary caregivers.

Importance of a Helping Alliance and Partnership With the Family

Many families at risk for neglect may not have had positive experiences with formal systems. A key component of many effective programs is to create a helping alliance and partnership with the family (Bean, 1994; Dore & Alexander, 1996; Kenemore, 1993). This requirement is especially challenging because some caregivers with neglect problems have difficulty forming and sustaining mutually supportive interpersonal relationships (Dore & Alexander, 1996; Gaudin & Polansky, 1986; Gaudin, Polansky,

Kilpatrick, & Shilton, 1993). One of the key challenges for practitioners is to form positive connections and partnerships with families so that they will have an opportunity to tackle the difficult challenges in their lives (McCurdy, Hurvis, & Clark, 1996). Successful engagement with families who may be resistant to intervention requires an ability to feel and demonstrate empathy with caregivers (Siu & Hogan, 1989) despite their initial resistance to intervention. Building relationships with caregivers models conflict resolution for building harmonious relationships that nurture the development of vulnerable family members (Bowlby, 1988; Crittenden, 1991). Crittenden suggests that when the practitioner sensitively attends to the affective communication of family members, a pattern of feedback loops leading to mutual accommodation and assimilation is established. These dialogues acknowledge and support caregiver strengths and provide family members with a secure base for developing communicative skills (Bowlby, 1988). Through this process, practitioners can create interventions tailor-made to each family's needs and competencies (Crittenden, 1991). To be effective over time, the intervention must help families develop more sustaining relationships with others. If intervention is neighborhood based, then these relationships are more likely to continue after intervention ends.

Importance of Empowerment-Based Practice

Several neglect-focused demonstration projects have reported on the importance of using empowerment approaches (Lee, 1994; Solomon, 1976) in their work with families (DiLeonardi, 1993; Landsman, Nelson, Allen, & Tyler, 1992; Mugridge, 1991; U.S.DHHS, 1993; Witt, Dayton, & Sheinvald, 1992; Zuravin & Shay, 1992). "Empowering families means carrying out interventions in a manner in which family members acquire a sense of control over their lives as a result of their efforts to meet their needs" (Dunst et. al., 1988, p. 88). To decrease the risk of neglect, interventions must help families learn to effectively manage the multiple stresses and conditions within the family and in their neighborhoods. Family members should be empowered to resolve their own problems and avoid dependence on the social service system (Lloyd & Sallee, 1994). Empowerment denotes a partnership between the practitioner and the family and involves the development and use of the capacities of the individual, family, organization, and community (Fraser & Galinsky, 1997). Drawing on these capacities helps families fully realize their own abilities and goals (Cowger, 1994; Guitierrez, 1990; Guitierrez, Glen Maye, & DeLois, 1995; Simon, 1994). The role of the helper becomes one of partner, guide, mediator, advocate, coach, and enabler.

Importance of Emphasizing Strengths

The strengths perspective is being increasingly applied with diverse populations (Saleebey, 1996, 1997; Trivette, Dunst, Deal, Hamer, & Prompst, 1990) and has particular relevance to families at risk for neglect and other forms of maltreatment (DePanfilis & Wilson, 1996). A strengths-based orientation helps build on a family's existing competencies and resources to respond to crises and stress; to meet needs; and to promote, enhance, and strengthen the functioning of the family system. Strengths-based practice involves a paradigmatic shift from a deficit approach, which emphasizes problems and pathology, to a positive partnership with the family. The focus of assessments (described earlier) is therefore on the complex interplay of both risks and strengths related to individual family members, the family as a unit, and the broader neighborhood and environment.

When a child's basic needs are unmet, we must understand what conditions within and outside the family may be contributing as well as what resources exist within and outside the family to help the family address the problem. The intervention, however, may not correct the problem but instead enable caregivers to meet the needs of family members who will be better able to have the time, energy, and resources for enhancing the well-being and development of the family (Dunst et al., 1988). As emphasized by Hobbs et al. (1984),

> Families are the critical element in the rearing of healthy, competent, and caring children. We suggest however that families—all families—cannot perform this function as well as they might unless they are supported by a caring and strong community, for it is community [support] that provides the informal and formal supplements to families' own resources. Just as a child needs nurturance, stimulation, and the resources that caring adults bring to his or her life, so too, do parents—as individuals and as adults filling socially valued roles (for example, parent, worker)—need the resources made possible by a caring community if they are to fulfill their roles well. (p. 46)

Importance of Culturally Competent Intervention

Risk and protective factors for child neglect may differ according to race and ethnicity. It is well established that families of color, and especially African American families, are disproportionately represented in the child welfare system (Children's Defense Fund, 1990; Leashore, Chipungu, & Everett, 1991; National Black Child Development Institute, 1990). Most often these families are poor and poorly educated (Brissett-Chapman, 1997). Furthermore, it is well documented that "children from African American, Hispanic, and other racial and ethnic backgrounds are subject to the direct and indirect effects of discrimination, compounding and exacerbating their risk for many kinds of problems" (Fraser & Galinsky, 1997, p. 272).

The need to increase cultural competency among helping professionals is a response to three factors in the United States: (1) increasing cultural diversity (Sue, Arrendondo, & McDavis, 1992), (2) the underrepresentation of professionals from diverse backgrounds in our helping institutions (McPhatter, 1997), and (3) inadequate delivery of social and mental health services to maltreated children and families of color (Gould, 1991). In particular, Gould suggests that families of color have received inadequate and often inappropriate and damaging child welfare services. There is compelling evidence to support this argument. For example, African American families and children have been denied access to many of the services of the child welfare system (Close, 1983), or they have received differential treatment within that system (Albers, Reilly, & Rittner, 1993; Stehno, 1982). Furthermore, minority children enter the foster care system disproportionately, partially influenced by poverty and by conversion of informal kinship arrangements to formal foster placements (Danzy & Jackson, 1997), and once in the system, they remain longer than Caucasian children, do not receive as many in-home support services as Caucasian children, and have a disproportionate number of undesirable experiences (Billingsley & Giovannoni, 1972; Gould, 1991; Mech, 1985). For example, African American children are more likely to be placed in transracial foster and adoptive homes than are Caucasian children and more likely to enter care as young children (Fein, 1991). Gould (1991) also suggests that African American children fare worse than white children or any other minority children on all measures of service delivery, such as recommended versus actual length of placement, number of services, adoption services, and worker contact with child and principal caregivers.

Because neglected children and their families continue to represent more than half of the caseload of our child welfare agencies (National Center on Child Abuse and Neglect, 1996), it is imperative that we work to increase the cultural competence of service providers. Basic cultural competence is achieved when organizations and practitioners accept and respect difference; engage in ongoing cultural self-assessment; expand their diversity knowledge and skills; and adapt service models to fit the target population's culture, situation, and perceived needs (Rauch, North, Rowe, & Risley-Curtiss, 1993). Culture is a set of beliefs, attitudes, values, and standards of behavior that are passed from one generation to the next. It includes language, worldview, dress, food, styles of communication, notions of wellness, healing techniques, childrearing patterns, and self-identity (Abney, 1996). Human beings create culture, and each group develops its own over time. Culture is dynamic and changing, not static; it evolves as conditions change. Every culture has a set of assumptions made up of beliefs that are so completely accepted by the group that they do not need to be stated, questioned, or defended. In brief, cultural competency is the ability to understand, to the best of one's ability, the worldview of our culturally different clients (or peers) and adapt our practice accordingly. To best meet the needs of families, practitioners must understand the world from the clients' points of view and help in a constructive manner.

At a symposium on neglect, Abney (U.S. DHHS, 1993) outlined needs of neglectful families that a culturally competent system should address. At the micro level, families need opportunities to build empowerment skills and to be involved in the advocacy process and peer support groups. At the macro level, families need financial assistance; housing; training focused on job retention; income augmentation to promote economic self-sufficiency; child care and health care; culturally sensitive research; substance abuse prevention and treatment programs; services that are geographically accessible, bilingual, and culturally sensitive; and greater participation in program planning and implementation by professionals of color and community representatives (U.S.DHHS, 1993).

Developmental Appropriateness of Interventions

It is critical that practitioners consider the developmental levels of children, caregivers, and the family as a system in their assessments and intervention strategies. For example, a child whose basic physical and emotional needs have been neglected will often suffer significant developmental delays (see Gaudin, Chapter 5, this volume). Interventions may need to offer opportunities for developmental remediation (e.g., therapeutic day care) while at the same time working on the attachment relationships between caregivers and children. Caregivers may bring a host of developmental issues to the family (e.g., unresolved losses, abuse, or deprivation during childhood) or may have difficulty assuming parental roles and responsibilities in adolescence. Described by Polansky, Chalmers, Williams, and Buttenwieser (1981) as "apathy-futility syndrome" or "psychological complexity" by Pianta, Egeland, and Erickson (1989), neglectful caregiving may be related to a failure of caregivers to have received nurturing as children. Cognitive interventions can help these caregivers change dysfunctional self-perceptions resulting from early neglect or abuse and break the intergenerational cycle of maltreatment (Egeland & Erickson, 1990). Last, the family may be stressed due to its developmental stage as a system (e.g., blended, young) or due to conflict in roles when the family is composed of caregivers across generations. As the drug epidemic has grown, we increasingly see grandparents raising their grandchildren due to neglect by drug-addicted parents. These newly constituted families often lack security due to informal arrangements and inadequate resources (financial and physical) to provide adequately for children (Kelley, 1996). Furthermore, the life cycle stages through which families evolve (Carter & McGoldrick, 1988) are interrupted; caregivers who thought that their childrearing days were over are unexpectedly unable to look forward to fewer demands during their retirement. In sum, it is essential that our interventions target the developmental needs of children, caregivers, and the family as a system.

INTERVENTIONS

The goal of intervention, to help families within communities meet the basic needs of their children, is to provide the mix and intensity of services appropriate to each family's need. Interventions are geared to increase the ability of families to successfully nurture their children by enabling families to use resources and opportunities in the community that will help them alleviate stress, overcome knowledge and skill deficits, and build and maintain caregiving competencies. Because the contributors to neglect are varied, interventions may be directed to developing or providing (or both) (1) concrete resources, (2) social support, (3) developmental remediation, (4) cognitive or behavioral interventions, (5) individually oriented interventions, (5) family-focused interventions, or (6) some combination of these (see Table 11.1).

Provision of Concrete Resources

Several types of neglect (e.g., household sanitation and safety, personal hygiene, nutritional neglect, and lack of supervision) may be the results of deficits in concrete resources. Furthermore, the stress of poverty and its many consequences (e.g., living in inadequate housing within crime-ridden neighborhoods) can contribute to a sense of powerlessness that further affects caregiving capacity to meet children's basic needs. Helping families access concrete resources supports adequate care of their children and is often crucial *before* families can address other factors in their lives that may affect care of their children. Examples include housing assistance; emergency financial, food, and energy assistance; affordable and quality child care; transportation; home management assistance; and free or low-cost medical care. These concrete resources are needed to help families move beyond mere survival to more optimal functioning, including improved care of their children (Nelson et al., 1993).

Social Support Interventions

Sufficient evidence exists that families who are socially isolated, experience loneliness, and lack social support in both rural and urban settings may be more prone to neglect than matched comparison groups (DePanfilis, 1996). A social network among a group of people serves to provide nurturance and reinforcement for efforts to cope with life on a day-to-day basis (Whittaker & Garbarino, 1983). Interventions are geared to provide or mobilize the personal social network of a family to serve one or more social support functions, including emotional, and material support, knowledge information, appraisal support (information pertinent to self-evaluation), and companionship. Studies on the stress-buffering role of social support and from intervention programs involving mobilization

TABLE 11.1 Interventions When Children Are Neglected.

Ecological (Concrete)	*Ecological (Social Support)*	*Developmental*	*Cognitive-Behavioral*	*Individual*	*Family System*
Housing assistance	Individual social support	Therapeutic day care	Social skills training	Alcohol or other drug in-patient and out-patient counseling, detoxification	Home-based family-entered counseling regarding family functioning, communication skills, home management, roles, and responsibilities
Emergency financial, food, or other assistance	Connections to church activities	Individual assistance with developmental role achievement (e.g., parenting)	Communication skill building	12-Step programs	Center-based family therapy
Clothing, household items	Mentor involvement	Public health visiting, with focus on developmental interventions, including attachment needs of family members	Teaching home management, parent-child interaction, meal preparation skills, and other life skills	Mental health in-patient and out-patient counseling	Mobilizing family strengths
Advocacy for availability or accessibility to community resources	Social support groups	Peer groups (often at schools) geared to developmental tasks (e.g., adolescence)	Teach new thought processes (e.g., regarding childhood history)	Crisis intervention	Nurturing family camps
Hands-on assistance to increase safety and sanitation of home (home management aides)	Development of neighborhood child care co-op	Mentors to provide nurturing, cultural enrichment, recreation, role modeling	Parenting education	Stress management counseling	Family sculpting
Transportation	Neighborhood center activities		Employment counseling or training (or both)	Play therapy	
Free or low-cost medical care	Social networking		Financial management counseling		
Low-cost but quality child care (parent aide, volunteer)	Recreation programs		Problem-solving training		
	Cultural festivals and other activities				

of social support suggest that both a confidant and a network help protect families against stress (Gottlieb, 1985).

To evaluate the meaningfulness of available social support, one must assess the *actual* network (accessibility, frequency of interaction, and closeness) and the *perceived* social support—from friends and from family (DePanfilis, 1996). Models for assessing the quantity and quality of a family's linkages with formal and informal supportive resources include (1) the Eco Map (Hartman, 1978); (2) the Social Network Map (Tracy, 1990; Tracy & Whittaker, 1990); (3) the Social Network Assessment Guide (Gaudin et al., 1990/91); (4) the Index of Social Network Strengths (Gaudin, 1979); (5) the Pattison Psychosocial Inventory (Hurd, Pattison, & Smith, 1981); (6) the Social Network Form (Wellman, 1981; Wolf, 1983); and (7) three instruments developed by Dunst et al. (1988): the Family Support Scale, the Inventory of Social Support, and the Personal Network Matrix. Each of these has its strengths and may be used in varied situations to enable families to identify individuals and systems in their lives that help them negotiate their often difficult life circumstances.

Once specific needs have been assessed, interventions vary from individual support by a paraprofessional or volunteer to parent groups geared to connect parents to each other within a neighborhood and community. Opportunities for helping families build the social supports they need are varied and multiple and offer hope that someone will "be there" for them, long after formal intervention has been discontinued. These services are crucial to an empowerment philosophy (DiLeonardi, 1993; U.S.DHHS, 1993; Witt et al., 1992; Zuravin & Shay, 1992).

There are advantages and disadvantages to both group and individual support intervention models. Because neglectful caregivers may lack basic verbal-social interaction skills (Gaudin, 1993a, p. 76; Gaudin et al., 1990/91), they may not easily develop positive social connections with others in a group setting. As a result, Gaudin (1993b) suggests that because neglectful caregivers may be ill at ease in groups, extra efforts must be made to engage these parents by providing child care, transportation, refreshments, and social activities; structuring group meetings; and limiting group size to 8 to 12 members. With these ingredients, caregivers are more likely to attend and to develop relationships with others in the group.

Intervention strategies that include lay services, such as parent aide counseling, have been shown to be more effective than traditional services in reducing the propensity for future maltreatment by neglectful parents (Cohn, 1979). Intensive contact with a volunteer, lay therapist, or parent aide helps expand and enrich impoverished networks and provides new information, positive norms, and helpful suggestions about child care. One of the advantages of this intervention is that services can be individualized, which is less likely in group interventions. However, when these services are delivered by paraprofessionals or volunteers, training, clear definitions of roles and tasks, and close supervision are critical (Videka-Sherman, 1988).

Developmental Remediation

Families with neglect problems have often experienced all types of loss in their lives. The developmental perspective provides a frame of reference for understanding the growth and functioning of human beings in the context of their families and their families' transactions with their environments (Pecora, Whittaker, & Maluccio, 1992). This perspective views human behavior and social functioning within an environmental context. It goes beyond ecology by including the stages and tasks of the family's life cycle, the biopsychosocial principles of individual growth and development, and goals and needs that are common to all human beings and families. In addition, a developmental perspective considers the particular aspirations, needs, and qualities of each person and each family in light of diversity in such areas as culture, ethnicity, race, class, and sexual orientation.

Intervention with families who have experienced difficulty meeting the basic needs of their children should be guided by an optimistic view of the capacity of children and adults to overcome early deprivation through nurturing experiences throughout the life cycle. This optimistic view should guide intervention but be balanced by a realistic appraisal of the capacity of caregivers to eventually meet the needs of their children.

Although few programs that offer therapeutic services geared to developmental issues have been evaluated, there are some promising approaches for helping children and their caregivers overcome serious caregiving deficits that may have evolved over generations. For children, preschool programs, such as Head Start, have demonstrated value in enhancing self-esteem and skills in disadvantaged children (Daro, 1988; Howing et al., 1989). Programs with therapeutic activities to provide cognitive stimulation, cultural enrichment, and development of motor skills and social skills were found to significantly improve children's functioning and the prevention of repeated maltreatment (Daro, 1988). Many therapeutic day care programs recognize that their interventions need to include the family. They may provide both child-oriented services, such as health, developmental, and psychological services, and involve caregivers in parent education and support groups (Miller & Whittaker, 1988).

Cognitive-Behavioral Interventions

Numerous studies support the effectiveness of using behavioral techniques in individual therapy with caregivers who have neglect or physical-abuse problems (Crimmins, Bradlyn, St. Lawrence, & Kelly, 1984; Crozier & Katz, 1979; Eyberg & Matarazzo, 1980; Reavley & Gilbert, 1979; Szykula & Fleichman, 1985; Wolfe et al., 1982; Wolfe, Sandler, & Kaufman, 1981). Specific techniques are selected after individual assessment and may include the following:

- Verbal instruction (e.g., about basic child care), often in combination with other techniques
- Social skills training, such as modeling, role-play, and behavior rehearsal (e.g., for preparation in handling specific child care tasks)
- Stress management, such as relaxation techniques and stress inoculation training, which involves relaxation training, cognitive coping skills, and behavioral rehearsal skills when caregivers are depressed or experience other negative effects of life stressors
- Cognitive restructuring, a process to assist clients to gain awareness of dysfunctional and self-defeating thoughts and misconceptions that impair functioning and to replace them with beliefs and behaviors that lead to enhanced functioning used when caregivers are feeling overwhelmed and powerless

These techniques are especially useful with neglectful families if they target both the environment and the individual. Project 12-Ways is one such program that uses an ecobehavioral approach (Lutzker, 1990; Lutzker & Rice, 1984, 1987) and reports success in reducing safety hazards in the home (Tertinger, Greene, & Lutzker, 1984). Using a home accident prevention inventory, practitioners formally assess the injury hazards that may be present in homes and then use several behavioral-educational treatment strategies to help families make their homes safer for children. Other improvements with such intervention strategies have been noted in the areas of nutrition, home cleanliness and personal hygiene, affective skills, and identification and reporting of children's illnesses (Lutzker, 1990). Azar

(1986) agrees that a cognitive-behavioral and developmental framework can focus not only on person-based deficits, such as parent-child interaction, impulse control, or parental cognitive dysfunctions, but also on environmentally based problems, such as stress level of a family and the social support network.

Other cognitive-behavioral interventions are geared to enable caregivers to modify negative, dysfunctional self-images incorporated as a result of early experiences of neglect and abuse. Project STEEP is an example of an intensive, individual, in-home counseling and group intervention program that seeks to change negative self-perceptions and break the intergenerational cycle of maltreatment (Egeland & Erickson, 1990). The effectiveness of this approach, however, has yet to be conclusively established.

Last, there are promising examples of group interventions (Daro, 1988; Gaudin et. al., 1990/91) that provide information on basic child care and skills, problem solving, home management, and social interaction skills. An example of a program that is designed to be offered in groups or in the home is the Nurturing Program (Bavolek, 1988). Implemented extensively throughout the United States and in parts of Europe and South America, the Nurturing Program evaluations show significant increases in knowledge of appropriate parenting skills and techniques; increased empathic awareness of children's needs; and decreased use of corporal punishment, inappropriate expectations, and parent-child role reversals (Bavolek, Comstock, & McLaughlin, 1983).

Interventions Focused on the Individual

Neglect often results due to multiple factors. Individually oriented intervention is sometimes needed to address problems that interfere with caregiving (e.g., mental health or drug problems) as well as child-specific interventions to help children overcome the consequences of neglect.

The needs of some children are neglected because their caregivers suffer from emotional and mental health problems. For example, Gaines, Sandgrund, Green, & Power (1978) found that mothers with neglect problems were functioning more poorly than abusive mothers relative to coping with stress and meeting their children's emotional needs. Similarly, in a study of low-income mothers in Baltimore, Zuravin (1988) found that as depression of mothers increased from mild to moderate to severe, the probability of neglect increased. Such findings suggest that following a comprehensive assessment of the family's needs and strengths, some caregivers require a mix of individual therapy and supports to help them overcome depression and other mental health problems that impair their ability to adequately care for their children.

Many professionals have also called attention to the fact that children from families with alcohol or other drug problems are overwhelming the service delivery capacities of the child protective services system (Besharov, 1994; Curtis & McCullough, 1993; Dore, Doris, & Wright, 1995). It is crucial that the comprehensive assessment evaluate the possibility of substance abuse (Olson, Allen, & Azzi-Lessing, 1996) and facilitate a treatment approach to help caregivers recover from their addiction and improve their abilities to provide care for their children. Olson et al., (1996) suggest that the risk of child maltreatment problems among families whose caregivers have a substance abuse problem is affected by eight dimensions: (1) commitment to recovery, (2) patterns of use, (3) effect on child caring, (4) effect on lifestyle, (5) supports for recovery, (6) parent's self-efficacy, (7) parent's self-care, and (8) quality of neighborhood.

Following the assessment, effective service to substance-abusing families requires the expertise of health care providers, substance abuse counselors, and child welfare workers. Collaboration among these service providers enhances interventions by increasing the family's access to services in the community. Major barriers to collaboration, such as interagency biases, differing philosophies, and control issues, may be overcome by joint planning and joint ownership of the service delivery program (Azzi-Lessing & Olsen, 1996; Denton, 1992; Kropenske & Howard, 1994).

Neglected children may require individual attention to help them overcome serious deficits in cognitive, academic, and social skills. For school-age children and adolescents, Gaudin (1993a) suggests that the following interventions may help: (1) special education programs to remedy deficits in cognitive stimulation and motivation to learn, (2) school- or community-based tutorial programs using professional teachers or volunteers to provide academic help and encourage relationships with nurturing adults, and (3) personal-skills-development classes for older children and adolescents to develop life skills appropriate to their ages and developmental levels.

Family-Focused, Home-Based Interventions

After a review of 19 demonstration programs, Daro (1988) concluded that interventions that included family members, rather than focusing on the primary caregiver, were more successful. Her findings further suggested that traditional, in-office, one-to-one counseling by professionals was ineffective with neglect. Polansky et al. (1981) drew similar conclusions and suggested that intervention is necessary with families to disturb the dysfunctional family balance to achieve a more functional family system that does not sacrifice the needs of the children. Gaudin (1993a) suggested that family interventions may "seek to reallocate family role tasks, establish clear intergenerational boundaries, clarify communication among family members, reframe parents' dysfunctional perceptions of themselves and their children, and enable parents to assume a strong leadership role in the family" (pp. 36-37).

Often, family-focused interventions are combined with the provision of concrete services, including the range of emergency and concrete resources previously discussed. Thus, a major part of family-focused intervention includes helping the family obtain concrete services, such as transportation, recreational opportunities, employment, financial assistance, housework assistance, child care, food assistance, medical care, toys and educational resources, utility assistance, and clothing assistance (Pecora et al., 1992). Family interventions are geared to empower the family to improve the safety of their environment and access resources needed to provide adequate child care. Homemaker services are an important support because primary caregivers may lack knowledge about basic household skills and homemakers can be effective role models. It is important that families learn more effective ways to manage their limited resources to avoid crises such as evictions, loss of food, and shortages of other resources to meet the basic needs of children.

CONCLUSIONS

Although strong empirical support for specific interventions is lacking, our combined practice wisdom does suggest some valuable principles for helping families provide adequate care for their children. These principles are rooted in an ecological developmental framework that targets intervention at the individual, family, and community system levels. Interventions must reach out to families in their communities and neighborhoods and include an individualized family assessment. Child neglect results from a complex interplay of both risk and protective factors; intervention should be tailored to meet the unique needs and strengths of each family. Integral ingredients in all interventions, however, are the development of a helping alliance and partnership with the family and empowering families to develop and use their strengths. Furthermore, practitioners must accept and respect differences and adapt service models to meet the needs of each family, its culture, situation, and perceived needs.

Following a comprehensive family assessment, promising interventions are directed to developing or providing concrete resources, social support, developmental remediation, cognitive or behavioral interventions, individually oriented interventions, and family-focused interventions. Services are geared to empower families to access the resources needed to manage the multiple stresses and strains in their lives so that they may provide children with adequate care and guidance. It is also essential that services are available to help children overcome developmental deficits that may have resulted from chronic inattention to their needs.

Because progress with families may be slow, programs should be designed flexibly, routinely (at least every 3 months) assess progress, and adjust treatment plans when necessary. In addition, there is evidence that addressing neglect takes more time compared with other types of child maltreatment (Cohn & Daro, 1987; Miller & Whittaker, 1988), particularly in cases involving chronic neglect and substance abuse (Nelson et al., 1993; Nelson, Landsman, Tyler, & Richards, 1996).

It must further be recognized that even under the best of circumstances, individual family-oriented intervention can only be expected to partially address the widespread problem of child neglect. There is an urgent need for policies to be targeted at social conditions that increase the risk of neglect. For example, we are currently at a crossroads as states implement welfare reform. These changes could lead to either improvement or deterioration in the economic circumstances of poor families and children, contributing to changes in the demand for child welfare services (Courtney, 1997). Because neglect is so directly linked to economic conditions and the availability of resources, states are challenged to implement plans that truly will lift families out of poverty and shift child care for children from daily supervision by ineffective parents to government-subsidized child care settings. On the other hand, families could also see a significant deterioration in their economic well-being as parents are forced to take low-paying jobs and settle for substandard child care. We are challenged to make the best of this hastily crafted reform to avoid increased societal neglect of our children.

Last, with respect to the family-level interventions that we do provide, it is imperative that we further efforts to evaluate outcomes toward learning what specific interventions are most effective in working with whom. In particular, our knowledge base is not refined to the level that we know what form(s) of intervention are best to meet the needs of families who are unmotivated to access needed services or specifically for what length of time services are needed. Although our models and evaluations are becoming more sophisticated, there is also a clear need to design programs that examine the cost-effectiveness of programs so that we have a better understanding of what types of interventions are best for addressing specific needs. At a minimum, our studies need to clearly describe the population that is being served (situational neglect, chronic neglect, specific subtypes of neglect), including differences between treatment and comparison groups, the intervention model (including specifically what types of services are provided to whom), the length and intensity of interventions, the treatment outcomes being targeted, and the standardized measures that are used for evaluating outcomes.

REFERENCES

Abney, V. D. (1996). Cultural competency in the field of child maltreatment. In J. Briere, L. Berliner, J. A. Bulkely, C. Jenny, & T. Reid (Eds.), *The APSAC handbook on child maltreatment* (pp. 409-419). Thousand Oaks, CA: Sage.

Albers, E. C., Reilly, T., & Rittner, B. (1993). Children in foster care: Possible factors affecting permanency planning. *Child and Adolescent Social Work Journal, 10,* 329-333.

American Professional Society on the Abuse of Children. (1995). *Psychosocial evaluation of suspected psychological maltreatment in children and adolescents.* Chicago: Author.

Anderson, C. M., & Stewart, S. (1983). *Mastering resistance: A practical guide to family therapy.* New York: Guilford.

Azar, S. T. (1986). A framework for understanding child maltreatment: An integration of cognitive behavioural and developmental perspectives. *Canadian Journal of Behavioural Science, 18,* 340-355.

Azzi-Lessing, L., & Olsen, L. J. (1996). Substance abuse-affected families in the child welfare system: New challenges, new alliances. *Social Work, 41,* 15-23.

Bavolek, S. J. (1988). *The nurturing programs for parents and children.* Park City, UT: Family Development Resources.

Bavolek, S. J., Comstock, C. M., & McLaughlin, J. A. (1983). *The nurturing programs: A validated approach for reducing dysfunctional family interaction* (Final report, Program No. 1R01MA34862). Rockville, MD: National Institutes of Health.

Bean, N. M. (1994). *Stranger in our home: Rural families talk about the experience of having received in-home family services.* Unpublished doctoral dissertation, Case Western Reserve University, Mandel School of Applied Social Sciences, Cleveland, Ohio.

Belsky, J. (1980). Child maltreatment: An ecological integration. *American Psychologist, 35,* 320-335.

Besharov, D. J. (1994). *When drug addicts have children.* Washington, DC: Child Welfare League of America.

Billingsley, A., & Giovannoni, J. M. (1972). *Children of the storm.* New York: Harcourt, Brace & Jovanovich.

Bloom, M., Fischer, J., & Orme, J. (1995). *Evaluating practice: Guidelines for the accountable professional* (2nd ed.). Boston: Allyn & Bacon.

Bowlby, J. (1988). *A secure base: Clinical applications of attachment theory.* London: Tavistock/Routledge.

Brissett-Chapman, S. (1997). Child protection risk assessment and African American children: Cultural ramifications for families and communities. *Child Welfare, 76,* 45-63.

Carter, B., & McGoldrick, M. (Eds.). (1988). *The changing life cycle—A framework for family therapy* (2nd ed.). New York: Gardner.

Children's Defense Fund. (1990). *A report card briefing book and action primer.* Washington, DC: Author.

Close, M. (1983). Child welfare and people of color: Denial of equal access. *Social Work Research and Abstracts, 19*(4), 576-577.

Cohn, A. H. (1979). Effective treatment of child abuse and neglect. *Social Work, 24,* 513-519.

Cohn, A. H., & Daro, D. (1987). Is treatment too late: What ten years of evaluative research tell us. *Child Abuse and Neglect, 11,* 433-442.

Courtney, M. E. (1997). Welfare reform and child welfare services. In S. B. Kamerman & S. J. Kahn (Eds.), *Child welfare in the context of welfare "reform."* New York: Columbia University School of Social Work.

Cowger, C. D. (1994). Assessing client strengths: Clinical assessment for client empowerment. *Social Work, 39,* 262-268.

Crimmins, D. B., Bradlyn, A. S., St. Lawrence, J. S., & Kelly, J. A. (1984). A training technique for improving the parent-child interaction skills of an abusive neglectful mother. *Child Abuse and Neglect, 8,* 533-539.

Crittenden, P. M. (1991). Treatment of child abuse and neglect. *Human Systems: The Journal of Systemic Consultation & Management, 2,* 161-179.

Crozier, J., & Katz, R. C. (1979). Social learning treatment of child abuse. *Journal of Behavior Therapy and Psychiatry, 10,* 213-220.

Curtis, P. A., & McCullough, C. (1993). The impact of alcohol and other drugs on the child welfare system. *Child Welfare, 62,* 533-542.

Danzy, J., & Jackson, S. M. (1997). Family preservation and support services: A missed opportunity for kinship care. *Child Welfare, 76,* 31-44.

Daro, D. (1988). *Confronting child abuse.* New York: Free Press.

Denton, I. (1992). *Challenges of collaborating to serve substance-abusing mothers and their children.* Paper presented at the conference Working Together: Linkages for Preserving Families Affected by Alcohol and Other Drugs, Richmond, Virginia.

DePanfilis, D. (1996). Social isolation of neglectful families: A review of social support assessment and intervention models. *Child Maltreatment, 1,* 37-52.

DePanfilis, D., & Wilson, C. (1996). Applying the strengths perspective with maltreating families. *The APSAC Advisor, 9*(3), 15-20.

DiLeonardi, J. W. (1993). Families in poverty and chronic neglect of children. *Families in Society, 74,* 557-562.

Dore, M. M., & Alexander, L. B. (1996). Preserving families at risk of child abuse and neglect: The role of the helping alliance. *Child Abuse and Neglect, 20,* 349-361.

Dore, M. M., Doris, J. M., & Wright, P. (1995). Identifying substance abuse in maltreating families: A child welfare challenge. *Child Abuse and Neglect, 19,* 531-543.

Dubowitz, H., Black, M., Starr, R. H., & Zuravin, S. J. (1993). A conceptual definition of child neglect. *Criminal Justice and Behavior, 20,* 8-26.

Dunst, C., Trivette, C., & Deal, A. (1988). *Enabling and empowering families.* Cambridge, MA: Brookline.

Egeland, F., & Erickson, M. F. (1990). Rising above the past: Strategies for helping new mothers break the cycle of abuse and neglect. *Zero to Three, 10,* 29-35.

Eyberg, S. M., & Matarazzo, R. G. (1980). Training parents as therapists: A comparison between individual parent-child interaction training and parent group didactic training. *Journal of Clinical Psychology, 36,* 492-499.

Fein, E. (1991). The elusive search for certainty in child welfare: Introduction. *American Journal of Orthopsychiaty, 61*(4), 576-577.

Fischer, J., & Corcoran, K. (1994a). *Measures for clinical practice: Vol. 1. Couples, families and children* (2nd ed.). New York: Free Press.

Fischer, J., & Corcoran, K. (1994b). *Measures for clinical practice: Vol. 2. Adults* (2nd ed.). New York: Free Press.

Fraser, M. W., & Galinsky, M. J. (1997). Toward a resilience-based model of practice. In M. W. Fraser (Ed.), *Risk and resilience in childhood: An ecological perspective.* Washington, DC: NASW Press.

Gaines, R., Sandgrund, A., Green, A., & Power, E. (1978). Etiological factors in child maltreatment: A multivariate study of abusing, neglecting, and normal mothers. *Journal of Abnormal Psychology, 87,* 531-540.

Gaudin, J. M., Jr. (1979). *Mothers' perceived strength of primary group networks and maternal child abuse.* Unpublished doctoral dissertation, Florida State University, Tallahassee.

Gaudin, J. M., Jr. (1988). Treatment of families who neglect their children. In E. M. Nunnally, C. S. Chilman, & F. M. Cox (Eds.), *Mental illness, delinquency, addictions, and neglect* (pp. 167-249). Newbury Park, CA: Sage.

Gaudin, J. M., Jr. (1993a). *Child neglect: A guide for intervention.* Washington, DC: National Center on Child Abuse and Neglect.

Gaudin, J. M., Jr. (1993b). Effective intervention with neglectful families. *Criminal Justice and Behavior, 20,* 66-89.

Gaudin, J. M., Jr., & Polansky, N. A. (1986). Social distances and the neglectful family: Sex, race, and social class influences. *Children and Youth Services Review, 8,* 1-12.

Gaudin, J. M., Jr., Polansky, N. A., Kilpatrick, A. C., & Shilton, P. (1993). Loneliness, depression, stress, and social supports in neglectful families. *American Journal of Orthopsychiatry, 63,* 597-605.

Gaudin, J. M., Jr., Wodarski, J. S., Arkinson, M. K., & Avery, L. S. (1990/91). Remedying child neglect: Effectiveness of social network interventions. *The Journal of Applied Social Sciences, 15,* 97-123.

Gottlieb, B. (1985). Theory into practice: Issues that surface in planning interventions that mobilize support. In I. G. Sarason & B. R. Sarason (Eds.), *Social support: Theory, research, and applications* (pp. 417-437). Dordrecht, Holland: Martines Nijjhof.

Gould, K. H. (1991). Limiting damage is not enough: A minority perspective on child welfare issues. In J. E. Everett, S. S. Chipungu, & B. R. Leashore (Eds.), *Child welfare: An Africentric perspective* (pp. 58-78). New Brunswick, NJ: Rutgers University Press.

Gutierrez, L. M. (1990). Working with women of color: An empowerment perspective. *Social Work, 35,* 149-154.

Guitierrez, L., Glen Maye, L., & DeLois, K. (1995). The organizational context of empowerment practice: Implications for social work administration. *Social Work, 40,* 249-258.

Hartman, A. (1978). Diagrammatic assessments of family relationships. *Social Casework, 59,* 465-476.

Hill, R. B. (1971). *The strengths of black families.* New York: National Urban League.

Hobbs, N., Dokecki, P. R., Hoover-Dempsey, K. V., Moroney, R. M., Shayne, M. W., & Weeks, K. H. (1984). *Strengthening families.* San Francisco: Jossey-Bass.

Howing, P., Wodarski, J., Gaudin, J., & Kurtz, P. D. (1989). Effective interventions to ameliorate the incidence of child maltreatment: The empirical base. *Social Work, 34,* 330-338.

Hudson, W. (1982). *The clinical measurement package: A field manual.* Homewood, IL: Dorsey.

Hurd, G., Pattison, E. M., & Smith, J. E. (1981, February). *Test-re-test reliability of social network self reports: The Pattison Psychosocial Inventory (PPI).* Paper presented to Sun Belt Social Networks Conference, Tampa, Florida.

Karls, J. M., & Wandrei, K. E. (Eds.). (1994). *Pie manual: Person in-environment system.* Washington, DC: National Association of Social Workers.

Kelley, S. J. (1996). *Neglected children in intergenerational kinship care* (Neglect demonstration project proposal submitted by Georgia State University to the National Center on Child Abuse and Neglect). Available from Dr. Susan Kelley, Georgia State University, Office of Research, College of Health Sciences, University Plaza, Atlanta, GA 30303.

Kenemore, T. K. (1993). The helping relationship: Getting in touch with the client's experience. In *National Center on Child Abuse and Neglect Chronic Neglect Symposium Proceedings, June 1993* (pp. 51-53). Chicago: National Center on Child Abuse and Neglect.

Kropenske, V., & Howard, J. (1994). *Protecting children in substance-abusing families.* Washington, DC: National Center on Child Abuse and Neglect.

Landsman, M. J., Nelson, K., Allen, M., & Tyler, M. (1992). *The self-sufficiency project: Final report.* Iowa City, IA: National Resource Center in Family Based Services.

Leashore, B. R., Chipungu, S. S., & Everett, J. E. (1991). *Child welfare: An Africentric perspective.* New Brunswick, NJ: Rutgers University Press.

Lee, J. A. B. (1994). *The empowerment approach to social work practice.* New York: Columbia University Press.

Lewis, H. (1969). Parental and community neglect: Twin responsibilities of protective services. *Children, 16,* 114-118.

Lewis, J. M., & Looney, J. G. (1983). *The long struggle: Well-functioning working class black families.* New York: Brunner/Mazel.

Lloyd, J. C., & Sallee, A. L. (1994). The challenge and potential of family preservation services in the public child welfare system. *Protecting Children, 10*(3), 3-6.

Lutzker, J. R. (1990). Behavioral treatment of child neglect. *Behavior Modification, 14,* 301-315.

Lutzker, J. R., & Rice, J. M. (1984). Project 12-ways: Measuring outcome of a large in-home service for treatment and prevention of child abuse and neglect. *Child Abuse and Neglect, 8,* 519-524.

Lutzker, J. R., & Rice, J. M. (1987). Using recidivism data to evaluate project 12-Ways: An ecobehavioral approach to the treatment and prevention of child abuse and neglect. *Journal of Family Violence, 2,* 283-290.

Magura, S., & Moses, B. S. (1986). *Outcome measures for child welfare services.* Washington, DC: Child Welfare League of America.

Magura, S., Moses, B. S., & Jones, M. A. (1987). *Assessing risk and measuring change in families: The family risk scales.* Washington, DC: Child Welfare League of America.

McCubbin, H., Thompson, A., & McCubbin, M. (1996). *Family assessment: Resiliency, coping and adaptation, inventories for research and practice.* Madison: University of Wisconsin Systems.

McCurdy, K., Hurvis, S., & Clark, J. (1996). Engaging and retaining families in child abuse prevention programs. *The APSAC Advisor, 9*(3), 1, 3-9.

McPhatter, A. R. (1997). Cultural competence in child welfare: What is it? How do we achieve it? What happens without it? *Child Welfare, 76,* 255-278.

Mech, E. V. (1985). Public social services to minority children and their families. In R. O. Washington & J. Boros-Hull (Eds.), *Children in need of roots* (pp. 133-186). Davis, CA: International Dialogue Press.

Miller, J. L., & Whittaker, J. K. (1988). Social services and social support: Blended programs for families at risk of child maltreatment. *Child Welfare, 67,* 161-174.

Mugridge, G. B. (1991, September). *Reducing chronic neglect.* Paper presented at the Ninth National Conference on Child Abuse and Neglect, Denver, CO.

National Black Child Development Institute. (1990). *The status of African-American children.* Washington, DC: Author.

National Research Council. (1993). *Understanding child abuse and neglect.* Washington, DC: National Academy Press.

Nelson, K., Landsman, M., Tyler, M., & Richardson, B. (1996, Fall). Examining the length of service and cost-effectiveness of intensive family service. *The Prevention Report, 2,* 13-17.

Nelson, K. E., Saunders, E. J., & Landsman, M. J. (1993). Chronic neglect in perspective. *Social Work, 38,* 661-671.

Olson, L. J., Allen, D., & Azzi-Lessing, L. (1996). Assessing risk in families affected by substance abuse. *Child Abuse and Neglect, 20,* 833-842.

Pecora, P., Whittaker, J., & Maluccio, A. (1992). *The child welfare challenge: Policy, practice, and research.* New York: Aldine.

Pianta, R., Egeland, B., & Erickson, M. F. (1989). The antecedents of maltreatment: Results of the mother-child interaction research project. In D. Cicchetti & V. Carlson (Eds.), *Child maltreatment: Theory and research on the causes of child abuse and neglect* (pp. 203-253). New York: Cambridge University Press.

Polansky, N. A., Chalmers, M. A., Williams, D. P., & Buttenwieser, E. W. (1981). *Damaged parents: An anatomy of child neglect.* Chicago: University of Chicago Press.

Rauch, J. B., North, C., Rowe, C., & Risley-Curtiss, C. (1993). *Diversity competence: A learning guide.* Baltimore: University of Maryland at Baltimore, School of Social Work.

Reavley, W., & Gilbert, M. T. (1979). The analysis and treatment of child abuse by behavioral psychotherapy. *Child Abuse and Neglect, 3,* 509-514.

Saleebey, D. (1996). The strengths perspective in social work practice: Extensions and cautions. *Social Work, 41,* 296-305.

Saleebey, D. (Ed.). (1997). *The strengths perspective in social work practice* (2nd ed.). New York: Longman.

Simon, B. L. (1994). *The empowerment tradition in American social work: A history.* New York: Columbia University Press.

Siu, S. F., & Hogan, P. T. (1989). Public child welfare: The need for clinical social work. *Social Work, 34,* 423-428.

Smale, G. G. (1995). Integrating community and individual practice: A new paradigm for practice. In P. Adams & K. Nelson (Eds.), *Reinventing human services community- and family-centered practice* (pp. 59-80). New York: Aldine De Gruyter.

Smokowski, P. R., & Wodarski, J. S. (1996). The effectiveness of child welfare services for poor, neglected children: A review of the empirical evidence. *Research on Social Work Practice, 6,* 504-523.

Solomon, B. B. (1976). *Black empowerment: Social work in oppressed communities.* New York: Columbia University Press.

Stehno, S. M. (1982). Differential treatment of minority children in service systems. *Social Work, 27,* 39-45.

Sue, D. W., Arrendondo, P., & McDavis, R. J. (1992). Multicultural counseling competencies and standards: A call to the profession. *Journal of Multicultural Counseling, 20,* 64-88.

Szykula, S. A., & Fleischman, M. J. (1985). Reducing out-of-home placements of abused children: Two controlled field studies. *Child Abuse and Neglect, 9,* 277-283.

Tertinger, D., Greene, B., & Lutzker, J. (1984). Home safety: Development and validation of one component of an ecobehavioral treatment program for abused and neglected children. *Journal of Applied Behavior Analysis, 17,* 159-174.

Thomlison, B. (1997). Risk and protective factors in child maltreatment. In M. W. Fraser (Ed.), *Risk and resilience in childhood: An ecological perspective.* Washington, DC: NASW Press.

Tracy, E. M. (1990). Identifying social support resources of at-risk families. *Social Work, 38,* 252-258.

Tracy, E. M., & Whittaker, J. K. (1990). The social network map: Assessing social support in clinical practice. *Families in Society, 7,* 461-470.

Trivette, C. M., Dunst, C. J., Deal, A. G., Hamer, A. W., & Prompst, S. (1990). Assessing family strengths and family functioning style. *Topics in Early Childhood Special Education, 10*(1), 16-35.

U.S. Department of Health and Human Services, National Center on Child Abuse and Neglect. (1988). *Study findings: Study of national incidence and prevalence of child abuse and neglect: 1988.* Washington, DC: Government Printing Office.

U.S. Department of Health and Human Services, National Center on Child Abuse and Neglect. (1993). *Chronic neglect symposium proceedings.* Washington, DC: Author.

U.S. Department of Health and Human Services, National Center on Child Abuse and Neglect. (1996). *Child maltreatment, 1994: Reports from the states to the National Center on Child Abuse and Neglect.* Washington, DC: Government Printing Office.

Videka-Sherman, L. (1988). Intervention for child neglect: The empirical knowledge base. *Child neglect monograph: Proceedings from a symposium* (pp. 46-63). Washington, DC: National Center on Child Abuse and Neglect.

Walmyr Publishing Co. (1990). *MPSI technical manual.* Tempe, AZ: Author.

Walmyr Publishing Co. (1992). *Walmyr assessment scales scoring manual.* Tempe, AZ: Author.

Wellman, B. (1981). Applying network analysis to the study of support. In B. H. Gottlieb (Ed.), *Social networks and social support* (pp. 171-200). Beverly Hills, CA: Sage.

Whittaker, J., & Garbarino, J. (1983). *Social support networks: Informal helping in the human services.* New York: Aldine.

Witt, C., Dayton, C., & Sheinvald, J. K. (1992). *The family empowerment program: A social group work model of long term, intensive, and innovative strategies to reduce the incidence of chronic neglect for at risk parents* (National Center on Child Abuse and Neglect, Grant # 90CA1392). Pontiac, MI: Oakland Family Services.

Wolf, B. M. (1983). *Social network form: Information and scoring instructions.* Unpublished monograph, Temple University, Philadelphia, PA.

Wolfe, D. A. (1993). Prevention of child neglect: Emerging issues. *Criminal Justice and Behavior, 20,* 90-111.

Wolfe, D. A., Sandler, J., & Kaufman, K. (1981). A competency-based parent training program for child abusers. *Journal of Consulting and Clinical Psychology, 49,* 633-640.

Wolfe, D. A., St. Lawrence, J., Graves, K., Brehony, K., Bradlyn, D., & Kelly, J. A. (1982). Intensive behavioral parent training for a child abusive mother. *Behavior Therapy, 13,* 438-451.

Zuravin, S. J. (1988). Child abuse, child neglect, and maternal depression: Is there a connection? In *Child neglect monograph: Proceedings from a symposium* (pp. 40-45). Washington, DC: National Center on Child Abuse and Neglect.

Zuravin, S. J., & DePanfilis, D. (1996). *Child maltreatment recurrences among families served by Child Protective Services: Final report* (National Center on Child Abuse and Neglect Grant #90CA1497). Baltimore: University of Maryland at Baltimore, School of Social Work.

Zuravin, S., & Shay, S. (1992). Preventing child neglect. In D. DePanfilis & T. Birch (Eds.), *Proceedings: National Child Maltreatment Prevention Symposium, June 1991.* Washington, DC: National Center on Child Abuse and Neglect.

12 Are Battered Women Bad Mothers?

Rethinking the Termination of Abused Women's Parental Rights for Failure to Protect

THOMAS D. LYON

It is often stated that intervention on behalf of abused and neglected children is intended to protect the child rather than punish the parent. This stance justifies a no-fault approach to child protection: If a child is being harmed and removal from the parents' custody is the only means to alleviate the harm, removal is justified. If reunification fails, regardless of whether the parent will not or cannot change, the termination of parental rights is justified. It matters not whether the parents acted to harm the child or failed to act to prevent harm. Nor does it matter whether the parents' action or inaction was intentional or unintentional, voluntary or involuntary. A parent who is unable to properly care for his or her child is as unfit as a parent who is unwilling to do so.

AUTHOR'S NOTE: Thanks to Amy Melner for sharing her research and to Hazel Lord and her staff at the University of Southern California Law Library.

Although the no-fault stance solves many dilemmas in theory, it is hard to maintain in practice. Anyone with any experience in child protection knows that the legal response to abusive and neglectful parents is experienced as punitive: certainly by the parents, most likely by the children, and often by the legal and social service professionals involved. Enforcers of child protection therefore feel much more comfortable taking action against morally blameworthy parents; such parents' pleas for sympathy sound hollow, because their deliberate harmful act is their own creation, separable from their horrible upbringing and hopeless circumstances. The hardest cases involve parents who are simply incapable of living up to minimal standards of care for their children; they can't be faulted for affirmatively acting to harm their children, for failing to love them, or failing to try to provide and protect. On the other hand, they can point to the failings of the system as the cause of their own deficiencies. With unlimited help from society, which they would gladly accept, they could live up to the standards of good care imposed by society. The neglectful parent is therefore more sympathetic than the abusive parent, the parent who fails to act more sympathetic than the parent who affirmatively causes harm.

Neglect and abuse overlap when a parent fails to protect a child against abuse by the other parent. If a parent knowingly and deliberately allows abuse to occur, it is not hard to assign blame. But if a parent is in some way helpless to prevent the abuse from occurring, one's belief in no-fault intervention is put to the test. What if the parent who fails to protect is an abused woman, abused by the same man who abuses her children? What if she is prevented from acting due to fear rather than lassitude? What if her attempts at self-help have failed because of society's own failings? Clearly, the abuser is blameworthy, and ought to suffer the consequences: Kick him out of the house until the abuse is stopped. But the realities of child protection are that if anyone goes, it is the child. From the perspective of the family involved, this response to abuse punishes each member of the family equally for what the abuser has done.

Social service agencies routinely add allegations of spouse abuse to dependency petitions, because it strengthens the case for removal. In Los Angeles County, the largest dependency court in the country, allegations of child abuse and neglect leading to removal of the child from the home are accompanied by reference to spouse abuse in about one third of the cases (Lyon & Saywitz, in press). The actual rate of overlap between child abuse and spouse abuse is probably even greater (Layzer, 1986 [one half of spouse abuse cases also involve child abuse]; McKay, 1994 [same]; Walker, 1984 [same]; Stark & Flitcraft, 1988 [one half of child abuse cases also involve spouse abuse]). The fact that the child abuser also abused the mother strengthens the claim that the mother was unable (and possibly unwilling) to protect the child from abuse. An abused woman is well aware of her spouse's violent tendencies and arguably aware that her children are at risk of abuse (*In the Matter of Katherine C.*, 1984) at the same time that the spouse abuse renders her less capable of protecting her children.

The fact that allegations of spouse abuse act to strengthen the resolve to remove children from abusive homes is consistent with a true no-fault philosophy. Again, however, the realities of practice may clash with the abstract principles espoused by child protection professionals. In my experience representing social services in child dependency proceedings, I frequently encountered punitive reactions to battered mothers. The impulse to blame the adult victim resolves ambivalence about taking a mother's children and offering little support to enable their return. Moreover, battered women appear blameworthy for their predicament when they fail to seek protection or, having sought protection, return to the abuser. When one squarely faces the structural and psychological obstacles that stand in the way of battered women seeking to protect their children and end their own abuse, it becomes more difficult to characterize spouse abuse as merely one more count against the mother's right to her children.

In this chapter, I take some tentative steps toward assessing the rights of battered women who fail to protect their children against abuse. Primarily, I seek to correct misconceptions in the case law regarding battered women and the reasons for their repeated victimization. Although I believe that correcting such misconceptions does not change the necessity for intervening when children are physically and sexually abused and the mother is powerless to help because of her own victimization, it does counsel greater deference to the parental rights of battered mothers when the termination of parental rights is considered. Given the more far-reaching proposals of recent commentary advocating greater rights for battered mothers, my recommendations are quite conservative. Indeed, I spend much of this chapter arguing why the actions of child protection workers are justified, even in the face of sympathetic portrayals of the difficulties encountered by battered women. Nevertheless, my recommendations would require a substantial shift in the way that many child protection professionals understand battered mothers.

In the second section, I outline the differences between battered women who fail to protect and another group of battered women who have received a great deal of attention in the case law: battered women who kill. I discuss why arguments advanced for expanding self-defense doctrine to excuse the actions of battered women who kill do not easily translate into arguments for greater rights for battered women who fail to protect.

In the third section, I discuss some specific suggestions made by legal commentators for the reform of child protection law with respect to battered mothers. I highlight the distinction between jurisdiction and removal on the one hand and termination on the other and suggest that reforms can occur at the termination stage without putting children at greater risk of further abuse.

In the fourth section, I criticize the case law on the termination of the parental rights of battered mothers. Specifically, I discuss the double standard for mothers and fathers, the unwarranted assumption that a battered woman who has escaped one abusive relationship will enter another, the lack of attention to adoptability and the parent-child relationship, and the problems presented by cases in which there is evidence that the mother was unwilling (rather than merely unable) to leave the relationship.

WHY IT'S BETTER TO KILL THAN STAY

There is a substantial literature defending battered women who kill their abusive spouses (e.g., Dutton, 1993; Schneider, 1992). Defense attorneys in such cases have had some success in presenting expert testimony on battered woman's syndrome to explain why battered women kill their abusers rather than leave.

Review of the case law reveals that similarly sympathetic treatment has not been given to battered women who lose parental custody because of allegations that they failed to protect their children against abuse. There are a number of reasons for this distinction. A relatively good reason is that child protection is a no-fault system, which has no room for sympathy: Inability is as damning as unwillingness when the child's safety is at stake. Practically speaking, however, sympathy plays a role in decision making, even when it is not supposed to. A second reason battered women who fail to protect are treated worse than battered women who kill is that it is more difficult to feel empathy for a woman who helplessly allows her child to be abused (no child deserves to be abused) than for a woman who kills her abusive spouse (he gets what he deserves). Moreover, the woman who kills overcomes her weakness and passivity and thus pleases those who bemoan the stereotypically feminine, whereas the mother who fails to protect can't even live up to society's minimal expectations for when a woman should take action—when the lives of her children are threatened. Indeed, many women muster the ability to leave (or to kill) when the spouse abuser begins to abuse the children (Browne, 1987 [spousal homicide sometimes triggered by child abuse]; Rounsaville, 1978 [child abuse related to decision to leave]; Snyder & Fruchtman, 1981 [same]; but see Strube & Barbour, 1984 [child abuse not related to decision to leave]).

Another reason that battered women who kill are treated better than battered women who fail to protect is that the purported effects of spouse abuse on the psychology of the victim have different implications for the woman who kills than for the woman who fails to protect. In criminal cases charging battered women with murder, battered woman syndrome (Walker, 1984) helps to explain why the woman kills instead of leaves. Her initial decision to remain in the relationship is largely due to what Walker calls the "cycle of violence," whereby the acute battering incident is followed by a period of repentance and pleas for forgiveness, which convinces the woman that the abuse will not recur. Her subsequent inability to leave is attributable to learned helplessness, whereby repeated attacks render her incapable of perceiving opportunities for escape. Battered woman syndrome also helps to explain why the woman perceived an imminent threat to her life when she killed, when the average bystander might be unaware that an attack was imminent (Schneider, 1992).

Traumatic bonding describes the process by which strong emotional attachments form between victim and abuser when the abuser is perceived as dominant and when the abuse is intermittent (Dutton & Painter, 1981, 1993). The process is said to occur between some hostage victims and their captors or between abused children and their abusive parents. Traumatic bonding helps to explain a battered woman's decision to return to her abusive spouse and her paradoxically positive feelings for the abuser.

If a woman has not killed her spouse, however, and has been charged with failing to protect her child against the batterer's abuse, the logic of the disorders (battered woman syndrome and traumatic bonding) suggests that the woman will remain in the relationship even if there are realistic opportunities for escape. A diagnosis of battered woman syndrome can thus *strengthen* a claim that a woman is unable to protect her child (*In re Interest of C.P.,* 1990; *In the Matter of Glenn G.,* 1992; Miccio, 1995).

Moreover, to the extent that learned helplessness and traumatic bonding affect the woman's motivation to leave, such that she appears unwilling rather than simply unable to sever the relationship, this strengthens a court's resolve that intervention (and ultimately, termination) is justified. Although learned helplessness was originally formulated as including an inability to learn that escape is possible (thus rendering one unable to leave), Strube (1988) states that there is little support for this aspect of learned helplessness and that "it appears that the self-perpetuating nature of learned helplessness arises primarily from the lack of motivation to emit new responses" (p. 243). Hence, an individual suffering from learned helplessness is capable of recognizing avenues of escape when they arise but is insufficiently motivated to pursue those avenues.

Recently, legal scholars have criticized the extent to which battered woman syndrome pathologizes the battered woman and characterizes their reluctance to leave as delusional, rather than recognizing the real barriers to successful escape from abuse and the woman's realistic perception of imminent danger (Dutton, 1993; Schneider, 1992). Browne (1993) points out that

> behaviors that outside observers may interpret as helplessness—such as staying with the abuser or refraining from initiating legal actions against him—may simply be accurate evaluations of the assailant's potential for violent responses and others' inability to intervene in time to guarantee safety. (p. 1080)

The real difficulties of leaving an abusive relationship are now well documented, including economic pressures (Strube & Barbour, 1983, 1984 [unemployment and self-reported economic hardship increases likelihood of staying]; but see Gelles, 1976 [employment unrelated to decision to leave]); inadequate police protection (Buzawa, 1982; Eisenberg & Moriarty, 1991; Elk & Johnson, 1989), insufficient shelters (Becker, 1995; Strube & Barbour, 1984 [having nowhere else to go predicts staying]), and increased risk of death following separation (Barnard, Vera, Vera, & Newman, 1982).

If battered women are more rational than pathological, and if their inability to separate is wholly (or even primarily) attributable to society's failure to offer them protection, termination of their parental rights is harder to justify. They are clearly willing to protect their children. Moreover, although they are technically unable to protect, one can no longer point to an inability that is specific to the individual. Recent commentary criticizing the harsh treatment of battered women by child protective services thus has emphasized the rationality of battered women's fears (e.g., Miccio, 1995). It is to that commentary that I now turn.

TEMPORARY REMOVAL VERSUS TERMINATION

Battered mothers' custody rights have become a popular topic among legal commentators. Miccio (1995) argues that dependency jurisdiction should not be taken against a parent when a "reasonably prudent parent, under like circumstances," would have failed to act. Miccio cites a case in which a mother failed to report her husband's sexual abuse of her daughter for more than 3 years due to his violence and threats, suggesting that under the proposed standard, the mother would not be held to have failed to protect (In the Matter of Glenn G., 1992). Enos (1996) similarly argues for an "objective standard" (which considers actions in light of what a reasonable person would do) for taking jurisdiction in child protection proceedings. Davidson (1995) and Dohrn (1995) argue that greater use should be made of protective orders, which would remove the spouse abuser and allow the mother and her children to remain together. Becker (1995) argues more generally that to justify civil action against battered women who fail to protect their children, society must make it easier for them to leave their abusive spouses.

The problem with these suggestions is that appreciation of the dangers of an abusive spouse and the failure of society to protect women against those dangers leads one to conclude that until society expends much more effort in protecting abused women, children who remain with their abused mothers will not be safe. Presumably, a reasonably prudent parent will not act should her life be in grave danger. Therefore, the more dangerous and persistent the abuser, the more likely an objective standard would necessitate leaving abused children in the home. Similarly, protective orders "work only if the assailant respects those orders or at least does no harm during times of violation" (Browne, 1993, p. 1080). If protective orders fail to keep abused women safe, they will hardly be more effective in protecting children. Society should make it easier for women to leave their abusive spouses, but the immediate needs of abused children cannot wait for such changes to occur. Dependency court is filled with sympathetic parents—with developmental disabilities, substance abuse problems—who might overcome their inabilities with greater social spending, yet we remove their children just the same.

Legal scholars are aware of these criticisms and sometimes express some ambivalence regarding their proposals. In an introductory footnote, Miccio (1995) calls her piece a "work in progress" and states her intention to write a "longer piece that infuses the voices of children as an integral part of the reconceptualization of protective statutes" (p. 1087). Becker (1995) emphasizes that "bias against mothers cannot preclude maternal responsibility unless we are willing to ignore harm to children (half of whom are girls)" (p. 22). (Cf. Watkins, 1995, p. 1420, who advocates greater deference to the rights of parents with developmental disabilities but emphasizes that he "does not advocate keeping children with parents who are . . . unable or unwilling to provide adequate care.")

A partial solution to the dilemma lies in recognizing the different phases of dependency jurisdiction, which include taking jurisdiction over a case so that services may be provided, removal of the child from the home pending rehabilitation of the parents, and the termination of parental rights in those cases where rehabilitation is not successful (e.g., California Welfare and Institutions Code, 1998). Commentators critical of the applicability of failure to protect laws to battered mothers often fail to clearly distinguish the different phases (Becker, 1995; Davidson, 1995, Enos, 1996). Yet the harms of failing to take action against an unfit parent vary, depending on the type of action contemplated. When serious abuse has occurred, failure to take jurisdiction and to remove the child from an abusive home places the child at immediate risk of future abuse.

Failure to terminate parental rights, on the other hand, does not return the child to an abusive home. The child is harmed if the failure to terminate prevents the child from establishing a secure relationship with an adoptive parent or guardian, and if the child's relationship with the parent is detrimental. However, unless prospective adoptive parents have been identified, it is unclear whether children of abused mothers will find greater permanence and safety if the mothers' rights are terminated. Indeed, premature termination before the mother has an opportunity to establish herself as a competent caretaker independent of the batterer jeopardizes the likelihood of a positive parent-child relationship.

In the Interest of Betty J. W. (1988) provides an example of the differing standards for removal and termination. In *Betty J. W.,* the Supreme Court of West Virginia overturned a trial court's termination of an abused mother's parental rights. The father had physically abused his five children and sexually abused his 17-year-old daughter. On the night of the sexual assault, the mother had "interceded and was beaten and threatened with a knife" (p. 332). On the day after the assault, the mother reported the abuse to the authorities and sought refuge with relatives. However, shortly before the termination petition was filed, the father, who had been out of the home, stayed overnight.

The fact that the father had returned to the household, albeit temporarily, is clearly cause for concern. On the other hand, the court noted that social services had done nothing to assist the mother in remaining apart from the father. By overturning the termination order and remanding the case for a consideration of temporary custody, the court made it possible for the mother to demonstrate her willingness to remain separate from the father and to regain full custody of the children during a reunification period. Hence, the children's safety was ensured, while the children's and mother's interest in maintaining their relationship was not prematurely sacrificed.

In what follows, I will outline what I believe to be a child-centered approach to issues concerning the proper treatment of battered women who fail to protect their children against abuse. The approach touches on several areas in which the courts have made unwarranted assumptions about battered women's behavior, beliefs, and responsibility.

UNFAIRNESS IN THE CASE LAW TERMINATING THE PARENTAL RIGHTS OF BATTERED MOTHERS

Double Standards for Mothers and Fathers

If the courts are sincere in applying a no-fault standard of neglect in failure to protect cases, then mothers and fathers ought to be equally susceptible to legal action when their children are maltreated. However, mothers are more often faulted for neglect than fathers (Becker, 1995; Dohrn, 1995).

An example of the different treatment of mothers and fathers is illustrated by two Illinois appellate court cases, decided one year apart. In *In the Interest of Dalton* (1981), an Illinois appellate court upheld the termination of parental rights of a mother whose two children had been physically and emotionally abused by their father, who was a convicted murderer and kidnapper. To prevent the mother from leaving with the children, the father had pointed a gun at the son's head, held one of the children outside a third-floor window, attempted to run over one of the children with a car, and followed the mother and kidnapped the children. These events were testified to by the mother and corroborated by two neighbors. The father had also abused the mother, including choking her until she had fainted and holding a gun to her head. At the time of the hearing, the father was serving a life sentence, and the mother's therapist noted that she was "employed and living in a suitable environment, was cooperative and sincere in her counseling effort, and had shown a genuine interest in improving the quality of her life" (p. 1230).

The court was unimpressed, however, emphasizing the mother's history:

> We believe that an adequate opportunity to flee could have presented itself within the seven-year period that respondent lived with Mr. Dalton. In fact, by respondent's own admission, during this seven year period, she and her children had lived apart from Dalton several times, but she continually chose to return to him. On one occasion, after reading in the newspaper of her husband's murder of a young woman, respondent still drove to Indiana to be with him. (p. 1232)

Notably, the court failed to understand why hearing proof of the abuser's ability to fulfill his threats might lead a battered woman to return to her abuser. One might excuse the court's incomprehension, however, given its appropriate emphasis on the mother's failure to present evidence of her current relationship with her children and the children's desire to remain apart from her. Perhaps had the children expressed a desire to maintain a relationship with the mother, the court would not have upheld termination. Moreover, one might defend the court by noting that it was merely upholding the well-established precedent that it is the "success of the parent's efforts" and not "the fact that efforts were made" that determines parental fitness (p. 1231).

What makes the result in *Dalton* troubling, however, is the holding by another Illinois appellate court, one year previously, in *In the Interest of Brown* (1980). That case terminated the rights of a mother whose daughter was abused by the stepfather. The stepfather had been convicted of killing the child's sister. The court concluded that the mother had herself abused the child but emphasized that even had she not done so, termination was warranted, because "any parent has the obligation to protect a child against harm." This aspect of the decision appears quite consistent with *Dalton*.

With respect to the child's noncustodial father, however, the court took a different approach. The court emphasized that the father had once reported the child's injuries to child protective services. Refusing to terminate his parental rights, the court sympathetically noted that he "was far in arrears in his child support and had no regular job or place of residence. The possibilities of obtaining a change of custody would be remote" (p. 491) The father's failure to *provide* for the child thus excused his failure to *protect* the child.

Last, relying on the fact that the stepfather had murdered a child, the court pointed out that the stepfather "appears to have been a violent man and any approach by [the father] by way of self-help would have led to reprisals of a demoniac variety" (p. 491). After all, the court concluded, the legal standard is that it is the father's "efforts to carry out [his] parental responsibilities, and not [his] success by which fitness is to be determined" (p. 491).

The legal standards enunciated by *Dalton* and *Brown* are diametrically opposed. Failure trumps efforts in *Dalton,* whereas efforts trump failure in *Brown.* It is difficult not to interpret the difference as a double standard for mothers and fathers. Selective application of a no-fault standard of parental fitness to mothers suggests that what no-fault really means is that the mother is always at fault. If courts sympathize with men who cannot face up to a violent child abuser, they ought to sympathize with women who are abused themselves. On the other hand, if they truly believe in a no-fault system of child protection, then blameless fathers ought to be found unfit.

Unwarranted Assumptions That the Abusive Relationship Will Be Repeated

One of the most common assumptions regarding battered women is that they are drawn toward abusive relationships. In support of such an assumption, one might point to the statistics on battered women who return to their abusive spouses. Reviewing the literature, Strube (1988) concluded that "about half of all women who seek some form of aid for spouse abuse can be expected to return to their partners" (p. 238). Strube found the rate particularly striking considering that many battered women seek help only when the abuse is life threatening. Moreover, given the brief follow-up periods used by most research, the actual rate of return is likely even higher. If women commonly exhibit a pattern of leaving and then returning, it seems reasonable to assume that a woman who has left her abuser is still likely to return to him, putting her children at future risk of further harm.

The problem with such reasoning is that it selectively ignores reasons why women seeking help at shelters (who make up the majority of battered women studied by researchers) ultimately return to the abuser. Although expressions of love and feelings of commitment predict return (Strube & Barbour, 1983, 1984), equally if not more important are economic and practical considerations, such as whether the woman is capable of establishing a separate residence after her stay at the shelter expires (Pfouts, 1978; Strube & Barbour, 1983, 1984). If a woman does establish a separate residence, this clearly evinces her economic and practical ability to remain apart from the abuser. Moreover, such a move is also stronger evidence than a shelter stay of her emotional commitment to permanent separation.

It is also unfair to point to the rates of battered women returning to their abusers to justify an assumption that a battered woman, once out of one abusive relationship, will enter another. It is one thing to predict return to a particular spouse and quite another to predict involvement with another abuser. Equating the two assumes that battered women suffer from a personality defect that renders them susceptible to abusive relationships.

One encounters such an assumption in the courts. In *In re Sunshine Allah V.* (1982), a New York appellate court overturned continued removal of a child in a case in which the mother had obtained an order of protection against the father, had not seen him for 2 years, and "indicated that if he returned she would call her family and the police" (p. 522). The lower court's opinion was founded on the fact that the mother "was equally submissive to her new husband" (p. 522), though there was no evidence he was abusive. In *In the Interest of A. V.* (1987), a Pennsylvania appellate court upheld the termination of a mother's parental rights whose husband had abused both her and her 6-month-old infant. The majority did not submit an opinion explaining their action. A dissent noted that the mother never witnessed abuse, that the explanations for the child's bruises were plausible, and that she was "now living separate and apart from her husband, and the evidence does not suggest that she is unable or unwilling to provide proper parental care or control for her daughter" (p. 781). Apparently, termination was justified on the basis of a psychologist's opinion that the mother had a "passive personality" (p. 781).

Courts might assume that abusive relationships frequently recur because reabuse is not uncommon among the cases they are asked to review (*In re Interest of M. H.*, 1985; *In the Matter of Dawn C.*, 1994; *In the Matter of Ettinger*, 1996). For example, in *Adoption of Paula* (1995), the Supreme Court of Massachusetts upheld the termination of a mother's parental rights to seven children despite the fact that she had successfully left the father. The reason? Her new companion (with whom she had an eighth child) was allegedly abusing his own children.

The research literature on spouse abuse emphasizes the extent to which battered women, once out of abusive relationships, are *not* likely to be abused again. Researchers who have documented the psychological effects of battering, whereby battered women remain with the abuser, emphasize that the ill effects are specific to the abuse relationship and not reflective of the victim's personality (Dutton & Painter, 1981, p. 144; Walker, 1979). Most women who have escaped abusive relationships do not then encounter further abuse (Hoff, 1990 [nine battered women who had been in shelter; 5-year follow-up found none abused by new partner]; Walker, 1979, p. 28 [120 battered women; few had more than one violent relationship]; Walker, 1984 [403 battered women, 75% of whom had left the batterer; "battered women were less likely to go into another relationship and, when they did, it was rarely another violent one," p. 148]). Moreover, most women currently in abusive relationships were not previously abused (Rounsaville, 1978, p. 16 ["Only 13% had been physically abused in a previous adult relationship"]). Although these limited data are based on unrepresentative samples and potentially biased self-reports, they suggest that the courts should be careful not to make general assumptions based on their limited experience with women who encounter a series of abusive partners.

On the other hand, if a woman *has* had a series of such relationships, fears of future abuse appear warranted. If the woman's latest relationship is abusive, it is unnecessary to speculate about her personality to conclude that her children are at risk. Reasonable conclusions regarding risk are sometimes obscured by critical legal commentary advocating greater rights for battered mothers. Enos (1996) cites *In re Interest of C. P.* (1990) as a case documenting society's failure to protect abused women and the reasonableness of a mother's decision to leave her child with the father despite her knowledge of the father's abusiveness. Before the child had turned 4 years of age, the mother had observed the father beating the child about the face and head with his fists and hitting the child with a stick, board, and belt. The mother had been severely abused by the father as well and had tried to leave with the child, only to see the child abducted by the father. The child was brought to the attention of the authorities when the father fatally abused her 18-month-old stepbrother.

Enos (1996) criticizes the Nebraska Supreme Court for slighting the mother's testimony that after separating from the father, she had attempted to obtain custody of the child by calling Child Protective Services and the police. Moreover, Enos argues that the court was insufficiently sympathetic to the mother's claim that the abuse prevented her from helping her child. The court's skepticism is more reasonable, however, when one reads that the mother had not visited her daughter for a year and that her justification for failing to visit was that she had remarried. The man she had remarried had since physically abused her other children.

A more difficult case presents itself when the mother has been involved in other abusive relationships but appears to have successfully extricated herself from the current abusive relationship and appears to be making progress in therapy at the time of the termination hearing. In *In the Matter of Farley* (1991), the Michigan Supreme Court refused to hear the appeal of an abused mother whose parental rights had been terminated due to her failure to protect her three children against physical and sexual abuse by the father. According to an opinion dissenting from the denial of review, the physical abuse had occurred when the mother was not at home, and the children had been told by the father not to tell. When told of the sexual abuse allegations, the mother initially expressed disbelief, but the following month asked the father to leave the home. At an evaluation session 5 months after the allegations surfaced, the mother held hands with the father, and either she or the father repeated a statement made by the child suggesting someone other than the father was the perpetrator. Nevertheless, she filed for divorce the following month (the divorce was finalized the following year, 2 months after the termination hearing).

At the time of the hearing, the mother had been living apart from the father for almost a year, had visited the children regularly, and had taken all the parenting classes required by social services. Her court-appointed therapist found that she had improved in therapy (as documented in part by her scores on the Minnesota Multiphasic Personality Inventory), that she was motivated, and that she was not at risk of abusing her children. The major reason for termination was the prognosis given by her therapist, as well as the concerns of two other mental health professionals, that she would return to her ex-husband or "might enter another abusive relationship and permit her children to be abused by that third party." The case is complicated by facts not mentioned in the dissent: The mother had been abused by the father for 8 years and had been in other abusive relationships before her marriage (Phillips, 1992, p. 1570). The difficult issue presented by *Farley* is whether a battered woman's progress is better measured by recent improvements or by more remote difficulties. As Phillips points out, the mother had never received counseling for domestic violence in the past. Her progress in therapy and her apparent success in independent living argue for giving her history of abuse less weight.

One might argue that the mother's year of independence from the father does not compare with her 8 years of abuse, justifying the assumption that her separate living arrangement is only temporary. However, such an assumption would lead to the termination of battered women's parental rights in many, if not most, of the cases in which children are removed from the mother's custody, because parents are given only 12 to 18 months to rehabilitate and reunify with their children. Termination decisions are necessarily made on the basis of short-term improvements in the parent's situation. Because a decision not to terminate parental rights does not mean immediate return of the children to the parents' custody, short-term improvements can be monitored while placement continues.

The Child's Need for Permanence: Insufficient Attention to the Mother–Child Relationship and the Adoptability of the Child

The rationale for termination after a relatively short period of reunification attempts is the child's need for permanence in her relationships with her caretakers. Foster parents attempt to avoid strong attachments with their foster children, even if they would like to adopt, lest reunification succeed and the children are returned to their parents' custody. If reunification efforts drag on too long, children suffer from the uncertainty of temporary placement and become too old to be attractive for adoption.

Was the children's need for a permanent parent-child relationship the motivating force in *Farley*? It is surprising that the opinion is silent regarding what would happen to the children post-termination. The children were 6, 9, and 13 years of age at the time of the termination hearing, and nothing was said regarding their adoptability should their mother's rights be terminated. Nor was anything said regarding the mother's relationship with the children other than the fact that she had faithfully exercised her right to visitation. Indeed, discussion of the mother-child relationship is notably absent from most of the termination cases I have reviewed here.

If a child is adoptable at the time termination is considered and the parent's rehabilitation is not complete, the child's need for permanence is thought to outweigh the benefits of maintaining the parent-child relationship. However, if the child is not adoptable, termination puts the child at risk of foster-care drift. Guggenheim (1995) has documented that legal reforms leading to an increase in the termination of parental rights have not led to a corresponding increase in the number of adoptions. Furthermore, if maintenance of the parent-child relationship is not harmful to the child, then the benefits of termination are unclear. Children form pathologically strong bonds to abusive parents (van der Kolk & Greenberg, 1987), paradoxically strengthened by the intermittent phases of affection and violence in the relationship. This is precisely the dynamic used to explain battered women's traumatic bonding to their abusive spouses (Dutton & Painter, 1981, 1993). It is possible that terminating a child's relationship with an unrepentant, maltreating parent is desirable, independent of the alternative long-term relationships immediately available. On the other hand, a mother who has never maltreated her child but was victimized by the same man as her child may not pose the same risks. The mother and child have lived through a shared trauma, much like a child and her maltreated sibling. The mother's affirmative steps to separate from the abuser are positive signs for the child. Although the relationship may be far from perfect, termination would sever the most fundamental, and often the only, long-term relationship the child has.

In *In the Interest of S. O., B. O., E. O., & C. B.* (1992), the Iowa Supreme Court upheld a trial court's termination of a mother's rights to her four children, ages 9, 8, 6, and 2. The father had abused the mother and sexually and physically abused the children. Although the mother had divorced the father, she "continued a pattern of sporadic cohabitation and visitation with him" (p. 603). Moreover, she had not fulfilled the goals of her case plan. Clearly, the mother had not taken the necessary steps to regain custody of her children.

However, given the mother-child relationship and the children's adoptability, the termination decision was necessarily a search for lesser evils. The intermediate court had held that the trial court should not have terminated the mother's rights to the 8-year-old and 9-year-old children, and the Iowa Supreme Court reversed. The court acknowledged that the children exhibited a "strong bond" with their mother: "Both children express their desire to rejoin their mother. They look forward to visits with her" (p. 604). The court dismissed the children's desires by pointing to expert testimony that the bond was unhealthy. A social worker noted that "an abused child may take on a parental protective role with the nonabusing parent" (p. 604). A therapist testified that the bond "had an intensity that is fueled by anger towards their mother" (p. 604).

One could quibble with the assumption that a child who is protective has thus formed a pathological bond with the nonabusive parent. Attachment through anger is clearly unhealthy, but abused children frequently express such anger at nonabusive mothers, even when the mothers take protective action (Herman, 1981). Nevertheless, one would be comfortable with such second-guessing of explicit preferences if there were an adoptive parent waiting in the wings, ready to form a healthier attachment with the children. There was not, and the experts could not agree whether the children were in principle "adoptable." The 8-year-old and 9-year-old had not even found a suitable temporary placement, having been removed from their foster homes due to behavioral problems. The court conceded, in an understatement, that they "may be difficult to place for adoption" (p. 604). Hence, the choice was between a bond of questionable quality and possibly no bond at all.

If termination is supposed to be about the interests of the child and not the fault of the parent, then the parent-child relationship and adoptability ought to be part of every termination decision. The assumption that the child does not benefit from continuing contact with an unrehabilitated parent is less compelling when that parent is attempting to overcome the continuing effects of the same kind of victimization that the child has suffered.

Words Versus Deeds

It is not uncommon for battered women to express love for their abusers (Bergman, Larsson, Brismar, & Klang, 1988 [of 49 battered women seeking medical care and accepting psychological treatment, 43% expressed love for the batterer]). A substantial proportion of battered women give "love" as the reason they do not leave the relationship (Strube & Barbour, 1983 [21% of 79 battered women visiting county attorney's counseling unit], 1984 [13% of 191 battered women visiting county attorneys' counseling unit]), and expressions of love reduce the likelihood that women will subsequently leave (Strube & Barbour, 1983, 1984). As Dutton and Painter (1981) note,

> While ambivalence may manifest itself behaviorally in battered women, most professionals would support the view that such women experience very strong emotional states post-traumatically, and that these states serve to push her out or pull her back into the battering relationship. (p. 146)

Expressions of love for the abuser understandably increase courts' willingness to terminate battered mothers' parental rights. Legal commentators arguing for greater deference to the parental rights of battered mothers (Davidson, 1995; Enos, 1996) often understate the extent to which battered women attribute their behavior to positive feelings for the offender. Perhaps they do so because acknowledgment of the positive feelings battered women often express for their abusers undercuts the assumption that battered women's failure to leave the abuser is solely motivated by fear.

In *In re Interest of J. B. and A. P.* (1990), the mother's 18-month-old child had been fatally abused by her male companion. The mother witnessed the man's abuse of her children and delayed seeking medical care for their injuries. The mother had left the man once due to the abuse, but because of his promises that he would no longer abuse the children, she returned. The court acknowledges that "there is some evidence that [the mother] is mildly retarded and was abused by, and fearful of, her husband. She claims this prevented her from protecting her children or leaving with them" (p. 482). It is this aspect of the case that Davidson (1995) emphasizes, and he points out that batterers frequently threaten to kill their spouses and their children if the spouse attempts to leave the relationship. Yet as

Davidson (1995) also acknowledges, and as the court emphasizes, "even as her 18-month-old child lay comatose at the hospital, [the mother] stated she would not leave her husband because she loved him" (p. 482).

In *In re Interest of C. D. C.* (1990), the Nebraska Supreme Court upheld the termination of the parental rights of the mother of a 7-month-old child who had been physically abused by the father and had suffered an unexplained skull fracture. The court acknowledged that the mother had "complied substantially with the plan prescribed for her, having cooperated in the various programs offered to her and having maintained very regular visitations with the child" (p. 806). Nevertheless, the court held that she had not maintained a safe environment, because of her continuing abuse by the father:

> The record establishes that the father continually moved in and out of the mother's life and that when he resided with her, he physically abused her. According to the evidence, on various occasions, the father had kicked the mother, given her a black eye, hit her in the chest, threatened her with a knife, burned her by throwing a cup of hot coffee on her, and caused bruises on her legs. . . . On another occasion, . . . he had dragged the mother by her hair across a parking lot. (p. 807)

Enos (1996) criticizes the court in *C. D. C.* for failing to refer to the abusive incidents in attempting to understand the mother's failure to remain separated from the father. She notes that the court "found that her *inability* to provide her child with a violence-free environment demonstrated a *willful* failure to meet the demands of her parental responsibilities" (p. 242 [italics added]). Yet what surely convinced the court that the failure was willful were the mother's statements to a rehabilitation counselor "that she was aware that she was choosing the father over her son" and her ability to recognize the father's abusiveness only when he was temporarily out of her life (p. 808).

Stronger evidence of the sometimes strong attachment between abuse victims and abusers can be found in cases in which battered women pursued relationships with their abusers even after the abusers had been imprisoned. In *In re Interest of Joshua M.* (1996), the father was convicted for sexually abusing two children, one of them the mother's child. The mother argued that she could not sever contact with the father because of his threats and abuse, which had led to her hospitalization at least once.

However, the court noted that she had attempted to visit the father in prison with all five of her children, in violation of the court order, and that she had written him letters "which make it clear she was desiring increased contact with him and expressing frustration because he did not want to see her any more" (p. 360).

Similarly, in *In the Interest of J. L. S.* (1990), the mother testified she had witnessed the father beat her infant child "about the head with his fists, biting her extremities, and force-feeding her scalding-hot formula" (p. 81) from the time the child was 3 months old to her removal at 9 months old. She testified that the father would beat her if she attempted to protect the child and that her fears of the father similarly prevented her from leaving him or reporting the abuse. Despite her claims that she had not contacted the father since his imprisonment, the State proved that she had sent the father photographs of the child, "which bore a loving message in [the mother's] handwriting," and that she had hitchhiked to visit the father in the penitentiary (p. 83).

That battered women often express strong feelings for their abusers should not be denied. To the extent that such feelings influence a mother's behavior, they are clearly relevant in the decision whether to terminate the mother's parental rights. However, an understanding of learned helplessness and traumatic bonding as potentially influencing battered women's motives and desires could enable courts to recognize cases in which a woman's explanation for her actions was the product of the situation rather than reflecting a long-standing attitude. If the courts can doubt a child's expressions of love for a parent on the grounds that the attachment is the unhealthy product of repeated abuse, they ought to treat a woman's prior statements with equal sophistication. When a woman has taken concrete steps to extricate herself from an abusive situation, prior statements should be given less weight than current actions.

A case that exemplifies the limited relevance of prior statements in light of affirmative actions by the mother is *In re D. K. W.* (1980), in which the Pennsylvania Supreme Court upheld the termination of a battered woman's parental rights. The court could have justified termination on the grounds that the mother had herself abused the child and had neither completed counseling nor exercised all her visitation rights. However, what most impressed the court was her failure to successfully separate from the abusive father, who had both abused the child and left the mother "covered from head to toe with bruises" (p. 71). The court was unpersuaded by her claims that her move out of the household and away from the father was sufficient:

> [The mother] further testified that she had done everything within her power to stay away from him, but it is clear that she has not rid herself of him or his violence. By appellant's own testimony at the May, 1979 hearing, [the father] continues to follow her, threaten her and fight with her. He also has broken into her home on several occasions and has waited for her many times while she was out. Thus, despite her recognition of and asserted attempts to remedy the problem, she has not succeeded. Though appellant may have moved away from [the father] for the purpose of improving her situation and regaining custody of her child, she clearly did not move far enough. (p. 72)

The court was influenced by the mother's statement that "she had experienced much violence in her own family while growing up, and, consequently, did not feel that she deserved anything better" (p. 72, n. 4). The mother's failure to move "far enough" was thus attributed to lacking motivation rather than the fanatical attempts of the abusive spouse to maintain contact. However, when a woman moves out and establishes a separate residence, that reflects a commitment to escape the abusive relationship. If the woman does not seek out contact with the abuser, his attempts to maintain contact with her may justify continued placement for the safety of the child but should be given less weight in determining whether her parental rights should be permanently severed. The courts should recognize that both previous failures to escape and statements justifying failure are often the products of the abuse.

CONCLUSION

I have argued that the courts should be more sympathetic to battered women whose children are also abused. Nevertheless, I do not advocate major changes in the law regarding the temporary custody of abused children whose mothers fail to protect. Removal and temporary placement of children should continue to be based on the safety of the child, regardless of the parents' fault or lack thereof. In this respect, I disagree with much of the legal commentary appearing in the past few years, which criticizes a "no-fault" approach to child protection.

However, I suspect that many commentators, were they to squarely face the issue, would not recommend return of a child to a battered woman's custody when the woman, despite her best efforts, could not keep a child-abusing spouse out of the home. They would advocate greater enforcement of restraining orders and the like (proposals with which I fully agree) but would acknowledge that the child's immediate safety is the first priority. In a perfect world, faultless mothers should always have custody of their children. In the real world, it is often more effective to remove the child than the abuser from the home.

Greater sympathy for battered women *should* affect judgments regarding the termination of parental rights. Understanding that the battered woman's continuing attachment to the abuser is a product of the abuse, her economic dependence, and her inability to find anywhere else to go enables one to reject stereotypes that suggest "once a battered woman, always a battered woman" (*In the Matter of Farley,* 1991, p. 998). When a woman finds a job and establishes a separate residence, this is evidence that she has largely overcome the forces that drive so many battered women back to their spouses. Moreover, concrete actions render previous professions of love for the abuser suspect, given the bonds attributable to trauma. Rather than seek out new abusive mates, women who have survived abuse most often choose their new mates with special care, aware of the entrapment that abuse creates. The courts should therefore treat apparent success in separation as such, particularly because to do so in a termination hearing does not place the child at risk of reabuse but allows the parent-child relationship to continue, pending potential return of the child to the mother's custody. Last, the courts should always consider the alternatives facing the child should termination occur; the mother-child relationship may be less than perfect but better than foster-care drift.

If my recommendations were adopted, I doubt that a large percentage of child protection cases involving spouse abuse would be resolved differently. In general, most cases in which children are removed for abuse or neglect end in the reunification of the child with his or her parents (Watkins, 1995). I would guess that most battered mothers are similarly reunited with their children. But although the relative number of cases in which battered mothers' parental rights are permanently severed may be small, the significance of such cases is substantial. A step as significant as termination should not be based on misconceptions and misplaced blame.

REFERENCES

Adoption of Paula, 651 N.E.2d 1222 (Mass. 1995).

Barnard, G. W., Vera, H., Vera, M., & Newman, G. (1982). Till death do us part: A study of spouse murder. *Bulletin of the American Academy of Psychiatry and Law, 10,* 271-280.

Becker, M. E. (1995). Double binds facing mothers in abusive families: Social support systems, custody outcomes, and liability for acts of others. *University of Chicago Law School Roundtable,* 2, 13-33.

Bergman, B., Larsson, G., Brismar, B., & Klang, M., (1988). Aetological and precipitating factors in wife battering. *Acta Psychiatrica Scandinavica, 77,* 338-345.

Browne, A. (1987) *When battered women kill.* New York: Free Press.

Browne, A. (1993). Violence against women by male partners: Prevalence, outcomes, and policy implications. *American Psychologist, 10,* 1077-1087.

Buzawa, E. (1982). Police officer response to domestic violence legislation in Michigan. *Journal of Police Science and Administration, 10,* 415-423.

California Welfare and Institutions Code, §§ 300-395 (West 1998).

Davidson, H. A. (1995). Child abuse and family violence: Legal connections and controversies. *Family Law Quarterly, 29,* 357-373.

Dohrn, B. (1995). Bad mothers, good mothers, and the state: Children on the margins. *University of Chicago Law School Roundtable, 2,* 1-12.

Dutton, D., & Painter, S. L. (1981). Traumatic bonding: The development of emotional attachments in battered women and other relationships of intermittent abuse. *Victimology: An International Journal, 6,* 139-155.

Dutton, D., & Painter, S. L. (1993). The battered woman syndrome: Effects of severity and intermittency of abuse. *American Journal of Orthopsychiatry, 63,* 614 622.

Dutton, M. A. (1993). Understanding the woman's response to domestic violence: A redefinition of battered women syndrome. *Hofstra Law Review, 21,* 1191-1242.

Eisenberg, H., & Moriarty, L. (1991). Domestic violence and local law enforcement in Texas: Examining police officers' awareness of state legislation. *Journal of Interpersonal Violence, 6,* 102-109.

Elk, R., & Johnson, C. W. (1989). Police arrest in domestic violence. *Response, 12*(4), 7-13.

Enos, V. P. (1996). Prosecuting battered mothers: State laws' failure to protect battered women and abused children. *Harvard Women's Law Journal, 19,* 229-268.

Gelles, R. J. (1976). Abused wives: Why do they stay? *Journal of Marriage and the Family, 38,* 659-668.

Guggenheim, M. (1995). The effects of recent trends to accelerate the termination of parental rights of children in foster care—An empirical analysis in two states. *Family Law Quarterly, 29,* 121-139.

Herman, J. L. (1981). *Father-daughter incest.* Cambridge, MA: Harvard.

Hoff, L. A. (1990). *Battered women as survivors.* London: Routledge.

In re D. K. W., 415 A.2d 69 (Pa. 1980).

In re Interest of C. D. C., 455 N.W.2d 801 (Neb. 1990).

In re Interest of C. P., 455 N.W.2d 138 (Neb. 1990).

In re Interest of J. B. and A. P. 453 N.W.2d 477 (Neb. 1990).

In re Interest of Joshua M., 548 N.W.2d 348 (Neb. Ct. App. 1996).

In re Interest of M. H., D. H., and P. T., 367 N.W.2d 275 (Iowa Ct. App. 1985).

In re Sunshine Allah V., 450 N.Y.S.2d 520 (N.Y. App. 1982).

In the Interest of A. V., 525 A.2d 778 (Pa. App. 1987).

In the Interest of Betty J. W., 371 S.E.2d 326 (W.Va. 1988).
In the Interest of Brown, 410 N.E.2d 486 (Ill. App. 1980).
In the Interest of Dalton, 424 N.E.2d 1226 (Ill. App. 1981).
In the Interest of J. L. S., 793 S.W.2d 79 (Tex. Ct. App. 1990).
In the Interest of S. O., B. O., E. O., & C. B., 483 N.W.2d 602 (Iowa 1992).
In the Matter of Dawn C., 1994 WL 506141 (Ohio App. 1994) [available on WESTLAW].
In the Matter of Ettinger, 923 P.2d 1290 (Or. Ct. App. 1996).
In the Matter of Farley, 469 N.W.2d 295 (Mich. 1991).
In the Matter of Glenn G., 587 N.Y.S.2d 464 (Fam. Ct. 1992).
In the Matter of Katherine C., 471 N.Y.S.2d 216 (Fam. Ct. 1984).
Layzer, J. (1986). Children in shelters. *Children Today, 15,* 5-11.
Lyon, T. D., & Saywitz, K. J. (in press). Young maltreated children's competence to take the oath. *Applied Developmental Science.*
McKay, M. M. (1994). The link between domestic violence and child abuse: Assessment and treatment considerations. *Child Welfare, 73,* 29-39.
Miccio, K. (1995). In the name of mothers and children: Deconstructing the myth of the passive battered mother and the "protected child" in child neglect proceedings. *Albany Law Review, 58,* 1087-1107.
Pfouts, J. (1978). Violent families: Coping responses of abused wives. *Child Welfare, 57,* 101-111.
Phillips, J. A. (1992). Re-victimized battered women: Termination of parental rights for failure to protect children from child abuse. *Wayne Law Review, 38,* 1549-1578.
Rounsaville, B. J. (1978). Theories in marital violence: Evidence from a study of battered women. *Victimology: An International Journal, 3,* 11-31.
Schneider, E. M. (1992). Describing and changing: Women's self-defense work and the problem of expert testimony on battering. *Women's Rights Law Reporter, 14,* 213-241.
Snyder, D. K., & Fruchtman, L. A. (1981). Differential patterns of wife abuse: A data-based typology. *Journal of Consulting and Clinical Psychology, 49,* 878-885.
Stark, E., & Flitcraft, A. H. (1988). Women and children at risk: A feminist perspective on child abuse. *International Journal of Health Services, 18,* 97-118.
Strube, M. J. (1988). The decision to leave an abusive relationship: Empirical evidence and theoretical issues. *Psychological Bulletin, 104,* 236-250.
Strube, M. J., & Barbour, L. S. (1983). The decision to leave an abusive relationship: Economic dependence and psychological commitment. *Journal of Marriage and the Family, 45,* 785-793.
Strube, M. J., & Barbour, L. S. (1984). Factors related to the decision to leave an abusive relationship. *Journal of Marriage and the Family, 46,* 837-844.
van der Kolk, B. A., & Greenberg, M. S. (1987). The psychobiology of the trauma response: Hyperarousal, constriction, and addiction to traumatic reexposure. In B. A. van der Kolk (Ed.), *Psychological Trauma* (pp. 63-87). Washington, DC: American Psychiatric Press.
Walker, L. E. (1979). *The battered woman.* New York: Harper & Row.
Walker, L. E. (1984). *The battered woman syndrome.* New York: Springer.
Watkins, C. (1995). Beyond status: The Americans with Disabilities Act and the parental rights of people labeled developmentally disabled or mentally retarded. *California Law Review, 83,* 1415-1475.

13 Child Neglect

Research Recommendations and Future Directions

MAUREEN M. BLACK
HOWARD DUBOWITZ

Child neglect accounts for more than half of the substantiated reports of maltreatment and almost half of maltreatment-related child deaths (Kadushin, 1988; McCurdy & Daro, 1994; U.S. Department of Health and Human Services [U.S.DHHS], 1996). Despite its prevalence, there are many unanswered questions regarding the etiology, treatment, consequences, and prevention of child neglect (Black, in press; Wolock & Horowitz, 1984). Several authors in this book have suggested specific areas for further research. This chapter builds on those suggestions by focusing on the major gaps in child neglect.

After reviewing the state of knowledge in the field of child maltreatment, the National Research Council (NRC; 1993) recommended that the research agenda be child oriented within an ecological framework to include "experiences of developing children and their families within a broader social context that includes their friends, neighborhoods, and communities" (p. 4). Although there is much to be learned from the existing child welfare system, the NRC encouraged broad-based research that examined "beyond what is—to what could be, if children and families were supported to attain healthy development" (p. 4). This chapter endorses the ecological perspective recommended by the NRC for guiding future research in child neglect.

THEORIES OF NEGLECT

The importance of ecological and transactional models in child maltreatment has been recognized for more than a decade (Belsky, 1980, 1993; Bronfenbrenner, 1993; Cicchetti & Rizley, 1981; Starr, 1978) yet has often been ignored both in research and in practice (NRC, 1993). Risk and protective factors are important constructs that can aid in understanding how ecological factors contribute to or ameliorate neglect; they can be conceptualized at the individual, family, and community levels (Garmezy, Masten, & Tellegen, 1984). Risk and protective factors differ in that risk factors are associated with increased likelihood of neglect and protective factors are associated with decreased likelihood of neglect. Although some have defined protective factors as the absence of risk or the opposite dimension of risk, Rutter (1987) argues that protective factors are conceptually distinct from risk factors. Protective factors, such as intelligence, an even temperament, and a relationship with a significant person, can have their own independent effects, or they can moderate (or buffer) the relationship between risk and neglect. Without theory to guide practice and research, clinicians and investigators cannot be assured of including critical variables that may help explain the relationships between risk and neglect and for protecting children against neglect. More research is needed in identifying factors that protect children from neglect. There is also a need to examine alternative theories on factors associated with neglect. For example, Crittenden's chapter in this volume (Chapter 3) proposes some new ideas to be tested.

DEFINITION OF CHILD NEGLECT

The current child welfare framework for defining neglect is to focus on omissions in care by parents or caregivers, resulting in actual or potential harm to children (U.S.DHHS, 1996). However, neglect is inherently difficult to define because the boundary between adequate and inadequate care is often not clear. The lack of a clear and agreed-on definition of neglect contributes to significant variability in policies and practice concerning neglect and hampers the comparison of research findings across studies on neglect.

One alternative is to eliminate the focus on parental responsibility and to define neglect based on the unmet basic needs of children. Thus, child neglect would be defined exclusively by children's basic needs not being met, regardless of the reason (Dubowitz, Black, Starr, & Zuravin, 1993; Giovannoni & Becerra, 1979; Wolock & Horowitz, 1984). However, the reasons and the context in which neglect occurs are important for guiding interventions.

Child protection is a basic tenet of all theories of child development, particularly during children's early years when they are most dependent on adult caregivers. However, societies have struggled with the task of differentiating between the responsibilities of parents and communities in raising and caring for children. Although families assume primary responsibility for protecting and nurturing their children, professionals, community agencies, and local institutions assist by assuming responsibility for adequate schools, safe neighborhoods, developmentally appropriate recreational facilities, accessible health services, and so forth (Garbarino & Collins, Chapter 1, this volume). Most of the research on the etiology of neglect has focused on parental behavior. This area would be enriched by examining the influence, direct and indirect, of other factors (e.g., neighborhood characteristics) on parenting and on children's well-being.

Community Standard

Several authors have attempted to clarify definitions of neglect by surveying community members and professionals (e.g., Dubowitz, Klockner, Starr, & Black, 1998; Giovannoni & Becerra, 1979; Polansky, Gaudin, Ammons, & Davis, 1985). Agreement on vignettes that may comprise neglect has been high across professional, disciplinary, racial, and class lines. Although this type of research provides information on community and professional standards, caution is warranted in assuming that common and acceptable practices are safe for children. For example, leaving young children home alone is dangerous, even if it is a common practice. Child neglect can undermine the integrity of the entire community by setting standards that are harmful to children (Garbarino, 1995; Polansky et al., 1985). Thus, neglect should be based on compelling evidence that a condition or circumstance harms children or puts them at risk for harm, regardless of community consensus. Equivocal situations (e.g., latchkey children) should be studied for their impact on children to examine whether they result in harm and should be considered as neglect. New knowledge improves our ability to meet children's needs (e.g., the benefit of car seats for young children) and correspondingly expands the definition of neglect when appropriate measures are ignored.

Poverty

Poverty often imposes limitations on families that interfere with children's well-being (Pelton, 1991). Nevertheless, most children raised in low-income families do not experience neglect (Zuravin, 1989), and within low-income communities, neglecting families are viewed as deviant (Polansky et al., 1985).

Although poverty often contributes to family dysfunction and may also directly deprive children of basic needs, poverty per se is not usually considered neglect by the child welfare system. Indeed, many state laws or regulations specifically exclude conditions that are associated with poverty, such as homelessness. Although additional research is not needed to document the detrimental effects of poverty on children, research is needed to understand how low-income families protect their children from the devastating effects of poverty and avoid child neglect. Research is also needed to examine how social policies and programs can reduce poverty and the neglect associated with it.

Multiple Sources of Information

Much of what is known about neglect is based on the definitions of state and local child protective service (CPS) agencies (Giovannoni & Becerra, 1979). However, there are referral biases suggesting that families who are minority, low income, or involved with social service agencies are disproportionately likely to be reported to CPS (English, Chapter 10, this volume; Wolock & Horowitz, 1984). Moreover, once a report is made, decisions regarding investigation and substantiation often vary by local policies and interpretations. Because CPS-defined cases of neglect are only a select subset of all neglect cases, research based on CPS-defined neglect is not representative of all child neglect.

Theoretically derived definitions of neglect developed by researchers are attempts to set objective criteria and to eliminate or reduce the bias often associated with CPS. Research definitions may be based on systematic observations of the home, including safety and parent-child or family interaction (Caldwell & Bradley, 1979; Magura & Moses, 1986; Trocme, 1996); specific behavioral criteria, such as missed appointments or school absenteeism; medical history; or self-report measures (Straus, Kinard, & Williams, 1996). Although research definitions may enhance theory on neglect, unique definitions may compromise the comparability of findings across studies and have little bearing on CPS cases. Some researchers (e.g., Harrington, Black, Starr, & Dubowitz, 1998) have combined CPS record reviews with research definitions as proposed by Zuravin (1991). However, most research teams have found substantial discrepancies in the identification of neglect across sources, posing the challenge of how to integrate the data. Additional research and guidance are needed to help researchers determine how to integrate information from multiple sources.

Children's Developmental Stages

There is little agreement on how to operationalize neglect from a developmental perspective, despite the recognition that definitions of neglect must consider children's age or developmental skills (Aber & Zigler, 1981). Thus, the decision whether a child who is home alone is experiencing neglect is dependent on the child's age or developmental status as well as the context in which the events occur. It may be developmentally appropriate for a 13-year-old to be alone for several hours during the day (particularly if there are neighbors or responsible adults nearby) but neglectful for a 3-year-old to be home alone. Additional research is needed to guide the assessment of possible neglect from a developmental perspective. For example, researchers could examine the impact of conditions and circumstances on children of different developmental levels, primarily in the realm of supervision and safety.

Potential Harm, Severity, and Chronicity

Investigators, clinicians, and policymakers dispute the importance of potential harm, severity, and chronicity (Cicchetti & Barnett, 1991). The potential for harm is difficult to measure, but epidemiological information may be helpful in establishing when children are at significant risk of harm. The risks associated with secondhand tobacco smoke or not being in a car seat are examples of such information. The severity of neglect may be assessed by the actual or potential degree of harm. Chronicity is often estimated by the duration of neglect, sometimes determined by the time period covered by multiple CPS reports, by falloffs in growth, or by documentation of non-adherence in medical or school records. Although CPS records have been used, they are a crude proxy for measuring chronicity. Additional research is needed to determine how to operationalize harm, severity, and chronicity of neglect.

Caregiver intentionality is sometimes considered in definitions of neglect (Dubowitz et al., 1993). However, caregiver attributions are extremely difficult to measure and often of limited value. If caregiver attributions are thought to be conceptually linked to neglect, then additional research is necessary to determine appropriate measurement strategies.

Types of Neglect

The definition of neglect is further complicated by the recognition that there are multiple subtypes of neglect. Several authors differentiate between physical and emotional neglect (Barnett, Manly, & Cicchetti, 1991, 1993; Cicchetti & Barnett, 1991), and educational neglect is usually considered separately. Zuravin (Chapter 2, this volume) has suggested multiple subtypes of neglect. Although some subtypes of neglect often co-occur (e.g., poor personal hygiene and household sanitation), others appear to be distinct (e.g., abandonment and not being enrolled in school). Just as the etiology and consequences for abuse and neglect may differ, they may also differ depending on the subtype of neglect. Research is needed on the relationships among subtypes of neglect and whether they have different etiologies and consequences. This type of information could improve the specificity of interventions.

Evolving knowledge and awareness has led to concern regarding possible "new" subtypes or manifestations of neglect. These include exposure to domestic and community violence, in utero drug exposure, inadequate protection in cars (i.e., car seats and belts), and secondary smoke, particularly when children have respiratory diseases. Additional research is needed to estimate the risks attached to these issues and how to determine neglect.

Co-Morbidity of Abuse and Neglect

Another definitional problem arises from the frequent co-occurrence of neglect and abuse (Ney, Fung, & Wickett, 1994), making it difficult to differentiate the two. Because abuse is related to a clearly defined act, children who are both abused and neglected may be classified as abused rather than neglected. To the extent that definitions, interventions, and consequences for abuse and neglect may differ, it can be difficult to extrapolate from studies in which abuse and neglect are operationalized as a single phenomenon. Yet, from a clinical perspective, because most maltreated children have experienced multiple forms of maltreatment, it is also important to consider research that addresses children who have experienced both abuse and neglect.

Thus, much additional research is needed on the definition of neglect. Not only is there a lack of conceptual clarity regarding the definition of neglect, but there is uncertainty regarding the optimal sources of information and the integration of information about the child, including developmental status and the context.

MEASURES AND METHODOLOGY

In addition to the lack of consensus regarding the definition of neglect, there are no agreed-on or community-accepted strategies to measure neglect. Clinicians, teachers, and others often rely on observable signs that children are not being adequately protected. Failure to thrive, poor hygiene, injuries, and failure to attend school or to comply with necessary health or medical recommendations are often seen as forms of neglect. However, these observable signs should not be construed as neglect without examining the context in which they occur. For example, failure to thrive has multiple causes beyond neglect (Black, 1995; Frank & Drotar, 1994).

Without clear standards of neglect, many clinicians and investigators develop their own operational definitions and measurements. Home observations provide valuable information on children and families, and there are at least three scales to classify neglect based on home observation. The Child Well-Being Scales (CWBS) (Magura & Moses, 1986) provide observational criteria that enable caseworkers to assess change within individual families. Although the CWBS have been used to identify neglect

(Harrington, Dubowitz, Black, & Binder, 1996), there are limited data on their validity, and their specificity may vary depending on whether the observations are conducted in the context of ongoing contact by caseworkers or single visits by researchers. The Child Neglect Index (Trocme, 1996) is similar to the CWBS; the initial findings on reliability and validity are promising, but further evaluation of this measure is needed. The Home Observation Measure of the Environment (HOME) (Caldwell & Bradley, 1979) is an observational measure of the child-centered quality of the home that has been used extensively in research on children's development.

Observations of children and parents during daily activities, such as meals and play, have been used to classify the quality of the parent-child interaction as ranging from neglectful to nurturant (Black, Hutcheson, Dubowitz, & Berenson-Howard, 1994). Although observational measures provide insight into how parents and children interact, they are only brief snapshots, usually conducted in highly structured settings (Black, Hutcheson, Dubowitz, Berenson-Howard, & Starr, 1996). Additional research is needed on field-oriented procedures for observing and scoring parent-child interactions, particularly with school-age children.

There are self-report measures in which parents are asked to report on their caregiving practices or on neglect experienced by their children. These measures enable respondents (usually adults) to report on neglect that they experienced during their childhoods (Straus et al., 1996). As these scales are used and data on their reliability and validity become available, their utility can be better assessed. However, because parents often want to portray themselves as socially desirable caregivers, it is difficult to establish validity in their reports. Although there are scales of social desirability (e.g., Crowne & Marlowe, 1964) to assess respondents' likelihood of providing truthful answers, additional research is needed on parental self-report measures.

Little is known about asking children to report on their own experiences of neglect. Additional research is needed to assess appropriate procedures and safeguards for children to report on their own experiences.

Most investigators have conceptualized neglect as a dichotomous variable, often guided by the demands of the child welfare or legal systems. However, neglect may exist on a continuum that extends from children's basic needs being adequately met, to vulnerability in one or more areas, to at least one need not being met. More research is needed to investigate the possibility of conceptualizing neglect along a continuum.

With limited measures to assess neglect, it is difficult to evaluate prevention or intervention programs. Thus, most programs have not been systematically evaluated. There is a need for a clear definition of neglect and better measurement strategies.

PREVENTION AND INTERVENTION

A recent report from the Institute of Medicine (Mrazek & Haggerty, 1994) includes a categorization of prevention programs that can be applied to the prevention of child neglect. *Universal* or population-based interventions are designed to prevent child neglect and to promote healthy development among the entire population (e.g., public service announcements). *Selective* interventions are directed toward families whose children are at increased risk of experiencing neglect (e.g., home interventions for adolescent mothers [Olds et al., 1997]). *Indicated* interventions are directed toward children of families who have been neglected. They are designed to prevent further neglect and to ameliorate the effects of neglect (e.g., foster care).

There has been widespread interest in home intervention as an effective strategy in promoting the health and development of young children (U.S. Advisory Board on Child Abuse and Neglect, 1991; U.S. General Accounting Office, 1990). A recent long-term evaluation of a home-visiting program initiated during pregnancy and extending through the first 2 years of the child's life showed a reduction in reports for abuse and neglect among the highest-risk families (Olds et al., 1997). However, many important questions remain concerning home visitation, including the optimal timing and duration of intervention, the frequency of the intervention, and the background of home visitors (e.g., nurses, social workers, paraprofessionals, or lay members of the community).

Much more research is needed to determine how to implement and evaluate universal and selective interventions so the need for indicated interventions is reduced. In addition to research on prevention programs targeted to individual children and families, research is needed on the design, implementation, and evaluation of prevention programs that move beyond individual levels to include community organizations. Community involvement is particularly important because it may enhance the sustainability of prevention programs if the community views the programs as worthwhile and develops a sense of ownership and responsibility.

Although the most proximal influences on children usually come from families, friends, and community institutions (e.g., school, church), these factors are not independent of one another and may be influenced by more distal neighborhood factors. For example, Brooks-Gunn, Duncan, Klebanov, and Sealand (1993) demonstrated that children from affluent neighborhoods had higher cognitive scores, fewer teenage births, and were less likely to drop out of school than children from low-income neighborhoods, even when differences in the socioeconomic characteristics of the families were controlled statistically. Thus, prevention programs that incorporate community resources and role models, such as Scouts, Big Brothers and Sisters, church programs, sports, and recreational centers, may protect children and reduce the likelihood of child neglect. Research involving these community programs may be helpful in learning how programs influence children and how to encourage children to take advantage of them. Engaging high-risk families in interventions can be very difficult. It would be helpful to clarify the barriers to participation and to develop strategies to overcome them.

Clinicians often focus on indicated interventions, which are designed to ameliorate the effects of neglect on children who have experienced neglect. Evaluations of research that are limited to process measures (e.g., number of children served, number of sessions conducted) or changes in parental attitudes are often insufficient. Policymakers are looking for convincing evidence regarding the impact interventions have on the prevention or amelioration of neglect and on children's behavior and development. Research on outcomes should be conducted using rigorous scientific methods, whether directed toward one child who has experienced neglect or toward a group of families whose children are at risk for neglect. Scientific methods, such as systematic record review by unbiased examiners, yield data that can be used to evaluate the impact and cost-effectiveness of intervention programs. Although the optimal design for evaluating interventions is often a randomized clinical trial (Meinert, 1986) in which a randomization procedure is used to assign participants to an intervention or control group, randomization is not always possible or desirable. There are quasi-experimental procedures, such as pretesting and posttesting, that can be introduced to reduce bias and ensure validity (Cook & Campbell, 1977).

There is also a need for further evaluations of interventions that are well-grounded in theory and that appear promising. Examples include The Nurturing Program (Bavolek & Comstock, 1983) and Project 12-Ways (Lutzker, 1990; Sarber, Halasz, Messmer, Bickett, & Lutzker, 1983). Cost is an overriding concern for all prevention and intervention programs, making it critical to examine the cost-effectiveness of programs. In summary, more research is needed to identify prevention and intervention strategies that reduce the occurrence of neglect and its harmful effects on children. In addition, it would be helpful to know under what circumstances prevention and intervention programs are likely to succeed.

WHERE IS RESEARCH NOT NEEDED?

Most of the research on the etiology of neglect has examined correlates of neglect cases involved with CPS. There is little need for more of these studies; instead, prospective and longitudinal research could refine our knowledge of risk factors and help guide selected preventive efforts. A fair amount has been learned about the negative consequences of neglect over the past few decades (NRC, 1993). Here too there is little need for additional cross-sectional descriptions of children who have experienced neglect. Rather, research is needed on the long-term outcomes and the risk and protective factors that influence these outcomes (e.g., what enables children to thrive under adverse conditions?). For some subtypes of neglect, the harm to children appears obvious (e.g., hunger, abandonment, homelessness), and there is little need to study the effects on children. Research should instead focus on interventions to address these problems. Investigations of the causes and consequences of child neglect should be theory driven. Single-factor, atheoretical investigations are unlikely to contribute to our understanding of the complex factors associated with the causes and consequences of child neglect.

Similarly, the child development literature has documented that optimal conditions for children include relationships with nurturant and consistent family members. Although research may be useful in learning how to help families provide the quality of care that children need, investigators should extend existing literature regarding the importance of relationships to children's development.

CONTEXT IN WHICH NEGLECT OCCURS

Neglect cannot be evaluated independent of the context and culture in which it occurs. Thus, in some cultures, young school-age children may be responsible for "baby-sitting" their younger siblings, whereas in the United States, this practice may be construed as neglectful. There is no guarantee that common or culturally acceptable situations are protective for children. For example, in households where cooking is done on an open fire in an area that is accessible to children, burns are more likely to occur. Or when children are raised in violence-ridden communities, they are more likely to be injured by stray bullets or by random acts of violence.

Research is necessary to examine the impact of different cultural and religious practices on children and to assess whether concern for children's well-being is justified (e.g., Asser & Swan, 1998). Sensitivity and knowledge regarding cultural differences are important concepts to consider in addressing this issue.

PARENTAL CHARACTERISTICS ASSOCIATED WITH NEGLECT

Regardless of whether neglect is conceptualized from a parental or a child perspective, it has been associated with a lack of social support and feelings of loneliness among caregivers (Gaudin, Polansky, Kilpatrick, & Shilton, 1993; Polansky et al., 1985). Caregivers of neglected children often live in low-income communities and have limited opportunities for social support (Vondra, 1990). In addition, they may have fewer social skills and be less likely to take advantage of available resources than caregivers of non-neglected children living in the same communities (Coohey, 1995; Polansky, Chalmers, Williams, & Buttenweiser, 1981). Without social support, caregivers may feel less satisfied and have less access to community norms of parenting. More research is needed on strategies that enable caregivers of children who have experienced neglect to build the skills necessary to access and use community resources, including informal supports.

Research is also needed on the role of parental mental health. Neglect has been associated with maternal depression and mood disorders (Gaudin, 1993; Vondra, 1990; Zuravin, 1989). Polansky et al. (1981) have described mothers of neglected children as having apathy-futility syndrome, a condition that resembles depression but does not meet the criteria for clinical depression. In addition, parents of neglected children have been described as immature with a tendency toward role reversal and difficulties establishing appropriate boundaries with their children (Polansky et al., 1981). Additional research is needed on the mental health problems of parents of neglected children and on strategies to enable them to take advantage of community programs that facilitate healthy parenting.

CHILD CHARACTERISTICS ASSOCIATED WITH NEGLECT

Associating child characteristics with neglect is controversial. Although caution is warranted not to blame the victim, there may be child characteristics that increase the likelihood of neglect. For example, children who are perceived by their caregivers as having a difficult temperament may be more likely to experience neglect (Famularo, Fenton, & Kinscherff, 1992; Harrington et al., 1998). Caregivers who rate their children as having difficult temperaments spend less time playing with them and are less responsive to their cues (Goodman-Campbell, 1979; Houldin, 1987; Milliones, 1978). In addition, caregivers reporting that their children are easily upset also report more negative affect than caregivers who report that their children are less easily upset (Mangelsdorf, Gunnar, Kestenbaum, Lang, & Andreas, 1990). It is unclear whether the potential link between temperament and neglect is related to the challenges of caring for a difficult child or to difficulties in information processing (Erickson & Egeland, 1996) or maternal functioning (Polansky et al., 1985), whereby children are perceived as difficult. However, these findings suggest that children who are perceived as being difficult may be more likely to be neglected. More research is needed that focuses on the characteristics of children, particularly as they are interpreted by caregivers, and on strategies that reduce the likelihood for neglect to occur.

POLICY IMPLICATIONS

Policy-oriented research is desperately needed in the area of child neglect. In the absence of clear findings, policymakers have to rely on emotional appeals or so-called best guesses in allocating resources to programs designed to alleviate or remediate neglect. The Personal Responsibility and Work Opportunity Reconciliation Act of 1996 led to the establishment of the Transitional Assistance for Needy Families, a program designed to move adults from welfare into the workforce. Although many children would benefit as their families achieve economic independence, children whose families are ineligible or unable to take advantage of federally funded programs may suffer by not having their basic needs met. Thus, research on federal economic programs should examine the impact on children and the possibility of child neglect.

Operations research is also needed to understand why federally funded programs, such as the Supplemental Food Program for Women, Infants, and Children, that have been shown to be effective in preventing low birth weight and undernutrition (Frisbie, Bieglar, deTurk, Forbes, & Pullum, 1997) are underused. Despite eligibility criteria that would enable more than 3 million children to receive supplemental food, thousands of families do not take advantage of the free services.

CONCLUSIONS

Neglect is a complex, multifaceted problem that can have profound effects on children. Unfortunately, there has been little research on the conceptualization, definition, measurement, prevention, treatment, or policy implications of neglect. What is known is that single-factor conceptualizations are too simplistic and will not lead to effective prevention or intervention programs. Conceptualizations regarding neglect are further complicated by the recognition that different forms of neglect may have differing etiological pathways and require differing interventions. Although effective interventions are likely to be expensive because they often require long-term, multidisciplinary collaboration (Gaudin et al., 1993), particularly given the associations between neglect and poverty, there is a national need to develop and evaluate policies and programs to help parents and communities protect and nurture their children.

REFERENCES

Aber, J. L., & Zigler, E. (1981). Developmental considerations in the definition of child maltreatment. *New Directions for Child Development, 11,* 1-29.

Asser, S., & Swan, R. (1998). Child fatalities from religion-motivated medical neglect. *Pediatrics, 101,* 625-629.

Barnett, D., Manly, J. T., & Cicchetti, D. (1991). Continuing toward an operational definition of psychological maltreatment. *Development and Psychopathology, 3,* 19-29.

Barnett, D., Manly, J. T., & Cicchetti, D. (1993). Defining child maltreatment: The interface between policy and research. In D. Cicchetti & S. L. Toth (Eds.), *Advances in applied developmental psychology: Vol. 8. Child abuse, child development, and social policy* (pp. 7-73). Norwood, NJ: Ablc.

Bavolek, S., & Comstock, C. M. (1983). *The nurturing program for parents and children.* Eau Claire, WI: Family Development Associates.

Belsky, J. (1980). Child maltreatment: An ecological integration. *American Psychologist, 35,* 320-335.

Belsky, J. (1993). Etiology of child maltreatment: A developmental-ecological analysis. *Psychological Bulletin, 114,* 413-434.

Black, M. M. (1995). Failure to thrive: Strategies for evaluation and intervention. *School Psychology Review, 24,* 171-185.

Black, M. M. (in press). Neglect: Long-term management: Psychological considerations. In R. M. Reece (Ed.), *Child abuse treatment.* Baltimore, MD: Johns Hopkins University Press.

Black, M., Hutcheson, J., Dubowitz, H., & Berenson-Howard, J. (1994). Parenting style and developmental status among children with nonorganic failure to thrive. *Journal of Pediatric Psychology, 19,* 689-707.

Black, M., Hutcheson, J., Dubowitz, H., Berenson-Howard, J., & Starr, R. H. (1996). The roots of competence: Mother-infant interaction among low-income, African-American families. *Applied Developmental Psychology, 17,* 367-391.

Bronfenbrenner, U. (1993). Ecological systems theory. In R. Wozniak & K. Fisher (Eds.), *Specific environments: Thinking in contexts* (pp. 3-44). Hillsdale, NJ: Erlbaum.

Brooks-Gunn, J., Duncan, G. J., Klebanov, P. K., & Sealand, N. (1993). Do neighborhoods influence child and adolescent behavior? *American Journal of Sociology, 99,* 353-395.

Caldwell, B. M., & Bradley, R. H. (1979). *Home observation for measurement of the environment.* Little Rock: University of Arkansas.

Cicchetti, D., & Barnett, D. (1991). Toward the development of a scientific nosology of child maltreatment. In W. Grove & D. Cicchetti (Eds.), *Thinking clearly about psychology: Essays in honor of Paul E. Meehl: Vol. 2. Personality and psychopathology.* Minneapolis: University of Minnesota Press.

Cicchetti, D., & Rizley, R. (1981). Developmental perspectives on the etiology, intergenerational transmission, and sequelae of child maltreatment. In R. Rizley & D. Cicchetti (Eds.), *Developmental perspectives on child maltreatment.* San Francisco: Jossey-Bass.

Coohey, C. (1995). Neglectful mothers, their mothers, and partners: The significance of mutual aid. *Child Abuse & Neglect, 19,* 885-895.

Cook, T. D., & Campbell, D. T. (1977). *Quasi-experimentation design and analysis issues for field settings.* Boston: Houghton Mifflin.

Crowne, D., & Marlowe, D. (1964). *The approval motive.* New York: John Wiley.

Dubowitz, H., Black, M., Starr, R. H., Jr., & Zuravin, S. (1993). A conceptual definition of child neglect. *Criminal Justice and Behavior, 20,* 8-26.

Dubowitz, H., Klockner, A., Starr, R. H., & Black, M. M. (1998). Community and professional definitions of child neglect. *Child Maltreatment, 3,* 235-243.

Erickson, M., & Egeland, B. (1996). Child neglect. In J. Briere, L. Berliner, J. A. Bulkey, C. Jenny, & T. Reid (Eds.), *The APSAC handbook on child maltreatment* (pp. 4-20). Thousand Oaks, CA: Sage.

Famularo, R., Fenton, T., & Kinscherff, R. (1992). Medical and developmental histories of maltreated children. *Clinical Pediatrics, 31,* 536-541.

Frank, D. A., & Drotar, D. (1994). Failure to thrive. In R. M. Reece (Ed.), *Child abuse: Medical diagnosis and treatment.* Philadelphia: Lea & Febiger.

Frisbie, W. P., Biegler, M., deTurk, P., Forbes, D., & Pullum, S. G. (1997). Racial and ethnic differences in determinants of intrauterine growth retardation and other compromised birth outcomes. *American Journal of Public Health, 87,* 1977-1983.

Garbarino, J. (1995). *Raising children in a socially toxic environment.* San Francisco: Jossey-Bass.

Garmezy, N., Masten, A. S., & Tellegen, A. (1984). The study of stress and competence in children: A building block for developmental psychopathology. *Child Development, 55,* 97-111.

Gaudin, J. M., Jr. (1993). Effective intervention with neglectful families. *Criminal Justice and Behavior, 20,* 66-89.

Gaudin, J. M., Jr., Polansky, N. A., Kilpatrick, A. C., & Shilton, P. (1993). Loneliness, depression, stress, and social supports in neglectful families. *American Journal of Orthopsychiatry, 1,* 597-605.

Giovannoni, J. M., & Becerra, R. M. (1979). *Defining child abuse.* New York: Free Press.

Goodman-Campbell, S. (1979). Mother-infant interactions as a function of maternal ratings of temperament. *Child Psychiatry and Human Development, 10,* 67-76.

Harrington, D., Black, M. M., Starr, R. H., & Dubowitz, H. (1998). Child neglect: A model incorporating child temperament and family context. *American Journal of Orthopsychiatry, 68,* 108-116.

Harrington, D., Dubowitz, H., Black, M. M., & Binder, A. (1996). Maternal substance abuse and neglectful parenting: Relations with children's development. *Journal of Clinical Child Psychology, 24,* 258-263.

Houldin, A. D. (1987). Infant temperament and the quality of the childrearing environment. *Maternal-Child Nursing Journal, 16,* 131-143.

Kadushin, A. (1988). Neglect in families. In E. W. Wunnally, C. S. Chilean, & F. M. Cox (Eds.), *Mental illness, delinquency, addictions, and neglect* (pp. 147-166). Newbury Park, CA: Sage.

Lutzker, J. R. (1990). Behavioral treatment of child neglect. *Behavioral Modification, 14,* 301-315.

Magura, S., & Moses, S. (1986). *Outcome measures for child welfare services: Theory and application.* Washington, DC: Child Welfare League of America.

Mangelsdorf, S., Gunnar, M., Kestenbaum, R., Lang, S., & Andreas, D. (1990). Infant proneness-to-distress temperament, maternal personality, and mother-infant attachment: Association and goodness of fit. *Child Development, 61,* 820-831.

McCurdy, K., & Daro, D. (1994). Child maltreatment: A national survey of reports and fatalities. *Journal of Interpersonal Violence, 9,* 75-94.

Meinert, C. L. (1986). *Clinical trials: Design, conduct, and analysis.* New York: Oxford University Press.

Milliones, J. (1978). Relationship between perceived child temperament and maternal behaviors. *Child Development, 49,* 1255-1257.

Mrazek, P. J., & Haggerty, R. J. (1994). *Reducing risks for mental disorders: Frontiers for preventive intervention research.* Washington, DC: National Academy Press.

National Research Council. (1993). *Understanding child abuse and neglect.* Washington, DC: National Academy Press.

Ney, P. G., Fung, T., & Wickett, A. R. (1994). The worst combination of child abuse and neglect. *Child Abuse & Neglect, 18,* 705-714.

Olds, D. L., Eckenrode, J., Henderson, C. R., Kitzman, H., Powers, J., Cole, R., Sidora, K., Morris, P., Pettitt, L. M., & Luckey, D. (1997). Long-term effects of home visitation on maternal life course and child abuse and neglect. *Journal of the American Medical Association, 278,* 637-643.

Pelton, L. H. (1991). Poverty and child protection. *Protecting Children, 7,* 3-5.

Polansky, N. A., Chalmers, M. A., Williams, D. P., & Buttenweiser, E. W. (1981). *Damaged parents: An anatomy of neglect.* Chicago: University of Chicago Press.

Polansky, N. A., Gaudin, J. M., Ammons, P. W., & Davis, K. B. (1985). The psychology ecology of the neglectful mother. *Child Abuse & Neglect, 9,* 265-275.

Rutter, M. (1987). Psychosocial resilience and protective mechanisms. *American Journal of Orthopsychiatry, 57,* 316 331.

Sarber, R. E., Halasz, M. M., Messmer, M. C., Bickett, A. D., & Lutzker, J. R. (1983). Teaching menu planning and grocery shopping to a mentally retarded mother. *Mental Retardation, 21,* 101-106.

Starr, R. H., Jr. (1978). The controlled study of the ecology of child abuse and drug abuse. *International Journal of Child Abuse and Neglect, 2,* 19-28.

Straus, M., Kinard, E. M., & Williams, L. M. (1996). *The neglect scale.* Durham: University of New Hampshire, Family Research Laboratory.

Trocme, N. (1996). Development and preliminary evaluation of the Ontario Child Neglect Index. *Child Maltreatment, 1,* 145-155.

U. S. Advisory Board on Child Abuse and Neglect. (1991). *Creating caring communities: Blueprint for an effective federal policy on child abuse and neglect.* Washington, DC: Government Printing Office.

U.S. Department of Health and Human Services, National Center on Child Abuse and Neglect. (1996). *Child maltreatment, 1994: Reports from the states to the National Center on Child Abuse and Neglect.* Washington, DC: Government Printing Office.

U.S. General Accounting Office. (1990). *Home visiting: A promising early intervention strategy for at-risk families* (Report No. GAO/HRD-90-83). Washington, DC: Government Printing Office.

Vondra, J. (1990). The community context of child abuse and neglect. *Marriage and Family Review, 15,* 19-38.

Wolock, I., & Horowitz, B. (1984). Child maltreatment as a social problem: The neglect of neglect. *American Journal of Orthopsychiatry, 54,* 530-543.

Zuravin, S. J. (1989). The ecology of child abuse and neglect: Review of the literature and presentation of data. *Violence and Victims, 4,* 101-120.

Zuravin, S. (1991). Research definitions of child physical abuse and neglect: Current problems. In R. Starr, Jr., & D. Wolfe (Eds.), *The effects of child abuse and neglect: Issues and research.* New York: Guilford.

14 Policy Issues in Child Neglect

RICHARD J. GELLES

It is both ironic and a major dilemma that the most common form of child maltreatment is the least well-understood and has the least clear policy response. Child neglect constitutes the largest portion of child maltreatment reports received, investigated, and responded to by the child welfare system. Neglect may have serious short-term and long-term harmful consequences for children. And yet, policy discussions, although not minimizing either the extent or consequences of child neglect, nearly always focus on the more sensational types of maltreatment, leaving neglect as a "residual" aspect of maltreatment, in terms of interventions, prevention programs, and public policy.

Although states have laws and policies for specific types of neglect, for example drug-exposed newborns, there is no overriding social policy for child neglect in general. A few factors have impeded the development of specific social policy aimed at the prevention and treatment of neglect. Although child maltreatment is difficult to define, neglect has proven even more difficult to define. There has been little research on the causes, correlates, and consequences of neglect. Because neglect tends to co-occur with other forms of maltreatment, it is difficult to identify the specific causes of neglect and to develop specific interventions. Last, there is a tendency for the child welfare and judicial systems to view neglect as less harmful to children, requiring a less intrusive response than physical or sexual abuse.

But neglect has a unique feature that further complicates definitions, assessment of causality and consequences, and interventions and prevention. When assessing physical abuse, one key question is whether the injury was inflicted or non-inflicted (i.e., accidental). When assessing sexual abuse, the key question often is, has abuse occurred? With neglect, the question is, given that neglect exists, could the parent have prevented the problem? Thus, the unique feature of neglect is locus of responsibility. It is often unclear whether neglect is due to a parent's omissions or due to absence of social, economic, or psychological resources. Thus, a frequent response to neglect is to assess whether parents could have met their children's needs given their resources. Compared to abuse, much of neglect may occur because of factors truly beyond the parents' control. Legal definitions of neglect attempt to resolve this problem by specifying that the behavior has to be avoidable and non-accidental. However, intentionality is difficult to assess, especially in neglect.

This chapter briefly reviews some material covered more extensively in previous chapters and focuses on social policy for child maltreatment and how social policy has generally ignored neglect. The neglect of children, more so than abuse, can be either a child welfare or a welfare issue depending on where the locus of responsibility is placed. Neglect cases are responded to by the child welfare system when the responsibility is placed on caregivers; when the responsibility is thought to lie elsewhere, the case may be referred to the welfare or health care or educational systems. Last, the chapter discusses how focusing more specifically on neglect can lead to better, more informed social policy.

CHILD NEGLECT: DEFINITIONS, EXTENT, CORRELATES, AND CONSEQUENCES

Definitions

The Child Abuse Prevention and Treatment Act (CAPTA) of 1984 defines child abuse and neglect as:

> the physical or mental injury, sexual abuse or exploitation, negligent treatment, or maltreatment of a child under the age of eighteen or the age specified by the child protection law of the state in question, by a person (including an employee of a residential facility or any staff person providing out-of-home care) who is responsible for the child's welfare under circumstances which indicate that the child's health or welfare is harmed or threatened thereby, as determined in regulations prescribed by the Secretary. (42 U.S.C. 5106g)

The federal definition was expanded in 1988 to indicate that the behavior had to be avoidable and non-accidental, to address the issue of intent (CAPTA, 1988). However, it still provided no clear guidance as to how to classify cases based on intent.

Beyond the federal definition, *child maltreatment* is a general term that covers a wide range of acts of commission and omission, either carried out by a caregiver or allowed to happen, which result in a spectrum of injuries, from death, to serious disabling injury, to emotional distress, to malnutrition and illness. Neglect constitutes three of the six main types of child maltreatment[1] in addition to physical, sexual, and emotional abuse:

1. *Physical Neglect:* Acts of omission that involve refusal to provide health care, delay in providing health care, abandonment, expulsion of a child from a home, inadequate supervision, failure to meet food and clothing needs, and conspicuous failure to protect a child from hazards or danger.

2. *Educational Neglect:* Acts of omission *and* commission that include permitting chronic truancy, failure to enroll a child in school, and inattention to specific education needs.

3. *Emotional Neglect:* Acts of omission that involve failing to meet the nurturing and affection needs of a child, exposing a child to chronic or severe spouse abuse, allowing or permitting a child to use alcohol or controlled substances, encouraging the child to engage in deviant or delinquent behavior, refusal to provide psychological care, delays in providing psychological care, and other inattention to the child's developmental needs.

Definitions of maltreatment generally fall short of providing a clear definition for human and social service providers or framers of social policy.

A major problem with federal and state definitions of maltreatment is that they assume that one can draw a clear line between acts of omission that are within the control of parents and those that are not. Is a child poorly fed or exposed to danger because of deliberate behavior of parents, or do such omissions occur because of structural and community problems that constrain parents' abilities to meet their children's needs? Indeed, most definitions focus on parental behavior without considering the structural, cultural, and community influences on parents.

A second problem is that definitions of neglect, by focusing on parental responsibility, avoid attention to social policies and institutions that directly harm children. If a child is poorly fed because the caregiver has exhausted her welfare benefits, who is responsible for the neglect—the mother or the state that established the time limit? More important from a policy perspective, is the appropriate policy to punish the mother or to find a program for her or to change the law that limited welfare benefits? In terms of educational neglect, who is responsible if a child's educational needs are not met—the parent or the school system? Whose contribution is greater? In New York City in 1987, the average expenditure per pupil was about $5,500, yet in neighboring suburbs, per-pupil expenditures were twice that (Kozol, 1991). It is hard to accuse parents of educational neglect when the education system has such immense inequities.

Ironically, child protective service (CPS) workers may find it easier to define neglect in affluent communities or in situations where social policies provide generous social and economic support than in poorer communities. A well-publicized example was the "home alone" case in Chicago a few years ago. Two parents left their preadolescent children alone at home and went on a week's vacation to Mexico. There was little debate as to whether this constituted neglect, because the parents obviously had the resources to find appropriate child care. The situation is more ambiguous when a mother on welfare, isolated from friends, family, and quality day care, leaves her children unattended when she goes to work.

Current definitions of maltreatment, including neglect, place a premium on responsibility and blame but focus only on caregivers, to the exclusion of institutions, social policies, and organizations that directly and indirectly neglect children. In some instances, it is easy to identify and label neglect; in other cases, the definition, and thus the appropriate social policy, are much less clear.

Extent

There are two main measures of the extent of child maltreatment in the United States, and both agree that neglect constitutes about half of all the cases of maltreatment each year.

The National Center on Child Abuse and Neglect (NCCAN) has conducted three surveys to measure the national incidence of recognized and reported child maltreatment (Burgdorf, 1980; NCCAN, 1988, 1996). The most recent survey estimated that in 1993, 2,815,600 children were maltreated (NCCAN, 1996).[2] Of this number, 1,961,300 children, or 70%, were "neglected," with 1,335,000 children physically neglected, 584,100 emotionally neglected, and 397,000 educationally neglected.

A second measure of the extent of child maltreatment is the National Child Abuse and Neglect Data System (NCANDS; U.S. Department of Health and Human Services, 1997),[3] based on official reports from 49 states and the District of Columbia. In 1995, states received 1.9 million reports of child maltreatment, representing 2,959,237 individual victims. Of the 1,000,502 child victims for whom maltreatment was indicated or substantiated and for whom there were data on type of maltreatment,[4] 244,903 experienced physical abuse, 523,049 experienced neglect, 29,454 experienced medical neglect, 126,095 experienced sexual abuse, 44,648 experienced emotional maltreatment, and 144,489 were classified as other forms of maltreatment. Thus, neglect constituted 55% of substantiated reports in 1995. The NCANDS data, although underrepresenting the true incidence of neglect, accurately measures the portion of child maltreatment investigations conducted for neglect.

It is clear that neglect is the most prevalent form of maltreatment, and cases of neglect constitute the largest portion of child welfare cases, investigations, and perhaps even interventions. Despite this, the more sensational physical and sexual abuse seems to evoke far more response and thus social policy.

Correlates

Garbarino and Collins (Chapter 1, this volume) and Crittenden (Chapter 3, this volume) address the social context of neglect and its causes. Thus, this section will briefly review some of the major factors contributing to neglect, especially those related to social policy.

There are multiple pathways and interactive factors that contribute to child maltreatment (National Research Council, 1993). In addition, children can experience multiple forms of maltreatment. Thus, disentangling correlates of child neglect from other forms of maltreatment is difficult.

From the complex constellation of factors related to neglect, poverty certainly emerges as a main risk factor (National Research Council, 1993). The results of the Third National Incidence Study of Child Abuse and Neglect (National Center on Child Abuse and Neglect, 1996) found that the incidence rate of recognized neglect in families with less than a $15,000 per year income was 27.2 per 1,000 compared with 11.3 per 1,000 for those with incomes from $15,000 to $29,999 and 0.6 per 1,000 for children in homes with incomes exceeding $30,000 per year.[5] Income was not related to emotional neglect, but it was related to physical and educational neglect (National Center of Child Abuse and Neglect, 1996). Although poverty contributes to neglect, it is important to note that all poor parents do not neglect their children. Thus, other factors must be considered. However, from a social policy perspective, it is clear that if poverty is a significant risk factor for neglect, policies to reduce economic disadvantage would diminish the risk and rate of neglect.

Neglect was more common in single-parent homes compared with two-parent households. Last, neglect was more common in homes with four or more children compared with homes with fewer than four children. However, homes with one child had higher rates of neglect than homes with two or three children (National Center on Child Abuse and Neglect, 1996). This unexpected finding may be because one-child homes have younger children and younger parents than households with two or three children. Here, we see stress (single-parent family, large number of children) as an important risk factor for neglect, implying that social policy must tackle the issues of single-parent families and high fertility rates if neglect is to be addressed.

Neglect may be an expression of pervasive and deeply rooted inadequacies in the parent. This condition has been termed a character disorder of neglectful parents, expressed as an "apathy-futility syndrome," and the "impulsive-ridden" character (Polansky, Chalmers, Buttenweiser, & Williams, 1981; Polansky, DeSaix, & Sharlin, 1972; Polansky, Gaudin, & Kilpatrick, 1992). Parents who neglect their children have been termed "childlike" or "infantile" (National Research Council, 1993). These findings suggest that for some neglectful parents, the appropriate intervention may be individual therapy.

Alcohol and substance abuse are often associated with maltreatment, but the association is not well understood (National Research Council, 1993). Much of the focus on the association has been on physical and sexual abuse, but alcohol and substance abuse appear to play a role in neglect as well, especially when, for example, neglect is defined as the birth of a drug-exposed baby.

Overall, effective social policies for neglect need to address economic disadvantage as well as illicit drug use. There is an obvious correlation between poverty, single-parent family structure, and substance abuse, and understanding how these factors are interrelated is key to developing appropriate interventions and social policy. Ironically, the welfare reform legislation of 1996 was designed to *reduce* the number of children born to single-parent mothers by limiting welfare benefits for these families. The unintended consequences of limiting benefits, at least in the short term, might be increased neglect and abuse. The vexing problem of teenage childbearing is closely related to child neglect, and successful social policies aimed at reducing out-of-wedlock teenage childbearing would likely reduce child neglect as well.

Consequences

Gaudin (Chapter 5, this volume); Bonner, Crowe, and Logue (Chapter 8, this volume), and Chasnoff and Lauder (Chapter 7, this volume) review the consequences of neglect, including fatalities, and the consequences of drug exposure for newborns.

Cognitive and behavior deficits and socioemotional problems have been found among neglected children, including lesser intelligence and language ability, undisciplined activity and extreme passivity, poor impulse control, and insecure attachments with adults (Wekerle & Wolfe, 1996). Erickson, Egeland, & Pianta (1989) report that compared with other maltreated children, neglected children have worse cognitive and academic achievement. More important, they found that children of psychologically unavailable mothers who were unresponsive to their children (Pianta, Egeland, & Erickson, 1989) had the worst problems at ages 5 and 6.

Although there are clear deficits in neglected children, these deficits are not always obvious to CPS workers or judges. Moreover, researchers and clinicians are often unable to disentangle the effects of the neglect from other problems associated with neglect, such as poverty. Whereas some of the deficits may be due to parental omissions in care, others may be due to poverty or the interaction of poverty, family structure, and parent characteristics. However, when researchers do disentangle the effects of other forms of abuse and the impact of poverty and structural influences, it appears that neglected children suffer the worst outcomes. This finding is even more striking in light of the apparent reluctance of the child welfare system and courts to view neglect as having serious consequences for children. Social policy appears to underemphasize the consequences of neglect when framing and developing legal and social interventions for neglected children.

SOCIAL POLICY AND CHILD MALTREATMENT

The Evolution of Child Welfare Social Policy

Child maltreatment, including neglect, has, for more than a century, been conceptualized as a child welfare problem that is best responded to by the social service or child welfare system. The basic assumption that guides intervention is that therapeutic approaches (i.e., social services and clinical interventions) are more effective in protecting children and preventing further abuse and neglect than punishment (i.e., arrest, prosecution, or other legal interventions). Because the essential philosophy of the child welfare system is compassion and not control (Rosenfeld & Newberger, 1977), the preferred response is to provide support for families as a means of protecting children.

At the core of the compassionate approach is the belief that children do best when cared for by their biological parents. The work on attachment (see, for example, Bowlby, 1958, 1969; Harlow, 1958, 1961; Lindsey, 1994) has been used to support this assumption, but even professionals and policymakers who are unfamiliar with research on attachment endorse the preferred approach to intervening in child maltreatment to preserve the family, so long as the child's safety is ensured.

The means by which child safety and parent attachment are balanced is through efforts to preserve families—either while allowing the maltreated child to remain in the home or while the child is temporarily placed outside of the home. Family preservation services aim to help families avoid out-of-home placement or separation.

The main exception to the policy of family preservation occurred in the wake of the rediscovery of child abuse in the 1960s. When Kempe, Silverman, Steele, Droegmueller, and Silver (1962) published their seminal paper, "The Battered Child Syndrome" in 1962, they focused on life-threatening acts of physical violence directed at young children. Kempe and the medical community called for mandatory reporting laws for child abuse so that serious inflicted injuries to children would be recognized and the circumstances addressed.

Mandatory reporting, combined with public awareness campaigns and technological developments, such as toll-free lines, led to extraordinary increases in reports. At the same time, because the medical and psychiatric communities were at the forefront of the campaign to identify child abuse as a serious problem, the prevailing causal model was a medical-psychiatric-psychopathological model that explained abuse as a function of parental psychopathology. Because the cause of abuse was thought to be a character or personality defect and because the form of abuse that framed social policy was child battering, for almost a decade, foster care became an important initial and long-term intervention. However, even during this period, it was rare that more than half of validated cases resulted in out-of-home placement.

By 1978, there were a little less than a million reports of child maltreatment. At the same time, there were 500,000 children in foster care (Pelton, 1989; Tatara, 1993). Although there was not a one-to-one relationship between maltreatment reports and foster care placement, most children in foster care were placed due to abuse or neglect. The combination of increased reports, more children in out-of-home placements, and the cost of such placements raised concerns across the child welfare system. At the same time, there was a shift in the explanation of child abuse and neglect. The shift changed the model from one that focused on parental psychopathology to a social psychological model that focused on poverty, social isolation, and social learning leading to the intergenerational transmission of violence and abuse and cultural support for physical punishment (Gelles, 1973; Gil, 1970; Parke & Collmer, 1975).

In addition, there was a consistent broadening of the definition of child maltreatment. The various forms of neglect were included under the federal definition of abuse and neglect, as was sexual abuse. The broadening of the definition had obvious consequences—more reports were received by state agencies, requiring more resources for investigation and services.

These shifts had a gradual but major impact on child welfare interventions and policy. Abusive parents, rather than being thought of as characterologically disordered and different, were now viewed as being at one end of a continuum of parenting. Their maltreating behavior was not seen as solely due to personality or psychiatric disorders but, rather, the result of a surplus of stressors and a deficit of resources. Anyone, this model proposed, could abuse or neglect a child, under certain circumstances. Even if there were signs of psychiatric disorder, these too were thought to arise from social and environmental conditions (see, for example, Gelles, 1973; Lindsey, 1994). This being the case, the major task of child welfare agencies became case management, to assist families in coping with stress and providing personal, social, and economic support.

By the late 1970s, the new model explaining child abuse and neglect was well integrated in the professional literature. At the same time, as noted earlier, out-of-home placements had reached 500,000 (Pelton, 1989; Tatara, 1993). And at the same time, neglect reports constituted approximately half of the maltreatment reports.

The Adoption Assistance and Child Welfare Act of 1980

The new child protection-family preservation policy that emerged in the late 1970s was crystallized by the federal Adoption Assistance and Child Welfare Act of 1980, considered the most significant legislation in the history of child welfare. The two major child welfare provisions of the act were on permanency planning and "reasonable efforts." Permanency planning was a response to concerns over what child welfare experts had labeled "foster care drift." Although data on foster care were limited, researchers and practitioners believed that too many children were lingering in the foster care system. These children existed in limbo, with few efforts made to either reunite them with their biological parents or to find permanent alternatives for them. Permanency planning mandated that states develop permanency plans for children—that they be returned to their birth parents, placed for adoption, or placed in another kind of permanent placement, within 18 months of entrance into the child welfare system. The second child welfare provision of the legislation was embodied in the two words "reasonable efforts." Again, aimed at reducing foster care drift and inappropriate out-of-home placement, the policy of "reasonable efforts" was stated in a brief, but important section of the legislation:

> In each case, reasonable efforts will be made (A) prior to the placement of a child in foster care, to prevent or eliminate the need for removal of a child from his home, and (B) to make it possible for the child to return to his home. (Public Law 96-272, Sec. 471a 15, p. 503)

States had to demonstrate that they made reasonable efforts and that they were in compliance with the permanency planning provision of the law to qualify for federal funding for adoption and foster care.

The central goal of the reasonable-efforts provision was to counter the apparent arbitrary decision making in case planning. Moreover, it was assumed that requiring reasonable efforts would motivate states to provide services for families and children rather than leaving children in foster care or terminating parental rights. The former addressed the issue of permanency, whereas the latter aimed to reduce the likelihood that parents' rights would be terminated without an opportunity to improve their caregiving abilities. For example, parents whose neglect was linked to drug abuse would be provided with drug treatment as part of reasonable efforts; parents with unreasonable expectations of their children's development would be provided with parenting classes; parents whose acts of omission seemed to be related to a lack of social and economic resources would receive assistance in terms of housing, job counseling, and so forth. The reasonable-efforts provision created one apparent safety valve in the child welfare system for parents whose acts of omission were mostly due to insufficient resources.

A third provision of the Adoption Assistance and Child Welfare Act (1980) stated that if children were placed outside the home, they had to be placed in the "least restrictive" environment; the least restrictive environment was defined as relative or "kin" care, the most restrictive, institutional care. This was another attempt to keep families together.

It appeared that the Adoption Assistance and Child Welfare Act of 1980 had the desired effect. Out-of-home placements declined to under 300,000 by the mid-1980s (Pelton, 1989; Tatara, 1993). However, by the 1990s, foster care placements approached 600,000 (Tatara, 1993).

SOCIAL POLICY AND CHILD NEGLECT

As noted earlier, there is no overriding social policy for child neglect. Policy appears to be driven by the more emotionally charged physical and sexual abuse. Only when there is a sensational case of neglect, such as the home-alone case or the instances of children found abandoned in squalid, roach- and rat-infested apartments (such as the Chicago "Keystone Kids," discussed later), does child neglect receive policy attention.

This policy gap is noteworthy because neglect may be increasing because of changes in other areas of social policy. During the 1980s, both the Reagan and Bush administrations reduced government spending on social programs, such as Aid to Families with Dependent Children, Food Stamps, job training, and supplemental Social Security; families may have been unable to meet their children's health, shelter, and even educational needs because of the elimination or reduction of social programs. It is unclear what the impact of the 1996 welfare reform legislation will be. This legislation required a percentage of welfare families in each state to work after receiving 2 years of welfare benefits, and it establishes a maximum 5-year lifetime limit for receiving welfare benefits. Although welfare reform legislation included substantial new federal funding for child care, it is not clear whether mothers who have received welfare benefits can work and adequately care for their children, as assumed by the framers of welfare reform. It is also unknown what will happen when families have exhausted their limit on benefits. It is reasonable to assume that more cases of neglect may occur because of the role strain of having to work and care for children and that neglect will increase when families become ineligible for benefits.

Lindsey (1994) observed that child abuse, and child neglect in particular, may have become a "means test" for families to receive public assistance. The means test notion is more complicated than it appears at first. First, because social programs are reduced or eliminated, caregivers may be more neglectful due to inadequate economic resources. Families ordinarily served by the welfare system may become child welfare cases. If a family exhausts its welfare benefits and the children are inadequately clothed, fed, or housed, the case may instead be served by the child welfare system. Thus, as Lindsey implies, parents and their children may have to be labeled "maltreator" and "maltreated" to receive services previously available to the needy. For many parents, the path to being considered neglecters of their children instead of needy may be as simple as having a label changed from "TANF (Temporary Assistance to Needy Families) eligible" to "child neglect." Second, parents may be more neglectful because of an interaction between reduced social and economic resources and personal factors. For example, a reduction in social resources may lead to more depression or more substance abuse, which may in turn lead to neglect.

When the public welfare safety net is inadequate, at least in theory, the child welfare system provides a finer meshed safety net. Yet the child welfare safety net comes with costs. First, parents and their children must be stigmatized with the labels "abuse," "neglect," and "maltreatment." Having these labels attached to you is a high price to pay for government and social assistance. Moreover, it is entirely possible, but largely unrecognized by those in the child welfare system, that such stigmatizing labels may be counterproductive in terms of motivating parents to engage in services. Thus, parents may expend more energy fighting the label and less energy using services.

Policy Dilemmas and Directions

Policy for child sexual abuse leans strongly toward using the criminal justice system and control approach. There is little argument that victims of child sexual abuse need to be protected from future harm and should not be left with either the abuser or a caregiver who is unable or unwilling to protect them from further victimization.

Policy for child physical abuse is more complex. On the one hand, some believe that compassion and family preservation are appropriate if the child's safety can be ensured. Others believe that child safety is too much of a gamble when children are left with or reunited with physically abusive parents (Gelles, 1996). Critics of reunification with physically abusive parents cite the lack of evidence that family preservation programs produce enough change to ensure child safety (Gelles, 1996). Supporters of family preservation point to anecdotes of children harmed or killed in foster care and point to the benefits of relationships with biological caregivers. Both sides often point to high-profile tragedies to support their positions, and as a result, social policy tends to move as a pendulum from child safety to family preservation, often in response to either the latest tragedy or advocacy effort (Lindsey, 1994).

One solution to the debate is for social policy to preserve families, as long as child safety is ensured. Yet such a logical compromise has problems. One reality of the child welfare system is that today's workers, even the best trained workers, are often ill-equipped to conduct comprehensive evaluations of the family and children as a basis for deciding on the appropriate placement. The science of risk assessment is still in an early stage. Moreover, the child welfare system is so biased toward the goal of preservation that it often waits too long before terminating parental rights. Even those children who are not scarred or damaged are unlikely to be adopted because many families interested in adopting prefer young children. Last, it is impossible to simultaneously reduce false positives (labeling someone dangerously abusive when he or she is not) and to reduce false negatives (labeling someone safe when he or she is not).

Policy for child neglect is even less clear. There are indeed high-profile cases of child neglect—home-alone cases, children in appalling conditions like the Keystone Kids, (McCormick, 1997),[6] "boarder babies"—children abandoned at birth in hospitals, and "crack babies." When the pendulum in child neglect cases moves toward safety and removal of children from dangerous homes, cases of inappropriately intrusive interventions are cited. In 1997, a Boston physician was investigated for neglect because she left her two daughters sleeping in the car while she ran to return videos. It was not a hot day and the mother never lost sight of the car, yet she was reported and investigated for child maltreatment. The resulting newspaper story caused the head of the Massachusetts Department of Social Services to announce a modification of how the department investigated reports of child maltreatment. Unfortunately, these rare cases mislead public opinion about child neglect *and* lead to the worst of all possible policy actions—public policy by anecdote. Tragic cases and mistakes are an important and useful window into the workings of the child welfare system. However, such cases are only a window and should not be the basis (as they sometimes are) of social policy.

Perhaps one major dilemma that needs to be resolved for there to be an appropriate policy for neglect is to revisit the definition as well as the causes of neglect. Although there have been numerous efforts to refine definitions of child maltreatment, these efforts have not yet produced operational definitions that clearly differentiate what acts of omission are the responsibility of the parent or due to social disadvantage. In revisiting the definition of neglect, it is important to shift the focus of the discussion from attributing blame and responsibility to a focus on children's basic needs and how to best ensure that children have the resources and caregiving that ensure their health, development, and well-being. Another question to be addressed is how far we expect parents to go to meet their children's needs in the face of economic disadvantage and discrimination.

Part of sorting out the definition is to revisit the issue of mandatory reporting and what should be reported. There has been debate over the past few years about whether child maltreatment is overreported or underreported (see Besharov, 1993, and Finkelhor, 1993, for a fuller discussion of this controversy). Those who argue that maltreatment is overreported note that the increasing number of reports has flooded the child welfare system and made it impossible to respond adequately to children in danger. Because neglect reports constitute nearly half of CPS reports, it may be a major component of what is labeled "overreporting." I have taken the controversial position against mandatory reporting (Gelles, 1996). Mandatory reporting, as currently carried out, focuses more on attributing blame than on meeting children's needs. Our three-decade experiment with mandatory reporting has convincingly demonstrated that mandatory reporting laws increase reports. However, child welfare agencies often are so understaffed that they can barely investigate the reports they receive, let alone provide necessary interventions. Professionals are required to report cases and turn over the responsibility for those cases to poorly trained CPS workers. Last, in terms of neglect, mandatory reporting channels families into the child welfare system instead of focusing on institutional and structural sources of the neglect. In addition, this channeling into the child welfare system can direct parents away from dealing with substance abuse problems that are closely connected to maltreatment. The channeling takes place because maltreatment becomes the primary diagnostic criterion, and intervention is governed by the need to balance child safety with family preservation. In Lindsey's (1994) terms, substantiated child neglect has become a "means test" for securing treatment for substance abuse. Given the paucity of resources available, families labeled "abusive" or "neglectful" are more likely to receive scarce resources than families with substance abuse problems or those labeled simply "needy."

Sorting out the definition is only a first step. For the definitions to be useful, they must become part of child welfare practice. Thus, CPS workers need to have means of differentiating unkept homes from dangerous homes, acceptable lapses from dangerous acts, disadvantage from deliberate omissions.

This sorting out will not be easy. The child welfare field has spent enormous energy assessing risk in terms of physical abuse and has not arrived at a consensus on how to conduct reliable and valid risk assessment. Child neglect poses an even more complex challenge.

If the child welfare field can ever resolve the definition and targeting issue, it will have to revisit the issues of reasonable efforts, reunification, and family preservation. Although supporters of the child welfare system protest that the system does not and should not apply "one-size-fits-all" interventions, it is quite clear that federal and state policy of reasonable efforts combines with a cultural preference for biological caregivers and a preference for compassion over control. The result is that preservation efforts and reunification are tantamount to a one-size-fits-all intervention—provide any service to keep a family together. Reasonable efforts often become "every possible effort" in daily practice, at least in terms of time, as there are no time lines or limits on how many services are provided or how long parents are given to change their behaviors. The child welfare system pays lip service to the need to be flexible and to consider the complex issues of neglect, whereas in practice, the system often applies one-size-fits-all interventions for the full range of child maltreatment. The broad principle of reasonable efforts makes sense, but in practice, this principle is unreasonably applied.

CONCLUSION

The child welfare system continues to be a well-intended dismal failure. In 1990, the U.S. Advisory Board on Child Abuse and Neglect declared that abuse and neglect in the United States represented a national emergency. The Board cited the scope of the problem and stated that

> [the] *system* the nation has developed to respond to child abuse and neglect is *failing*. It is not a question of acute failure of a single element of the system; there is a chronic and critical multiple organ failure. (U.S. Advisory Board on Child Abuse and Neglect, 1990)

Subsequent Advisory Board reports were equally critical of the child welfare system.

There is a long-standing tradition of responding to child maltreatment with more compassion than control. Although the system attempts to balance child safety and family preservation, the policy of reasonable efforts and the belief in the effectiveness of intensive family preservation prioritize preservation over safety. Recently, however, there have been calls for more control and a greater emphasis on a child-centered rather than a family-centered system (Gelles, 1996; Lindsey, 1994). Child neglect, however, continues to receive much less attention, despite being nearly half of CPS reports.

In an ideal world, social policies would be implemented that provided sufficient child and family support, without the label of neglect when a lack of resources is largely to blame. Achieving this ideal is crucial because the child welfare system is *not* the appropriate institution to provide a social safety net for families and children. The application of a stigmatizing label is rarely constructive or a motive for change.

However, regardless of what is the cause of neglect, substance abuse, personality disorder, or economic or social stress, child welfare policy must prioritize the best interests of the child and child safety. This does not mean abandoning efforts to preserve families. Many families may respond to family preservation services. However, because neglect tends to be a chronic condition, child welfare policy needs to recognize that changing neglecting caregivers may take considerable time, and this wait may damage children. Thus, a central component of decision making should be a realistic assessment of the time expected for parents to change and the impact this wait will have on the children. Children must not be denied permanence, moved from foster home to foster home, and back and forth between in-home and out-of-home placements while parents are given chance after chance to change, especially in the absence of progress.

Needed Policy Improvements

1. The most important feature of a child welfare policy for neglect is that caseworkers be capable of conducting a comprehensive evaluation of the family and children, to determine dangerousness and prospects for change (Gelles, 1995). Such an evaluation is necessary to appropriately tailor interventions to the needs of the child and family.

2. A second important feature of child welfare policy is that there should be specific acts of omission and commission that are considered so dangerous that they do not generate a family-preservation-and-reunification response; instead, child safety and permanence should be expedited. There is some agreement that caregivers who kill or severely injure children should not have an opportunity to repeat such acts. More controversial is the new policy in New York City that states that giving birth to a cocaine-positive child is a "rebuttable presumption of unfitness." Such a policy preserves due process for neglecting parents but places the burden of proof for reunification on the parent, not the child welfare agency.

3. A third needed improvement to child welfare policy and practice is the need to evaluate the effectiveness of interventions. After more than three decades of effort to identify child maltreatment and provide ameliorative interventions, there is still only a minimal understanding of what interventions are effective (National Research Council, 1993, 1998). Without a scientific knowledge base on which interventions are effective under what conditions, and wedded to the goal of preserving families, the child welfare system lacks the flexibility to recognize interventions that do not work.

4. Another critical component of child welfare policy for neglect is to create time lines for change. An example is a Rhode Island law (94-H8625, Substitute A. An Act Relating to Domestic Relations–Adoption of Children, 1994) that states that "the fact that a parent has been unable to provide care for a child for a period of twelve months due to substance abuse shall constitute prima facie evidence of a chronic substance abuse problem." Evidence of a chronic substance abuse problem is grounds for termination of parental rights, if there is clear and convincing evidence of such a condition. The right to due process is preserved, and the termination of parental rights is not automatic. But such a policy elevates child safety, permanence, and a child's sense of time above the usual priority given to biological parents.

Challenges

1. The most important challenge to improving policy responses to neglect is to try to draw a clear line between less than optimal but acceptable care and clearly inadequate care.

2. Closely tied to the first challenge is discriminating between parent behavior due to factors beyond their control and circumstances over which parents reasonably do have control.

3. An equally important challenge is whether or not this society will provide resources for children and families *before* they fall into the child welfare system. Children are inextricably linked to any policy that affects families. A change in social programs or welfare policy automatically affects children. Similarly, it is difficult to develop a policy for children that can be implemented independent of their caregivers. Health care, child care, food, housing, clothing all reach children through their caregivers. The current debate over welfare reform finds a significant nexus over this very

issue. The proponents of welfare reform work rules and time limits minimized the obvious fact that when benefits are cut off from parents, the benefits to their children are also cut; those opposed to the reform emphasized the potential harm to children.

4. A final challenge is whether social policy will establish interventions, with children as the priority. Because the lives of parents and children are inextricably linked, social policy often aims to assist parents, presuming a "trickle down" benefit to children. But, if children must linger in limbo or be in homes where they are harmed, one cannot presume that helping parents automatically helps children. Children must come first for neglect policy and child welfare policy if their safety, well-being, and developmental potential are to be ensured.

NOTES

1. The three national incidence studies of child abuse and neglect categorize child abuse and neglect into these six categories for purposes of measuring the extent of recognized and reported child abuse and neglect. Although there are other means of categorizing child maltreatment, this chapter employs the six types used in the national incidence surveys (Burgdorf, 1980; National Center on Child Abuse and Neglect, 1988, 1996).

2. The most recent survey of reported and recognized child maltreatment employed two definitions of child maltreatment. The first, a "harm standard," was a stringent standard that required that a child had demonstrable harm as a result of maltreatment. A child would have to have been *seriously harmed* by neglect to be included in the neglect estimate. The second standard of "endangerment" was a more relaxed measure, with the child not having to be harmed to be included in the measure (National Center on Child Abuse and Neglect, 1996, p. 2-9). The incidence data reported here use the endangerment standard.

3. Prior to 1992, state reports of child maltreatment were collected and analyzed by the American Association for Protecting Children (1988, 1989). During 1987, the last year the survey was conducted, 2,178,384 children were reported to state agencies for suspected child abuse and neglect. Of these, it is estimated that 686,000 reports were substantiated by the state CPS.

4. A *victim* is defined as a child whose case was either "substantiated" or "indicated" after a CPS investigation. *Substantiated* is used when the allegation of maltreatment is founded by the CPS investigation. This is considered the highest level of finding by a state agency. *Indicated* is used when maltreatment cannot not be substantiated, but there is reason to suspect that the child may have been maltreated or was at risk of maltreatment (U.S. Department of Health and Human Services, 1997).

5. These incidence statistics are for what the Third National Incidence Study of Child Abuse and Neglect labeled "the harm standard," which is the most stringent definition of child maltreatment (National Center on Child Abuse and Neglect, 1996, p. 2-9).

6. The "Keystone Kids" story began when 19 children were found jammed into a cold and squalid apartment on Keystone Avenue in Chicago in February 1994. Conditions inside the

home included roaches, rat droppings, bowls of rotten food, and two toddlers who shared a bone with a dog in the apartment. The six mothers of the children hung out together and collected a total of $4,692 per month in welfare and food stamps.

REFERENCES

Adoption Assistance and Child Welfare Act of 1980, Pub. L. 96-272, 42 U.S.C. 1396s (1980).

American Association for Protecting Children. (1988). *Highlights of official child neglect and abuse reporting, 1986.* Denver, CO: American Humane Association.

American Association for Protecting Children (1989). *Highlights of official child neglect and abuse reporting, 1987.* Denver, CO: American Humane Association.

Besharov, D. J. (1993). Overreporting and underreporting are twin problems. In R. J. Gelles & D. Loseke (Eds.), *Current controversies on family violence* (pp. 257-272). Newbury Park, CA: Sage.

Bowlby, J. (1958). The nature of the child's tie to his mother. *International Journal of Psychoanalysis, 39,* 350-373.

Bowlby, J. (1969). *Attachment and loss: Vol. 1. Attachment.* New York: Basic Books.

Burgdorf, K. (1980). *Recognition and reporting of child maltreatment.* Rockville, MD: Westat.

Child Abuse Prevention and Treatment Act, Pub. L. 93-247, 42 U.S.C. 5101 (as revised in 1984).

Child Abuse Prevention and Treatment Act, Pub. L. 93-247, 42 U.S.C. 5101 (as revised in 1988).

Erickson, M. F., Egeland, B., & Pianta, R. (1989). The effects of maltreatment on the development of young children. In D. Cicchetti & V. Carlson (Eds.), *Child maltreatment: Theory and research on the causes and consequences of child abuse and neglect* (pp. 647-684). New York: Cambridge University Press.

Finkelhor, D. (1993). The main problem is still underreporting, not overreporting. In R. J. Gelles & D. Loseke (Eds.), *Current controversies on family violence* (pp. 273-287). Newbury Park, CA: Sage.

Gelles, R. (1973). Child abuse as psychopathology: A sociological critique and reformulation. *American Journal of Orthopsychiatry, 43,* 611-621.

Gelles, R. J. (1995, July). *Using the Transtheoretical Model of Change to improve risk assessment in cases of child abuse and neglect.* Paper presented at the 4th International Family Violence Research Conference, Durham, NH.

Gelles, R. J. (1996). *The book of David: How preserving families can cost children's lives.* New York: Basic Books.

Gil, D. (1970). *Violence against children: Physical child abuse in the United States.* Cambridge, MA: Harvard University Press.

Harlow, H. (1958). The nature of love. *American Psychologist, 13,* 673-685.

Harlow, H. (1961). The development of affection patterns in infant monkeys. In B. M. Foss (Ed.), *Determinants of infant behavior, Vol. 1.* London: Metheun.

Kempe, C. H., Silverman, F. N., Steele, B. F., Droegmueller, W., & Silver, H. K. (1962). The battered child syndrome. *Journal of the American Medical Association, 181,* 107-112.

Kozol, J. (1991). *Savage inequalities: Children in America's schools.* New York: Harper Collins.

Lindsey, D. (1994). *The welfare of children.* New York: Oxford University Press.

McCormick, J. (1997, March 24). Chicago hope. *Newsweek,* 68ff.

National Center on Child Abuse and Neglect. (1988). *Study findings: Study of national incidence and prevalence of child abuse and neglect: 1988.* Washington, DC: U.S. Department of Health and Human Services.

National Center on Child Abuse and Neglect. (1996). *Study findings: Study of national incidence and prevalence of child abuse and neglect: 1993.* Washington, DC: U.S. Department of Health and Human Services.

National Research Council. (1993). *Understanding child abuse and neglect.* Washington, DC: National Academy Press.

National Research Council. (1998). *Assessing family violence interventions.* Washington, DC: National Academy Press.

Parke, R. D., & Collmer, C. W. (1975). Child abuse: An interdisciplinary analysis. In M. Hetherington (Ed.), *Review of child development research, Vol. 5* (pp. 1-102). Chicago: University of Chicago Press.

Pelton, L. (1989). *For reasons of poverty: A critical analysis of the public child welfare system in the United States.* New York: Praeger.

Pianta, R., Egeland, B., & Erickson, M. F. (1989). The antecedents of maltreatment: Results of the Mother-Child Interaction Research Project. In D. Cicchetti & V. Carlson (Eds.), *Child maltreatment: Theory and research on the causes and consequences of child abuse and neglect* (pp. 203-253). New York: Cambridge University Press.

Polansky, N. A., Chalmers, M. A., Buttenweiser, E., & Williams, D. P. (1981). *Damaged parents: An anatomy of child neglect.* Chicago: University of Chicago Press.

Polansky, N. A., DeSaix, C., & Sharlin, S. (1972). *Child neglect: Understanding and reaching the parent.* New York: Child Welfare League of America.

Polansky, N. A., Gaudin, J. M., & Kilpatrick, A. C. (1992). Family radicals. *Children and Youth Services Review, 14,* 19-26.

Rosenfeld, A., & Newberger, E. H. (1977). Compassion vs. control: Conceptual and practical pitfalls in the broadened definition of child abuse. *Journal of the American Medical Association, 237,* 2086-2088.

Tatara, T. (1993). *Characteristics of children in substitute and adoptive care.* Washington, DC.: Voluntary Cooperative Information System, American Public Welfare Association.

U.S. Advisory Board on Child Abuse and Neglect. (1990). *Child abuse and neglect: Critical first steps in response to a national emergency.* Washington, DC: Government Printing Office.

U.S. Department of Health and Human Services, National Center on Child Abuse and Neglect. (1997). *Child maltreatment, 1995: Reports from the states to the National Center on Child Abuse and Neglect.* Washington, DC: Government Printing Office.

Wekerle, C., & Wolfe, D. A. (1996). Child maltreatment. In E. J. Mash & R. A. Russel (Eds.), *Child psychopathology* (pp. 3-60). New York: Guilford.

Index

About the Contributors

Maureen M. Black, Ph.D., is Professor in the Department of Pediatrics at the University of Maryland School of Medicine and Director of the Growth and Nutrition Clinic, a multidisciplinary, family-focused clinic for children with failure to thrive. She is a fellow of the American Psychological Association, president of the Society of Pediatric Psychology, and a past president of the Division of Child, Youth, and Family Services of the APA. Her clinical and research interests involve nutritional and family-focused interventions with children and families from low-income urban communities to promote growth and development, follow-up of children exposed to substances prenatally, and evaluation of multigenerational programs to promote adolescent development and parenting skills among adolescent mothers and fathers.

Barbara L. Bonner, Ph.D., is a clinical child psychologist and Director of the Center on Child Abuse and Neglect in the Department of Pediatrics at the University of Oklahoma. Her research interests include child abuse-related fatalities, children and adolescents with inappropriate or illegal sexual behavior, and the effectiveness of family preservation and family support programs. She recently completed a 5-year treatment outcome study funded by the National Center on Child Abuse and Neglect on children with sexual behavior problems. She is past president of the American Professional Society on the Abuse of Children (APSAC) and is treasurer of the International Society for the Prevention of Child Abuse and Neglect (ISPCAN). She serves on the Editorial Boards of *Child Maltreatment, Journal of Pediatric Psychology,* and *Child Abuse and Neglect,* and she has published many articles on child maltreatment.

Ira J. Chasnoff, M.D., is President of the Children's Research Triangle and Professor of Pediatrics at the University of Illinois College of Medicine in Chicago. He is one of the nation's leading researchers in the field of maternal drug use during pregnancy and the effects on the newborn infant and child. His research projects include a study of the long-term cognitive, behavioral, and educational developmental effects of prenatal exposure to alcohol, cocaine, and other drugs; the effects on birth outcome of prenatal treatment and counseling for pregnant drug abusers; and the effectiveness of both outpatient and residential treatment programs for pregnant drug abusers. He is the author of four books and numerous articles on the effects of drug use on pregnancy and on the long-term cognitive, behavioral, and learning outcomes of prenatally exposed children. His most recent book, *Understanding the Drug-Exposed Child,* has been cited as an important addition to the literature on helping children at risk of educational failure.

Cyleste C. Collins is a research assistant at the Family Life Development Center at Cornell University in Ithaca, New York.

Patricia McKinsey Crittenden, Ph.D., M.Ed., M.A., is a consultant on social ecology and development, University of Virginia, Family Relations Institute. Her primary interest is developmental psychopathology. Her work with maltreating mothers and children and later administering a family support center for at-risk families in a housing project is central to her understanding of both child neglect and the process by which early exposure to threatening conditions affects later psychological and interpersonal functioning. She has published empirical research on the functioning of maltreating families and contributed to the development of theory regarding developmental psychopathology. Currently, she teaches, in universities and health organizations around the world, research and clinical assessment methods tied to dynamic-maturational theory of the development of interpersonal strategies for protecting the self and one's children.

Sheila M. Crow, M.A., is Assistant Director of the Center on Child Abuse and Neglect and Director of the Center's Administrative Programs in the Department of Pediatrics at the University of Oklahoma Health Sciences Center. She also serves as the Administrator of the Oklahoma Child Death Review Board. Her primary research interest is in child fatalities, with a focus on child maltreatment-related deaths. She is past co-chair of the American Professional Society on the Abuse of Children's (APSAC) Child Fatality Task Force and is editor of *The Link,* the official newsletter of the International Society for the Prevention of Child Abuse and Neglect (ISPCAN). She has published reports on child fatalities and child maltreatment-related disabilities.

Diane DePanfilis, Ph.D., M.S.W., is Assistant Professor at the University of Maryland School of Social Work. With more than 25 years of experience in the child welfare field as a caseworker, supervisor, program manager, national trainer, consultant, and researcher, she is a frequent consultant to child welfare agencies. She is currently principal investigator of a demonstration project funded by the National Center on Child Abuse and Neglect that is providing early intervention to families at risk of neglect and is coediting *Child Protection Practice Handbook* (Sage Publications, forthcoming). Recent research and publications relate to child maltreatment recurrences; CPS risk assessment and decision making; the relationship between adolescent parenting and child maltreatment; intergenerational transmission of child maltreatment; the role of social support in preventing neglect; and family-focused, outcome-based intervention to reduce risk of neglect. She is currently president of the National Board of Directors of the American Professional Society on the Abuse of Children.

Howard Dubowitz, M.D., M.S., is Professor of Pediatrics at the University of Maryland School of Medicine and Director of the Child Protection Program at the University of Maryland Medical System. He is Chair of the Child Maltreatment Committee of the American Academy of Pediatrics, Maryland Chapter, and he is on the Executive Committee of the American Professional Society on the Abuse of Children (APSAC). His clinical work has included all forms of child maltreatment with a special interest in neglect. His research has been in the areas of child neglect, sexual and physical abuse, kinship care, physician training in child abuse, and the prevention of child maltreatment. He has been actively involved in child advocacy at the state and national levels, and he chairs the Legislative Committee of APSAC. He has presented at numerous local, regional, national and international conferences, and he has published widely in the field of child abuse and neglect.

Diana J. English, M.S.W., Ph.D., is affiliated with the Department of Social and Health Services at the University of Washington, Seattle, and is the director of a public child welfare research center located in a public child welfare agency. Her research interests include risk assessment in child protection, factors that influence child protective services decision making, the long-term effects of child maltreatment on children's growth and development, and the effectiveness of public service interventions.

James Garbarino, Ph.D., is Co-Director of the Family Life Development Center and Professor of Human Development at Cornell University. He served as President of the Erikson Institute for Advanced Study in Child Development from 1985–1994. Garbarino is author or editor of seventeen books, including *Understanding Abusive Families* (second edition, 1992); *The Psychologically Battered Child* (1986); *What Children Can Tell Us* (1989); *Children in Danger: Coping With the Consequences of Community Violence* (1993); and *Raising Children in Socially Toxic Environment* (1995). He has served as a scientific expert witness in criminal and civil cases involving issues of violence and children. The National Conference on Child Abuse and Neglect honored Garbarino in 1985 with its first C. Henry Kempe Award, in recognition of his efforts on behalf of abused and neglected children. In 1994, the American Psychological Association's Division on Child, Youth, and Family Services presented him with its Nicholas Hobbs Award. Also in 1994, he received the Dale Richmond Award from the American Academy of Pediatrics Section on Behavioral and Developmental Pediatrics.

James M. Gaudin, Jr., Ph.D, is Professor at the University of Georgia School of Social Work. He has been principal investigator for research on child neglect and incarcerated mothers and their children over the past 17 years. His research has been funded by the U.S. Department of Health and Human Services, National

Center on Child Abuse and Neglect, University of Georgia Research Foundation, and private foundations. He is author of 30 articles in refereed journals, two books, and three book chapters. He authored *Child Neglect: A Guide for Professional Helpers,* one of the *User Manual Series* published by the National Center on Child Abuse and Neglect. He is recognized nationally and internationally as one of the leading researchers in child abuse and neglect, and has given workshops on child neglect to professional groups throughout the southeastern United States. He has more than 25 years of experience as a clinical practitioner, supervisor, administrator, program developer, teacher, and researcher in the field of family and child welfare.

Richard J. Gelles, Ph.D, holds the Joanne and Raymond Welsh Chair of Child Welfare and Family Violence in the School of Social Work at the University of Pennsylvania. His book *The Violent Home* was the first systematic investigation of family violence and continues to be highly influential. He is the author or coauthor of 23 books and more than 100 articles and chapters on family violence. His latest books are *The Book of David: How Preserving Families Can Cost Children's Lives* (1996) and *Intimate Violence in Families, Third Edition* (Sage, 1997). He is a member of the National Academy of Science panel on "Assessing Family Violence Interventions." He is also vice president for publications for the National Council on Family Relations. He edited the journal *Teaching Sociology* from 1973 to 1981 and received the American Sociological Association, Section on Undergraduate Education, "Outstanding Contributions to Teaching Award" in 1979. He has presented lectures to policy-making groups and media groups, including *The Today Show, CBS Morning News, Good Morning America, The Oprah Winfrey Show, Dateline,* and *All Things Considered.* In 1984, *Esquire* named him as one of the men and women who are "changing America."

E. Wayne Holden, Ph.D., is employed by Macro International Inc. as principal investigator of the national evaluation of the Comprehensive Community Mental Health Services for Children and Their Families program, sponsored by the Substance Abuse and Mental Health Services Administration. He was a faculty member in the Department of Pediatrics at the University of Maryland School of Medicine from 1988 to 1998. He has published extensively in the area of children's mental health and specifically in the area of child maltreatment.

Jill E. Korbin, Ph.D., is Professor of Anthropology at Case Western Reserve University. She received the 1986 Margaret Mead Award from the American Anthropological Association, served as a Society for Research in Child Development Congressional Science Fellow in 1985-86 in the offices of Senator Bill Bradley, and was a Scholar-in-Residence at the Kempe National Center in 1977-78. She has published numerous articles on culture and child maltreatment, including her edited book, *Child Abuse and Neglect: Cross-Cultural Perspectives* (1981). She has conducted research on women incarcerated for fatal child maltreatment, on child and elder maltreatment in Ohio, on the impact of neighborhood factors on child maltreatment in Cleveland, and on health and childrearing among Ohio's Amish population.

Mary Beth Logue, Ph.D., is a pediatric psychologist and Assistant Professor in the Department of Pediatrics at the University of Oklahoma Health Sciences Center. Her research interests include physical symptom presentations of psychological disorders, ethical decision making by health professionals, and other topics related to child maltreatment. Her clinical practice includes working with medically ill children in both inpatient and outpatient settings, as well as children and families with a variety of problems. She is a member of the Child Protection Committee at Children's Hospital of Oklahoma, the American Psychological Association, Oklahoma Psychological Association, and the American Professional Society on the Abuse of Children (APSAC).

Lee Ann Lowder, J.D., is an attorney who supervises appeals for the Office of the Cook County Public Guardian. The office represents 43,000 abused and neglected children in the juvenile court in Chicago. About 85% of the parents of the Public Guardian's child clients have substance abuse problems. The Illinois Department of Children and Family Services has a policy of referring women whose newborns test positive for cocaine and other illegal substances to drug treatment programs. A woman's first cocaine baby is rarely brought to the attention of the court. Consequently, the most common new case in Cook County juvenile court is brought on behalf of the second or third cocaine baby born to a mother, and the mother's older children.

Thomas D. Lyon, J.D., Ph.D., is Associate Professor of Law at the University of Southern California Law School. He worked as an attorney for the Children's Services Division of the Los Angeles County Counsel's Office from 1987 to 1995, representing the Department of Children's Services in dependency proceedings alleging child abuse and neglect. His dissertation was named the outstanding dissertation in developmental psychology by the American Psychological Association in 1995. He is associate editor for legal issues for the *Advisor,* a publication of the American Professional Society on the Abuse of Children (APSAC), and he is also on APSAC's board of directors. His work has appeared in *Child Development, Contemporary Psychology, Cornell Law Review, Pacific Law Journal, Harvard Women's Law Journal,* and *Psychology, Public Policy, and Law.*

Laura Nabors, Ph.D., is on the faculty of the Division of Child and Adolescent Psychiatry at the University of Maryland School of Medicine. She completed a postdoctoral fellowship at the Frank Porter Graham Child Development Center at the University of North Carolina at Chapel Hill. Her research interests include examining risk and resilience factors and their influence on the lives of children and families; conducting program evaluation and quality improvement activities in children's mental health services; increasing knowledge about the impact of abuse, neglect, and violence on children and the prevention of these problems; and ways in which to improve educational opportunities for and the social development of young children with special needs.

James C. Spilsbury, M.P.H., is a doctoral student in the Department of Anthropology at Case Western Reserve University. He has worked in international health projects in sub-Saharan Africa and Haiti for eight years. He has developed an interest in the anthropology of childhood and is currently conducting his dissertation research on inner-city children's perceptions of safety and danger in Cleveland, Ohio.

Susan J. Zuravin, Ph.D., M.S.W., is Associate Professor at the University of Maryland School of Social Work. Her primary research focus is child welfare. She has received funding from the National Center on Child Abuse and Neglect to conduct studies both on the etiology and sequelae of child abuse and neglect and on the characteristics and outcomes of the public foster care system. Published papers from these studies have examined the relationship between maternal depression and both child physical abuse and neglect, the ecological correlates of child maltreatment, the childbearing and contracepting patterns of maltreating families, the intergenerational transmission of child maltreatment, and various long-term sequelae of child sexual abuse.